WEAVING FAMILY TAPESTRIES

CONSTRUCTION OF FAMILIES

Second Edition

Helen Gore-Laird, Ph.D.
Lori M. Selzer, M.Ed.
JoAnn W. Hazard, M.Ed.

PEARSON

Custom
Publishing

Cover Art: *In the Neighborhood*, by Peter Arvidson.

Printed in the United States of America

10 9 8 7 6 5 4 3 2

ISBN 0-536-81351-5

BA 999224

AK/KW

Please visit our web site at *www.pearsoncustom.com*

PEARSON
Custom
Publishing

PEARSON CUSTOM PUBLISHING
75 Arlington Street, Suite 300, Boston, MA 02116
A Pearson Education Company

COPYRIGHT ACKNOWLEDGMENTS

CONTENTS

ACKNOWLEDGMENTS

What ever is worth doing at all is worth doing well.

—Lord Chesterfield

Doing something well, especially a book, requires many people who provide support and encouragement. Without their help, we could not have accomplished the completion of this book. We would like to acknowledge those who, by their support and guidance, made this book possible.

Before we ever considered constructing a book, many people in our lives provided us with the encouragement and love to tackle endeavors we believed impossible. Those who have contributed to our success along the way have been (for Helen) her father, William H. Gore; (her mother) Dorothy Dunn Gore, (her grandmother) MayBelle White Gore, and her loving husband, Glenn W. Laird; (for Lori) Rose Schlanger (her grandmother who always supports her, no matter how crazy the idea), Barbara and Jerry Selzer (her parents), and all of her brothers, sisters and nieces; (for JoAnn) Rick Hazard (her loving husband), her children—Nicole, Kristen, and Ryan, Sadie and James Woodward (her mother and father).

We wish to thank both Glenn W. Laird and Rick Hazard for being incredibly helpful and patient while we worked late into the night preparing the manuscript. Without their support, this would have been a much more difficult task.

We additionally wish to thank Elizabeth Laird for doing some of the typing and Tanya Laird and Nathan Walther for helping in the process of finding a name for the book. Tanya was the one who planted the seed for the title to grow into its current version.

We also wish to thank Leslie Noles, of Allyn and Bacon Longman for first suggesting that we do this book and to Judson Harper, for his patience as he walked us through the process and waited (and waited) for the final manuscript to be handed to him.

There are many others in our lives, who we have not mentioned, that have provided support and encouragement to us. To those unmentioned, we also give thanks.

It is our hope that we have done our work well and made those close to us proud of the accomplishments that they knew we could achieve.

Helen M. Gore-Laird, Ph.D.
Lori M. Selzer, M.Ed.
JoAnn W. Hazard, M.Ed.

Section A:
COURSE WORKBOOK

1
CALCULATING YOUR SEMESTER GRADE

Your exams and class assignment grades are weighted. The letter grade that you earn is transformed into a numbered system for easy calculation of your grades. Below is a conversion table that will aid you in calculating your semester grade.

To calculate your grade, take the converted number, multiply it by the weighted percentage, and enter that number into the weighted grade column. At the end of the semester, add the weighted grade column and convert that number to the corresponding letter grade. (Note: Your grade will be rounded to the next highest number. For example, if you have 4.55, your grade is considered 5, which converts to a C.)

Letter Grade	Convert to	Letter Grade	Convert to	Letter Grade	Convert to
A	11	B-	7	D+	3
A-	10	C+	6	D	2
B+	9	C	5	D-	1
B	8	C-	4	F	0

GRADE CALCULATOR

	Letter Grade	Converted Number Grade	Weighed %	Weighted Grade
Participation (Total of 11)			10%	
Writing Response 1			5%	
Writing Response 2			5%	
Writing Response 3				
Family Research 1			5%	
Family Research 2			5%	
Family Research 3			5%	
Family Study Paper			25%	
Exam 1			10%	
Exam 2			10%	
Exam 3			10%	
Exam 4			10%	
Course Grade				

Extra credit: Add to two lowest exam scores if you did both; to lowest exam score if you did one

2

PARTICIPATION
ACTIVITY WORKSHEETS

PARTICIPATION ACTIVITY WORKSHEET

Activity 7

Last Name: _____ **First Name:** _____

Date: _____ **SSN:** _____ **Section #:** _____

PARTICIPATION ACTIVITY WORKSHEET

Activity 2

PARTICIPATION ACTIVITY WORKSHEET

Activity 8

Last Name: _____ **First Name:** _____

Date: _____ **SSN:** _____ **Section #:** _____

PARTICIPATION ACTIVITY WORKSHEET

Activity 9

Last Name: _____ **First Name:** _____

Date: _____ **SSN:** _____ **Section #:** _____

PARTICIPATION ACTIVITY WORKSHEET

Activity 10

Last Name: _____   **First Name:** _____

Date: _____   **SSN:** _____   **Section #:** _____

_____

_____

_____

_____

_____

_____

_____

_____

_____

_____

_____

_____

_____

_____

_____

_____

_____

_____

_____

_____

PARTICIPATION ACTIVITY WORKSHEET

Activity 11

Last Name: _____ **First Name:** _____

Date: _____ **SSN:** _____ **Section #:** _____

Writing
Response Papers

3

WRITING RESPONSE PAPERS

INSTRUCTIONS AND GRADING CRITERIA

General Format:

The goal of the Writing Response Paper is to promote critical thinking. Each Writing Response Paper should be formatted as an opinion paper. Your opinion must be supported by evidence found in your assigned readings and/or your class lectures for this course. Directions for formatting your Writing Response Paper can be found below.

Each Writing Response Paper must . . .

- be no more than one and one half (1½) pages in length
- be double spaced
- be typed (no handwritten papers will be accepted)
- have margins that are one (1) inch
- be left justified
- be formatted to 12 point type in either Arial or Times New Roman
- have your name and other information right justified at the top of the *first page* of your paper. The following is an example:

First Name Last Name
Last four digits of SSN
Date

- have the appropriately numbered cover sheet stapled to the front of the Writing Response Paper
- be stapled all together in the top, left hand corner

Citation Information

- You must cite your references in your paper. For efficiency, you may use the following abbreviations followed by the page number(s) you found your information on:
  WFT = *Weaving Family Tapestries: The Construction of Families*
  DF = *Diversity in Families*
- Use the following examples as your guide in making your citations:
  (WFT, p. A86); (WFT, p. B224) or (DF, p. 43)

- Only use course textbooks and lecture notes for citations.
- If you are citing from lectures, use the professor's name followed by the date of the lecture to which you are referring. Use the following format: (Selzer, 01/18/2003)
- Do not cite names that are in your readings—you are not using the original source material, therefore you only need to use the title(s) of your textbook(s).

Grammar:

Grammar represents 50% of the overall grade for each Writing Response Paper. Your papers will be graded for correct spelling, syntax, sentence structure, and punctuation. Below are some hints for having a well-written paper:

1. Have someone else read your paper for you.
2. Read the paper aloud to yourself.
3. Run both, spell check and grammar check, on your paper, but do not exclusively rely on the spell check or grammar check program for accuracy.
4. Write your paper ahead of time and reread it the next day.

Content:

Content represents 50% of the overall grade for each Writing Response Paper. This portion of your grade will reflect your level of understanding of the subject matter. It will also demonstrate your ability to critically analyze the material you are learning. The point of view that you take in your paper is not as important as how well you argue and support your point. The following hints will help you write a better response:

1. Reiterate any points from the original work that you wish to agree or disagree with.
2. Your agreements or disagreements should be argued logically.
3. Supporting your arguments with factual information always makes a defensible case. You will want to use materials from your textbooks and lectures.

WRITING RESPONSE GRADING SCALE

Grammar:

A paper that is scored in this range will have . . .

7.5–6.8	no more than four spelling errors and/or four grammatical errors
6.7–6.0	five to seven spelling errors and/or five grammatical errors
5.9–5.1	eight to ten spelling errors and/or six grammatical errors
5.0–4.0	eleven to thirteen spelling errors and/or seven grammatical errors
3.9–0.1	fourteen or more spelling errors and/or eight or more grammatical errors

Content:

A paper that is scored in this range will be . . .

7.5–6.8	excellent (logically developed; textbooks/class lectures well referenced)
6.7–6.0	good (logically developed; textbooks/class lectures referenced)
5.9–5.1	satisfactory (somewhat developed argument; some textbook/class lecture references)
5.0–4.0	poor (poorly developed argument; few textbook/class lecture references)
3.9–0.1	unsatisfactory (underdeveloped, not logically developed or lacks argument; no textbooks/class lectures referenced)

Total Grade:

15.0–14.0	A	(11 points)		10.4–10.0	D+	(3 points)
13.9–13.5	A-	(10 points)		9.9–9.4	D	(2 points)
13.4–12.8	B+	(9 points)		9.3–9.0	D-	(1 point)
12.7–12.5	B	(8 points)		8.9 ↓	F	(0 points)
12.4 –12.0	B-	(7 points)				
11.9–11.3	C+	(6 points)				
11.2–11.0	C	(5 points)				
10.9–10.5	C-	(4 points)				

Writing Response B

Cover Sheet

You must staple this cover sheet to the front of your work.

Last Name: _____ **First Name:** _____

SSN: (Last 4 digits only) _____ **Date:** _____

Instructor: _____ **Section #:** _____

In *Diversity in Families,* Baca Zinn and Eitzen identified the term, *the new poor.* How are the *new poor* defined? What are the consequences to the families who are defined as the *new poor*? Use Bronfenbrenner's Ecological Systems Theory to explain the phenomena of the *new poor*. Do you agree or disagree with Baca Zinn and Eitzen's notion that the *new poor* exists? Why or why not?

Grammar	
Content	
Total	

Student Comments: _____

_____

_____

Grader Comments: _____

_____

_____

_____

_____

WRITING RESPONSE C
Cover Sheet

You must staple this cover sheet to the front of your work.

Last Name: _____ **First Name:** _____

SSN: (Last 4 digits only) _____ **Date:** _____

Instructor: _____ **Section #:** _____

Using both, the cultural and structural explanations, present and evaluate why there are variations in divorce statistics by race. Do you think this adequately explains divorce rate differences by race? Why or why not?

Grammar	
Content	
Total	

Student Comments: _____

_____

_____

Grader Comments: _____

_____

_____

_____

_____

WRITING RESPONSE C

Cover Sheet

(You must attach this cover sheet to the front of your paper)

Last Name: _____   First Name: _____

Shift (Check a single one): _____   Date: _____

Section: _____   Section #: _____

WRITING RESPONSE D
Cover Sheet

You must staple this cover sheet to the front of your work.

Last Name: _____ **First Name:** _____

SSN: (Last 4 digits only) _____ **Date:** _____

Instructor: _____ **Section #:** _____

Many individuals who live in the United States today choose friends, dates, or partners with the idea that they have complete freedom of choice. Think about the last three people you have dated or become close friends. Discuss the elements of those relationships, such as belief systems, ethnicity, class, race, and/or gender. Be sure to address homogeneity in conjunction with your thoughts. How do your own experiences compare with the views of the authors of your textbooks?

Grammar	
Content	
Total	

Student Comments: _____

_____

_____

Grader Comments: _____

_____

_____

_____

WRITING RESPONSE E
Cover Sheet

You must staple this cover sheet to the front of your work.

Last Name: _____ **First Name:** _____

SSN: (Last 4 digits only) _____ **Date:** _____

Instructor: _____ **Section #:** _____

Despite the idea that we often do not consider children to be a means of parental social-ization, they do play a role in their parents interactions with others. In what way(s) can you identify that your parents changed their way(s) of thinking and/or behaving after hav-ing children? Did the way(s) they think or behave change based on the development of their children? What influence do you think children have (or will have) on your parent-ing style? Explain your answer (be sure to use your textbooks and/or lectures to support your answer).

Grammar	
Content	
Total	

Student Comments: _____

_____

_____

Grader Comments: _____

_____

_____

_____

WRITING RESPONSE G
Cover Sheet

You must staple this cover sheet to the front of your work.

Last Name: _____   **First Name:** _____

SSN: (Last 4 digits only) _____   **Date:** _____

Instructor: _____   **Section #:** _____

Many families in the United States today are choosing to live in non-traditional house-holds. What do you view as the social structures that affect this choice? Do you agree or disagree with people living in non-traditional household? Why or why not?

Grammar	
Content	
Total	

Student Comments: _____

_____

_____

Grader Comments: _____

_____

_____

_____

WRITING RESPONSE H
Cover Sheet

You must staple this cover sheet to the front of your work.

Last Name: _____ **First Name:** _____

SSN: (Last 4 digits only) _____ **Date:** _____

Instructor: _____ **Section #:** _____

Choose two myths identified by Baca Zinn and Eitzen in *Diversity in Families* (chapter one) and explain why they are considered myths. Compare these myths with your own family experiences. Do you agree or disagree that these are myths? Why or why not?

Grammar	
Content	
Total	

Student Comments: _____

_____

_____

Grader Comments: _____

_____

_____

_____

WRITING RESPONSE I

Cover Sheet

You must staple this cover sheet to the front of your work.

Last Name: _____ **First Name:** _____

SSN: (Last 4 digits only) _____ **Date:** _____

Instructor: _____ **Section #:** _____

With the advent of industrialization, the "Cult of True Womanhood" emerged. Define the phrase, "Cult of True Womanhood." How did this affect gender roles within the family? Do you think this affects families today? Why or why not?

Grammar	
Content	
Total	

Student Comments: _____

_____

_____

Grader Comments: _____

_____

_____

_____

_____

WRITING RESPONSE J
Cover Sheet

You must staple this cover sheet to the front of your work.

Last Name: _____ **First Name:** _____

SSN: (Last 4 digits only) _____ **Date:** _____

Instructor: _____ **Section #:** _____

Instructor's Choice

_____
_____
_____
_____
_____
_____

Grammar	
Content	
Total	

Student Comments: _____
_____
_____

Grader Comments: _____
_____
_____
_____

Family
Research Assignments

4

FAMILY RESEARCH ASSIGNMENTS

INSTRUCTIONS AND GRADING CRITERIA

General Format:

Each Family Research Assignment must . . .

- be typed (no handwritten papers will be accepted)
- include the appropriately numbered cover sheet
- have the cover sheet stapled to the front of the assignment
- be stapled all together in the top, left hand corner
- have margins that are one (1) inch
- be left justified
- have your name and other information right justified, at the top of the *first page* of your paper. The following is an example:

First Name Last Name
Last four digits of SSN
Date

- be formatted to 12 point type in either Arial or Times New Roman.

Format for Questions & Answers:

Each Family Research Assignment must . . .

- have each question numbered and typed, singled spaced, above your answer. The question must be typed exactly as it appears on the assignment, including the information in parentheses.
- have double spaced answers to the single spaced questions
- have each question answered in complete and grammatically correct sentences
- have answers that are no more than three-quarters (¾) of a page, unless otherwise noted

Notes to Remember:

- Make a copy of each assignment before you turn it in so that you will have it available for writing your major paper, the Family Study Paper.

- Please see your instructor *before* your paper is due if you are having difficulty with any part of the assignment.

- **NO LATE PAPERS WILL BE ACCEPTED!**

Grammar:

Grammar will represent 50% of the overall grade for each Family Research Assignment. Your papers will be graded for spelling, syntax, sentence structure, and punctuation.

Some hints for having a well-written paper are:

1. Have someone else read your paper for you.
2. Read the paper aloud to yourself.
3. Run both spell check and grammar check on your paper, but do not exclusively rely on the spell check and grammar check programs for accuracy.
4. Write your paper ahead of time and reread it the next day.

Content:

Content represents 50% of the overall grade for each Family Research Assignment. Your answers to the questions are not graded on specific content; however, graders will grade your work as to how well you answer each question asked and how well you address the issues that the question raises.

Some questions may make you feel uncomfortable, or you may not know the information. If this occurs, you must explain why you are not able to answer the question(s). Any question or part of question left unanswered will be assumed to be disregarded and will be reflected in your overall grade.

Confidentiality Statement:

All information that you report when answering family research questions will remain confidential. Only the instructor, the grader, and the coordinator for the course have access to your papers.

Some questions may make you feel uncomfortable, or you may not know the information. If this occurs, please see your instructor and explain why you are not able to answer the question(s). Your instructor will be able to help you determine the best way to answer the question(s).

FAMILY RESEARCH ASSIGNMENT GRADING SCALE

Grammar:

A paper that is scored in this range will have . . .

7.5–6.8	no more than four spelling errors and/or four grammatical errors
6.7–6.0	five to seven spelling errors and/or five grammatical errors
5.9–5.1	eight to ten spelling errors and/or six grammatical errors
5.0–4.0	eleven to thirteen spelling errors and/or seven grammatical errors
3.9–0.1	fourteen or more spelling errors and/or eight or more grammatical errors

---

Content:

A paper that is scored in this range will be . . .

7.5–6.8	excellent (logically developed and all sections of the questions are developed)
6.7–6.0	good (logically developed but some missing items)
5.9–5.1	satisfactory (somewhat developed answers and some missing items)
5.0–4.0	poor (poorly developed answers and missing items)
3.9–0.1	unsatisfactory (underdeveloped answers and many missing items)

Total Grade:

15.0–14.0	A	(11 points)	10.4–10.0	D+	(3 points)
13.9–13.5	A-	(10 points)	9.9–9.4	D	(2 points)
13.4–12.8	B+	(9 points)	9.3– 9.0	D-	(1 point)
12.7–12.5	B	(8 points)	8.9 ↓	F	(0 points)
12.4 –12.0	B-	(7 points)			
11.9–11.3	C+	(6 points)			
11.2–11.0	C	(5 points)			
10.9–10.5	C-	(4 points)			

FAMILY RESEARCH ASSIGNMENT 1

Due: _____

QUESTIONS: (THERE ARE 5 QUESTIONS TO THIS ASSIGNMENT)

1. What is the culture and/or ethnic background(s) of your family of origin (the family in which you were raised)? How long has your family been in the United States? How did they come to the United States (if known)? Why did your family (ancestors) move to the United States? What events might have led them to decide to leave their home country? (You may have to do some research to find out what was happening in the country of origin when your family left.) Where in the United States does your family now live? How did you come to live in this area?

2. Who are your grandparents (their names)? Give a brief description of each of your grandparents (if one or more of your grandparents are deceased, write what you know or remember about them). What do you know about your great-grandparents (write a brief description about them)? What role did your grandparents/great-grandparents play in your life?

3. Who are your parents (their names)? What is unique about each of them? What special activities did/do you share with each of your parents?

4. Who are your siblings (from oldest to youngest, include names and birth dates)? Give a brief description of each of your siblings (including yourself). What is unique about each sibling? What role does each sibling (including yourself) play within the structure of the family (examples—baby, trouble-maker, mama's helper, confidant, peacemaker, etc.)?

5. Give a favorite family story that is often shared within your family. How does this story illustrate the character of your family? (You are limited to one page or less.)

FAMILY RESEARCH ASSIGNMENT 2

Due: _____

QUESTIONS: (THERE ARE 5 QUESTIONS TO THIS ASSIGNMENT)

1. Discuss four (4) values and beliefs that your family considers to be important. Why are they important to your family? (Examples of *values*—honesty, fidelity, trustworthiness; examples of *beliefs*—religious beliefs, roles of males and females, discipline of children)

2. What religions do the members of your family of origin practice? What are some of the religious traditions that your family practices (Christmas, Rosh Hashanah, Ramadan, Kwanza, etc.)? How does your family celebrate the traditions, either religious or non-religious, that are important to them?

3. How important is the role of education in your family? What types of certifications or degrees do your family members hold? (You might want to name some institutions your family has attended, graduated from, or supported in some manner.) What types of things have supported or interfered with the education of family members? How has education affected the socioeconomic level of your family? Are your views concerning education the same as your family's? Why or why not?

4. What types of occupations have your family members held? Is there a generational occupational trend in your family? If so, what is it? Why do you think it exists? If not, why do you think your family members have had various types of occupations?

5. What types of recreational activities does your family value and enjoy doing together? Are there any special events in which your family participates in annually or on another regular basis (Examples: Fourth of July picnic, family vacation, family reunion)? Describe how your family celebrates, plans, or participates in these activities.

FAMILY RESEARCH ASSIGNMENT 3

Due: _____

QUESTIONS: (THERE ARE 6 QUESTIONS TO THIS ASSIGNMENT)

1. Describe how your parents met. How long have (were) they been engaged in a relationship? Does your parents' relationship characterize the history of relationships in your family of origin? Why or why not?

2. Are there any divorces, separations, and/or remarriages in your family of origin? If so, describe how the family handled the situation. Would you report that separations, divorces, and/or remarriages are common or uncommon in your family? What reasons would you give for this situation being either a common or uncommon occurrence? Are you from a blended family? If so, describe how the family members handled the "coming together" of the different family units. (You are limited to one page.)

3. Are there any medical trends in your family (Examples: sickle cell disease, Tay Sachs, heart disease, cancer, schizophrenia, depression, etc.)? If so, how does the family handle these medical trends? If your family does not have any identified medical trends, why do you think your family is healthy? Discuss how medical costs, access to doctors, and/or access to medication have affected your family.

4. What is your family's attitude towards each of the following (use complete sentences to answer this question)? Do you agree with your family's position on these issues? Why or why not? Please do not list.

Abuse Issues	Pregnancy Issues
Alcohol Abuse	Birth Control (rhythm method, pill, condom, diaphragm, Depo-provera shot, etc.)
Illegal Drug Use (abuse/recreational use)	Out-of-Wedlock pregnancies/births
Legalized Drug Use/ Abuse	Abortion
Cigarette Use	Adoption

5. What is your family's attitude towards violence in the family? Many of us know someone in our family or someone close to us who has experienced violence. We even experience family violence vicariously when watching television shows or movies. What happens when violence occurs in families? How do you think your family would handle the situation? Whether your family has experienced domestic altercations or not, how does your family handle anger?

6. What is your family's attitude towards physical, sexual, or emotional abuse? How do you think families handle physical, sexual, or emotional abuse? What consequences does abuse have on family functioning? Parents have different ways of disciplining their children. How was discipline handled in your family? Do you agree or disagree with your parents' way of discipline? Why or why not?

Family
Study Paper

5

FAMILY STUDY PAPER

INSTRUCTIONS FOR THE FAMILY STUDY PAPER

You will be required to write one (1) major paper, the Family Study Paper. The Family Research Assignments are designed to prepare you to write the Family Study Paper. The family that you will be researching will be your own family of origin. You will apply the concepts and theories learned in this course to your family. You must follow the instructions below, as well as any verbal instructions given in class.

INSTRUCTIONS:

1. The first page of the paper will be your cover page. The cover page should include the following information and be in the same style as the following example:

> The Title of Your Paper
>
>
>
> Your Name
> Date
> Name of Instructor
> Course Identification

2. The second page of your Family Study Paper will be your grade sheet (found in this course workbook).

3. The body of your paper is next. The body of your paper must be five to seven (5-7) pages in length. You should make sure that your paper is in the correct format, grammatically correct, and free of spelling errors. You must make theoretical connections to the research you have done on your family and what you have learned in this class. Make sure you support your thoughts and opinions about your family by citing class lectures and readings.

4. You must use American Psychological Association (APA) format. (The authors of your textbooks write your books in APA format.) The exceptions to formal APA format are:

- You will be allowed to use the following abbreviations when citing materials from your readings:

  WFT = *Weaving Family Tapestries: The Construction of Families*

  DF = *Diversity in Families*

- You are not required to include a reference page.

5. You must staple your paper in the top left-hand corner. **No paper clips, crimped corners, plastic report covers, special binding or folders will be accepted.**

6. Each page (except the cover sheet and grade sheet) must be numbered in the upper right-hand corner (right justified). You should have a running header with the first letter of your last name and the last four digits of your social security number. It should look like the following if your name is Linda Fisher and your social security number is 421-09-6431:

F6431— 1

PAPER FORMAT:

Family Study Papers must . . .

- be typed.
- be doubled spaced.
- have one (1) inch margins
- be left justified.
- be formatted in 12 point type in Arial or Times New Roman.
- be constructed in the following order

  A. Cover Sheet

  B. Grade Sheet

  C. Body of Paper (5 to 7 pages)

FAMILY STUDY PAPER GRADING SCALE

25.0–24.0	A	(11 points)
23.9–22.0	A-	(10 points)
21.9–21.0	B+	(9 points)
20.9–19.0	B	(8 points)
18.9–18.0	B-	(7 points)
17.9–17.0	C+	(6 points)
16.9–16.0	C	(5 points)
15.9–15.0	C-	(4 points)
14.9–14.0	D+	(3 points)
13.9–13.0	D	(2 points)
12.9–12.0	D-	(1 point)
11.9 ↓	F	(0 points)

FAMILY STUDY PAPER SUGGESTED OUTLINE

Below is a *suggested* outline for your Family Study Paper. It is not the only way you may construct the paper, just a suggestion to aid you in getting started.

I. Introduction
(The introduction includes a global statement about the family, explains why you are writing the paper, what and how you will discuss/address the issues.)

II. Family History (use your Family Research Assignments to help you construct this section)
—Write a brief autobiography of your family
—This section is best done when you can include Part III concurrently

   A. Discuss your family in terms of issues/values/beliefs that you identify as important from the Family Research Assignments.

   B. Use a family story (or stories) to illustrate the main issues/values/beliefs your family faces

III. Application of theory from class lectures and course readings to your family system (Do not use outside sources beyond your class lectures and course readings)

   A. Note the differences and similarities of your family to the family forms studied in the course

   B. Apply Bronfenbrenner's Ecological Systems Theory to discuss your family system from your viewpoint.

   C. Draw material from your textbooks and lectures that support or oppose your identified family values, beliefs, and ways of daily operation (Example: divorce, child discipline; violence).

   D. Use the cultural and/or the structural approach in terms of understanding your family.

IV. Conclusion (Do not introduce any new information at this point.)

Extra Credit Assignments

6

EXTRA CREDIT ASSIGNMENTS

INSTRUCTIONS AND GRADING CRITERIA:

Extra credit is allowed in this course as an opportunity to enhance your overall grade, as well as an opportunity to learn and apply the theoretical concepts learned throughout this course.

Extra credit assignments are optional. You may choose to do one, two, or none of the assignments. As a student, the choice of which extra credit is strictly up to you. Each assignment is worth up to five (5) points. Extra credit points will be added to your exam grades, as follows:

- Two extra credit assignments—points will be added to your two lowest exam grades. The points will be distributed between the two exams to give you the best possible grade.

- One extra credit assignment—points will be added to your lowest exam grade.

Extra credit assignment due dates are listed in your course syllabus. **The extra credit assignment must be turned in only on that date.** No late extra credit assignments will be accepted. The following procedures must be followed:

1. You are to turn in only one extra credit assignment on each of the two due dates found on your course syllabus calendar.

2. You may not turn in extra credit assignments at any other time.

3. You may not repeat the same assignment twice.

4. You must include the assignment cover sheet, stapled to the front of the assignment. Failure to include the cover sheet will result in no credit being issued for that assignment.

5. You must fill out the cover sheet completely. If any component is missing, it will not be accepted and you will not get credit for the assignment.

6. All extra credit assignments must (unless otherwise noted in the assignment):
   - be typed
   - be double spaced
   - have 12 point font
   - have one (1) inch margins

EXTRA CREDIT ASSIGNMENT A

Prepare a Family Budget

Based on the following scenario, prepare an itemized budget. Be sure to make the budget as realistic as possible. (Hint: Use the Sunday newspaper advertisements as a guide for pricing items or check prices when shopping at your local stores.)

An eighteen-year-old female, Angela, is a single mother of a nine-month-old child, Darrius. Angela is taking General Equivalency Degree (GED) classes in the morning in order to earn her high school degree. Her parents are not allowing her to live at home. As a result, she is currently living in a transitional living shelter. Angela works twenty hours a week at a drug store, which is within walking distance from the shelter. She is a cashier and earns $5.50 per hour.

The transitional living shelter provides Angela with an apartment and partial day care. She is responsible for paying for one week of daycare each month, providing food for herself and Darrius, and purchasing everyday necessities, including diapers.

The transitional living program requires that she save twenty-five percent (25%) from her job earnings each month.

Angela's monthly income and resources are as follows:

INCOME	RESOURCES
$350.00 after taxes (Drug store)	$240.00 Food Stamps
	WIC Vouchers*

Note: Food stamps may only be used for food purchases. Other household supplies cannot be purchased with these funds.

*WIC vouchers can only be used for designated items: milk, cereal, rice, beans, formula, cheese, peanut butter and frozen juices.

Based on the above information, prepare a monthly budget for Angela. Be sure to include diapers, baby wipes, clothing, feminine needs (such as tampons), and other household needs.

EXTRA CREDIT ASSIGNMENT B

Research the Day, Month, and/or Year You Were Born

This project allows you to explore the concepts presented in Bronfenbrenner's macrosystem and chronosystem. Many things were happening in the world on the day you were born. To do this exercise, you will need to do some research. You can find information through Internet links, newspaper archives, "This Day in History," books, and/or the "The Year You Were Born" cards.

This project must not be any larger than ledger size (11x17). Your cover sheet must be securely attached to your project. Additionally, you must cover a minimum of ten (10) different subject areas (see suggestions below).

Items to look for during the time you were born include, but are not limited to:

- Historical events
- Popular music of the time
- Popular books of the time
- Hair, clothes, shoe styles of the time
- Best film of the year, best actor, best actress
- The cost of housing, cars, gasoline, bread, milk, eggs, etc.
- The marriage and divorce trends of the year
- Popular leisure activities of families
- Best job opportunities of the year you were born
- Popular sayings and phrases of the year
- New inventions of the year
- The best selling car of the year
- The most popular toys of the year

Use your creativity in preparing this extra credit opportunity. For example:

- Create a picture book.
- Create a scrapbook.
- Create your own birthday card that includes birthday facts found in your research
- Write a letter to your future grandchild.
- Write a two to three (2-3) page paper.

You are only limited by your own imagination!

EXTRA CREDIT ASSIGNMENT C
Read and Analyze a Children's Book

This project requires that you choose a children's book from the list provided and analyze the family image portrayed in the book in terms of what you have learned from your textbooks and class lectures. You will write a one to two page paper.

Be sure to use citations from the textbooks and class lectures to support your thoughts. No reference page is required.

Approved Children's Book List:

Book	*Author*
1. *A Story, A Story: An African Tale*	Gail Haley
2. *Love You Forever*	Robert Munsch
3. *Legend of the Bluebonnet*	Tommie dePaola
4. *Mufaro's Beautiful Daughters*	John Steptoe
5. *Something Beautiful*	Sharon Dennis Wyeth
6. *Nana Upstairs, Nana Downstairs*	Tommie dePaola
7. *Heather Has Two Mommies*	Leslea Newman
8. *Black Is Brown Is Tan*	Arnold Adoff
9. *It Is Not Your Fault, Koko Bear*	Vicki Lansky
10. *Dinosaur's Divorce*	Laurence Brown and Marc Brown
11. *The New Baby*	Joanna Cole and Margaret Miller
12. *Family Pictures/Cuadros de Familia*	Carmen Lomas Garza
13. *Alexander, Who Does Not Want to Move*	Judith Viorst

EXTRA CREDIT ASSIGNMENT D

A Family Study:
Looking for Your Roots

Choose one of the following two assignments:

Assignment One: "Geneogram"

To do this project, you will need to either go to the library or the bookstore to look at one or both of the following books:

Geneograms: Assessment and Interventions by Monica McGoldrick (preface), Randy Gerson and Sylvia Shellenberger
Geneograms by Emily Marlin

Your geneogram must be legible and be no larger than a legal size piece of paper. Try to identify as many generations of your family as possible. Ask your parents, grandparents, and/or other family members to help you.

Use colored pencils or markers to help make clear connections and identify trends. Be sure to include a legend.

Assignment Two: "Family Tree"

Go to a website that allows you to research information to construct your family tree. Example sites:

- *http://www.all-surnames.com*
- *http://www.rootsweb.com*

You may be creative in how you develop your family tree. Your family tree must be legible and be no larger than a legal size piece of paper. Try to identify as many generations of your family as possible. Ask your parents, grandparents, and/or other family members to help you.

These projects will take time to complete. It cannot be done overnight. So, if you plan to do this assignment, plan your time to work on it over a period of several days. The time you spend on this project will be a rewarding experience as you learn about your family's history and relationships.

EXTRA CREDIT ASSIGNMENT E

A Day in the Life of a Pre-Schooler

Observe three hours of interaction at the Human Development Lab School (see university website for location). While observing, be sure to note the following:

- Note at least three examples of teacher/child interactions

  - Write down the objective interaction (exactly what happened—the activity).

  - Record the teacher's action and the child's action (the response to the activity).

  - Record the length of the interaction (time).

  - What was the outcome of the interaction?

- From your observations, how are the rules established and implemented? Give example(s).

- How do the teachers and/or the children handle conflict? Give example(s).

EXTRA CREDIT ASSIGNMENT F

Be a Volunteer!

To better understand the stresses that a family faces in times of crisis, hardship, and in every day life, volunteer for a minimum of ten (10) hours at one of the suggested settings or in a setting approved by your instructor. Before you begin volunteering at any site, seek prior approval from your instructor to insure the appropriateness of the setting.

For this extra credit you will need to do the following:

- Keep a journal of your daily experiences and volunteer activities (be sure to include how this project is making you feel or think)

- Connect experiences to information learned in this course. This needs to part of your journal.

Suggested Settings for Volunteering:

- Head Start

- Nursing Homes

- Daycares

- Educational Settings

- Shelters

- Social Services Agencies

- Hospitals

EXTRA CREDIT ASSIGNMENT G
Music to My Ears

Many songs have been written about relationships and families. Choose a song that has relevance to relationships and families. It can be from any genre that you choose. You are to analyze the song in reference to the material you have learned in this course. You are to write a one (1) to two (2) page paper of your analysis. Be sure to reference course materials by using citations. You must attach a copy of the song lyrics.

You may use any of the following examples of songs, but your choices are unlimited as long as the song is applicable to this course.

Examples:

- *My Boyfriend's Back* - The Angels - gender relationships and roles

- *Papa Don't Preach* - Madonna - teenage pregnancy and parental relationships

- *China* - Tori Amos - relationship/communication/breakup

- *Ours* - Sugar Ray - complex relationship involving a married woman and another man

- *Your Cheatin' Heart* - Hank Williams - extramarital affair

- *Stand by Your Man* - Tammy Wynette - gender roles and expectations

- *Tears in Heaven* - Eric Clapton - death of a child

- *Born to the Breed* - Judy Collins - the struggle of a single parent

- *Family Portrait* - Pink - adolescent's view of divorce

- *Cats in the Cradle* - Jim Croce - father/son relationship/family time/family values

- *Daddy's Hands* - Holly Dunn - family values, love

- *Teach Your Children Well* - Crosby, Stills, Nash, and Young - family values/parent responsibilities

- *Fast Car* - Tracy Chapman - alcoholism, poverty

- *Maria* - Stephen Sondheim - love, romance, intimacy

- *America* - Stephen Sondheim - immigration

- *America* - Neil Diamond - immigration

EXTRA CREDIT ASSIGNMENT H
Pass the Popcorn, please!

Movies often depict families in real life situations. We can gain understanding of many family situations by watching a movie and then applying what we have learned in this course.

Choose one of the following approved movies and then write a one (1) to two (2) page paper. Be sure to use citations from your textbooks and lectures to support your thoughts.

APPROVED MOVIES:

- *Not Without My Daughter*
- *The Next Best Thing*
- *Mrs. Doubtfire*
- *How Stella Got Her Groove Back*
- *The Color Purple*
- *Barbershop*
- *Divine Secrets of the Ya-Ya Sisterhood*
- *About Schmidt*
- *The Joy Luck Club*
- *Bringing Down the House*
- *American Pie I, II, or III*
- *Parenthood*
- *My Big Fat Greek Wedding*

Extra Credit Assignment I
Who Me, Violent?

Theorists and others have argued that the root of violence in America can be located in the media children view today. They especially point to children's cartoons. For this assignment, watch two (2) hours of children's cartoons. Write a one (1) to two (2) page paper. Be sure to use citations from your textbooks and lectures to support your thoughts.

Include the following elements in your paper:

- The name of the cartoon

- The time and day of the show

- The television channel on which the show appeared

- The age of the child at which the show is targeted

- The types of commercials that are broadcasted with the cartoon show

- Count the number the number of violent acts

- Describe what happened in each violent act and why you judged the act to be violent

- Given that you have viewed two (2) hours of cartoon material, how would you plan a children's cartoon that would be free of violence, but still entertaining?

EXTRA CREDIT ASSIGNMENT J

Tell the Story of Your Life

For this extra credit project, you will create a scrapbook that represents significant experiences that have had an impact on your life. Things that you may want to include in your scrapbook are **copies** of childhood pictures, family photographs, letters of achievement, letters from relatives, report cards, and other types of memorabilia. Your scrapbook may contain artwork, poems, letters, and objects that are meaningful to you.

The purpose of this project is to help you identify meaningful relationships and experiences in your life. Understanding how we are connected to others, what we have contributed and achieved, and why our lives are meaningful, helps us to prepare for our eventual death. It is hoped that this scrapbook of your life will become a work "in progress" (as is your life) and that you will continue to add to it and expand it through the years of your life.

Your scrapbook should meet the following criteria:

1. Organization of the scrapbook—

   - Is it chronological (tells your life story)?

   - Is it neat?

   - Is the placement and arrangement of items done in a creative, but thoughtful manner?

2. Does your scrapbook contain a variety of items from various periods of your life?

Your creativity is only limited by your imagination!

EXTRA CREDIT ASSIGNMENT K

Planning Ahead: My Funeral Plan

For most of us, we rarely have the opportunity to make funeral plans and we seldom think about making our own. In this extra credit opportunity, you will develop a plan for your funeral. This process typically includes several elements—

1. Disposal of the body. There are a variety of methods in which one may dispose of a body, including burial, burial at sea, cremation, excarnation (having the elements and small rodents do the dirty work), Cryogenics, etc . . . You will need to choose a method for disposal of your body that is comfortable for you.

2. Obituary. What do you want your obituary to say about you? Write your own obituary. Do you want the obituary to be in the newspaper, a brochure given out at the funeral service, or given out in some other form?

3. Invitees. Who would you like to invite to your funeral?

4. Ritual. This may include: music, poems, prayers, final statements, gifts, etc . . .

5. Memorial: This might include a tree being planted in your name, a grave marker, or any other objects that allow your friends and family to have a connection to your life.

As part of your funeral plan, consider how much you would want someone to spend on your funeral (use today's dollars). Be sure to consider the cost of the coffin, the burial plot or cremation urn or mausoleum or other place of rest, etc . . . You may want to contact a funeral home and talk with them about funerals or you may go online to—

1. google.com

2. type "funeral plans" in the search window

3. go to several of the sites and use information gained from these sites to aid in the development of your funeral plan.

EXTRA CREDIT ASSIGNMENT L

Write Your Own Ticket!

There are many ideas that you may have that may work for an extra credit assignment. If you have an idea, discuss it with your instructor and get their approval prior to embarking on this extra credit assignment.

Submit the following information for approval.

Your Name: _____ **SSN#:** _____

Class Section: _____ **Date of Submission:** _____

Description of your idea: _____

_____

_____

_____

❑ **Approved**   ❑ **Disapproved**

_____   _____
Instructor's Signature   **Date of Approval**

Instructor's Comments: _____

_____

_____

_____

Exam
Requirements

7

EXAM REQUIREMENTS

INSTRUCTIONS FOR EXAM DAY PREPARATION

For each exam you will need the following items:

- Blue scantron sheet

- Two or three #2 pencils sharpened with erasers

- Picture ID (driver's license or college identification card)

- The appropriate "Cheat Sheet" form, completed in your own handwriting and removed from your textbook. (The cheat sheet is optional.)

Hints to help you prepare for your exam:

- Keep up with your readings daily. Do not wait until the day before the exam to read all the assigned materials.

- After class, reread your class notes and make any corrections or additions to your notes while the information is still fresh in your mind.

- Study a little each day by going back over the previous material. Make notes on how certain ideas connect to previous ideas mentioned in class or to other readings.

- Take notes on your readings.

- As you read, note the things that are confusing to you or that you do not understand. Bring these questions up in class. (Hint: You could be the class hero/heroine because you may be the only one brave enough to bring up the issue.)

- Form a study group and meet often. Discuss your ideas. Some study groups assign readings to each member and then they exchange notes after discussing the readings among themselves.

- The night before the exam, get a good night's rest.

- On the morning of the exam, eat a nutritious breakfast. It will help you be alert for the exam.

- Arrive early for the exam, find your seat, and relax.

If you have done all of the above, you will be more than prepared for the exam.

Hints for preparing a helpful "Cheat Sheet":

- Remove the "Cheat Sheet" form from the course packet to use.

- Prepare your cheat sheet in your own handwriting.

- You may use both the front and the back of the form.

- Your cheat sheet must be prepared on the form provided. If the form from the course packet is not used, you will be unable to use your cheat sheet.

- The cheat sheet should be organized by related ideas and themes.

- When organizing the chapters from your textbooks, your readings, and lectures, use different colors to designate themes across chapters, readings, and lectures.

- Charting ideas and themes is a helpful way of organizing all of your data.

"CHEAT SHEET" FOR EXAM 2

Date of Exam: _____

Name: _____

SSN: _____   **Section #:** _____

Remove this sheet from your workbook and prepare your cheat sheet on it. You may use both sides. Your cheat sheet must be on this form in order for you to use it for the exam. You must complete this sheet in your own handwriting.

"CHEAT SHEET" FOR EXAM 3

Date of Exam: _____

Name: _____

SSN: _____ **Section #:** _____

Remove this sheet from your workbook and prepare your cheat sheet on it. You may use both sides. Your cheat sheet must be on this form in order for you to use it for the exam. You must complete this sheet in your own handwriting.

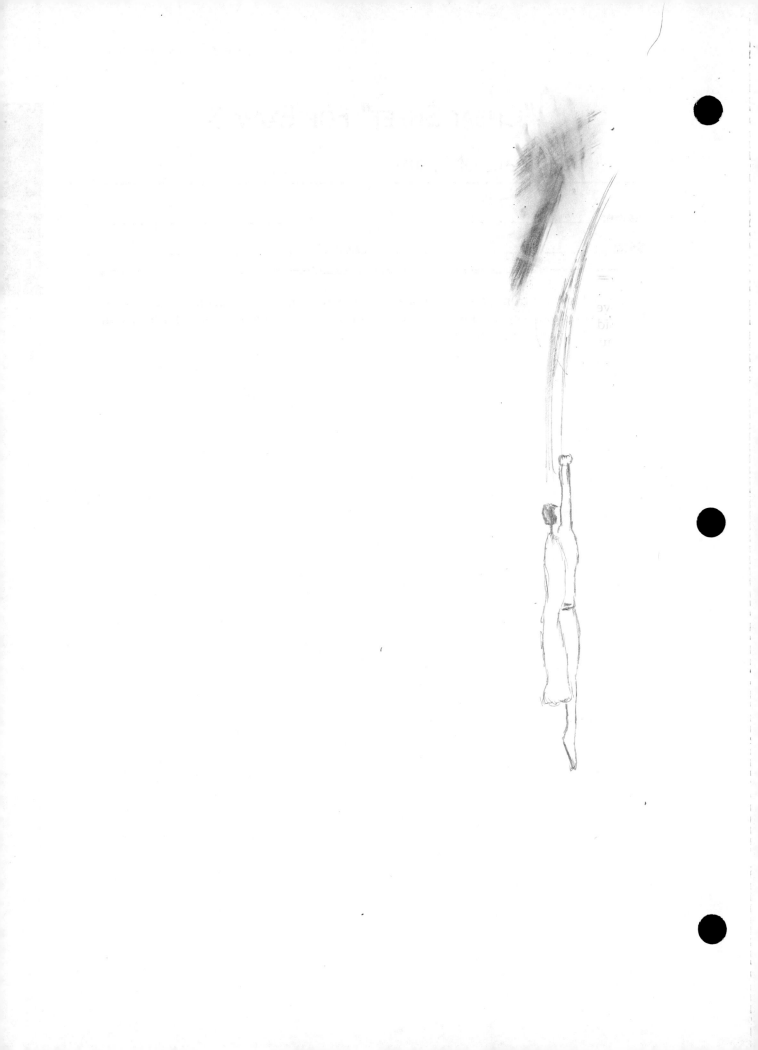

"CHEAT SHEET" FOR EXAM 4

Date of Exam: _____

Name: Saul Picazo

SSN: _____   **Section #:** 01319

Remove this sheet from your workbook and prepare your cheat sheet on it. You may use both sides. Your cheat sheet must be on this form in order for you to use it for the exam. You must complete this sheet in your own handwriting.

dual-earner

8

EXAM STUDY GUIDES

STUDY GUIDE: DIVERSITY IN FAMILIES
BACA ZINN AND EITZEN

For each chapter, know and be able to apply . . .

Chapter 1:

- the obstacles to studying the family objectively
- the three distinct images of families in the United States
- the myths about the family
- the micro level and macro level of relationships between society and families
- the vital resource for many poor women ("Norma", box 1.3)
- keywords:
    backstage and front stage behavior
    nuclear family
    monolithic family form
    patriarchy
    human agency
    family paradigm
    family
    household

Chapter 2:

- family based economy and family wage economy
- the marriage customs of the colonial period and of the "modern" family
- the role and view of colonial children
- changes in family life with the emergence of the "modern" family
- differences between middle class women and working class women
- sources to use when researching your family
- keywords:
  "modern" family
  family reconstitution
  aggregate data analysis
  godly family

Chapter 3:

- the characteristics of the "cult of true womanhood"
- the changing view of childhood and adolescence
- women's work in factories
- Gutman's findings on slave families
- work and gender roles in Black and Chicano families
- the life of street children in New York
- keywords:
  social production
  social reproduction
  doctrine of two spheres
  chain migration/stage migration
  matriarchal family households
  compadrazgo system
  accordion households

Chapter 4:

- the three societal "earthquakes"
- "structured inequality" and what it is a function of
- forces transforming the economy and jobs in the United States
- what has been the middle class "American Dream" and why it is hard to obtain today
- coping strategies for Americans
- demographic trends
- affects of immigration on Latinos and Asians
- the consequences and problems facing the elderly in our society
- the four major personality types among people who are seventy (70) years old and older
- keywords:
    sunrise and sunset industries
    the "new poor" and the "old poor"
    postmodern family
    transnational family/binational family
    fictive kin
    machismo
    downward mobility

Chapter 5:

- the difference between the cultural and structural approach to studying families
- understand and be able to apply the cultural approach views of class, race, and gender
- understand and be able to apply the structural approach views of class, race, and gender
- understand the shortcomings of each approach
- the Panel Study of Income Dynamics (P.S.I.D.) study results (box 5.1)
- define each social class
- survival strategies of poor mothers (box 5.2)
- the importance of kinship networks to Blacks and Latinos
- types of patriarchy
- the factors influencing the high rate of black single female-headed households
- the sex role approach and its shortcomings
- keywords:
  social stratification
  matrix of domination
  culture of poverty
  racial formation
  institutional racism
  compulsory heterosexuality
  household augmentation
  "underclass"
  class privilege
  gender

Chapter 6:

- the changes in men's and women's participation in the labor force and what caused these changes
- the consequences to family of contemporary work patterns (shift, increased hours etc.)
- the different effects on the family of various types of work situations (professional, blue collar etc)
- research on teens who work
- gender differences with work in the home
- types of invisible work women do
- the components of the Family Leave Act
- coping strategies for workers from both employers and employees
- keywords:
    work-family role system
    spillover
    family interference
    invisible work
    sequencing
    mommy track
    second shift
    unpaid work

Chapter 7:

- dating and courtship practices and influences (heterosexual couples)
- differences in race, class
- "his" and "her" sex and love characteristics
- factors contributing to the sexual revolution
- influences on mate selection
- how race, class, gender, and sexual preference influence dating practices, intimacy
- what research concluded about sexuality
- sex and poor teens
- teenage childbearing
- new data on AIDS
- keywords:
    homogamy
    heterogamy
    hypogamy
    hypergamy
    principle of least interest
    sexual identity
    sexual orientation

Chapter 8:

- recent trends of marriage
- the benefits of marriage/ revisited comparing husband's and wife's marriage
- effects on women of delayed marriage
- five types of enduring marriages
- factors that correlate to a stable marriage
- types of "power" used in marriages
- four characteristics of a peer marriage
- what the text concludes about the future of marriage
- keywords:
    marital quality
    homogamous marriage
    role fit
    patriarchy
    machismo

Chapter 9:

- what is meant by the social construction of parenting
- changes related to family composition/ fertility rates
- benefits/ costs of parenting
- gendered parenting
- birth order characteristics
- homosexual parenting
- social supports to parents—positions of liberals and conservatives
- research on daycare
- keywords:
    pronatalism
    boomerang generation
    sandwich generation
    bi-lateral model of parent child relations

Chapter 10:

- how society sanctions violence
- spousal abuse
- conditions that favor abuse
- difficulties obtaining data
- why women stay in abusive situations
- issue of power and control in family violence
- the major determinant in violence against women
- what is child abuse?
- factors contributing to abuse
- effects of incest on victims
- types of elder abuse
- unique problems associated with domestic violence in same sex relationships
- social and legal remedies for family violence in the United States and Sweden
- keywords:
  patriarchal terrorism
  ageism
  learned helplessness

Chapter 11:

- correlates of divorce/ who is most at risk for divorce
- differences between "his" and "her" divorce
- effects of divorce on children
- race and divorce/ religion and divorce
- factors which contribute to high divorce seen in African American population
- sources of income for divorced women/ problems associated with these sources
- advantages/disadvantages to remarriage
- lack of societal help for blended families
- keywords:
  feminization of poverty
  reconstituted family
  blended family
  "thin kin"

Chapter 12:

- five global trends in family formation
- correlation between gender, race and singlehood/ rise in single population
- problems and benefits cited for heterosexual cohabitation
- characteristics of same sex families
- rights that homosexuals are seeking for social and economic benefits
- pros and cons of commuter marriages
- keywords:
    chosen family
    transnational family
    commuter family
    non-family household
    marriage squeeze
    domestic partner movement

Chapter 13:

- ideological fault lines between conservatives and progressives
- be able to compare the values and views of conservatives and progressives *with:*

    the cultural and structural approach, strict father and nurturant parent *on:*

    birth control, abortion and welfare reform

- research data on the distribution of condoms in high schools and who supports this
- what is missing in welfare reform
- major problems affecting poor children
- relationship between poverty of the elderly and poverty of children
- the premise of Head Start, who it serves, and its effectiveness
- the proposals to guide family policy
- keywords:
    deep poverty
    family policy
    latch key children

STUDY GUIDE: READINGS

Essential Families: Biological Fact or Social Fiction?
Helen M. Gore-Laird, Ph.D.

- Know the term "biological essentialism"

- Understand the difference between "biological essentialism" and "evolutionary process"

- Know and understand the various social forms discussed in the article

- Know and understand which primate species and which human cultures are examples of each type of social forms

- Understand why the author argues that the nuclear family is not "hard wired" to the human specie

- Know Morgan's three stages of human evolution of human societies as described by Engles

- Know Engles' evolutionary steps in family forms

- _____

- _____

- _____

Historical Basis of Anglo Families in America
Glenn W. Laird

- Know the seven types of folkways discussed in lecture as they apply to the four Anglo-American family groups

- Be able to distinguish the folkway characteristics of each group

- _____

- _____

- _____

Genealogical Research: Developmental Perspectives
Helen M. Gore-Laird, Ph.D. and Glenn W. Laird

- Know the difference between primary and secondary sources

- Know the difference between the terms, *sasha* and *zamani*

- Know how to get started in genealogical research

- _____

- _____

- _____

The Way We Weren't: The Myth and Reality of the 'Traditional' Family
Stephanie Coontz

- Know how Coontz defines "traditional family" and why it is a myth

- Know the various ways in which families were structured for the different eras identified in the reading

- _____

- _____

- _____

Urie Bronfenbrenner: Ecological Systems Theory
Helen M. Gore-Laird, Ph.D.

- Know the basic premise underlying Bronfenbrenner's Ecological Systems Theory

- Know and be able to apply the characteristics of the following systems . . .

  - microsystem

  - mesosystem

  - exosystem

  - macrosystem

  - chronosystem

- Understand the nature of each of the following terms (know what they are and how to apply them):

  - ecology/ecological

  - systems

  - theory

- _____

- _____

- _____

Discovering What Families Do
Urie Bronfenbrenner

- Understand the five propositions and be able to apply them

- Know why the five propositions are key to the development of the child

- _____

- _____

- _____

Individual Development: A Holistic, Integrated Model
David Magnusson

- Know what is meant by "development of living organisms"
- Understand the basic premise of the article: that we need to study individuals in a holistic manner
- Know what it means to study an individual holistically and what it constitutes
- Understand the concepts of:
  - mentalistic
  - biological
  - environment
  - behavior
- _____
- _____
- _____

Two Ideal Parenting Models: Making Sense of Them
Helen M. Gore-Laird, Ph.D.

- Know the characteristics of the "Strict Father" model and the "Nurturant Parent" model
- Know the key factors of each of the models
- Be able to distinguish the two models in an applied manner
- Know how Kohlberg and Loevinger would explain the two models
- _____
- _____
- _____

Jobless Ghettos and the Social Outcome of Youngsters
William Julius Wilson

- Know the effects of the following . . .
  - family management
  - neighborhood social organizations
  - unsupervised peer groups
  - ghetto-specific cultural practices
- Know and be able to apply the terms:
  - new urban poverty
  - social organization
- _____
- _____
- _____

The Basic Tenets of Polyamory
Lori M. Selzer, M. Ed.

- Understand the term "polyamory"
- Know and be able to apply the internal key components of polyamorous relationships
- Know and be able to apply the external key components of polyamorous relationships
- Know and be able to apply the different models of polyamorous relationships
- _____
- _____
- _____

Growing Up Without "Dad"
JoAnn Hazard, M. Ed.

- Know why the author feels it is difficult to study fatherlessness
- Know what the researchers say about the advantages to children raised with a father in the home
- Understand other variables (besides an absent father) that could account for differences in development between children raised with a father and children raised without a father in the home
- Know the proposals suggested by both the conservatives and the progressives.
- Know the problems faced by families where grandparents raise grandchildren.
- Know the differences between families where the single parent is the father instead of the mother.
- _____
- _____
- _____

Parenting in Diverse Cultures
Tommie J. Hamner

- Know how the quality of the home environment affects children
- Know the diverse view points in African-American culture
- Know how the characteristics of the African-American culture affects child rearing
- Know the characteristics of the Mexican-American parenting style
- Know how Native Americans interact with their children
- Know how Asian Americans parent their children
- _____
- _____
- _____

Vietnamese American Families
Nazli Kibria

- Know how the Vietnamese culture feels about divorce and what values and beliefs contribute to these feelings
- Know how the Vietnamese construct extended families
- Know what the family roles are in Vietnamese families
- _____
- _____
- _____

Ain't Misbehavin': Discipline and Parenting
Anne C. Beal, Linda Villarosa, and Alison Abner

- Understand the "four walls" of parenting
- Know the four identified parenting styles
- Know how discipline is different for each age group
- Know the negatives of spanking
- Know and understand the effects of shaken baby syndrome
- _____
- _____
- _____

The Two Sexes and Their Social Systems
Eleanor Maccoby

- Know the factors that Maccoby reports which influence the development of gender identity and gender roles
- Know what Maccoby sees as the weakness of the argument she presents
- Recognize the differences of the various ages (birth to adolescence) of each gender
- _____
- _____
- _____

Family Time, Family Values
Mark Mellman, Edward LaZarus, and Allan Rivilin

- Know the "family values" authors highlight and why Americans find them important

- Know what "personal values" Americans consider to be important

- Be able to distinguish between "family values" and "personal values"

- Know the two "central fault lines" identified by the authors that underlie value preferences

- Know what suggestions the authors make to improve family life

- _____

- _____

- _____

Section B:
READINGS

1

THE "ESSENTIAL" FAMILY: BIOLOGICAL REALITY OR SOCIAL FICTION?

Helen M. Gore-Laird, Ph.D.[1], University of Houston

Most of us have grown up accepting, without question, the idea that we are biologically "hard-wired" to become part of a nuclear family form. That supposed innate tendency is the desire to mate and reproduce with only one person. But, what if we are not innately wired for only this type of family paradigm? What if other family forms are just as viable, or even more viable than nuclear monogamy? What does this mean for us as individuals? What does this mean for us as a society? As a specie?

Biological essentialism refers to the idea that men and women are intrinsically different due to some internal "essence." For those who ascribe to the tenets of biological essentialism, gender differences are not really differences in gender but a biologically based difference that is consistent across cultures. Furthermore, biological essentialists stipulate that there is no variation in the expression of biologically essential characteristics. Extending this logic to families, biological essentialism makes the assumption that we are "hard wired" to have one mate for life and one family form. Biological essentialists believe that there is something about our biology that makes us what we are as genders. To them, it is biological essentialism which places the construction of gender outside society. It is this construction of gender, combined with our need to reproduce, that creates the need for families. Thus, the nuclear family form becomes the dominant cultural norm for how we think about our sexuality as well as how we assign gender roles. In assigning the explanation of family to biology, we, in reality, are socially constructing our understanding of gender. In other words, saying that family is an effect of biology is itself a creation of our culture and thus, is a particular kind of social construct. Biological essentialism, as applied to families, does not allow for any diverse forms of family to be considered as "normal." Thus, same sex unions, cohabitation, polyamourous relationships, polygamous relationships, *et cetera*, are excluded as legitimate forms of family.

If we assume that we are not "hard wired" to have monogamous relationships which result in a nuclear family form, we must assume that some evolutionary force is at work in the establishment of family form. If we accept the evolutionary explanation, then all forms of family become legitimate.

To determine which viewpoint is correct, or if there is some interaction between the two positions, essentialism or evolution, we must ask what determines family form? Additionally, we will want to know how any specific form of the family supports both the societal needs of a particular group and the needs of the individual. How are children raised and treated in these alternative forms of family? And then we must ask are these alternative styles of being family deviant and in need of "treatment" or are they actually adaptive? And finally, we must ask how understanding and knowing about the different family forms effect our western understanding of family?

SOCIAL ANIMALS AND THE CONSTRUCTION OF RULES OF BEHAVIOR

All social animals require rules of behavior for the group to function. Rules can be either descriptive or prescriptive (DeWaal, 1996). Descriptive rules can apply to both animate and inanimate objects. A descriptive rule describes a typical behavior (i.e., a man throwing a stone or a mother breast-feeding her child). Prescriptive rules are those which are actively enforced through rewards and punishment. Marriage, and the social customs that surround marriage, are rules of a society which are enforced through the reward of acceptability or the punishment of exclusion or ridicule. These rules reflect the moral perspective of a society. They define what is right and what is wrong; what is acceptable and what is unacceptable. Yet, one must ask if there is only one morality or one right way to form a family? If so, who determines what that correct morality, and thus, family form, is? If not, can we have multiple moral forms that allow us to have more than one "right" way to form a family?

What we know to be true is that multiple perspectives—and thus multiple moral forms—do exist. We also can find diversity in how family is structured throughout the world. One can find diversity in how marriage occurs and how children are raised from culture to culture, community to community, and from era to era. The rules that direct the construction of family change over time and thus, the given family structure changes. Many forms of family exist today and/or have existed in the past. Family function, and thus structure, has changed over time to ensure the survival of the specie and also as a response to economic and political pressures of a given time period (i.e. the Victorian Era). However, we often accept as true that "everyone" has the same moral understandings and that we all accept for true that the nuclear family is the ideal family form. Thus, the nuclear family becomes the "measuring stick" by which we judge all other forms of relationships. In our modern world, despite access to more knowledge about how others form relationships, we make the assumption that "family values" and the nuclear family are being corrupted by the entrapments of a changing world.

We are correct to understand that today the family form is changing. However, it is not breaking apart or disintegrating. To be a part of a family, whatever its form, is to engage in a time honored process that is dynamic, not static. We live in a diverse world, with diverse family forms. Thus, in an effort to gain an understanding of the diversity found in family structures, I will trace the origin of family from its roots to its modern form.

THE "FAMILIES" OF PRE-HUMAN HOMINIDS

One possible means of determining the origins of the family form most common to us today would be to study our ancient animal ancestors. The origins of *Homo sapiens* have been traced back millions of years, to include a number of long-extinct species. One of the numerous Australopithocene species appears to have given rise to *Homo habilis* in the savannahs of eastern Africa roughly 2.4 million years before the present (B.P.), which in turn gave rise to *Homo erectus* approximately 1.8 million years B.P. *(http://www. archaeologyinf.com/species.htm).* These various hominid species, like most primate species (and most mammals, for that matter), appear to have been social species. As such, the survival of the group—rather than specific individuals—was paramount to the long-term viability of the specie. Therefore, group and individual behaviors had to be adapted to insure success of the group. Reproductive strategies, nutritional strategies, as well as group social dynamics were all evolved to that end. The scarce physical evidence that has been gathered thus far affords scientists clues as to what these strategies may have been. We can know, within a limited range of certainty, overall physical characteristics of these creatures, the types of foods they consumed, the tools they made, *et cetera*.

Unfortunately, behaviors—including "family" formation—can only be inferred from what we already know. It is easy to assign our known behaviors to these extinct species. Thus, we must be careful in our analysis of the data. We must maintain strict rules of interpretation. Thus, the behaviors regarding "family" formation can only be inferred, but not imposed. This is the process of assuming that our behaviors today (within a particular social setting) are the behaviors of the past. The only currently available hard evidence of social interaction for early hominids is a 3.56-million-year-old set of *Australopithecus afarensis* footprints in volcanic ash near Laetoli in Tanzania. This set of prints suggests a lone male walking close to a lone female, which appeared to be carrying a burden (assumed to be a child) on one hip *(http://www.archaeologyinf.com/australopithecusafarensis.htm).* Many, particularly biological essentialists, have jumped to the conclusion that this is "proof" of the long-term existence of monogamous, nuclear families among our human ancestors. However, the physical evidence can at best only prove that—at that moment in time, at that place—one male and one female were walking close together. Other conclusions that could just as easily be drawn are: 1) that the female's imbalanced gait could be the result of an injury or congenital condition; 2) the pair could have been siblings, with the brother protecting his sister from the volcanic ashfall; or, 3) a male from one band may have been "herding" a female captured from another band back to his own band's campsite. Given the paucity of unambiguous evidence about our distant ancestors, we can probably only conclude that they lived in small bands that cooperated for survival. But, we cannot know if they formed families as we know them or if sexual pairings for reproduction were monogamous, promiscuous, or polygynous. However, we might look to our closest contemporary kin for hints at the biological origins of the modern family.

"FAMILIES" OF OUR CLOSEST KIN: THE MODERN PRIMATES

The orang-utans (*Pongo pygmaeus*), the gorillas (*Gorilla beringei* & *Gorilla gorilla*), the chimpanzees (*Pan troglodytes*), and the bonobos (*Pan paniscus*), collectively known as the "great apes," have been recognized as our closest modern kin on the primate family tree. Studies of these species could yield insights into our own biological tendencies. If there is a consistent "family" form among these great apes, especially among the chimps and bonobos (our very closest kin), then perhaps a case can be made for the essential biologic family "type" for humans.

Research on animals over the last few decades has shifted focus from merely attempting to describe physical characteristics and cataloging species in the accepted taxonomic framework to attempting to understand the full range of behaviors for each specie. This is most often accomplished by long-term observation in both captivity and in the wild. The most popularly known of these studies is that of chimpanzees (*Pan troglodytes*) initiated by Jane Goodall. Her observation of the chimps at Gombe National Park in Tanzania began in 1960 and spans several generations. Almost as well known is the work of the late Dian Fossey with mountain gorillas (*Gorilla beringei beringei*) in Rwanda between 1967 and her murder by gorilla poachers in 1985. Other less well known studies include those of bonobos (*Pan paniscus*) by Franz de Waal at the Yerkes Center for Primatology at Emory University and by Takayoshi Kano in their natural range of the Lomako Forest near Wamba in The Congo.

Until recently, it was thought that orang-utans (which means "old man of the forest" in the language of the locals) lived in virtual solitude in the jungles of Borneo and Sumatra, with males and females interacting only to mate, leaving the females to raise their young alone. What we have recently come to know about them is that two females will sometimes form groups consisting of them and their off-spring, sometimes accompanied by one male. Females do not appear to mate with only one male over their lifespan.

The popular conception of mountain gorilla society is that, in all cases, each family group is headed by a single dominant male (known as a "silverback") who is the exclusive sexual mate to all females in the group. In other words, they practice the patriarchal form of family: polygyny. In reality, only 61% of all mountain gorilla groups have just one male with several females. Fully 36% of all groups are comprised of two or more males with females; the remaining 3% of groups are temporary agglomerations of all males. Within the multi-male family groups (those with females), "affairs" between non-dominant males and group females have been documented.

Chimpanzees, with whom humans have been most often compared, were once thought to be polygynous, like the majority of gorillas. However, the research of the last few decades has revealed a very complex social form referred to as a "fission-fusion" society (Jane Goodall Institute: *http://www.janegoodall.org/chimps/social.html*). Basically, this means that the size and composition of the social group varies throughout the year, depending on specific situations and/or activities (O'Neil, 2002). The males of a group, usually always related at some level, rarely leave to join another group, although adolescent females will. Males will form constantly shifting sub-groups (fission) for foraging, hunting, and the development of alliances for "political" advantage. Females form and reform even more complex relationships on an ongoing basis. The group as a whole (fusion), often containing 40 to 60 individuals, serves as the "family" unit. Mating patterns, which occur only during female estrus, are of three basic types. The most prevalent is for all or most of the males in the group to attempt to mate with a female in estrus, with only one or a few being accepted by the female. The second most common is for the alpha male of the group to attempt to keep all other males away and gain exclusive mating rights. The third type is the "consort" arrangement, in which a sub-dominant male will persuade a female to accompany him to an isolated part of the group's range and keep her isolated until she comes into estrus (Jane Goodall Institute: *http://www.janegoodall.org/chimps/social.html*).

According to recent DNA testing, the bonobo is our closest relative, sharing over 98% of the same genetic material (de Waal, 1995). The best evidence indicates that bonobos and our direct ancestors diverged in East Africa roughly 6 to 8 million years ago, with chimps diverging from bonobos within the last approximately 4 million years. Like their cousins, the chimps, bonobos live in fission-fusion societies. The only association that is anything other than temporary, is the one between a mother and her dependent offspring. However, the alliances between bonobo females play essentially the same role as that of males among chimps, with high-ranking female groups exercising a form of dominance over males in most situations. Mating among the bonobos is controlled more by the females than by the males (de Waal, 1995).

The most important finding in studies of bonobos, however, is the centrality of sex in group life. Sex among this specie is in no way exclusively heterosexual or monogamous, with sex acts of many types (copulation, mutual genital stimulation, tongue kissing, and oral sex) being performed male-to-female, female-to-female, or male-to-male. Sex is used to facilitate food sharing, to resolve conflicts, and to prevent conflicts. Sex is also apparently used purely for pleasure, with masturbation being noted often (de Waal, 1995).

When we look at all of these apes, along with other primate species, six basic social group patterns are seen. They are 1) a single female with her offspring, 2) a monogamous family group, 3) a polyandrous group (one female mated to several related males), 4) a one-male/several females group (known as polygynous or a male with a "harem"), 5) a multi-male/multi-female group, and 6) a fission-fusion society (Chart 1) (O'Neil, 2002).

CHART 1

"Family Forms" Among the Primate Species

Social Group Pattern	*Primate Species Following This Pattern*
single female & her offspring	orang-utans, mouse lemurs, and galagos
monogamous family group	titi monkeys, gibbons, siamangs, indris, tarsiers and some pottos
polyandrous family group	marmosets and tamarins
one-male/several-female group	gorillas, hamadryas baboons, langurs, and howler monkeys
multi-male/multi-female group	savanna baboons, macaques, colobus, and some New World monkeys
fission-fusion society	chimpanzees and bonobos

EVOLVING HUMAN FAMILY FORMS

Having failed to identify a consistent family form among our closest primate kin in our search for the "essential" family, we are left to look at family forms we are aware of in human history and which are found in various societies around the world today. Work in this search began in the Nineteenth Century with early anthropologists, most notably the American, Lewis H. Morgan. The work of Morgan and others was summarized and given an evolutionary framework in Frederick Engels' famous book, *The Origin of the Family, Private Property, and the State,* originally published in 1884. In this book, Engels described a progressive evolution of human societies from "savagery" through "barbarism" to "civilization". Relying on Morgan's construct, Engels specifically defined these stages as follows:

> Savagery—the period in which the appropriation of natural products, ready for use, predominated; the things produced by man were, in the main, instruments that facilitated this appropriation. Barbarism—the period in which knowledge of cattle breeding and land cultivation was acquired, in which methods of increasing the productivity of nature through human activity were learnt. Civilization—the period in which knowledge of the further working-up of natural products, of industry proper, and of art acquired. (Engles, 1972, p. 44)

As can be seen, each step along the way was generally characterized by changes in the underlying economic form of the societies, which necessitated evolving family forms. This conclusion was based largely on studies of "savage" and "barbaric" societies still in existence in the Nineteenth Century and from historic sources by Greeks and Romans of contacts with such peoples. Some forms of "earlier" family forms had been observed in certain "primitive" peoples, and others were implied to have existed based on terms for relationships that survived in the indigenous languages. The specific evolutionary steps in family forms identified by Engels were "promiscuous," group marriage, pairing marriage, and monogamy (Engels, 1972, pp. 44–82).

The promiscuous stage of reproduction, is described by Engels and his sources as a sexual free-for-all with no incest prohibitions and no family formation (Engels, 1972). This stage was tied to a human economy not dissimilar to that of the great apes. This would have consisted of group foraging mainly for plants (leaves, nuts, fruits, roots, etc.) with some protein gathered from insects (ants, termites, locust, grubs, etc.) and macro-invertebrates (crayfish, clams, etc.). This diet was occasionally supplemented with small vertebrates (lizards, snakes, small primates, etc.) hunted by groups of males using crude tools of wood, bone, and stone. Engels gives no specific examples of such a society, leaving the impression that the existence of such an arrangement was purely speculative.

The first stage of family development was called the "Consanguine" family, which was described as the earliest form of "group marriage" (Engels, 1972, pp. 51–52). According to Engels and his sources, this group marriage arrangement was thought to be composed of natural brothers and sisters being "married" as a group, with sexual relations between adults and their natural offspring forbidden. This arrangement mirrored the sort of fission-fusion society typical of chimps and bonobos. Morgan tied this family form to the end of the early stage of savagery, which is referred to as the paleolithic or "old stone" age. Today, the concept of consanguine family is more complex and is not based on a reproductive relationship that we would consider to be incestuous, but rather indicates relationships based on descent from one mother.

Following his discussion on the "Consanguine" family form, Engles moves into his description of the more "advanced" group marriage form, which Morgan had designated by the Hawaiian term *punaluan* (Engels, 1972, pp. 52–59). In this arrangement, all or some of the sons of one mother will be married to all or some of the sisters of another mother. Children would be raised jointly by all adult members and all cultural property would be in communal ownership inherited from the mother (lands were owned by the tribe). Morgan had tied this family form to the middle and later stages of savagery, which bridged from the late paleolithic through the mesolithic, or "middle stone" age, encompassing the use of fire, the bow and arrow, and basket weaving. The overarching social structure would be that of the matrilineal "gens" (clan) or tribe.

The next family form mentioned by Engels was that of the "pairing marriage" (Engels, 1972, pp. 59–71). This form progresses into the situation of one man taking one wife, or more commonly two or more wives (polygyny). This form arises in the early stages of barbarism (the neolithic or "new stone" age), which is characterized by a gradual shift to pastoralism and seasonal farming, through the Bronze and Iron Ages, and carrying over into the earliest stages of "civilization." The line of inheritance of major property—originally herds of cattle, and then land itself—is now through the father ("patrilineal"). Engels describes the shift from a more-or-less matriarchal family form to a decidedly patriarchal one during this period (Engels, 1972).

According to Morgan, the final family form to arise in this vast march of history is the "monogamian" (Engels, 1972). Arising out of the pairing marriage forms of the barbarian epoch, Engels describes it as being "based on the supremacy of the man; its express aim is the begetting of children of undisputed paternity, this paternity being required in order that these children may in due time inherit their father's wealth as his natural heirs (Engels, 1972, pp. 71–72)." In order to insure this, although the man is still allowed extra-marital relations, the wife must be totally faithful in order to assure paternity. When personal property was inherited through the mother (all land belonging to the tribe or clan), paternity was never an issue. However, when large amounts of male-owned private property, including land, became a issue, certitude of paternity was paramount. According to Engels, these changes went hand-in-hand with the creation of the state (originally monarchies) and the advancement of mass agriculture and the formation of class systems.

VARIETIES OF FAMILY FORMS TODAY

These Victorian Era understandings of Engels and his sources are still somewhat helpful in understanding the changes in family forms that were responses to changes in the way people earned income or supported their families. However, our current understandings on the construction of family forms indicate the past and current existence of far more diverse forms and a much less linear evolution of forms. Since most societies in the world today are still tribal in organization, we would expect pairing marriage forms, especially polygynous ones, to predominate. According to the Department of Anthropology at the University of California at Davis, a recent survey of 849 societies around the globe showed that only 16% of them were monogamous, 0.5% were polyandrous, and the remaining 83.5% are almost exclusively some form of polygynous (Stewart, 1997). Even this finding over-simplifies the full picture of global family diversity. The following discussions illustrate several types of family forms which exist today, some of which are consistent with Engel's view, and some of which are not.

The Na of China: A Consanguine Family System

The Na are a small ethnic group of about 30,000 living in the Yongning Basin on the border between the Yunnan and Sichuan provinces in southwestern China. They migrated to the area around the end of the first century C.E. from the Tibetan plateau to the northwest. They are primarily a farming people, raising crops of Dekkan wheat, corn, potatoes, and vegetables. They also raise buffalo, cows, horses, and mules, and supplement their incomes with various crafts, especially weaving (Hua, 2001).

What makes the Na unique in the region, if not in the modern world, is their family form. This form apparently originated many millennia in the past, most likely long before they became agrarian. This particular consanguine family form is characterized by all the offspring of one or more mothers (who are sisters) living together as "brothers" and "sisters" in one household. Each line, called a *lignée*, is descended from the oldest known female ancestor (Hua, 2001). The men live in one wing of the large house—in what is essentially a dormitory—and primarily tend to the farming and animal husbandry and dealings with the wider world. The women live in another wing—each having her own bedroom—and are mainly engaged in care of the house, raising the children, and production of craft goods. All members partake in the raising of the family's children, although the "grandmothers" and "great-uncles" bear the greater burden owing to their more extensive life experience.

In traditional Na society, no one ever gets "married" in any sense. Procreation results from the practice of the "visit," in which liaisons between one man of one lignée and one woman of another lignée are arranged during the day, and consummated at night (sibling incest is strictly forbidden). The visit always occurs at the home of the woman. In what is known as the "furtive" visit (Hua, 2001), the man arrives at the pre-arranged time (usually after midnight) and either climbs in the woman's bedroom window or uses a particular knock so that only the woman who is being visited will answer the door. Long-term, relatively committed relationships, use an out-in-the-open visit, known as the "conspicuous" visit (Hua, 2001). In either case, the couple may spend the entire night in her room, but the man must be gone before dawn and back to his own home in order to fulfill his daily responsibilities (Hua, 2001). The number of "lovers" any member of Na society may have over the course of their life can range widely, from only a handful, to scores. Monogamous relations are rare, despite decades of central communist government pressure on the Na to adopt monogamous marriage (Hua, 2001).

Children are considered purely the offspring of the mother, although many Na today realize the biology of procreation. Since matrilineal descent is all that matters, paternity—even if it is known or suspected—is essentially ignored. This pattern is so ingrained in the society, that the Na have no words for "father" or "marriage." A child of one family calls her mother and all her mother's sisters (including first cousins) "mother." The child recognizes all of its mothers' male siblings (and first cousins) as "uncles." The next older generation in the household is comprised of "grandmothers" and "great-uncles." All children of one generation consider all girls—no matter the biological mother—sisters, and all boys brothers.

The Na think that their family form is vastly superior to that of the nuclear, monogamous one. From their perspective, it is an utterly non-sensical endeavor for two young people to attempt to raise children by themselves. To them, it is far less stressful to let the young adults produce the children and have the older and wiser generation, of several individuals, do most of the child-rearing.

The survival of the family form used by the Na provides some affirmation that Morgan's conclusions about the evolution of family forms have credibility. However, the survival of the form well into a sedentary agrarian way of life, at the very least, smudges the boundaries of transition predicted by Morgan and Engels.

The !Kung, san of the Kalahari: Pragmatic Serial Monogamy

The *!Kung*, san, known to us as the "Bushmen," are a society of hunter-gatherers who continue to exist as they may have for roughly 125,000 years in and about the Kobe area of the Kalahari Desert of southern Africa. The Human Genome Project has concluded that all modern humans appear to be descended from these Khoisan-speaking people. The !Kung have an unusually egalitarian society, with little discernible social stratification, and virtual equality between men and women (Shostak, 1981). Although the normative !Kung family is monogamous, up to 5 percent of families are polygynous at any given time (Shostak, 1981). Upon reaching puberty, a young woman may have one or more "trial marriages"—typically to a man 5 to 15 years her senior—until she becomes pregnant, whereupon she becomes "officially" married (Shostak, 1981). Most !Kung have one long-term marriage, but divorce is common and many will have several marriages over the course of their life. Among the !Kung, it is felt that it is far better to terminate a bad marriage than to allow people to be unhappy (Shostak, 1981). Sex is a very important part of life for these people (it is even referred to as "food"), and is both practiced often and talked about openly (Shostak, 1981). Extra-marital affairs are common for both sexes, but are kept as discreet as possible so as not to bring shame or hurt to the other partner (Shostak, 1981). Children are spaced about four years apart and are nursed for about the same length of time (Shostak, 1981). Child-rearing is primarily the responsibility of the mother, although she is often assisted by her mother, sisters, co-wives, or friends.

Obviously, !Kung society has evolved to some degree over the last 125,000 years. However, Morgan and Engels would have predicted that such a "primitive" hunting and gathering people should be practicing some form of group marriage.

Engels' Marxist certitude would never have allowed for a predominance of monogamous marriages among such people.

The Canela of Brazil: Open Marriage

The Canela are a Native American people living in a single village roughly 400 miles southeast of the mouth of the Amazon River in central Brazil. When first contacted by Europeans around 1700, they were still a society of hunter/gatherers. Due to severely diminished hunting range (only 5% remains), the approximately 1,300 surviving Canelas now practice intensive agriculture. One of their society's most outstanding characteristics, that of sharing freely, still largely survives, but is rapidly waning in the face of expanding contact with modern materialist society (Smithsonian Institute).

The family form of the Canela is similar to that of the Na, in that it is consanguine, with several generations of women and their spouses living in the "long-house" of the common female ancestor. However, monogamous marriage is the norm. In a manner similar to the !Kung, beginning at age 11 to 13, a girl enters her first "trial" marriage. Upon becoming pregnant and giving birth, she is fully married. Even then, both partners may have numerous love affairs. Many Canela festivals and rituals, including the harvest festival and the puberty ritual for young men, involve much group sex. Refusal to participate by the woman, or the woman's husband forbidding her participation due to jealousy, were once considered serious breaches of the Canelas' value of open sharing. Since the 1980s, when contact with western civilization (especially with Christian missionaries) began to intensify, jealousy and selfishness have increased significantly, leading to the diminishing of the former sexual openness (Socioambiental).

As can be seen, the traditional Canela family structure appears to possess characteristics of other family types, forming what seems a blend of forms. While the consanguine relationship system hints at former group marriage, the "monogamy" which has replaced it was, until the last few decades, very porous. It too is a form which approximates one of the systems predicted by Morgan and Engels, but contains characteristics which are quite unique.

The Neslilik of the Arctic: Patriarchy In a Harsh World

The Neslilik is a small community of Inuit peoples (usually around 200) which is isolated and rarely interacts with other tribes. In Neslilik tradition all male first cousins are called brothers and all female first cousins are called sisters (Oswalt, 2002). For the Neslillik, marriage of first cousins is expected (Oswalt, 2002). The newly formed family unit lives with or near the husband's family (partilocal marriage residence). The extended family consists of two or more consanguineal families spanning a number of generations, i.e. two brothers, their wives, and children (Oswalt, 2002).

In general, the early Inuit tribes, who lived in central, Northern Canada, and the Arctic, viewed the selection of a mate for marriage as a personal preference (Bonvillain, 2001). However, in central Canada, arranged marriages were not uncommon. There was no formal marriage ceremony, but the union was marked by the couple beginning to live together (Bonvillain, 2001). Once the couple decided they would live together, the couple would live with or near the wife's family (matrilocal residence) until the birth of the first child, when the couple usually moved near the husband's family (patrilocal residence) (Bonvillian 2001). For the Inuit, divorce was easy (Bonvillain, 2001). So, while a couple was expected to be in a monogamous relationship, the ease with which they could divorce made serial monogamy common.

Children are treated with great affection and indulgence among the Neslilik. In learning their own gender related tasks, the daughters and sons are often taught the duties associated with the opposite gender. Those children who learned both gender responsibilities became more valuable as a spouse because they have a dual set of skills (Oswalt, 2002). Thus, androgynous roles were favored over gender-specific roles in mate selections. However, we do find that in Inuit relationships there is a tendency toward male dominance, especially in the central arctic (Oswalt, 2002). Therefore, while androgynous skills are valued, the need for the hierarchical pattern of male dominance is also needed to assure survival in a harsh environment.

The harsh environment requires that men do most of the hunting of seals and whales. Cooperative hunting of caribou is done by men, women, and children. Women are responsible for preparing the skins and the meat that are brought back from the hunts. The women's work was very important because the skills used in the preparation of the skins (for warmth) and the food (for substance throughout the winter) determined the survivability of the group.

It is required that before leaving on whale hunting expeditions, men are to abstain from sexual intercourse and from eating certain foods (Oswalt, 2002). When going whaling, the men choose a leader called an *Umialik*. The Umialik's wife holds an important role in the society. She is responsible for making new clothes for the whalers and performing ritual ceremonies related to the capture of the whale.

Two or more related families live together, travel together, share food and other resources. They follow a bilateral descent mechanism. In the spring, small groups of related people separate from the larger group, which had assembled together in the winter time, and form temporary camps. The small camps usually consists of an older couple and the families of their grown sons, therefore the married daughters go with their husband's families. Wife-beating and wife-stealing is tolerated in the Neslilik culture. In the past, this often led to disputes among men which resulted in the killing or maiming of men.

While monogamous relationships are the norm for the Neslilik and the Inuit in general, the ability to easily obtain a "divorce" and the toleration of "wife-stealing" supports serial monogamy. The Neslilik family form and way of life have characteristics of Morgan and Engel's descriptive system, yet it also contains some unique ways of functioning as a community and as a family unit.

The Innu of Sub-Arctic Canada: Open Marriage

The Innu are a tribe found in sub-arctic central and southeastern Canada. Their name is derived from the original name for themselves, "Innuat", which means human being. Hunting and fishing were the primary sources of work for the males. Women made clothes (preparing the hides) and cured the meats gained in the hunt. Their lifestyles were not easy and food was not plentiful. They were often hungry, even though the Innu had available to them a variety of resources (Bonvillian, 2001, p. 520). This was due the migratory nature of the animals that lived in their territory. The economic system of the Innu is centered on hunting and fishing while the gathering of plants provides a minor part of their diet (Bonvillian, 2001). For the most part, they do not engage in farming activities. In general they live in a harsh environment that requires special skills to survive. Most modern

Innu do not follow the aboriginal practices of their forefathers, but a significant minority do continue to engage in the traditional hunting and fishing activities (Bonvillain, 2001).

They were nomadic and each winter camp contained no more than three or four extended nuclear families. The summer camps could number as many as a 1000. These camps could be either patrilineal or matrilineal. Men and women cooperatively constructed their lodges. Cheerfulness was valued as a social comfort and humor was seen as the best medicine for illness.

The Innu stress "generosity, hospitality, cooperation, and loyalty (Bonvillain,2001, p. 525)." People are expected to share resources and engage in communal work. They do not tolerate coercion either within households or within the community. They seek advice from knowledgeable others in the village. Decisions for the group are made jointly by all who are affected. Thus, the Innu society is one of egalitarian principles.

The Innu view marriage as a contract by the man and woman but also accept marriages arranged by parents (Bonvillain, 2001). Even when the parents have not arranged the marriage, parental guidance is often sought in contracted marriages. Innu men and women usually engaged in premarital sex with each other or with others. No strict rules governed premarital sexual activity. Within the marriage, the Innu normative expectations are that partners show each other mutual respect and they do not tolerate family violence. Both men and women may engage in extramarital sex. A divorce may be obtained by either partner if they are not satisfied with the marriage arrangement. Cross-cousin marriages are the preferred marital affiliation. Polygynous marriages (men having many wives) are possible because men have a high mortality rate. That is, in terms of the ratio of men to women, there are more women than men. The Innu observe a bilateral lineage pattern of descent.

The Innu do not believe in any forms of corporal punishment for the discipline of children. Neither do parents tolerate verbal chastisement of their children. When Catholic missionaries arrived in Quebec and encountered the Innu, the Jesuits wanted to take the children from the homes of their parents because the Jesuits believed that corporal punishment and chastisement would have a positive effect on the adult personality of children.

The aboriginal tribes practiced equalitarian gender roles. Women and men were both valued as autonomous individuals. Household duties, while gendered theoretically, were in actuality conducted by both males and females. Men's and women's influence and authority waxed and waned depending upon the situation. Coercion of others, either male or female, was not tolerated and therefore was rarely attempted. The Innu valued autonomy, patience, and cooperation. They would avoid those who exhibited anger, superiority, haughtiness, and boastfulness. Avoidance essentially devalued one as a group member and thus became a powerful social sanction on one's behavior. Under the Jesuit influence, the Innu were coerced into developing a hierarchical system of relations in which the female and children were submissive to the male. This system, while imposed upon the Innu, was resisted and only reluctantly incorporated into their lifestyle.

The aboriginal Innus would have been classified by Morgan as barbaric. Today, there are characteristics of both the barbaric and civilized classifications among these people. It is interesting to note that the "civilized" form brought by the Jesuits undermined the norms of the Innu that support egalitarianism, sharing, caring, tolerance, and generosity. The Jesuits introduced a system that did not support the open marriage concept adopted by the Innu and invalidated their non-violent approach to rearing their children. Today, many Innu have resisted the changes brought to their way of live by outsiders such as the Jesuits.

RELIGION AND ITS INFLUENCE ON FAMILY FORM

Many would argue that the nuclear family form has been ordained by God. But we must ask "which God?" Worldwide, there is great diversity in religious practices and belief in God. Most religions prescribe for their believers rules of conduct and behavior, including marriage practices. However, even within the same religious practice, the rules and standards have changed over time (see Chart 2). In the United States, the issue of "family" or "family values" has been central to public discourse on what some characterize as the "disintegrating" family. This discourse often resides in the realm of our religious beliefs as well as our political orientation.

The United States is a microcosm of the major world religions. Yet, central to our belief, as a society, is that we are a "Christian nation." This has led to a great debate that centers on family form versus family function. Barbara Dafoe Whitehead (1993) stated that the growing divorce rate and remarriage, as well as the growing number of single-parent households, have harmed our children and represent the weakening of our social fabric. This perspective promotes the nuclear family (man and woman joined in marriage and with children) as the normative family form. This implies that all other forms of being family are deviant. Yet, even while in the United States the nuclear family is promoted as the normative form, many other forms of family are practiced—some of which are acceptable to the general public while others are not. In general, single parenthood, divorce, remarriage, and blended families are acceptable alternative forms of family. Other forms, such as Gay or Lesbian parenthood, polyamourous families, cohabiting families, and other alternative forms are less acceptable.

On the other hand, Mark Kowalewski (1998a) argues that family form is less important than family function. He uses his Biblical knowledge to build his argument that no one family form is delineated in the Bible, but instead he argues that the focus is on family function. Kowalewski states that "each Christian household is a little church where the values of mutual love, community, hospitality, egalitarianism, inclusion and fidelity have the opportunity to grow (p. 3)." Kowalewski's view allows for tolerance of diversity in family forms, while setting the rules and standards for behavior regarding family function. Kowalewski (1998b) further argues that it is "difficult to untangle the effects of family structure from the whole web of other forces influencing children's well-being (p. 1)." To emphasize his point, he quotes from the inaugural conference of the Council on Contemporary Families held in Washington, D.C. in November 1997, which states that

> It is not family form or structure in itself that makes a difference in how families and children fare, but rather the kinds of relationships and processes which their various strengths, resources, supports, vulnerabilities, stresses, and challenges set in motion. Rather than faulting families, the task is to identify and build upon their strengths, to determine their needs and to devise strategies and policies to meet them (p. 6 from Council on Contemporary Families).

Thus, even when we look to religion to support the notion that the monogamous nuclear family form is normative and ordained by God, the results are not unanimous. We find that there are examples of both monogamous nuclear family forms and alternative family forms supported by religious rules and standards. What we can conclude is that family diversity is found not only through out the world, but also in the United States. The monogamous nuclear family, we must infer, develops in response to social expectations that are rooted in the societal economic system, political system, and cultural norms.

CHART 2
SOCIAL CONSTRUCTS OF FAMILIES
CORRELATIONS WITH MAJOR RELIGIONS

Religion	Period/Form	Family Form(s)
Judaism	Archaic	Monogamy with polygyny for wealthy (Abraham, Jacob, Solomon, etc.)
	Modern	Monogamy
Hinduism		Polygyny allowed for upper castes (Brahman and Kshatriya); monogamy for all others
Buddhism		Monogamy is ideal; celibacy for monks and nuns (pragmatic reasons); variations depending on ethnic/tribal groups (fraternal polyandry—Lhopas of Nepal; consanguine non-marriage—Na of southwestern China)
Christianity	Pre-Nicene	Monogamy (Greco-Roman cultural model)
	Roman Catholic	Celibacy is ideal; strict monogamy for procreation only (reflects influence of gnostic dualism, i.e. - hatred of the "flesh")
	Eastern Orthodox	Monogamy
	Protestant	Monogamy
	Latter-Day Saints	Early: Polygyny normative (especially for wealthy); Current: Monogamy official w/polygyny "underground"
Islam		Polygyny allowed, but not encouraged; practice varies with ethnic/tribal cultures

CONCLUSION

Thus, if we accept the notion of biological essentialism as true, then we must assume that our need for the monogamous family form lies within the realm of naturalism. This is because naturalism assumes explanation through natural scientific methods. Therefore, from a natural scientific method we can argue that we are biologically hard wired as a species to have nuclear families and all other forms must be rejected. However, if we reject biological essentialism as an explanation for the existence of the nuclear family form, then the evolutionary understanding of the existence of a multiplicity of family forms must follow, with the nuclear family being only one of many forms.

With the variety of forms or topologies of families that exist today, it is erroneous to assume that the only correct form for the family is the monogamous nuclear family. Each family must be understood within the context of its economic, political, and communal situations. We must understand how the structure and form of family arrangements allow for the survival of the social group through the process of adaptation. The nuclear family structure as we know it today developed in response to modernity and industrialization. It was a family structure that adapted to changing times and has generally been accepted as the norm in Western societies for several centuries. When we find extra-familial networks, they take on a significance "in collective life—friendships, memories of neighborhood proximity, and solidarity, places of worship, forms of leisure, and so forth—and take on more immediate meaning and become urgently needed (Goulbourne, 2003, p. 8)." We see in alternative forms of family structure the process of adaptability to environmental pressures—political, economic, and social—that allows the family to function in a loving and caring manner to nurture and protect the members of that family in order to assure its survival. Alternative family structures are not deviant from the accepted norm of the nuclear family, but instead demonstrate how different people have accommodated to diverse environmental conditions. Thus, the question of biological essentialism in terms of family can be answered: the nuclear family is not a product of biological essentialism but a socially constructed myth that promotes one form of family as correct while assigning all other forms to deviant categories.

Referring back to the earlier table which related social group patterns to the primate species which employed them, Chart 3 compares the familial primate relationships to examples in modern human societies:

CHART 3

SOCIAL GROUP PATTERNS OF THE PRIMATES APPLIED TO MODERN HUMAN SOCIETIES

Social Group Pattern	Human Societies Following This Pattern
single female & her offspring	Many Modern Societies, especially urban societies
monogamous family group	Practiced in most modern societies
polyandrous family group	Lhopas of Nepal
one-male/several-female group	Certain sects of the Church of Jesus Christ of Latter-Day Saints; many tribal societies in Africa and Aisa
multi-male/multi-female group	Polyamourous family groups (alternative form that is formed by choice) and some Polynesian groups before the intrusion of Christian Missionaries (all sisters from one family marry all brothers from another family)
fission-fusion society	Innu

Family diversity is the true biological norm. Family is a socially constructed reality which reflects the manner in which people have adapted to the economic, polictical, and cultural expectations of their society. Family form is dynamic. It is forever changing to meet the "modern" needs of the specie. What can be consistent across cultural groups, economic systems, and political systems is family functioning; and that is what we should focus on. We should promote those ideals which enable people to have healthy relationships and raise children who do not fear their parents.

[1]Many thanks to Lucinda Carspecken who helped me gain insight into the North American Indians and who spent many hours helping formulate the ideas about family and how it applies to American Indians. Thanks to Phil Carspecken and Barbara Korth for their insight and helpful dialogue which guided me in shaping this paper. Also, I am grateful for the knowledge, insight, support, and time given by husband, Glenn W. Laird, that enabled me to write this paper.

REFERENCES

Bonvillain Nancy (2001). *Native Nations: Cultures and Histories of Native North America.* Upper Saddle River, NJ: Prentice Hall.

De Waal, Frans B.M. (1995). "Bonobo Sex and Society" *Scientific American.* March 1995. Pp. 82–88.

De Waal, Frans B.M. (1996). *Good Natured: the origins of right and wrong in humans and other animals.* Cambridge, MA: Harvard University Press.

Engels, Frederick (1972). *The Origin of the Family, Private Property, and the State.* New York: Pathfinder Press.

Goulbourne, Harry (April 2003). "Editorial: Caribbean families and communities." *Community, Work & Family.* Oxfordshire, OX: Taylor & Francis Ltd. (6, 1)

Hua, Cai (2001). *A Society Without Fathers or Husbands: The Na of China.* Cambridge, MA: MIT Press.

Kowalewski, Mark (Winter, 1998a). *Forming our Families in God's Image: A Christian Vocation.* Millennium3, *http://www.millennium3.org/Winter1998/feature.htm*

Kowalewski, Mark (Fall, 1998b). *Building Bridges: A Response to Don Browning.* Millennium3, *http://www.millennium3.org/Fall%2011998/03kowalewski.htm*

O'Neil, D. (2002). *Primate Behavior: Social Structure. http://www.palomar.edu/behavior/social.htm.*

Oswalt, Wendall H. (2002). *This Land was Theirs: A Study of Native Americans.* Seventh Edition. Boston: McGraw-Hill.

Shostak, Marjorie (1981). *Nisa, the Life and Words of a !Kung Woman.* Cambridge, MA: Harvard University Press.

Stewart, Kelly (1997). "Honey, We're Home!" *The Davis Enterprise,* June 20, 1997. *http://www.anthro.ucdavis.edu/features/stp/stphoney.htm*

Whitehead, Barbara Defoe (April, 1993). *Dan Quayle was Right.* Atlantic Online, The Atlantic Monthly. *http://www.theatlantic.com/politics/family/danquayl.htm.*

2

THE HISTORICAL BASIS OF ANGLO-AMERICAN FAMILIES

Glenn W. Laird

One thing that will be emphasized many times in this text is the fact that there is not now—and has never been—any one single form of the "American Family." Reaching even as far back as pre-Columbian times, no single family form could be identified which manifested itself among all of the many aboriginal tribes and bands that were spread across the North American continent. Family forms, values, and functions varied depending on the specific environment and the social and economic adaptations of each society. They continue to do so today. Because this is a book about the modern American Family, one must turn to the roots of the predominant culture of today—Great Britain—in order to gain a relevant appreciation of family variations over time.

This article will draw heavily from a work by David Hackett Fischer, *Albion's Seed: Four British Folkways in America.* Fischer's book documents an exercise in **cultural history**, looking at the four fundamental types of English families that shaped the **mythic** notion of what it was to be "American." Fischer studied what is referred to as the **"folkways"** of the four major immigrant societies that peopled the Eastern Seaboard from 1607 until 1775. Fischer defines a folkway as *"the normative structure of values, customs and meanings that exist in any culture."* (Fischer, 7) For each of the four main groups—the **Puritans**, the **Cavaliers**, the **Quakers**, and the **Border Peoples**—he discusses at length the following twenty-four folkways:

Speech ways	*Age ways*	*Work ways*
Building ways	*Death ways*	*Time ways*
Family ways	*Religious ways*	*Wealth ways*
Marriage ways	*Magic ways*	*Rank ways*
Gender ways	*Learning ways*	*Social ways*
Sex ways	*Food ways*	*Order ways*
Child-rearing ways	*Dress ways*	*Power ways*
Naming ways	*Sport ways*	*Freedom ways*

For purposes of this exercise, we will concentrate on the seven folkways which have greatest bearing on issues of family form, functions, and values: **family ways, marriage ways, gender ways, sex ways, child-rearing ways, work ways,** and **social ways**. A summary discussion of each of the four cultural groups and their peculiar manifestations of each of these seven folkways follows.

THE PURITAN FAMILY

These were the original "Yankees" of New England. They arrived in the Massachusetts Bay Colony, Plymouth Colony, Rhode Island, Maine, New Hampshire, and Connecticut mostly from 1629 to about 1641 (the beginning of the English Civil War). The majority of the roughly 80,000 immigrants came from East Anglia. They were Puritan (Calvinistic) in their religious beliefs and middle-class in social status. They were a most rigid and intolerant lot, coming to the New World not so much to escape religious persecution at home, but to become the majority that could persecute in its on right. For the core of this population, religious beliefs drove almost every aspect of life. They had come to establish a theocracy, with the religious and civil authorities virtually indistinguishable one from the other, not unlike Iran today.

Family Ways

The Puritans saw their entire world as a hierarchy of covenants—a covenant being best defined as a contract between unequals. There existed a covenant between God and his Chosen People (the Puritans), a covenant between the civil/religious authorities and the rest of the society, and a covenant between a man and his family. The Puritan family was decidedly patriarchal. It was nuclear and large, with six to 12 or more children being the norm. The household might also contain a servant or two. The family was expected to be very orderly, and its behavior was regulated by the civil/religious authorities. Each family literally had an official—called a "tithingman"—who openly spied on family interactions and reported deviations from social morés to the higher authorities.

Marriage Ways

Despite the Puritan emphasis on religion, marriage was viewed as a civil contract. A marriage license was required, and the wedding was officiated, not by a clergyman, but by a magistrate. Social pressure was high for marriage, with roughly 95% of adults being married. Single adults were rare, and were forced to live with a family chosen by the magistrates. Marriage came relatively late, with both partners averaging in their mid-twenties. Marriages were based on mutual affection. They were not arranged, but the consent of both sets of parents was required.

Gender Ways

The Puritans preached "equality in spirit" between men and women, but practiced inequality in all else. There existed clear gender roles within the family, with women being expected to be subservient to their husbands. Despite this repression of women, they were legally protected, due to the viewpoint within the society that women were the "weaker" sex.

Sex Ways

To these people, sex was viewed matter-of-factly. It was considered to be good and wholesome within the context of marriage, but it was also supposed to be a strictly private matter between the husband and wife. Leaving a bedroom door ajar or a window open during intercourse—if observed by the tithingman—would bring humiliation before the congregation. Sex outside of marriage was strongly condemned, but—despite the impression left by Hawthorne's novel *The Scarlet Letter*—men were more strongly punished than women. This was due largely to the fact that women were seen as weaker, and would most likely be the victims of a dominating male.

Child-Rearing Ways

The Puritans were steeped in the concept of "Original Sin." To them, every child was born ignorant and depraved: full of sin and the Devil. Their response is described by Fischer as "breaking the will" of the child. The object was to repress any manifestations of self esteem in the child so that it would grow to be an obedient servant of God and of the society. Corporal punishment was frequent and severe, and little or no affection was shown toward a child. Once the child reached adolescence, he or she was "sent out" to have their rearing completed in the household of a non-related family. In this practice, the natural outpouring of teenage rebellion against their parents was thwarted.

Work Ways

The Puritans had developed a very strong work ethic back in England and brought it with them to the Colonies. From this cultural group is the origin of what we refer to as the "Protestant Work Ethic." To them, work was seen as a calling by God for the good of society and not for selfish gain. They were expected to work hard, but not get wealthy. This created a real conflict of values, since hard work often led to personal gain. This "Catch-22" led to both intra-personal and intra-societal conflict among the Puritans.

Social Ways

The Puritans in New England lived in what are referred to as "nucleated villages." In this arrangement, everyone lived in houses on small lots in a village, with each family having a farming lot, a grazing lot, and a wood lot outside of town. The center of the village contained the Meeting House (Congregational Church), the Town Hall, the Commons, and various merchant shops, inns, etc. On the surface, it would appear that they lived in this manner in order to maximize protection from predations of savage Indians. In point of fact, their villages back in England looked almost exactly the same. It was a settlement pattern that reflected their desire to keep an eye on one another to be sure that everyone was following the rules set down for them by God. It was the fear of God's Law that drove them to live in close proximity and to be constantly involved in each others' lives.

THE CAVALIER FAMILY

These were the wealthy planter families of the "Old South," arriving mostly between 1642 (the second year of the English Civil War) and 1675 (the "Restoration"). The core came mainly from the south and southwest of England into the "Tidewater" areas of Virginia and Maryland first, and then the Carolinas. They were mostly of old Saxon warrior stock, led by the second sons of landed gentry. To them, the possession of large amounts of land was vital, for it represented wealth and power. They were arrogant, refined folk who had for centuries believed that they were the superior people of the earth, and that all other people (no matter race, religion, or gender) had been placed on earth to serve them and them alone. They came dragging hordes of indentured servants, and later resorted to Native American and lastly to African slaves to raise their crops and children and respond to their every whim (One can see here visions of Tara and Scarlet O'Hara from the novel and movie, *Gone With the Wind*). The Cavaliers themselves constituted less than one-fifth of the total of more than 70,000 immigrants that came to the Tidewater during this period. The remainder consisted of a few artisans, craftsmen, and merchants, with a multitude of indentured servants. The Cavaliers were strong supporters of the English Crown and of the Anglican Church. They were about maintaining their privileged lifestyle above all else, while religion, education, and work all were secondary (and often bothersome) concerns.

Family Ways

Among the Cavaliers, extended family was of extreme importance. One's cousins were often one's best friends, and the appellation "cousin" applied to a non-relative was a compliment of the highest order. Family "character"—as well as one's place in the universe—was considered to be hereditary. Families, both extended and nuclear, were patriarchal. A Cavalier household would be much larger than that of a Puritan family, although there would normally be only half as many children. The difference was made up by a bevy of servants, who hovered about tending to the family's every need and whim.

Marriage Ways

Marriage was considered a "sacred union" among this cultural group. The wedding was first solemnized in the Anglican church in town. Afterwards, the party would retire to the plantation home for the big reception, during which the couple would recreate the ancient (pre-Christian) Saxon custom symbolizing the establishment of a new domestic arrangement: jumping the broom. On average, women were about 18 when they married, while men were about 28. These marriages were, for all intents and purposes, arranged. They were not arranged in the sense of being actually negotiated, contractual arrangements between two sets of parents while the children were still young, but in the sense of subtle pressures and contrivances to push the two together. The importance of steering certain young men and women together was to insure that property retention was insured. In fact, marriages between first cousins were not at all uncommon. This was an effective way to keep the property in the family.

Gender Ways

Despite the nominally patriarchal nature of this society, the "battle of the sexes" was a near constant reality among the Cavaliers. Young women brought up in an environment where they were as catered to by servants and other social "underlings" as their male counterparts, and who came into a marriage with nearly as much property as their husbands, were not given to suddenly becoming meek and mild subjects of their spouse. Major fights were common, and women often ended up leaving the big plantation and setting up housekeeping in the house in town. Many marriages were very stormy, although divorce was rare.

Sex Ways

In this society, males were expected to be sexual predators. Good examples of this way of life, as lived in England, can be seen in the movies *Tom Jones* and *Gosford Park*. On the other hand, the women—especially those married or to be married—were expected to be chaste. This dichotomy was seldom reconciled, with 20% to 33% of women being pregnant at the time of marriage. Having an "illegitimate" child was punished for practical reasons (a potential drain on the county coffers) rather than moral reasons. Adultery applied to married women only, and rape was lightly punished.

Child-Rearing Ways

The goal of bringing up children—especially the boys—was to develop a strong will and a sense of autonomy. At the same time, a clear understanding of the rigid social hierarchy and each family's place in it was inculcated in every child. One might feel themselves to be the "crown of creation," but must also know who were your "betters" and to behave accordingly. Fischer refers to this process as one of "bending the will," in which self-restraint was important. This would lead in time to a type of stoicism and even fatalism among those caught in the upper-middle tiers of the society. Corporal punishment was rare, but psychological abuse was common.

Work Ways

The Cavaliers themselves were basically a lazy lot, working only out of necessity. It was for this reason that they were surrounded by servants to do all of their work for them. The journal of one Cavalier planter in colonial times expressed his desire to "live idly and without manual labor." They loved money and all it brought them, but did not like the daily bother of it, depending on bookkeeper servants to take care of financial matters and give them cash on demand.

Social Ways

The settlement pattern in the southern colonies was one of large, scattered estates (plantations) with small market towns where business was conducted and the local church was found. For the Cavaliers, life was one big traveling party, with first one family and then another hosting a big party at their plantation home. The plantation houses had to be very large, not only to accommodate the large number of household servants, but to be able to bed and entertain numerous other families from time to time.

THE QUAKER FAMILY

These people, who called themselves the Society of Friends, were a truly persecuted religious minority in England, especially after the Restoration. They came mostly from the North Midlands of England, but also from Wales and Ireland. About 23,000 of them found refuge in the "Middle Colonies" of Pennsylvania, Delaware, and New Jersey from 1675 to 1725. Religious and cultural tolerance was a cornerstone of their philosophy, and they welcomed many German, Dutch, and Swedish Pietists to their colony. In fact, their universalist view of God's grace and their egalitarian rejection of hierarchies in general made them hated by the Puritans and the Anglicans respectively. The majority of Friends were of the lower middle class, consisting of "husbandmen, craftsmen, laborers, and servants." They were pacifists and believed strongly in education.

Family Ways

Fischer describes the Quaker family as "child-centered, fond-fostering, nuclear," usually having between five and eight children. Each family was set in the context of the "family of God," which was the way in which the Quakers viewed mankind in general and their own society in particular. Love was the basis for all family life and the life of the community. There was great equality among family members, just as there was in their society as a whole.

Marriage Ways

Marriage was imaged as a "union of sweethearts." If a couple fell in love, they had to seek the consent of their respective families and of the Meeting (the Quaker congregation). This was done in a lovingly critical manner, the intent being to help the couple understand clearly if they were suited for one another. The last thing the wider community wanted was an unhappy marriage with unhappy children several years down the road. When the time came, the couple wrote their own wedding vows. They tended to marry late, with men typically being 26 to 32 years old and the women 21 to 30. This insured greater maturity and responsibility of the partners.

Gender Ways

Like the Puritans, the Quakers believed that all were equal "in spirit." Unlike them, the Quakers practiced real equality in everyday life. Decision-making within a family involved every member, including the children. Both mates viewed each other as "help meets." There were gender roles for some types of work, but they were based more on pragmatic considerations than religiously derived rules. There were many women preachers among the Quakers, which was an especial abomination to the Puritans, who would torture and kill them if they came to New England.

Sex Ways

The Quakers were probably more "puritanical" than the Puritans when it came to sexual matters. For them, sex was strictly for marriage, and then mainly for procreation. They saw love as distinct from lust: the former being of a spiritual and affectionate nature, the latter being purely self-gratifying and physical. Extended periods of sexual abstinence were common for many early Quakers, especially if they were not trying to have another child. In their society, modest attire and behavior were demanded.

Child-Rearing Ways

"Bracing the will" was the intent as expressed by Fischer. Developing healthy self-esteem and self-confidence was paramount. Love was the guide. There was little or no corporal punishment among the Quakers, who chose rewards and praise for good behavior. Unlike the Puritans, who focussed on catching a child "doing something wrong" and then severely punishing them, the Quakers ignored "bad" behavior and watched for "good" behavior which was reinforced through reward. The Quakers recognized developmental stages in children three hundred years before modern psychologists. They came to realize that all behavior is learned and that a two-year-old cannot be expected to know what an adult or even an eight-year-old can. They saw child-rearing as a communal process, as were most other social activities. Most important, they saw children as equals and treated them accordingly.

Work Ways

The work ethic of the Quakers was, in terms of outward manifestations, essentially identical to that of the Puritans. The primary difference lay in their view that it was God's love they were responding to rather than God's law in seeing work as a calling for the good of the society.

Social Ways

Quakers lived in what they called a "loving neighborhood." Physically, their settlement patterns looked very much like those of the Puritans. The town lots tended to be a bit larger than those of the Puritans, but all the fields still were located outside of town. They came together happily for mutual aid and socializing. They lived close to one another, not to spy on each other to keep everyone in line, but to notice problems that might require assistance. Again, God's love rather than God's law was the driving force in their society.

THE "REDNECK" FAMILY

These were the peoples referred to by Fischer as the "Border Peoples," since the vast majority came originally from the border areas of the southern Scottish Lowlands and Northumbria in England. Most were Protestants (especially Presbyterians), many of whom were transported to Ulster (Northern Ireland) in the early 1600s by Queen Elizabeth I to work the plantations given to mostly Cavalier landlords as part of her program of subduing the Irish. They were mostly poor, illiterate tenant farmers who were fiercely independent and unbearably proud. The names "red-neck," "hoosier," and "cracker" were applied to them in England centuries before and followed them here. They were highly clannish, very conservative, and intolerant of other ethnic groups and social classes. They came from an old warrior society that never achieved the material success of the other peoples of the British Isles. This tide of immigrants arrived in the North American colonies from about 1717 until the outbreak of the American Revolution, and consisted of upwards of 400,000 individuals. Arriving last among the four groups, they found all of the good land along the coast and the Piedmont from New England southward already taken. Consequently, they kept moving westward until they found land that was occupied only by scattered Native Americans. This land was in the Appalachian Mountain chain and its foothills. Their settling in this location led to the first truly "American" designation for them: "hillbillies."

Family Ways

Extended family was very important in this culture. The notion of a clan, a group of families united by intermarriage, was central for these people. Each nuclear family was nurtured and supported by the clan. Each nuclear family was highly cohesive and very large, with numbers of children similar to those in Puritan families. Large numbers of children meant more warriors and workers for the clan.

Marriage Ways

In the distant past, in the areas of their origins, these warrior people practiced cattle stealing and "bride abduction." By the time they reached America, bride abduction had become ritualized. Once a couple decided they wished (or had) to get married, the date was set (based on the next visit from the circuit-riding preacher). On the prescribed morning, the clan of the groom-to-be would gather at his parents' cabin. The men would proceed to get well lubricated with whiskey, then ride over the ridge to the home of the bride-to-be. A few would dismount, run inside, grab the young woman, throw her over a horse, fire their guns in the air, whoop and yell, and ride off in the direction from which they had come. This was a signal for the family of the bride to run out, shout indignantly, mount their horses, and ride in hot pursuit with guns and whiskey jugs in tow. Once all were together, the party would begin, replete with much eating, drinking, and fighting. Somewhere in the middle of it all, the preacher would perform the wedding ceremony. Once the party was over (sometimes days later), everyone would retire to their homes to leave the newlyweds to begin their life together. These marriages occurred early—usually in late teens or early twenties—with a large majority of the women obviously pregnant.

Gender Ways

Like most warrior cultures around the world, this was a very patriarchal system. Gender roles were very clearly defined. Men were warriors; women were workers. While farm work was shared almost equally between husband and wife, the housework was purely "women's work." Married life was often characterized by a cycle of intense feelings of love, punctuated by outbursts of violence—usually fueled by large amounts of alcohol—followed by deep remorse and reconciliation.

Sex Ways

Among these people, sexual talk and behavior was very open. Outsiders of the time were usually appalled by the amount of skin displayed by the women, and flirting was frequent and unabashed. Sex was for fun; procreation was a side benefit. Body parts and functions were widely discussed and often displayed. Place names in the areas where they settled were sprinkled with "racy" terms.

Child-Rearing Ways

As in most warrior societies worldwide, "building the will" was the intent . . . for the males. Girls were taught to be hardworking and self-sacrificing. Techniques employed for raising boys centered on permissiveness ("boys will be boys") punctuated by random outbursts of violence. The point was to raise a man to be ready and able to defend himself in a fight at any provocation.

Work Ways

In this society, men did only work that was absolutely necessary, preferring instead to hunt, drink, and fight. Women did the bulk of the actual work—half the farm work and all of the housework. The work was grueling, with hoe husbandry and cattle herding being the mainstay.

Social Ways

The settlement patterns of these folk were of clusters of homesteads of closely related families in geographic proximity to clusters of other clan families. Outsiders were always viewed with suspicion ("You're not from around these parts, are you?") Mobility was common, partly due to the lack of a history of rootedness and partly due to the fact that the soils they farmed were poor and soon exhausted. Their homes—log cabins—were temporary structures created from the buy-products of clearing a patch of forest for farming. Clan groups practiced "serial migration." This usually occurred when restless young men would leave to find better land to the west, and upon locating some would send word back for the rest of the group to follow. This rootlessness continues today in the form of the mobile home and a constant moving to find work.

CONCLUSION

As can be seen from the discussion above, although all of these people were "Englishmen," they represented four distinct cultural groups. As such, their social values varied, their ways of making a living varied, and their family forms varied. That diversity has not gone away over the last 200 to 300 years. In fact, it has intensified, with other cultural groups immigrating to the United States and all of them interacting in various ways at the same time that we have moved from an agrarian to an industrial and now to a technological economy.

REFERENCES

Fischer, David Hackett. *Albion's Seed: Four British Folkways in America*. Oxford University Press. New York. 1989.

THE HISTORICAL BASIS OF ANGLO-AMERICAN FAMILIES

	THE PURITAN FAMILY	*THE CAVALIER FAMILY*
FAMILY WAYS	"covenanted" (internally, with greater society, and God); nuclear; large (6-12+ children); orderly; constantly regulated by church/civil authority	patriarchal; extended family very important ("cousins"); family "character" considered heredi- tary; surrounded by servants; 4-6 children
MARRIAGE WAYS	civil contract (magistrate); late (mid-20s); 95%; not arranged, but consented by parents; based on love	sacred union; Anglican ceremony & "jumping the broom"; women about 18/men about 28; essen- tially arranged; cousin marriages common
GENDER WAYS	equality in "spirit" (more women "churched"); inequality in all else; clear gender roles; women legally protected as "weaker"	major conflicts in outward social expectations and reality; women fought for equality constantly in the household
SEX WAYS	sex within marriage seen as good and wholesome (but private); sex outside of marriage was strongly condemned (men punished more severely than women)	Males were expected to be sexual predators; 20-33% of all women pregnant at time of marriage; bastardy punished for financial rather than moral reasons; adultery applied to married women only
CHILD-REARING WAYS	steeped in concept of Original Sin; children born ignorant and depraved; "breaking the will" was key element; little or no affection; much corporal punish- ment; "sent out" for training in vocation	goal was to develop strong will and autonomy (especially boys), while bowing to rigid social hierarchy; "bending the will" (to self-restraint); stoicism
WORK WAYS	strong work ethic; seen as call- ing of God for good of society and not for selfish gain	worked out of necessity; aspired to "live idly and without manual labor"; loved money but didn't want to bother with it
SOCIAL WAYS	nucleated central villages; strong sense of community; everyone involved in lives of others	small market villages & large, scattered estates; traveling party; honor was of great importance

THE HISTORICAL BASIS OF ANGLO-AMERICAN FAMILIES

	THE QUAKER FAMILY	*THE "REDNECK" FAMILY*
FAMILY WAYS	"child-centered, fond-fostering, nuclear"; 5-8 children; set in context of the "family of God"; love was basis of all family life; great equality	very clannish (extended family very important); marriage ties weaker than blood; nuclear family highly cohesive and large (8-12+ children)
MARRIAGE WAYS	a union of "sweethearts"; consent of couple, families, meeting; married late (men 26-32/women 21-30); wrote own vows	"bride abduction" in fact or ritual; lots of drinking and fighting; married early (men 20-21/women 19-20)
GENDER WAYS	equality in "spirit" and in everyday life; mates were "help-meets" with gender roles, but equal decision-making (old Viking ways); women preachers	man = warrior/woman = worker; farm work shared almost equally; house work was for women; totally patriarchal; love and violence
SEX WAYS	sex was for marriage, especially for procreation; love was seen as distinct from lust; extended abstinence was common; modest attire and behavior was demanded	sexual talk & behavior very open; high rates of pre-nuptial pregnancy and bastardy
CHILD-REARING WAYS	"bracing the will" was intent; little or no corporal punishment; rewards instead; recognized developmental stages of children; communal process; saw children as equals	typical of warrior societies worldwide; for boys: mostly very permissive w/ outbursts of violence ("building the will"); for girls: taught to be self-sacrificing
WORK WAYS	strong work ethic; seen as calling of God for good of society and not for selfish gain	men worked when necessary (preferred to fight); women did much work in fields and home; hoe husbandry and cattle herding
SOCIAL WAYS	a "loving neighborhood"; clustered small lots surrounded by larger fields; happily came together for mutual aid and socializing	constantly moving (log cabin & mobile home); serial migration; scattered isolated homesteads; clan proximity; down on strangers

ADDITIONAL NOTES ON
EARLY ANGLO FAMILIES IN AMERICA

ADDITIONAL NOTES ON
EARLY ANGLO FAMILIES IN AMERICA

3

GENEALOGICAL RESEARCH: DEVELOPMENTAL PERSPECTIVES

Helen M. Gore-Laird, Ph.D., University of Houston

Glenn W. Laird

We have been conducting family history research for nearly twenty years. It began with a carbon copy on onion-skin paper of some genealogical notes on one family line done in the 1930s. Given to Glenn by his maternal grandmother years before, it became an increasingly intriguing stimulus to look into our origins. The search has been at times frustrating, but mostly rewarding, as amazing facts have emerged and some old myths have been proven wrong. Along the way, our initial mere curiosity gave way to an increasingly organized, scientific research project. We have learned much, not just about our families, but about the methods necessary for uncovering the past lives of long-ago dead people. We have also learned much in the process of how our own attitudes and values had their roots in the lives of our ancestors. The following is a sharing of those discoveries.

WHY DO FAMILY HISTORY RESEARCH?

We have found that people do family history research for a wide variety of reasons. Some hope to prove they are descended from someone famous (royalty is preferable). Some want to discover if they might carry a gene that predisposes them to a deadly disease. Some may want to achieve status through being admitted to the Daughters of the American Revolution (DAR) or the Sons of the American Revolution (SAR). Many, like us, may simply be curious. We suspect that most—in this era of a frenetic, rootless, throw-away society—want to find out where they came from . . . to feel grounded.

Whatever the reason, one thing is certain, the history of your ancestors has done much to shape who you are. Your family of origin—and the families from which it sprang—provide a framework in which the most primary interactions can occur. This is the environment in which you begin to learn about life and how to be part of society. It shapes your view of the world. The socio-economic status, value systems, life styles, and world views of you and your immediate family are most likely direct products of the situations and experiences of your ancestors. The past is not deterministic of the future, but it carries a heavy influence. Therefore, one way to obtain insight into how you became who you are is to look carefully at the history of your family. While looking at the history of your family of origin may reveal many of the details of the dynamics of your socialization, going back many generations can add a broader social-context perspective.

If your ancestors were white and here before the American Revolution, knowing to which of the four major English social groups they belonged can say volumes about your current situation. These four were:

- the Puritans of New England (the classic "Yankees")
- the Cavaliers of the Tidewater Region (the old Southern Aristocracy)
- the Quakers of Pennsylvania, and
- the "Border Peoples" who settled the back country in the 50 years prior to the revolution (the "Hoosiers", "Crackers" and "Rednecks")

The same is true for every ethnic group that came to America along the way and fell into the mythical "melting pot":

- the Germans, Irish, Italians, Poles, Scandinavians, Chinese, and Jews who arrived between 1840 and 1930
- those who have come since World War Two, including people from the Indian Subcontinent, Asia, Southeast Asia, the Near East, Africa, Latin America, and the Caribbean.

People whose ancestors were Native Americans (including the *mestizos* and Indians of Latin America) and those descended from African slaves, have still different histories that uniquely shape them to this day. Each group has contributed attitudes, beliefs, clothing, words, and food (to name just a few) to "American" society in general, and to their descendants in particular.

THE BASIC APPROACH

One key to this or any type of research is to be sure that the information you collect is <u>verifiable</u>. Get primary source material wherever possible (actual documents or copies of those documents). Family stories of past generations, despite the sincerity of personal belief in their veracity, need to be backed up with solid evidence.

Do not be afraid to discover "embarrassing" truths. For example, Glenn can boast a witch and a bastard half-breed slave among his direct ancestors. His maternal grandmother's ancestors did not have a castle in Germany, despite a family myth created by a fake genealogy produced in the 1930s. You may also discover marvelous things no one knew before. For instance, Glenn is distantly related to Stephen F. Austin (2nd cousin, 7 times removed). Erastus Milo Cravath (founder and first president of Fisk University) is his 2nd great-granduncle, Calvin Coolidge is his 4th cousin, twice removed, and he is a 9th great-grandson of George Bunker (remember the hill?). And, despite Glenn's loss of a castle in Germany, Helen's ancestors (Clan Lamont) in Scotland had two castles (Toward & Asgog). Helen also discovered that all was not well in the household of Jacob and Rachel Gore (early 1800s). Several newspaper clippings reading "Rachel has left the bed and board of Jacob Gore. He will no longer be responsible for her debts," showed that Rachael frequently left Jacob. This was also a clue that Rachel had money of her own and could afford to leave her plantation owning husband.

People in your family that you interview may discourage you, refuse to discuss certain people or events, or have unreasonable gaps in their memories. There are probably very interesting stories behind each of these. We would advise you to keep looking for the buried treasures.

A METHODOLOGICAL APPROACH

Like all scientific endeavors, genealogical research (a subset of historical research), if done properly, adheres to the following cyclical process:

Existing Knowledge → **Develop Hypothesis** → **Gather Data** → **Analyze Data Critically** → **Draw Conclusions** (revised knowledge base) → **Develop New Hypothesis**

Genealogical research is, by necessity, data research (although the burgeoning field of DNA research may eventually add an entirely new dimension). Depending on the location and time period, records may be excellent or fragmentary. Much work is done by inference. Trial and error and process of elimination are the daily bread of this work.

In historical research of any kind, documents are the main source of information. Documents fall into two basic types: **Primary Source Materials** and **Secondary Source Materials.**

Primary Source Materials are documents which record facts relating to an event at the time of the event. These include the following:

- Census Records

- Marriage Certificates

- Birth Certificates

- Baptismal Records

- Death Certificates

- Personal Diaries

- Family Bibles

- Deed Records

- Wills

- Tombstone Inscriptions

Secondary Source Materials are documents which compile or summarize many Primary Source documents. These include the following:

- Indexes of Primary Source Materials, such as county marriage records, deed records, court proceedings, vital statistics, military records, immigration records, etc.

- A book of local history (church congregation, town, county, region, state, etc.)

- A book written about a particular family history

Secondary Sources should always be used to get a "big picture" and to point the way to Primary Sources. To be certain of your findings, always try to get copies of the Primary Source Materials in order to confirm the facts. Some people who compile indexes may misread names or miss families altogether. In the end, only Primary Sources are considered valid data.

The following steps are a recommended approach to do effective genealogical research:

1. **Start with what you know**. Collect all of the family papers, Bibles, stories, and artifacts you can. Write this information down in outline form.

2. *Interview* every member of the oldest generation of each ancestral line to get as much information about who, what, where, and when for every deceased ancestor that they personally knew. One African cultural group refers to these as the *sasha* or "living-dead." They are the people who "live on" in the memories of those who knew them.

3. If your ancestors have lived in the United States for a long time, it is vital to know names and places of residence of known ancestors in 1930, 1920, 1910, and 1900, if possible. These are the dates of the latest Census Records that have been released by the Census Bureau.

4. Spend the next block of time doing *library research*. Houston has an excellent resource in the Clayton Library on Caroline at Calumet north of Hermann Park. The collection and staff are totally oriented to family history. Several local LDS Churches have Family Research Centers. There are many resources on the Internet.

5. Get census data, starting in 1930 or 1920 and work backwards.

6. Get birth, marriage, and death records, where possible.

7. Look in indexes for military records and immigration lists.

8. As you go back in time, you will discover more details about the ancestors you have heard stories of. You will also uncover the names of and information regarding the ancestors you have never heard of. In the same African source as before, these are known as the *zamani* or "truly-dead."

9. Once you know where certain people were at certain times, you may wish to go a step further and visit the **state archives** for that state and the **county courthouses** and/or local libraries of the area where they actually lived.

10. Deed, tax, church, and court records can help to flesh out the lives of these people with details that make them more real.

11. Microfilm copies of old local newspapers can also be a good source of information.

12. State and local histories can give you insights into the historical and cultural contexts of your ancestors. You may discover their ties to major historical events and places.

At every step, with every bit of data, think *critically* about it. Take *nothing* at face value. This is real detective work, and the slightest clue, if overlooked, can cause you to miss a major find. For instance, until the middle of the Nineteenth Century, traditional naming systems were often followed. Paying careful attention to the names of children can provide clues to identifying their grandparents as you go further back in time. Look at neighboring families for clues to the maiden names of wives. Also, during certain census years, an agricultural census was conducted which would detail the number and types of livestock, crops produced, etc., giving further insight into the economic status of particular families.

A final word of warning: Genealogical research is highly addictive, and there is no 12-step program to recovery!

4

THE WAY WE WEREN'T: THE MYTH AND REALITY OF THE "TRADITIONAL" FAMILY

Stephanie Coontz

Many politicians and religious leaders have urged a return to the "traditional" family. However, historian Stephanie Coontz argues that this supposed "traditional" family is actually mythological. In this article, she provides snapshots of family life from colonial to present times. By doing so, she reveals that none of these family structures protected people from inequalities based on race, class, gender, or interpersonal conflict.

COLONIAL FAMILIES

American families always have been diverse, and the male breadwinner-female homemaker, nuclear ideal that most people associate with "the" traditional family has predominated for only a small portion of our history. In colonial America, several types of families coexisted or competed. Native American kinship systems subordinated the nuclear family to a much larger network of marital alliances and kin obligations, ensuring that no single family was forced to go it alone. Wealthy settler families from Europe, by contrast, formed independent households that pulled in labor from poorer neighbors and relatives, building their extended family solidarities on the backs of truncated families among indentured servants, slaves, and the poor. Even wealthy families, though, often were disrupted by death; a majority of colonial Americans probably spent some time in a step-family. Meanwhile, African Americans, denied the legal protection of marriage and parenthood, built extensive kinship networks and obligations through fictive kin ties, ritual co-parenting or godparenting, adoption of orphans, and complex naming patterns designed to preserve family links across space and time.

The dominant family values of colonial days left no room for sentimentalizing childhood. Colonial mothers, for example, spent far less time doing child care than do modern working women, typically delegating this task to servants or older siblings. Among white families, patriarchal authority was so absolute that disobedience by wife or child was seen as a small form of treason, theoretically punishable by death, and family relations were based on power, not love.

THE NINETEENTH-CENTURY FAMILY

With the emergence of a wage-labor system and a national market in the first third of the nineteenth century, white middle-class families became less patriarchal and more child-centered. The ideal of the male breadwinner and the nurturing mother now appeared. But the emergence of domesticity for middle-class women and children depended on its absence among the immigrant, working class, and African American women or children who worked as servants, grew the cotton, or toiled in the textile mills to free middle-class wives from the chores that had occupied their time previously.

Even in the minority of nineteenth-century families who could afford domesticity, though, emotional arrangements were quite different from nostalgic images of "traditional" families. Rigid insistence on separate spheres for men and women made male-female relations extremely stilted, so that women commonly turned to other women, not their husbands, for their most intimate relations. The idea that all of one's passionate feelings should go toward a member of the opposite sex was a twentieth-century invention—closely associated with the emergence of a mass consumer society and promulgated by the very film industry that "traditionalists" now blame for undermining such values.

EARLY TWENTIETH-CENTURY FAMILIES

Throughout the nineteenth century, at least as much divergence and disruption in the experience of family life existed as does today, even though divorce and unwed motherhood were less common. Indeed, couples who marry today have a better chance of celebrating a fortieth wedding anniversary than at any previous time in history. The life cycles of nineteenth-century youth (in job entry, completion of schooling, age at marriage, and establishment of separate residence) were far more diverse than they became in the early twentieth-century. At the turn of the century a higher proportion of people remained single for their entire lives than at any period since. Not until the 1920s did a bare majority of children come to live in a male breadwinner-female homemaker family, and even at the height of this family form in the 1950s, only 60% of American children spent their entire childhoods in such a family.

From about 1900 to the 1920s, the growth of mass production and emergence of a public policy aimed at establishing a family wage led to new ideas about family self-sufficiency, especially in the white middle class and a privileged sector of the working class. The resulting families lost their organic connection to intermediary units in society such as local shops, neighborhood work cultures and churches, ethnic associations, and mutual-aid organizations.

As families related more directly to the state, the market, and the mass media, they also developed a new cult of privacy, along with heightened expectations about the family's role in fostering individual fulfillment. New family values stressed the early independence of children and the romantic coupling of husband and wife, repudiating the intense same-sex ties and mother-infant bonding of earlier years as unhealthy. From this family we get the idea that women are sexual, that youth is attractive, and that marriage should be the center of our emotional fulfillment.

Even aside from its lack of relevance to the lives of most immigrants, Mexican Americans, African Americans, rural families, and the urban poor, big contradictions existed between image and reality in the middle-class family ideal of the early twentieth century. This is the period when many Americans first accepted the idea that the family should be sacred from outside intervention; yet the development of the private, self-sufficient family depended on state intervention in the economy, government regulation of parent-child relations, and state directed destruction of class and community institutions that hindered the development of family privacy. Acceptance of a youth and leisure culture sanctioned early marriage and raised expectations about the quality of married life, but also introduced new tensions between the generations and new conflicts between husband and wife over what were adequate levels of financial and emotional support.

The nineteenth-century middle-class ideal of the family as a refuge from the world of work was surprisingly modest compared with emerging twentieth-century demands that the family provide a whole alternative world of satisfaction and intimacy to that of work and neighborhood. Where a family succeeded in doing so, people might find pleasures in the home never before imagined. But the new ideals also increased the possibilities for failure: America has had the highest divorce rate in the world since the turn of the century.

In the 1920s, these contradictions created a sense of foreboding about "the future of the family" that was every bit as widespread and intense as today's. Social scientists and popular commentators of the time hearkened back to the "good old days," bemoaning the sexual revolution, the fragility of nuclear family ties, the cult of youthful romance, the decline of respect for grandparents, and the threat of the "New Woman." But such criticism was sidetracked by the stock-market crash, the Great Depression of the 1930s, and the advent of World War II.

Domestic violence escalated during the Depression, while murder rates were as high in the 1930s as in the 1980s. Divorce rates fell, but desertion increased and fertility plummeted. The war stimulated a marriage boom, but by the late 1940s one in every three marriages was ending in divorce.

THE 1950s FAMILY

At the end of the 1940s, after the hardships of the Depression and war, many Americans revived the nuclear family ideals that had so disturbed commentators during the 1920s. The unprecedented post-war prosperity allowed young families to achieve consumer satisfactions and socioeconomic mobility that would have been inconceivable in earlier days. The 1950s family that resulted from these economic and cultural trends, however, was hardly "traditional." Indeed it is best seen as a historical aberration. For the first time in 100 years, divorce rates dropped, fertility soared, the gap between men's and women's job and educational prospects widened (making middle class women more dependent on marriage), and the age of marriage fell—to the point that teenage birth rates were almost double what they are today.

Admirers of these very *nontraditional* 1950s family forms and values point out that household arrangements and gender roles were less diverse in the 1950s than today, and marriages more stable. But this was partly because diversity was ruthlessly suppressed and partly because economic and political support systems for socially-sanctioned families were far more generous than they are today. Real wages rose more in any single year of the 1950s than they did in the entire decade of the 1980s; the average thirty-year-old man could buy a median-priced home on 15 to 18% of his income. The government funded public investment, home ownership, and job creation at a rate more than triple that of the past two decades, while 40% of young men were eligible for veteran's benefits. Forming and maintaining families was far easier than it is today.

Yet the stability of these 1950s families did not guarantee good outcomes for their members. Even though most births occurred within wedlock, almost a third of American children lived in poverty during the 1950s, a higher figure than today. More than 50% of black married-couple families were poor. Women were often refused the right to serve on juries, sign contracts, take out credit cards in their own names, or establish legal residence. Wife-battering rates were low, but that was because wife-beating was seldom counted as a crime. Most victims of incest, such as Miss America of 1958, kept the secret of their fathers' abuse until the 1970s or 1980s, when the women's movement became powerful enough to offer them the support denied them in the 1950s.

THE POST-1950S FAMILY

In the 1960s, the civil rights, antiwar, and women's liberation movements exposed the racial, economic, and sexual injustices that had been papered over by the Ozzie and Harriet images on television. Their activism made older kinds of public and private oppression unacceptable and helped create the incomplete, flawed, but much-needed reforms of the Great Society. Contrary to the big lie of the past decade that such programs caused our current family dilemmas, those antipoverty and social justice reforms helped overcome many of the family problems that prevailed in the 1950s.

In 1964, after 14 years of unrivaled family stability and economic prosperity, the poverty rate was still 19%; in 1969, after five years of civil rights activism, the rebirth of feminism, and the institution of nontraditional if relatively modest government welfare programs, it was down to 12%, a low that has not been seen again since the social welfare cutbacks began in the late 1970s. In 1965, 20% of American children still lived in poverty; within five years, that had fallen to 15%. Infant mortality was cut in half between 1965 and 1980. The gap in nutrition between low-income Americans and other Americans narrowed significantly, as a direct result of food stamp and school lunch programs. In 1963, 20% of Americans living below the poverty line had *never* been examined by a physician; by 1970 this was true of only 8% of the poor.

Since 1973, however, real wages have been falling for most Americans. Attempts to counter this through tax revolts and spending freezes have led to drastic cutbacks in government investment programs. Corporations also spend far less on research and job creation than they did in the 1950s and 1960s, though the average compensation to executives has soared. The gap between rich and poor, according to the April 17, 1995, *New York Times*, is higher in the United States than in any other industrial nation.

FAMILY STRESS

These inequities are not driven by changes in family forms, contrary to ideologues who persist in confusing correlations with causes; but they certainly exacerbate such changes, and they tend to bring out the worst in *all* families. The result has been an accumulation of stresses on families, alongside some important expansions of personal options. Working couples with children try to balance three full-time jobs, as employers and schools cling to policies that assume every employee has a "wife" at home to take care of family matters. Divorce and remarriage have allowed many adults and children to escape from toxic family environments, yet our lack of social support networks and failure to forge new values for sustaining intergenerational obligations have let many children fall through the cracks in the process.

Meanwhile, young people find it harder and harder to form or sustain families. According to an Associated Press report of April 25, 1995, the median income of men aged 25 to 34 fell by 26% between 1972 and 1994, while the proportion of such men with earnings below the poverty level for a family of four more than doubled to 32%. The figures are even worse for African American and Latino men. Poor individuals are twice as likely to divorce as more affluent ones, three to four times less likely to marry in the first place, and five to seven times more likely to have a child out of wedlock.

As conservatives insist, there is a moral crisis as well as an economic one in modern America: a pervasive sense of social alienation, new levels of violence, and a decreasing willingness to make sacrifices for others. But romanticizing "traditional" families and gender roles will not produce the changes in job structures, work policies, child care, medical practice, educational preparation, political discourse, and gender inequities that would permit families to develop moral and ethical systems relevant to 1990s realities.

America needs more than a revival of the narrow family obligations of the 1950s, whose (greatly exaggerated) protection for white, middle class children was achieved only at tremendous cost to the women in those families and to all those who could not or would not aspire to the Ozzie and Harriet ideal. We need a concern for children that goes beyond the question of whether a mother is waiting with cookies when her kids come home from school. We need a moral language that allows us to address something besides people's sexual habits. We need to build values and social institutions that can reconcile people's needs for independence with their equally important rights to dependence, and surely we must reject older solutions that involved balancing these needs on the backs of women. We will not find our answers in nostalgia for a mythical "traditional family."

QUESTIONS

1. Describe how children and childhood were perceived in colonial times. How does this perception compare to our view of children today? What changes in society caused us to change our perspective?

2. If you were a white female, in which historical period would you choose to live? Which historical period would you select if you were African American? Explain why you made these choices.

3. According to Coontz, what puts stress on families today? What can we do to relieve some of this stress?

4. Suppose that an editorial appearing in your local newspaper called for a return to the traditional family values of the 1950s as a way to save the family. Write a letter to the editor explaining why this plea is neither feasible nor desirable.

5

Urie Bronfenbrenner Ecological Systems Theory: An Overview

Helen M. Gore-Laird, Ph.D., University of Houston

Who Is Urie Bronfenbrenner?

Urie Bronfenbrenner (2002) was born in Moscow, Russia in 1917. He immigrated to the United States with his parents at the age of six. He received his bachelor's degree, with a double major in psychology and music, from Cornell University in 1938. He received his master's degree in Developmental Psychology from Harvard University and his doctorate from the University of Michigan in 1942. The day after receiving his doctorate, he was inducted into the army (World War II). While in the United States Army, he served as a psychologist in a variety of assignments. Following the war, he accepted a faculty position at the University of Michigan. In 1948, he accepted a faculty position at Cornell University. Today, he is Professor Emeritus at Cornell University.

Bronfenbrenner's work has been influenced by the works of Kurt Lewin, George Herbert Mead, Sigmund Freud, William I. and Dorothy S. Thomas, Edward C. Tolman, Lev Vygotsky, Kurt Goldstein, Otto Rank, Jean Piaget, and Ronald A. Fisher (Bronfenbrenner, 1979). While Bronfenbrenner acknowledges that he stood on the shoulders of these scholarly "giants" he states that

> the seeds of the ecological conceptions developed here had been planted long before
> I entered college. It was my good fortune to have been brought up on the premises
> of a state institution for those who were then called 'feebleminded,' where my father
> was a neuropathologist (Bronfenbrenner, 1979, xi)

His growing up in this environment allowed him to witness not only the effects of community interaction, but also the effects of the larger systems on the lives of those in the institution, especially when the government stopped the programs which allowed those institutionalized to work on the farms and shops of the institution.

While grounded in the concrete experiences of his childhood, his theory on ecological systems and individual development began to take root as he engaged in discussions at faculty seminars. Bronfenbrenner's (Bronfenbrenner, 1979, 2002) work has been guided by three mutually reinforcing themes. Those guiding themes have been

1. to develop theory, corresponding research designs and pilot studies which are at the forefront of developmental science;
2. to design implications and applications of theory and research findings for policy and practice; and
3. to conduct seminars for, and supervise projects carried out by, graduate students and upper-class majors that prepare them for work in the public world.

In other words, Bronfenbrenner did not just want to develop theories; he wanted his work to be applicable to the experiences of people in the real world. He also wanted to prepare graduate and upper-class students for work the public sphere. To this end, Bronfenbrenner (2002) became a prolific writer and is active in both the public and private sector. He is a major contributor in the design of developmental programs in the United States and elsewhere. He is one of the founders of a nationwide educational program for disadvantaged young children, Head Start.

Bronfenbrenner (2002) has received many awards and honors in his lifetime. In 1996, he received the "Lifetime Contribution of Developmental Psychology in the Service of Science and Society" award. This award is now given annually in Bronfenbrenner's name.

BRONFENBRENNER'S ECOLOGICAL SYSTEMS THEORY

When we try to pick up anything by itself we find it is attached to everything in the universe.

—John Muir

THE BASIC PREMISES OF SYSTEMS THEORY

Systems theory is based in the three major aspects of human beings that the ancient Greeks identified and studied—*the mind, the body, and the spirit* (Greek Philosophy). As noted in the quote from John Muir, we live in a world of connectedness. Individuals who work with systems theories understand that human beings do not develop in isolation; they develop in a variety of contexts. The environments which surround the individual human being, and the constant interaction of the individual and their environment, play major roles in the individual's development. Heylighen and Joslyn (1992) noted that systems theory is interested in the "arrangement of and relations between the parts which connect them into a whole." Ashby (cited in Heylighen and Joslyn, 1992) recognized that systems are dynamic; they are "open to, and interact with, their environments, and that they can acquire qualitatively new properties through emergence, resulting in continual evolution." Bronfenbrenner's Ecological Systems Theory (1979) recognizes that the developing person is in constant interaction with his/her environment and that this interaction shapes the person's personality and his/her behavior.

When working with individuals, one may assume that the system theory model considers the four major components of the individual at work. These systems are

1. the *cognitive system* which perceives, stores, processes, and retrieves information;
2. the *affective system* which is the seat of interaction that modifies perceptions and thoughts before and after they are processed cognitively;
3. the *regulatory system* which directs and manages input and output functioning;
4. the *behavioral system* which represents the output of the individual and controls the overt action of a human being.

These systems do not work independently of each other. They are interconnected in such a manner that if one system is not functioning well, other systems are affected. For example, if one has a migraine headache, their cognitive system is impaired. The person may become anxious, which affects the respiratory system, which in turn, may affect one's behavior. How we behave is also influenced by the culture in which we are raised. For instance, our cultural heritage may expect us to hide the outward display of our feelings when we are hurting, thus we keep how we are feeling to our self.

Because we do not live in isolation, other factors influence our development and behaviors. The ecological systems model developed by Bronfenbrenner, incorporated these factors within a model containing five layers of context or ecology which interact with the individual. Bronfenbrenner (1979) states that these layers or systems are "a set of nested structures, each inside the next, like a set of Russian dolls (p. 3)." These five interlocking systems are the microsystem, the mesosystem, the exosystem, the macrosystem, and the chronosystem.

The ecological systems model hypothesizes that an individual's thinking (cognition), feeling (affect), and willing (conation), as well as one's overt behavior develops as a result of a four-part interactional process (the action occurs between the parts). This process includes the *transactions* among the various components of the individual as influenced by the *biological maturation* and bodily functioning of the individual as the individual receives *stimuli* from the environment or context in which he or she is involved, and the *feedback* received by the individual from the environment as a result of an individual's overt behavior. This process is interconnected and ever repeating. The individual is constantly adapting to the surrounding environment. However, the environment is also changing as a result of its interactions with the individual. In other words, syngery between the individual and the environment exists. As Bronfenbrenner (1979) states,

> the ecology of human development involves the scientific study of the progressive, mutual accommodation between an active, growing human being and the changing properties of the immediate settings in which the developing person lives, as this process is affected by relations between these settings, and by the larger contexts in which the settings are embedded (p. 21).

While these interactions may not effect great change on the larger environment or public policy, we through our interactions with our immediate environment exact a change within ourselves as well as change the environment in which we are interacting.

Dr. Martin Luther King, Jr., and Mohandas Gandhi are good examples of how one's interaction with the environmental shapes their development, which in turn can cause a change in the larger environment. Dr. Martin Luther King, Jr., grew up in an era of "separate but equal" racial treatment in the United States. These early childhood experiences eventually led to his becoming the civil rights leader in the 1950s and 1960s. The Civil Rights Movement eventually led to changes in public policy regarding the treatment of blacks in America. Gandhi, a well-educated man from India, suffered the indignities of discrimination when he traveled to South Africa. These experiences eventually led him to become the leader of India and to help the Indian people gain self-respect and to regain control of their country.

THE ECOLOGICAL SYSTEMS MODEL

Bronfenbrenner understood this four-part interactional process. He also understood that forces outside our control influence our development and behavior. For example, decisions made at the political level can affect the school age child's learning. In 1946, Harry Truman signed into law The National School Lunch Act. This act allowed poor children to receive free or reduced rate lunches at school. Poor children, who often came to school hungry, were now able to get a healthy lunch. Studies have clearly demonstrated that children who are better nourished can perform better in school. Thus, the lunch program, which later expanded to include breakfast, allowed disadvantaged children to get much-needed nourishment, which in turn allowed the children to perform better in school.

An overview of Bronfenbrenner's (1979) ecological perspective yields four major points. These major points are.

1. that the focus is on the individual's relationship within his/her social contexts,
2. that human development occurs in a set of overlapping ecological systems,

3. that all of these systems operate together to influence what a person becomes as he/she develops, and

4. that chronology (the study of time) helps in understanding how changes in the macrosystem affect the developing individual.

These points elucidate the premise of Bronfenbrenner's Ecological Systems theory. The important issue in understanding Bronfenbrenner's theory is that the development of the individual-in-context is the central focus. The basic interaction of the individual is that of the dyad, which is two persons interacting. Examples of dyads are the mother rocking and singing to her baby or a father playing catch with his daughter in the backyard.

WHAT IS AN ECOLOGICAL SYSTEMS THEORY?

Bronfenbrenner has created a *model*, a description or analogy used to help visualize something that cannot be fully observed, to explain human behavior. In order to understand his theory, it is best to first understand the terms. First, *ecology* is the branch of science which is concerned with the interrelationships of organisms and their environment. *Systems* refers to a regularly interacting or interdependent group of items forming a unified whole. The use of *theory* allows one to develop a plausible or scientifically acceptable general principle or body of principles which explain phenomena. Consequently in systems theory, individual behavior is explained by the interaction of the individual with his/her environment. A study of these interactions can lead us to predictions about behavior. For example, we can predict (*theory*) the behaviors of men who abuse women (a *system* of abuse) by understanding how the interrelationships which occur in their environmental influences them (*ecology*).

The five ecological structures identified by Bronfenbrenner (1979) which affect individual development are the microsystem, the mesosystem, the exosystem, the macrosystem, and the chronosystem. Each of these interlocking systems can be conceived "topologically as a nested arrangement of concentric structures, each contained in the next (Bronfenbrenner, 1979, p. 22). These structures will be defined in the following paragraphs.

The **microsystem** is the system nearest the individual where interactions occur at an immediate, face-to-face level. This is where, for the developing child, the most important aspects of the patterns of behavior, roles, and relationships in the home, school, workplace, the playground, etc., are shaped. Bronfenbrenner (1979) defines the microsystem as

> . . . a pattern of activities, roles, and interpersonal relations experienced by the developing person in a given setting with particular physical and material characteristics (p. 22).

The most critical aspect of this system is found in the word "experience" (Bronfenbrenner, 1979). For Bronfenbrenner our experiences include not only the elements explicit in the environment but how the experiences are perceived by the individual. An example of a microsystem interaction would be a mother redirecting the attention of her child from the electrical outlet to an appropriate toy with which to play. In this example, the child might perceive the experience as a loving caring act. Had the mother slapped the child's hand, the child could develop a fear of his mother because his perception is that she hurts him. As one mother noted, she spanked her son until one day, when he was about three, she bent down to hug him and he recoiled believing he was about to be hit (Murphy, 1999). She goes on to add that she promised her son that she would never hit him again and kept her promise.

The **mesosystem**, the next level in the system, surrounds and incorporates the microsystem of the individual. In this system, the interaction occurs between two or more microsystems, such as a parent-teacher conference or overtime at work. Bronfenbrenner defines the mesosystem as

> . . . the interrelations among two or more settings in which the developing person actively participates (such as, for a child, the relations among home, school, and neighborhood, peer groups; for an adult, among family, work, and social life). (p. 25)

Think of the mesosystem as a "system of microsystems." For example, in the movie, *Parenthood*, Gil and Karen are the parents of Kevin. Kevin has had some emotional problems which has concerned his teachers. A school psychologist was called in to observe and test Kevin. Gil and Karen are called to the school where they engage in a conversation regarding Kevin's future. Here we have several microsystems operating in a mesosystem setting—Gil and Karen; Gil and Kevin; Karen and Kevin; the school principal and the school psychologist; the school principal and Gil, etc.

The **exosystem**, the third level in the ecological system, includes social settings that the individual never experiences directly, but in which decisions are made that will affect the individuals who do interact directly with the developing individual, such as neighborhood/community structures that affect the functioning of smaller systems such as newspapers, parent's workplace, or local governments. Bronfenbrenner defines the exosystem as

> . . . one or more settings that do not involve the developing person, as an active participant, but in which events occur that affect, or are affected by, what happens in the setting containing the developing person.

In the example above, the psychologist made the decision that Kevin should go to a special school for emotionally disturbed children. He made this decision based on his observations and testing of Kevin and in conjunction with the school principal. They did not involve Kevin in the decision-making process, yet he would have been affected by the decision made. This is an example of the exosystem at work.

The **macrosystem**, the fourth level in the ecological system, includes the "blueprints" for defining and organizing the institutional life of the society, including overarching patterns of culture, politics, economy, etc. Thus, the macrosystem has embedded within it the subcultural and cultural contexts of the micro-, meso-, and exo-systems and therefore, explains how development is affected by different historical events and different cultures. Bronfenbrenner defines the macrosystem as

> . . . [the] consistencies, in the form and content of lower-order systems (micro-, meso-, and exo-) that exist, or could exist, at the level of the subculture or the culture as whole, along with any belief system or ideology underlying such consistencies.

For example, all cultures experience death. Yet, each culture and subculture has different attitudes toward death, encounters with death, and death-related practices.

The **chronosystem**, the temporal dimension in the ecological system, provides the context in which our lives occur. This not only takes into account maturational attributes, but it also includes the cohort effect of the major events in our lives which affect our life course. For example, those who lived or were born during the Great Depression were greatly affected by the event. Another example would be the age of a child when their parents divorced. The chronosystem represents time. So, to truly understand a person's development, we need to also know the era (or time in history) into which that person was born and what events occurred during their lifetime that would affect their development.

THE ASSUMPTIONS OF THE ECOLOGICAL SYSTEMS THEORY

Every theorist makes assumptions about the nature of the environment and the individual. The assumptions made by Bronfenbrenner's theory are as follows:

1. The guiding metaphor for humans under this model is the historical event.
2. The nature of humans is that an individual is part of an ever changing person/environment relationship.
3. The individual takes an active role in his/her own development.
4. The environment also takes an active role in the development of the individual.
5. The ecological systems model takes both a continuous and discontinuous approach to development.
6. Development of the individual is multidimensional.
7. The ecological systems theory is not a stage theory.

THE STRENGTHS AND WEAKNESSES OF THE ECOLOGICAL SYSTEMS THEORY

Every theory has strengths and weaknesses. Bronfenbrenner's theory is no different. The following are some of those strengths and weaknesses:

The **strengths** of the ecological systems theory lies in the fact that it emerged in response to the deficiencies of the earlier stage theories and learning theories that attempted to explain individual development. The strengths of his theory lie in the following factors.

a. Bronfenbrenner and others like him have attempted to explain the complex nature of human development by emphasizing that development *does* occur in a context.
b. The ecological systems theory underscores the notion that people do change their environment and actively contribute to their own development.
c. The understanding that development occurs multi-directionally and that we can not predict where our lives are going unless we look at the transactions which transpire between the individual and the environment.

As strange as it may sound, the **weaknesses** of Bronfenbrenner's Ecological Systems Theory lie in its strengths.

a. While the ecological systems theory gives us an understanding of how a person's development grows out of interactions between the person and his/her environment which is steered by social and historical forces, it does not give a very clear picture of the course of human development.
b. Because of the nature of the ecological systems theory, the theory may never be able to provide a coherent developmental theory.

Web Sites and Readings on Bronfenbrenner's Theory

http:/www.human.cornell.edu./facultybio.cfm?netid=ubl 1 &facs-1

http:/www.people.cornell.edu/pages/ubl 1

http:/www.parenthood.library.wisc.edu/Bronfenbrenner.html

http:/www.personal.spu.edu/faculty/n/x/nxd10/siblings.pdf

Bronfenbrenner, U. (1979). The Ecology of Human Development: Experiments by Nature and Design. Cambridge, MA: Harvard University Press.

Moen, Phyllis; Elder, Glen H. Jr.; Lüscher, Kurt, Eds. (1995). *Examining Lives in Context: Perspectives on the Ecology of Human Development*. Washington D.C.: American Psychological Association.

References

Bronfenbrenner, U. (1979). *The Ecology of Human Development: Experiments by Nature and Design*. Cambridge, MA: Harvard University Press.

Bronfenbrenner, U. (2002) Urie Bronfenbrenner: Retrieved May 1, 2002, from Cornell University Bronfenbrenner Web site: *http:/www.people.cornell.edu/pages/ub11/*

Heylighen, F. and Joslyn, C. (1992). What is Systems Theory? Revised May 1, 2002, from Principia Cypernetica Web Site: *http:/pespmc1.vub.ac.bc/SYSTHEOR.html*

Greek Philosophy. Retrieved May 1, 2002, The Internet Encyclopedia of Philosophy from University of Tennessee at Martin Web site: *http:/www.utm.edu/research/iep/g/greekphi.htm*

Murphy, A.P. (Ed.) (1999). *It Worked for Me, Parent's Magazine*. New York: St. Martin's Griffin.

6

DISCOVERING WHAT FAMILIES DO

Urie Bronfenbrenner

Today we are witnessing two revolutions: one in society, the other in science. Although these revolutions are occurring in different domains, both center on the same phenomenon: the dramatic changes taking place in family life across the world and the consequences of these changes for the development of human competence and character, both in present and in future generations. In turn, the results of the social revolution are being newly illumined by today's scientific revolution—the research conducted over the past two decades in the field of human development.

The changes now taking place in contemporary family life are better documented for industrial nations, but they are no less and, indeed, are perhaps even more profound in developing countries. In fact, although differing in appearance, the underlying dynamics and ultimate effects of family change are strikingly similar around the globe. We now know that the stresses being experienced today by families everywhere have common roots and call for common strategies grounded in the basic requirements for the survival and growth of all human beings in all human ecologies.

Yet this knowledge creates an unwelcome paradox. It appears that the more we learn about the conditions that undergird and foster the development of human competence and character, the more we see these same conditions being eroded and destroyed in contemporary societies, both developing and developed. Given this paradox, this essay has three aims.

- First, I shall summarize the main findings of the scientific revolution that has occurred in the study of human development.

- Second, I shall indicate the implications of the new research findings for the changes that have been taking place in contemporary family life.

- And third, in light of these widespread changes and of the knowledge we are acquiring about their consequences, I shall suggest some practical implications for both public policy and private social action.

What are the conditions and processes that undergird and foster the development of human competence and character from early childhood onward? The requirements for

Urie Bronfenbrenner is Professor of Human Development and Family Studies and of Psychology at Cornell University in Ithaca, New York. This essay is based on an address, "Who Cares for Children?" delivered to UNESCO in Paris in September 1989.

developing competence and character appear to be universal, deriving from the basic biological nature of the species *Homo sapiens*, thus cutting across culture, nationality, and class.

Note the qualifying phrase "appear to be." The findings of science are tentative by definition. Moreover, in my view, the results of research in this particular sphere should be subject to validation by human experience. For this reason, I confine myself to those findings from systematic studies that also have some support from the observations of professionals and paraprofessionals working in the field as well as from families themselves. I begin with those facts that are most clearly established from both perspectives.

First and foremost, all children require good health care and adequate nutrition. Yet millions of children in today's world lack these essentials.[1] Accordingly, many outstanding organizations and agencies have dedicated themselves to meeting these primary needs.

Assigning top priority to this task is unquestionably necessary and urgent. Indeed, recent research only underscores its importance. At the same time, however, the new findings do call into question a policy that makes the provision of health and nutrition its top and *only* priority. Such a policy appears to assume that nothing else is of comparable importance and that once these basic necessities are made available, the achievement of at least normal development for the great majority of young children is, by and large, a likely outcome.

By contrast, the scientific investigations of the past two decades reveal that basic medical services and adequate diet, while essential, are not enough by themselves to insure normal physical and psychological development, particularly for children of families who have been exposed to biological, economic, and social stress. Beyond health care and nutrition, certain other essential requirements must also be met.

A recent UNICEF seminar on early childhood development summarized the issue:

> It has long been accepted that good health and nutrition support the psychological and social development of the young child. Less widely recognized are the more recent findings that developmentally sensitive interaction with a child, namely interaction which satisfies the child's need to grow socially, psychologically, and cognitively, has a direct and measurable impact on the physical health of the child. While the implications of these interaction effects are of considerable importance for the health and well-being of children, they have been seriously neglected in development planning.[2]

Although "developmentally sensitive interaction" lies at the heart of the matter, it is not the whole scientific story. Nor is it easy to convey the full scope of that story in a necessarily brief chapter. I shall try to do so in a series of five propositions, each followed by some explication and one or more examples.[3]

PROPOSITION I

> In order to develop—intellectually, emotionally, socially, and morally—a child requires participation in progressively more complex reciprocal activity, on a regular basis over an extended period in the child's life, with one or more persons with whom the child develops a strong, mutual, irrational, emotional attachment and who is committed to the child's wellbeing and development, preferably for life.

Although this proposition has the merit of being fairly compact, it is also complex. Therefore we will examine its key elements one by one.

What is meant by "progressively more complex reciprocal activity"? Perhaps an analogy will help. It's what happens in a ping-pong game between two players. As the partners become familiar with each other, they adapt to each other's style. The game starts to move faster, and the shots in both directions tend to become more complicated, as each player, in effect, challenges the other.

In families, who challenges the other the most—the child or the adult? Research evidence indicates that in the beginning the infant calls most of the shots and, so to speak, "teaches" his or her parents or other caregivers.

Almost all adult human beings are adept learners in this situation—males no less than females—provided, of course, that they are willing and able to pay attention to the teacher and go to school almost every day over a long period of time. And there's the rub! In contemporary societies, it is becoming increasingly difficult to maintain the regular attendance and the high level of alertness that such learning requires. In short, while virtually everyone has the needed aptitudes, the learning process is not easy. Indeed, microphotographic studies of parent-infant interaction reveal it to be extraordinarily and increasingly complex as the process evolves.

This increasing complexity develops in two ways. Not only does the same game become more complicated, but new games are added by both parties. This phenomenon is seen especially clearly in early childhood. For example, a longitudinal study in which children were followed from birth through the eighth year of life revealed a progressive sequence in the young child's responsiveness and initiatives toward others. Thus, at birth, infants are especially responsive to vestibular stimulation (being picked up and held in a vertical position close to the body), which has the effect of soothing the baby so that it begins to engage in mutual gazing. By three months, visual exploration extends beyond proximal objects, and the mother's voice is most likely to elicit responses, especially in the form of reciprocal vocalizations. From about six months on, the infant begins actively to manipulate objects spontaneously in a purposeful way and to rearrange the physical environment. By now, both vocalization and gesture are being used to attract the parents' attention and to influence their behavior. In addition, the child increasingly, across modalities, initiates and sustains reciprocal interaction with a widening circle of persons in the immediate environment. The sequence reaches a new climax with the emergence of language as a medium of social interchange. By the age of two or three, the informal play between child and adult becomes a major vehicle of cognitive, emotional, and social development.

Crucial to the establishment and maintenance of this progressive trajectory is the ready responsiveness by a familiar adult to the young child's initiatives as well as the introduction by the adult of activity-engaging objects and experiences appropriate to the youngster's evolving capacities. In the absence of such adult responsiveness and presentation of opportunities, general psychological development is retarded, particularly for children who have been exposed to biological, economic, or social stress.

By now it should be clear that what is made possible by "progressively more complex reciprocal interaction" is a process of mutual "education." The child "teaches" the adult and the adult "teaches" the child. However, a caveat is critical here:[4] the kind of teaching that takes place in this context is quintessentially informal and even unconscious. The young child is not trying to teach the caregiver to respond in a particular way. He or she is simply expressing an evolving repertoire of behavioral initiatives and reactions. Nor can the adult caregiver foresee what the young child will do and thus plan in advance how he or she will respond to the young child's actions. The most the adult can do is to be ready and willing to react and to act in ways that will attract or hold the child's attention.

In sum, we are not dealing here with education in its traditional meaning of formal instruction.[5] Rather, such extended informal activities serve as a necessary prerequisite to formal schooling. This point must be borne in mind when we consider the design of policies and programs for enhancing child development.

Yet as already noted, informal education is no less demanding than its formal counterpart; it too takes a long time. Neither the young child nor the adult caregiver can learn much from each other if they get together only now and then for short periods with frequent interruptions. Hence, the specification, as a second key element in Proposition I, of joint activity "on a regular basis over an extended period in the child's life."

Thus far, it would appear that any person who repeatedly engages in progressively complex reciprocal activity with a child will be equally effective in furthering the child's physical and psychological development. The final clause of Proposition I, however, imposes some restrictions in that regard: specifically, the other person must be someone *"with whom the child develops a strong, mutual, irrational emotional attachment and who is committed to the child's well-being and development, preferably for life."*

What is "an irrational emotional attachment"? It means that an adult regards a particular child as somehow special—especially wonderful, especially precious—even though objectively the adult may well know that this is not the case. It is the illusion that comes with love. The illusion flows in both directions: for the child, the adult is also special—someone to whom the child turns most readily when experiencing both trouble and joy and whose comings and goings are central to the child's experience and well-being.

What is the relevance of this mutual emotional relationship for processes of "progressively more complex reciprocal interaction" between child and adult? Research evidence indicates that such interaction requires high levels of motivation, attentiveness, sensitivity, and persistence on the part of both participants and that *these requisite qualities are more apt to arise and to be sustained in relationships characterized by strong, mutual, emotional attachment.*

Moreover, once such a strong mutual attachment is established, it tends to endure, thus enhancing the likelihood of a continuing pattern of reciprocal interactions at successively more complex levels throughout the child's life. The two parts of Proposition I also have a reciprocal relationship. Thus, one reason mutual attachments tend to endure is that the recurring patterns of reciprocal interactions that they encourage in turn enhance the intensity of the mutual emotional tie.

In sum, it can be said that human development occurs in the context of an escalating psychological ping-pong game between two people who are crazy about each other.

As implied in the preceding exposition, once the processes stipulated in this first proposition become established, they activate and enhance additional potentials for development. Prominent among these are responsive and active orientations, not just toward persons but toward certain other features of the child's immediate environment. One of the earliest and strongest potentials to become activated in this way is the subject of the next proposition.

PROPOSITION II

The establishment of patterns of progressive interpersonal interaction under conditions of strong mutual attachment enhances the young child's responsiveness to other features of the immediate physical, social, and—in due course—symbolic environment that invite exploration, manipulation, elaboration, and imagination. Such activities, in turn, also accelerate the child's psychological growth.

For young children today, how available are objects and settings that meet the developmental criteria set forth in Proposition II? Consider, from this perspective, the wide array of manufactured toys, games, and play equipment produced in modern technological societies. To name a few: battery-powered play vehicles; automated figures of animals, humans, and monsters; playgrounds with special equipment for children of different ages; graduated series of puzzles, construction sets, and board games; and all manner of audiovisual devices and computer games for successive age levels. Many of these products are quite expensive.

Yet upon examination, many of these items hardly fulfill the requirements stipulated in Proposition II. Specifically, they do not invite exploration, manipulation, elaboration, or imaginative activity on the part of the child. They fail primarily because they are so rigidly structured as to allow little opportunity for introducing any spontaneous variation. To be sure, many products of modern technology do meet the criteria stipulated in Proposition II or can be designed to do so. These products should be praised and recommended to parents, professionals, and the public at large.

Objects and settings that meet the specified developmental criteria are by no means limited to products of modern technology. They are as readily found in traditional and transitional cultures as they are in so called "post-industrial" societies. To cite a few examples: objects in nature—both animate and inanimate, large and small—such as domestic animals, stones and shells, trees and caves; objects that can be put inside one another or used to build things that can be broken down again; anything that can make rhythmic and musical sounds, such as pots, pans, and soup spoons; materials that can be used to draw, paint, or mold shapes and forms. More broadly, whatever induces sustained attention and evolving activity of body and mind, such as songs, dances, stories, dolls and stuffed animals that become friends, picture books, and, of course, books that can be read, then reimagined and retold on one's own.

But some children may not respond, even when provided with a range of objects and opportunities for activity. An obvious prerequisite is that the environment include materials appropriate to the child's developing physical and psychological capacities. In addition, the youngster's active orientation toward the physical and symbolic environment is powerfully mediated by prior and persistent patterns of interpersonal interaction in the context of a strong, enduring emotional relationship with one or more adults, almost always including the child's parents. These ongoing experiences remain a potent liberating and energizing force, not only in relation to the physical environment but to the social world as well. Thus they enable the child to relate to persons beyond the immediate family, including peers as well as adults, and to involve them effectively in meeting the child's own developmental needs. At a broader level, the child's newly acquired abilities make it possible for her or him to benefit from experiences in other settings, most notably to learn in school.

In short, the *informal education* that takes place in the family is not merely a pleasant prelude, but rather a powerful prerequisite for success in *formal education* from the primary grades onward. This empowering experiences reaches further still. As evidenced in longitudinal studies, it appears to provide a basis, while offering no guarantee, for the subsequent development of the capacity to function responsibly and creatively as an adult in the realms of work, family life, and citizenship.

This does not mean, however, that the absence of early opportunities for interactive experiences in the context of a mutual emotional attachment precludes the possibility of later achieving adult effectiveness. Other routes to the acquisition of competence and character exist. The problem is that these routes are far less efficient and far more expensive, both in time and money.

Thus, taken as a whole, the research evidence indicates that when the elements stipulated in the first two propositions are provided on a continuing basis, the positive effects on children's development are indeed substantial. Accordingly, a society that seeks the well-being and development of its children is well advised to provide them with the kinds of environments and experiences specified in these two propositions.

But there is a catch. Research findings also reveal that the processes of interaction between child and environment that foster development described in Propositions I and II operate efficiently only under certain conditions existing in the broader environment in which these proximal processes occur. The remaining three propositions deal with the nature of these enabling and disabling circumstances. Thus the next proposition sets a qualifying proviso to Proposition I.

Proposition III

The establishment and maintenance of patterns of progressively more complex interaction and emotional attachment between caregiver and child depend in substantial degree on the availability and involvement of another adult, a *third party* who assists, encourages, spells off, gives status to, and expresses admiration and affection for the person caring for and engaging in joint activity with the child.

It also helps, but is not absolutely essential, if the third party is of the opposite sex from that of the person dealing with the child. Isn't science wonderful? We've rediscovered the wheel!

I am sometimes asked up to what age do the foregoing principles apply. The answer is debatable, but I would say anytime up to the age of, say, 99.

The research evidence in support of the third proposition comes mainly from studies of a phenomenon that constitutes one of the main changes occurring in contemporary family life: the rapid rise in the proposition of single-parent households in both the developed and developing world. The overwhelming majority of such homes are those in which the father is absent and the mother bears full responsibility for the upbringing of the child. A large number of investigations of developmental processes and outcomes in families of this kind have now been conducted across a range of cultural and social class groups, including socialist countries and some developing nations as well. In general, the findings lead to two complementary conclusions.

First, results indicate that, controlling for associated factors such as low income, children growing up in such households are at greater risk for experiencing a variety of behavioral and educational problems, including extremes of hyperactivity or withdrawal, lack of attentiveness in the classroom, difficulty in deferring gratification, impaired academic achievement, school misbehavior, absenteeism, dropping out, involvement in socially alienated peer groups, and, especially, the so-called "teenage syndrome" of behaviors that tend to hang together—smoking, drinking, early and frequent sexual experience, a cynical attitude toward work, adolescent pregnancy, and, in the more extreme cases, drugs, suicide, vandalism, violence, and criminal acts. Most of these effects are much more pronounced for boys than for girls.

More intensive investigations of these phenomena have identified a common predisposing factor for the emergence of such problem behaviors, namely, a history of impaired parent-child interaction and relationships beginning in early childhood.

Not all single-parent families, however, exhibit these disturbed relationships and their disruptive effects on development. Systematic studies of the exceptions have identified what may be described as a general "immunizing" factor: children of single-parent mothers are less likely to experience developmental problems in those families in which the mother receives strong support from other adults living in the home or from nearby relatives, friends, or neighbors; members of religious groups; and, when available, staff members of family support and child-care programs.

Interestingly enough, the most effective agent of third-party support (in the minority of instances in which such assistance is provided) appears to be the child's father. And what counted most was not the attention given to the child, important as this was, but the assistance provided to the mother herself by serving as a back-up in times of crisis, doing errands, spelling her off, sharing responsibility for discipline, and providing needed advice and encouragement. It appears that, in the family dance, "it takes three to tango."

The developmental risks associated with a one-parent family structure are relatively small, however, in comparison with those involved in two other types of environmental context. The first and most destructive of these is poverty. Because many single-parent families are also poor, parents and their children are in double jeopardy. But even when two parents are present, research in both developed and developing countries reveals that in households living under stressful economic and social conditions, processes of parent-child interaction and environmentally oriented child activity are more difficult to initiate and to sustain. Much more effort and perseverance on the part of parents are required to achieve the same effect than are required in families living under more favorable circumstances, particularly when, as is often the case, the mother is the only parent or even the only adult in the home.

To be sure, research also indicates that when the mother, or some other adult committed to the child's well-being, does manage to establish and maintain a pattern of progressive reciprocal interaction, the disruptive impact of poverty on development is significantly reduced. But, among the poor, the proportion of parents who, despite their stressful life circumstances, are able to provide quality care is, under present conditions, not very large. And even for this minority, the parents' buffering power begins to decline sharply by the time children are five or six years old and exposed to impoverished and disruptive settings outside the home.

What is the impact of poverty on children's development? The consequences of economic hardship are similar to those for single parenthood in the absence of a third party, but the risks are substantially higher and the effects more pronounced, typically persisting well into adulthood (except in those as-yet-infrequent instances in which opportunities for continuing rehabilitative experiences become available).

Developmental processes are now at risk not only for poor and single-parent families. During the '70s and '80s, other highly vulnerable contexts have evolved that cut across the domains of class, family structure, and culture. Recent studies reveal that a major disruptive factor in the lives of families and their children is the *increasing instability, inconsistency, and hectic character of daily family life.* This growing trend is found in both developed and developing countries, but has somewhat different origins in each. However, the debilitating effect on child-rearing processes and outcomes is much the same. Let's begin with examples from the so-called postindustrial world, since they may be more familiar. The following description is based on observations of the American scene.

> In a world in which both parents usually have to work, often at a considerable distance from home, every family member, through the waking hours from morning till night, is "on the run." The need to coordinate conflicting demands of job and child care, often involving varied arrangements that shift from day to day can produce a situation in which everyone has to be transported several times a day in different

directions usually at the same time—a state of affairs that prompted a foreign colleague to comment: "It seems to me that in your country, most children are being brought up in moving vehicles."[6]

Many other factors also contribute to the disruption of daily family life: long commutes to and from work; jobs that require one or the other parent to be away for extended periods; frequent changes in employment; the associated moves for the whole family or those that leave the rest of the family behind waiting till the school term ends or adequate housing can be found; and the increasing number of divorces, remarriages, and redivorces. In this regard, the most recent evidence suggests that the disruptive effects of remarriage on children may be even greater than those of divorce.

A parallel disorganization of family life in Third-World countries has been reported in a number of field studies but was perhaps best described by participants from the developing world at the 1982 UNESCO seminar "The Child and the Family in a Changing World." Experts spoke of the breakdown of family traditions and of the reinforcing role of tribal customs and community life through the disruptive inroads of Westernization and urbanization.

What are the developmental outcomes of the hectic character of family life? Once again, the observed consequences are educational impairment and behavior problems, including long-term effects that now also encompass children of the well-educated and the well-to-do.

Obviously, if we are to deal with such deeply rooted societal phenomena as poverty and the hectic pace of daily family life, we must restructure the social order. Nevertheless, the destructive impact of both these forces on the competence and character of future generations is so enormous that their elimination must be given the highest priority at the national and international level.

But such an undertaking is a long-term endeavor, and children can't wait. Some immediate and practicable short-term strategies, however, can reduce the social disarray and human damage produced by both destructive forces. The general nature of these strategies is indicated in the next proposition.

PROPOSITION IV

The effective functioning of child-rearing processes in the family and other child settings requires establishing ongoing patterns of exchange of information, two-way communication, mutual accommodation, and mutual trust between the principal settings in which children and their parents live their lives. In contemporary societies, these settings are the home, child-care programs, the school, and the parents' place of work.

Why the parents' workplace? Research shows that one of the principal sources of stress and disarray in the lives of families and their children lies in job stress—the conflict between the needs of the family and the demands of the job.

But which parent's job stress has the greater disruptive effect on the child.' Although the answer may appear counterintuitive, available evidence points to the father. Why? The most apt response to this question was given by the distinguished American sociologist Robin M. Williams. Commenting upon this differential effect of stress on the job, he pointed out, "the mothers absorb it all, and the fathers don't even know that there's anything to be absorbed."

Practically speaking, what kind of mutual accommodations can be made between the two domains of family and work? Particular policies and measures, of course, differ from one society to the next, but here are a few examples:

- Flexible work schedules

- Availability of part-time jobs (for both men and women) without loss of job benefits and opportunities for advancement

- Establishment at each work organization of a family resources office or specialist who serves as an advocate in relation to family-work issues; maintains a file of nontechnical publications and resource materials relating to child development and parenthood; provides referral to family services available in the community; serves as a stimulus and resource for introducing cost-effective policies and practices in the workplace that can reduce unnecessary stress resulting from the conflicting demands of work and family life, with due regard to the primary need of the work setting to fulfill its productive and service responsibilities.

What is the *quid pro quo?* Studies indicate that such measures reduce absenteeism and job turnover and lead to improved employee morale and quality of performance.

The fifth and final proposition lays out the principal directions to be pursued in policies and practices aimed at enhancing child development and family life in contemporary societies.

PROPOSITION V

The effective functioning of child-rearing processes in the family and other child settings requires public policies and practices that provide place, time, stability, status, recognition, belief systems, customs, and actions in support of child-rearing activities not only on the part of parents, caregivers, teachers, and other professional personnel, but also relatives, friends, neighbors, co-workers, communities, and the major economic, social, and political institutions of the entire society?[7]

With Proposition V, 1 complete my effort to convey the general findings of recent research on factors affecting early child development as they relate to the revolution in family life that has been occurring around the globe. In order to link research to reality, the implications of these findings for policy and practice have been incorporated into the presentation of the five propositions summarizing the principal conclusions indicated by the scientific evidence. These implications deal with priority principles and processes applicable at successive levels, beginning with the child in the family and in other care settings, then proceeding to more distant contexts of the workplace, the community, and the society at large.

Today, new grounds exist for believing that national action based on the foregoing principles may at last be possible. The new element in the picture is the increasing recognition and concern on the part of leaders in both the public and private sector with respect to two escalating economic problems. The first is the enormous cost of providing for, or (alternatively and more frequently) neglecting, the growing segments in the population of so-called "uneducables" and "unemployables." The second relates to the quality and dependability of the available work force in an age of increasing economic competition with both developed and developing nations. But this is neither the preferred nor the most potent dynamic for success. The most powerful force is the new hope for families and nations of seeing children seemingly fated to a life of failure and pain bloom into competent and caring human beings.

NOTES

1. For a recent assessment of the nature and scope of the problem on a worldwide basis, see *Strategies for Children in the 1990s* (New York: UNICEF, 1989).

2. *Innocent Update*, Proceedings of the First Innocent Global Seminar: Early Child Development (Florence, Italy: UNICEF International Child Development Center, No. 3, July 1989), p. 1.

3. The research on which these propositions are based is summarized and cited in the following publications by the author: "The Ecology of Cognitive Development: Research Models and Fugitive Findings," in R. H. Wozniak and K. Fischer, eds., *Specific Environments Thinking in Context* (Hillsdale, NJ: Erlbaum, in press); "Ecological Systems Theory," in R. Vasta, ed., *Six Theories of Child Development* (Greenwich, CT: JAI Press, 1989), pp. 185–246; "Ecology of the Family as a Context for Human Development," *Developmental Psychology* 22 (No. 6, 1986), pp. 732–742.

4. This caveat is signaled by the quotation marks I have placed around each of the traditional pedagogical terms.

5. This restricted connotation of the concept is particularly characteristic of English. In a number of other languages, a broken contract exists that encompasses both formal and informal aspects of childbearing, for example *éducation* in French, *Erziehung* in German, *vospitaniye* in Russian.

6. Urie Bronfenbrenner. "The Changing Family in a Changing World," unpublished paper delivered at the UNESCO conference "The Child and the Family in a Changing World," Munich, November 1982.

7. Urie Bronfenbrenner, "Family Support: The Quiet Revolution," in S. L. Kagan, D. R. Bowell, B. Wersbound, and E. E. Zigler, eds. *America's Family Support Program Perspectives and Prospects* (New Haven, CT: Yale University Press, 1987), pp. xi–xii.

7

INDIVIDUAL DEVELOPMENT:
A HOLISTIC, INTEGRATED MODEL

David Magnusson

As the title of the chapter suggests, the aim of this chapter is to present and discuss the main elements of an integrated, holistic model for individual functioning and development, which can serve as a general theoretical framework for planning, implementation, and interpretation of empirical research on specific aspects of individual development. The motive for such a model is discussed on the background of an analysis of the present state of affairs, which is characterized more by fragmentation of developmental subfields than by integration, which is a prerequisite for further success.

The old holistic view has got new clothes and an enriched content from three sources during recent decades. The first source is the modern models for dynamic, complex processes, which have meant a theoretical and empirical revolution in disciplines that are concerned with such processes in natural sciences, biology, and medicine. These models emphasize the holistic character of the processes and the need for integration of all operating factors in the theoretical models, which serve as the theoretical framework for planning, implementation, and interpretation of empirical research. The second source is the rapid development in scientific disciplines in which research has contributed knowledge about the role of biological aspects of individual functioning and development: developmental biology, pharmacology, endocrinology, neuropsychology, and other disciplines. The third source is the conceptual analyses of the role of environmental factors, at different levels of organization, for which Bronfenbrenner (1977, 1979a, 1979b, 1993) has been a pioneer.

The chapter is mainly devoted to the presentation of a theoretical outline of a holistic, integrated model for individual development. The research strategy and methodological implications of such a model are far-reaching, and it would lead too far to deal with them more comprehensively in this connection (see Bergman, 1988, 1993; Magnusson, 1988, 1993; Magnusson, Andersson, & Törestad, 1993; Magnusson & Bergman, 1988; Magnusson & Törestad, 1993, for further discussions).

INDIVIDUAL DEVELOPMENT: A DEFINITION

Psychological research on individual development is concerned with individual functioning in terms of thoughts, feelings, actions, and reactions studied across the lifetime of the individual.

Development of living organisms refers to progressive or regressive changes in size, shape, and function during the lifetime. Psychological research on individual development covers this process from conception to death. In this definition, two concepts are essential: change and time. *Time is not the same as development, but development always has a temporal dimension.* Therefore, if a person's distinctive pattern of characteristics remains unchanged across time, no development has occurred. Consequently, processes that go on in an unchanged manner, within existing structures, do not constitute development. Thus, developmental models should be distinguished from models that analyze and explain why individuals function as they do in terms of their current psychological and biological dispositions. Because the current functioning of an individual is a result of earlier developmental processes in his or her life course and because this current functioning, at the same time, forms the basis for later stages, models for current functioning and developmental models are complementary.

SCIENTIFIC PROGRESS: THE NEED FOR A GENERAL MODEL OF *HOMO*

In the empirical sciences, one characteristic feature of real scientific progress is increasing specialization. When specialization in a subfield of the natural sciences has reached a certain level, it becomes apparent that further progress lies in integration with what has been achieved in neighboring disciplines. During recent decades, the most important steps forward in natural sciences have been taken by integration within the interface of what earlier had been conspicuously different disciplines. This happened first in the interface of physics and chemistry and recently in the interface of biology, chemistry, and physics. The earlier unambiguous and clear boundaries between subdisciplines have disappeared.

Also in empirical research on individual functioning, specialization takes place. In some areas, specialization has been very productive and has offered important contributions. However, despite the recent indications of more integration among disciplines, for example, between brain research and cognitive psychology, research in behavioral sciences in general is still characterized by what Toulmin (1981) once described as "sectarian rivalry" (p. 267). During the eighties, researchers, discussing the future prospects of psychology, described this lack of integration as one of the main obstacles for further, real scientific progress in behavioral sciences (de Groot, 1990; Thomae, 1988). As a matter of fact, this was also an issue of great concern for Stern (1911) in the beginning of this century.

Thus, fragmentation is still a characteristic of psychological research on individual functioning at all levels, that is, diversification of research in specialties with little or no contact across domains. Fragmentation involves content, concepts, research strategies, and methodology. At a metatheoretical level, it has its roots in the existence of three main explanatory models: mentalistic, biological, and environmental. (The models are, of course, not mutually exclusive; each one is a matter of emphasis.) The distinction between these explanatory models is not only of theoretical interest. Each of them has had and still has a far-reaching impact on fundamental aspects of societies: social welfare, politics, culture, education, the causes and treatment of mental illness, criminal behavior, and alcohol and drug abuse, to mention only a few (see Magnusson, 1988).

According to a mentalistic approach, the main explanation for an individual's way of functioning is to be found in the functioning of the mind and can be discussed and explained in terms of intrapsychic processes of perceptions, thoughts, values, goals, plans, and conflicts. To this approach belong personality theories in general, as well as the mainstream of research on intelligence, cognitive processes, and learning—with repercussions in research on artificial intelligence. A strong representative of this approach is, of course, Piaget.

The biological model identifies biological factors as having primary influence on individual functioning. Its roots can be traced back to the very old notion of individual differences in temperament as dependent on the predominance of one of the four basic body fluids: blood, phlegm, black bile, or yellow bile. When modern biological models of individual development are applied, the major determining guiding factors are genetic and maturational. In its extreme version, this model implies that individual differences in the course of development have their roots in genes, with little role played by environmental and mental factors. This view was characterized by Cairns (1979a) in terms of the organism as a "gene machine" (p. 165). The view was discussed and criticized by Hunt (1961), who characterized the main elements of it in terms of "predetermined development" and "fixed intelligence." Research in behavioral genetics, pharmacology, endocrinology, and neuropsychology during recent decades has strengthened the biological explanation of individual functioning.

The environmental model locates the main causal factors for individual functioning in the environment. It is reflected in theories and models at all levels of generality, from Marxist models for the society to stimulus–response models for very specific aspects of behavior as it is studied in the mainstream of experimental psychology. In developmental research, there are various environmental streams with different sources. A strong and very influential exponent is, of course, behaviorism (cf. Skinner, 1971; Watson, 1930). Another is *psychoanalytic theory*, which refers to early experiences of the environment as guiding forces for the individual's way of functioning later in life. An additional influential line, which strongly influenced developmental psychology during the sixties, seventies, and eighties, is rooted in sociology, in which the basic formulations about the strong environmental impact on individual development were formulated by Durkheim (1897). This view is reflected in the vast amount of research in which individual differences in various aspects of the life course have been studied as the result of differences in upbringing environments (cf. Bronfenbrenner & Crouter, 1983, and their discussion of the "new demography").

An old controversy in developmental research is that between a biological and an environmentalistic view: the *nature–nurture issue*. The debate can be traced back to the early times of our civilization. Plato in his *Republic* discussed the central issue of justice in the perspective of human character as determined by nature [*physics*] and nurture [*trophe*]. In the modern history of psychology; the biological view was formulated and strengthened by the work of Galton and the publication of his influential book *Hereditary Genius* (1869). With respect to intelligence, his line of reasoning was followed in the beginning of this century by Terman, Goddard, and Yerkes, among others, all of whom believed that the intelligence tests that had been constructed at that time actually measured fixed and innate intelligence.

As pointed out by Eccles and Robinson (1985), it was chiefly in the eighteenth century that the thesis of environmentalistic determinism became "official," much influenced by the empiristic psychology of Locke. A view emphasizing the role of environment and the possibilities to influence individual development by environmental factors was advocated by Binet (1909). He strongly argued against the view of intelligence as an inherited, fixed quantity: "We must protest and react against this brutal pessimism. With practice, enthusiasm, and especially method, one can succeed in increasing one's attention, memory and judgement, and in becoming literally more intelligent than one was before" (Binet, 1909, p. 126). Binet also took the consequence of this view and worked out a program of "mental orthopaedics" as a method of improving the intelligence of mentally retarded children (pp. 127–128). A recent contribution to this nature–nurture debate was presented by Bronfenbrenner and Ceci (1994).

A somewhat younger controversy is that between the mentalistic and the environmentalistic perspective, which is reflected in the debate between proponents of a cognitive approach (cf. Piaget, 1948) and proponents of a socialization approach (cf. Miller & Dollard, 1941) to social development and behavior. An example drawn from theories of moral development may illustrate the issue. For Kohlberg (1969), moral development is closely related to cognitive development. In contrast, both Marx and Freud, from very different perspectives, regarded conscience, as the base for moral choice, as being instilled from the outside through a process of socialization beyond the individual's control.

Of course, nothing is wrong with each of the three general explanatory models per se. What is wrong occurs when each of them claims total supremacy, and that has been the case to an extent that has hampered real progress both in research and in application.

Now, a basic question to be answered is the following: When research in natural sciences is characterized by the iterative process of specialization and integration, why is behavioral research, including developmental research, on the whole characterized by specialization with only little integration? The reason is probably complex, but let me point to a possible explanation.

One condition that facilitates the iterative process of specialization and integration in natural sciences is the existence of a general theoretical framework, a general model of nature, for theorizing and conducting empirical inquiry. The fact that we lack a corresponding general theoretical framework for the formulation of problems, for the development of a common conceptual space, and for the development and application of adequate methodologies is, in my opinion, an essential obstacle for further real progress in the behavioral sciences. We need the formulation of a general model of homo, which synthesizes and integrates the three metatheoretical models briefly described earlier. A modern, integrated holistic model meets this requirement.

BASIC PROPOSITIONS OF AN INTEGRATED, HOLISTIC VIEW

A modern, integrated, holistic model for individual functioning and development rests on three basic propositions:

> 1. *The individual functions and develops as a total integrated organism. Development does not take place in single aspects, taken out of context.*

As a general statement, this view is old. It is reflected in the assumption about the four basic temperaments, in the typologies, and in the discussion about an idiographic versus a nomothetical approach and about statistical versus clinical prediction in empirical research. In developmental research a holistic view was advocated in the beginning of this century (see, e.g., Stern, 1911). During recent decades, it has had its proponents in Block (1971), Cairns (1979a, 1983), Magnusson (1988), Sameroff (1983), Sroufe (1979), and Wapner and Kaplan (1983), among others. In a volume that did not receive the attention it deserved, Cairns (1979a) expressed this view in the following formulation: "Behavior, whether social or nonsocial, is appropriately viewed in terms of an organized system, and its explanation requires a 'holistic analysis' " (p. 325) Sroufe (1979) expressed the same general view: "There is a logic and coherence to the person that can only be seen in looking at total functioning" (p. 835).

In a modern holistic model, individual functioning and development is best described as a series of dynamic, complex processes; that is, many factors are involved and operate simultaneously in an individual, most often in a nonlinear way. For understanding such processes in general, the mainstream models of dynamic, complex processes—chaos theory (Basar, 1990; Gleick, 1987), catastrophe theory (Zeeman, 1976), and general systems theory (Bertalanffy, 1968)—must be considered. They have been formulated in the scientific disciplines concerned with dynamic processes (e.g., meteorology, ecology, biology, brain research, and chemistry) and have had a far-reaching, almost revolutionary influence on theorization and empirical research in these fields (see, e.g., Bothe, Ebeling, Kurzhanski, & Peschel, 1987). A consequence of the formulation of the modern models for complex, dynamic processes has been the development of adequate methodologies for the study of such processes, for example, the revival of nonlinear mathematics and methods for the study of patterns.

These models for dynamic, complex processes have important implications, if adequately applied, also for theorization and empirical research on the dynamic, complex process of individual development. When the methodologies developed for such models are considered in psychology, we have to avoid the mistake we made when we took over models and methods from natural sciences, particularly physics, in the beginning of this century. By doing this without careful analysis of the phenomena that were the objects of our interest and without consideration of these phenomena's characteristics, we applied models and methods from physics in an inappropriate way. Most researchers now agree that this had a hampering effect on real scientific progress in psychological research.

Thus, although it is important to consider the modern models for dynamic, complex processes mentioned above, it is equally important to be careful with their application in research on individual functioning. There are some similarities between the structures and processes studied in natural sciences and the structures and processes investigated in psychological research. But there are also essential differences, particularly when the interest is in the functioning of the total organism. At that level, fundamental characteristics and guiding elements in the dynamic, complex process of individual functioning are intentionality, linked to emotions and values, and lessons learned from experience. This fact must be taken into consideration when methods derived for the study of dynamic, complex processes, which do not have these elements, are applied in planning and implementing of empirical research in psychology.

One basic formulation in modern models for complex, dynamic processes has direct and important application for empirical research on individual functioning. It states that the total process cannot be understood by studying one aspect (variable) after the other in isolation from the other, simultaneously operating elements. The total picture has an information value that is beyond what is contained in its specific parts (the doctrine of epigenesis). This property of dynamic, complex processes has important consequences for the planning, implementation, and interpretation of empirical developmental research.

2. *The individual functions and develops in a continuously ongoing, reciprocal process of interaction with his or her environment.*

This proposition forms the basic feature of classical interactionism. It has been advocated and elaborated for a long time by researchers from very different perspectives, both in research on personality and in research on developmental issues. Baldwin (1895) explicitly discussed ontogenetic and evolutionary development in such terms in the 1890s. And as suggested by Cairns and Cairns (1985), there is a direct line from Baldwin to Piaget and Kohlberg and those who have influenced various areas of developmental research. During the last decades, the role of person–environment interaction for individual development has become accepted by most developmentalists.

Particularly by his theoretical contributions, including the conceptual analyses of the environment and its function, at different levels of organization, in the person–environment interaction process, Bronfenbrenner (1977, 1979a, 1979b, 1989, 1993) has played a leading role in this development.

3. The third basic proposition integrates mental factors, biological factors, behavioral, and environmental factors in a dynamic-process model. As was underlined in the introduction, two models are needed: one for current functioning of the individual within given structures and one for the individual developmental process. Thus, the third basic proposition has two complementary subpropositions: one for current individual functioning (3a) and one for individual functioning in a developmental perspective (3b).

3a. *At each specific moment, individual functioning is determined in a process of continuous, reciprocal interaction between mental factors, biological factors, and behavior—on the individual side—and situational factors.*

The way this process in an immediate situation evolves can be described with reference to Figure 1. The figure gives a simplified (but on the main points correct) picture of what happens psychologically and biologically in a certain situation with specific features. (Note that the figure is only a summarized description of a temporal sequence of events, not a neural network or a neuropathway.)

Assume that an individual encounters a situation that he or she interprets as threatening or demanding. The cognitive act of interpreting the situation stimulates, through the hypothalamus, the excretion of adrenaline from the adrenal glands, which in turn triggers other physiological processes. The cognitive–physiological interplay is accompanied by emotional states of fear, anxiety, or generally experienced arousal. In the next stage of the process, these emotions affect the individual's behavior and handling of the environment. They also influence his or her interpretation of the sequence of changes in the situational conditions and thereby his or her physiological reactions in the next stage of the process.

Thus, the perceptual–cognitive system and the biological system of an individual are involved in a continuous loop of reciprocal interaction. The way this process functions is contingent, among other things, on the environment, as it is perceived and given meaning by the individual. The outcomes of such situation–individual encounters will set the stage for subsequent reactions and actions to psychologically similar situations, as interpreted by the individual in his or her perceptual–cognitive system. In the developmental process, this interaction process affects both the mental system—for example, in the interpretation of certain types of situations and in the response to such situations—and the physiological system. Frequent encounters with stressful situations may affect the immune system and lead to psychosomatic symptoms (Farmer, Kaufmann, Packard, & Perelson, 1987; Öhman & Magnusson, 1987).

3b. *The individual develops in a process of continuous reciprocal interaction among psychological, biological, and environmental factors.*

Stattin and Magnusson (1990) illustrated this process by assessing the implications of biological maturation rate for the developmental process of girls. When the girls were 14

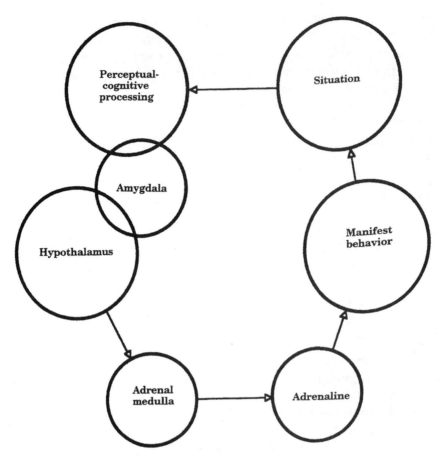

Figure 1
A simplified picture of the interplay of environmental, cognitive–emotional, physiological, and behavioral factors for an individual in a specific situation.

years and 5 months, on average, Stattin and Magnusson found a strong relation between different aspects of norm-breaking behavior (e.g., alcohol consumption) and the age at which each girl had reached menarche. In a follow-up study of the girls when they reached the age of 26, there was no systematic relation between various aspects of social adaptation (e.g., alcohol consumption) and each girl's age at menarche. However, there was a systematic relation between other aspects of adult life (e.g., family, children, education level, and job status) and age at menarche. Further analyses showed that the important mediating factor behind the more advanced social behavior among early-maturing girls was association with older, working boys. Early-maturing girls without this association did not demonstrate socially advanced behavior. The early-maturing girls who associated with older, working boys also differed from girls without this association with respect to mental factors, such as self-perception.

Thus, to understand and explain the role of biological factors, here the rate of biological maturation in the developmental process, we have to consider mental factors, biological factors, behavior, and environmental factors operating simultaneously (Pulkkinen, 1992).

Together, these propositions form the main elements of modern interactionism. What distinguishes modern interactionism from classical interactionism or developmental contextualism is the introduction of biological factors in individual functioning and the ongoing reciprocal interactive processes of biological and mental factors in the individual.

THE MENTAL SYSTEM IN A HOLISTIC PERSPECTIVE

A basic element of an interactionistic, holistic view is that a person is not only a passive receiver of stimulation from the environment, but also an active, purposeful agent in the person–environment interaction process (Endler & Magnusson, 1976). Thus, a guiding principle in the individual's inner and outer life is in the functioning of the perceptual–cognitive system (including worldviews and self-perceptions) with attached emotions, motives, needs, values, and goals. It can be briefly summarized as the integrated mental system.

The dynamic conception of mental processes as activities, rather than as the reception and processing of information, was advocated early by the act psychologists in Europe, such as Brentano (1874/1924) and Stumpf (1883). In the United States, James was a proponent of the same view. The intentional character of the individual's way of functioning was stressed by Tolman (1951), among others, and more recently the individual as an active, purposeful agent has been emphasized in action theory (cf. Brandtstädter, 1993; Strelau, 1983; see also Pervin, 1990).

By selecting and interpreting information from the external world and transforming this information into internal and external actions, the mental system plays a crucial role both in the process of interaction between mental and physiological factors within the individual and in the process of interaction between the individual and his or her environment. Not only does the mental system permit the organism to shape its effective environment, but also it provides a rapid and reversible strategy for organisms to adapt to changing environments. The mental system serves as a leading edge for adaptation in individual development in that it mobilizes neurobiological and physiological modifications and environmental changes.

Congenital factors (including genetic factors) set the stage for the development of an individual's mediating mental system. Within the restrictions, and using the potentialities of these biological factors, the structure and functioning of an individual's mediating mental system are formed. This system changes slowly in a process of maturation and experience that takes place in the continuous, bidirectional interaction between the individual and the environment. Thus, the mediating system is a function of the individual's interaction with the environment in the course of individual development, and it plays a crucial, guiding role in that interaction process at each stage of the developmental process.

In some psychodynamic models of individual development and the functioning of the mental system, the concept of unconscious processes has played a central role. This debate has been given new fuel during the past few decades through the growing interest in and understanding of the parallel processes of controlled (conscious, attended to, and thus subject to critical analysis) versus automatic (out of attentional focus and awareness) processing of information (see, e.g., Bowers, 1981; Brewin, 1986; Greenwald, 1992; Norman & Shallice, 1980). This continuously ongoing processing of signals impinging on the senses subliminally renders new importance to the perceptual–cognitive system; at the same time, it plays down the central role earlier ascribed to its conscious functioning.

BIOLOGICAL FACTORS IN A HOLISTIC PERSPECTIVE

Two lines of research on biological factors are of interest in this connection:

1. As discussed in the introduction, an issue of debate since ancient times has concerned nature versus nurture: the relative role of hereditary and environmental factors in individual functioning, currently and in a developmental perspective.

Since the beginning of the history of differential psychology, the role of genetic factors has been a main issue (Galton, 1869). After a period, starting during the 1960s, in which genetic factors were almost abandoned from the agenda, the development in human genetics has led to a renewed interest. That various aspects of individual functioning are, to some extent, determined by inherited properties of the body is supported by much empirical research (Cairns & Nakelski, 1971; Lagerspetz & Lagerspetz, 1971; Pedersen, 1989; Plomin, Chipuer, & Loehlin, 1990).

The traditional view on the role of genetic factors has been a unidirectional, cause–effect relation. At a most basic level, the onset and course of certain developmental sequences may be determined genetically to the extent that they are common to all individuals. However, even such developmental sequences as the onset of the menstrual cycle in girls and the regulation of growth in height are somewhat modifiable by environmental factors. The individual phenotype develops in the framework offered by the genotype in a reciprocal interaction process with the environment, a process that starts at conception and goes on through the life span. On the scene set by inherited factors, many different plays are possible (Waddington, 1962). Within the limits set by inherited factors, there are large potentialities for change, because of the interplay with environmental factors.

Thus, that there is a hereditary predisposition for a certain type of behavior does not mean that it cannot be changed by environmental influences (cf. Angoff, 1988). Cairns (1979), in his evaluation of the role of heredity and environment in individual differences in aggression, drew the conclusion that the differences obtained by selective breeding show strong environmental specificity and can be modified by environmental social conditions to such an extent that the inherited differences no longer matter. In well-planned longitudinal studies of newborns, Meyer-Probst, Rössler, and Teichmann (1983) demonstrated that favorable social conditions acted as protective factors for later social development among children identified at birth as biologically rich.

In this perspective, current individual functioning is the result of a life history of a person–environment interaction, in which environmental and inherited factors participate in a process for which it is not possible to disentangle their relative role at the individual level. The outcome of the process, at a certain stage of development, depends on the potential resources and limitations of the individual from the start and the properties of the environment with which the individual interacts during the life course.

2. The interaction process in which an individual is involved with the environment can be described in terms of an active adaptation process (Lerner, 1991). In this adaptation process, physiological factors, in constant interaction with cognitive–emotional factors, play an important role. On the biological side of this internal process, the endocrine system, in particular the sympathetic–adrenal and pituitary–adrenal systems, is of special importance. Cannon (1914) pointed to the role of the sympathetic–adrenomedullary system in emergency situations and demonstrated that adrenaline and noradrenaline are released as an effect of sympathetic innervation in response to threatening stimuli, as an adjustment mechanism to prepare the body for fight and flight (see Figure 1 and the discussion under 3a, pp. 27–29).

The rapid developments in neuropsychology, endocrinology, and pharmacology during the last decades have brought new knowledge about the role of physiological factors for the way that people think, feel, act, and react (cf. Magnusson, af Klinteberg, & Stattin, 1993; Rutter & Casaer, 1991; Zuckerman, 1980). Recent research on temperament has demonstrated the biological basis for temperament at an early age (Kagan, 1989, 1994). The relation of thoughts, emotions, and behavior to physiological processes has been elucidated in much recent empirical research (see, e.g., Gunnar, 1986, for a review). The role of individual differences in biological maturation during adolescence was elucidated in the study by Stattin and Magnusson (1990), presented above. That physiological factors are involved in the developmental process has been empirically demonstrated in a number of studies on antisocial behavior (cf. Magnusson, af Klinteberg, & Stattin, 1994).

BEHAVIOR IN A HOLISTIC PERSPECTIVE

As shown in the interactive model presented in Figure 1, behavior in all its manifestations, including verbal and motor behavior, plays an essential role in the total interaction process and, thus, also in individual development. In the interaction process, behavior is influenced by cognitive interpretations of what happens in the outer world (embedded in worldviews, self-perceptions, emotions, values, and needs), by subconscious automatic processing and by physiological processes. At the same time, it has a functional role in the total interaction process in two interrelated respects: first, by activities to reach short-term and long-term goals (Pervin, 1983), such as changing the situational conditions to satisfy personal short-term and long-term needs and to avoid negative cognitive, mental, or biological experiences (Magnusson, 1981) and, second, by adaptation to other individuals' behavior to develop and maintain working social relations (Cairns, 1994). The way the behavioral system of a person functions in a particular situation at a particular stage of the life cycle, and how successfully, is a result of the process of maturation and learning across development.

THE ENVIRONMENT IN A HOLISTIC PERSPECTIVE

In the developmental process of a person, environmental factors play a decisive role (see, e.g., Maccoby & Jacklin, 1983; Radke-Yarrow, 1991). Contact with others is necessary for the development of speech and language as a tool for thought and for communication (Camaioni, 1989; Tomaselli, 1992); for the development of adequate worldviews and self-perceptions (Epstein & Erskine, 1983); and for the development of well functioning, integrated norm and moral systems (Wilson, Williams, & Sugarman, 1967). The importance of contact with others for physical health has been emphasized in the increasing number of reports from research on social networks (e.g., Wills, 1984; Wortman & Dunkel-Schetter, 1987).

The individual and his or her environment do not form separate entities. The individual is an active, intentional part of the environment with which he or she interacts. Individuals meet their environment most directly in specific situations, which, in turn, are embedded in the larger environment with physical, social, and cultural properties operating both directly and indirectly at all levels of specificity–generality in the person–environment interaction (Barker, 1965; Bronfenbrenner, 1977, 1979a, 1979b, 1993; Magnusson, 1981).

The actual, physical environment acts on the individual in important respects that can be reacted to without an intermediate process of interpretation. The view of the environment as a source of stimulation that elicits and releases individual responses was bluntly expressed by Skinner: "A person does not act upon the world, the world acts upon him" (Skinner, 1971, p. 211). This conception of the environment is inherent in much developmental research in which various aspects of the upbringing environment in the home and at schools have been regarded as causes in the developmental process of individuals, with reference to a one-direction cause–effect model.

In a holistic, interactionistic perspective, the main role of the environment in the functioning and development of an individual is to serve as a source of information. This assumption contributes to understanding the way an individual interacts with the environment at various levels of complexity as conceptualized and discussed by Bronfenbrenner in various connections. This view is reflected in modern social learning theory, which assumes that an individual's way of dealing with the external world develops in a learning process in which two types of perceived contingencies are formed: (a) situation–outcome contingencies (implying that certain situational conditions will lead to certain outcomes) and (b) behavior–outcome contingencies (implying that certain actions by the individual will have certain predictable consequences; cf. Bolles, 1972). The formation of situation–outcome and behavior–outcome contingencies constitutes one source for the stability and continuity of individuals' functioning in relation to the environment in current situations and for the development of well functioning mental systems in the individuals.

The environmental influence on the developmental process differs among individuals with respect to size and type of consequences. Of particular interest in this connection is the occurrence of significant single events that may have profound impact on the life course of a person. Some such events occur seemingly randomly, but also as a consequence of the person's readiness for a certain type of action or reaction (e.g., a marriage or a new job) and an opportunity offered by the environment (e.g., meeting a special, matching person or receiving an offer of a new job). In other cases, a significant event may be the result of deliberate action by the person himself or herself or by individuals whose actions influence others.

Significant single events may occur over the whole life span, the character depending on the readiness of the individual, both mentally and physically, to act and react in relation to the opportunities and restrictions offered by the environment.

The effect of significant events is to change the direction of the life course. For example, buying a new house in a certain area with specific characteristics in terms of neighbors, opportunities or jobs, schooling, and cultural and leisure activities—instead of in an area with other characteristics—may have far-reaching effects on the direction of the future life course of all family members. Sometimes the effect is not immediately visible, but grows slowly and ends up having decisive effects on the person's life in a manner that is characteristic of the so-called butterfly effect in chaos theory. In other cases, the effect is more direct and leads to what has been discussed in terms of *turning points* (Pickles & Rutter, 1991).

THE TOTAL PERSON–ENVIRONMENT SYSTEM

The fact that the mental factors, behavior, biological factors, and environmental factors have been discussed separately does not imply that they function as four independent systems, operating interactively in the dualistic sense of a Cartesian view. They represent different aspects of a system of personal and environmental factors, which together constitute an integrated whole and operate as such (see also Schneirla, 1966).

The view reflected in the second proposition (p. 33) concerned with person–environment interaction and referred to as *classical interactionism* has been advocated and discussed by researchers under various headings. For example, Pervin (1968) adopted the term *transactionism*, and Bandura (1978) the term *reciprocal determinism* for individual functioning in a current perspective. Baltes, Reese, and Lipsitt (1980) used the term *dialectic–contextualistic;* Bronfenbrenner and Crouter (1983), the term *process–person–context model;* and Lerner and Kauffman (1985), the term *developmental contextualism*, for their view on the person–environment process.

Here and in other connections, I have consistently over the years used the terms *interaction* and *interactionism*. My reason is simple. They are terms well established in all other life sciences to cover the essence of the life processes of living organisms. Recently, a Swedish cell biologist used the title "Life Is an Interaction" for a public lecture on his discipline (Lindberg, 1992). It can only be harmful and detrimental to progress in our own discipline and to collaboration with neighboring sciences if we always try to invent and use new terms instead of adopting concepts well established in sciences with which we want to collaborate.

Causality: The Central Role of Dynamic Interaction

When I use the term *interaction* here, it refers to lawful dynamic interaction as a basic principle in the process of individual functioning. This meaning of the term has to be distinguished from statistical interaction in experimental designs for the study of individual differences.

An essential common characteristic of the explanatory models, which were briefly described in the introduction, is the view of unidirectional causality for the relation among variables. For a long time, the dominating general view, reflected in the experimental designs in the distinction between dependent and independent variables and between predictors and criteria, has been that biological and environmental factors are causes and that mental phenomena are results. The notion of stimulus–response (S–R) relations has been one of the most influential views in psychology. Many personality models also assume a unidirectional relation between cognitive–emotional factors and behavior.

In contrast to this traditional view, a central element in an interactionistic model is the reciprocal interaction among operating factors (Magnusson, 1990, 1993; Magnusson & Törestad, 1993). Interaction among operating factors is a fundamental characteristic of the processes of all living organisms. (Interaction among elements is also a central aspect of *relational holism* in physics; Zohar, 1990). It is central at all levels of individual functioning, from the functioning of single cells and how they organize themselves into systems in a lawful manner to fulfill their developmental role in the total organism (Edelman, 1987) to the functioning of a person in relation to his or her environment (Endler & Magnusson, 1976). In the interaction process, psychological factors can operate as causal factors, and biological factors can influence psychological phenomena. What starts a specific process and what maintains it vary. A psychological factor can start a biological process that is then maintained by physiological factors, and psychological factors can start and maintain a process that has been triggered by biological factors. Environmental factors influence a person's physical and mental well-being, and at the same time, an individual affects his or her own environment in many different ways.

The example presented in Figure 1 illustrates how the mental, behavioral, and biological systems of a person are involved in a continuous loop of reciprocal interaction in a current situation. The example illustrates how this process is dependent on the character of the specific, proximal situation that the individual encounters, particularly the situation as it is perceived and interpreted by the individual. The empirical example about maturing girls from Stattin and Magnusson (1990) shows how the developmental processes of the girls and their outcomes in the long range were dependent on the psychological and biological dispositions of the girls; the properties of the social, economic, and cultural environments in which the specific situations that the girls encountered were embedded; and the interaction among these factors.

DEVELOPMENTAL CHANGE: LAWFUL PROCESSES IN THE PERSON–ENVIRONMENT SYSTEM

A fundamental characteristic of the developmental process of a person is that the total person–environment system of operating factors—biological, psychological, and social—changes across time (Gottlieb, 1991). In the balance between the built-in resistance to change in the total system and subsystems once established, on the one hand, and sensitivity to factors in the individual and in the environment that work for change, on the other, the total system is in continuous transition into new states across the lifetime. In this process, both individuals and environments change and interact as totalities: individuals as a result of biological changes (e.g., growth or myelinization of the brain), as well as cognitive and emotional experiences, and environments as a consequence of societal changes and of individuals' direct and indirect actions in and on them, among other things. The fact that both persons and environments change across the life span leads to changes in the character of the interaction between them. The interaction process per se will thus precipitate development. For example, the character of the interactive process within a family changes across time.

A consequence of the perspective applied here, with methodological implications, is that changes do not take place in single aspects isolated from the totality. The extent to which different aspects of individual functioning are influenced by environmental factors in this process varies. For example, in sexual development, some features, such as gonadal structure and function, are strongly regulated by biological factors. On the other hand, other aspects of individual functioning, such as choice of peers and type of sexual relations, may be strongly open to experiential influences (Cairns, 1991).

Much debate has been devoted to the issues of stability versus change and continuity versus discontinuity in individual development. Characteristics of most of these studies are (a) that they deal with data for single variables one at a time, for example, aggressiveness, intelligence, and hyperactivity and (b) that they express temporal consistency of single variables in terms of relative stability, that is, in terms of stable rank orders of individuals across time for the variable under consideration (Weinert & Schneider, 1993).

As emphasized above, a fundamental characteristic of individual functioning as a holistic, dynamic process implies, among other things, that individuals do not develop in terms of single variables but as total integrated systems. In this perspective, all changes during the life span of a person are characterized by lawful continuity (Magnusson & Törestad, 1992); the functioning of a person at a certain stage of development is lawfully related to the functioning of the individual at earlier and later stages, but is not necessarily predictable. Each change in the process of human ontogeny is understandable and explainable in the light of the individual's previous life history and the functioning of the environment at the time for the change. This is true even for changes that are so abrupt that they seem to break a stable direction of development; for example, changes that have been characterized as turning points sometimes appear as a result of chance events or significant events. This view makes the dispute about whether individual development is characterized by continuity or discontinuity a pseudoissue in developmental research. The interesting aspect of this issue is what determines abrupt changes in the life course of a person and the kind of mechanisms that underlie such changes.

Individual development is not a process of accumulation of outcomes; it is rather, at the individual level, a process of restructuring of subsystems and the whole system within the boundaries set by biological and social constraints. If one aspect changes, it affects also related parts of the subsystem and sometimes the whole organism. For example, if one of the necessary operating factors in the coronary system totters, the whole coronary system and the whole organism may be affected. At a more general level, the restructuring of processes and structures at the individual level is embedded in and part of the restructuring of the total individual–environment system.

Much developmental research on stability and change has concentrated on stability and change in quantitative terms, and the issue has often been whether individual development is characterized by more of the same in a way that is reflected in statistical stability of rank orders of individuals for the specific variable under consideration. It should be recognized that the process of developmental change in an individual is characterized by both quantitative and qualitative change. The psychological significance of a certain state of a certain variable depends on the context of other, simultaneously operating variables in the system under investigation (i.e., on the pattern of operating factors to which the variable under consideration belongs).

These points have the implication—stressed by modern models for dynamic, complex processes, which were briefly referred to above—that the functioning of the total process cannot be understood by the study of single aspects, taken out and studied in isolation from their context with other operating factors. Developmental change does not take place in single variables. It is the total individual that changes in a lawful way across time.

THE PATTERNING OF OPERATING FACTORS

A basic, well-documented principle in the development of biological systems is their ability for self-organization (Barton, 1994; Eigen & Schuster, 1979; Kaplan & Kaplan, 1991; Kauffman, 1993; Nicolis & Prigogine, 1977). From the beginning of the development of the fetus, self-organization is the guiding principle (Hess & Mikhailov, 1994). Within subsystems, the operating components organize themselves in a way that maximizes the functioning of each subsystem with respect to its purpose in the total system. At a higher level, subsystems organize themselves to fulfill their role in the functioning of the totality. We find this principle in the development and functioning of the biological systems of the brain, the coronary system, and the immune system. It can also be applied to the development and functioning of the cognitive systems and manifest behavior.

For the discussion here, two aspects of the self-organizing processes are essential. First, individuals differ in the way operational factors are organized and function within subsystems, such as the perceptual–cognitive–emotional system, the immune system, the coronary system, and the behavioral system. Individuals also differ in subsystem organization and function. These organizations can be described in terms of patterns of operating factors within subsystems and in terms of patterns of functioning, cooperating subsystems. As an example, Weiner (1989) discussed the oscillations produced by natural pacemakers of the heart, the stomach, and the brain in terms of patterns.

Second, the number of ways in which operating factors in a certain subsystem can be organized in patterns, for the subsystem to play its functional role in the totality, is restricted. The goal for empirical research is then twofold: (a) to identify the possible operating factors in the subsystem under consideration and (b) to identify the ways in which these factors are organized (i.e., the actual working patterns of operating factors).

An empirical illustration to this view is presented by Gramer and Huber (1994). In a study of cardiovascular responses in what was assumed to be a stressful situation, they found that the subjects could be classified in three groups on the basis of their distinct pattern of values for systolic blood pressure, diastolic blood pressure, and heart rate (see Figure 2).

These data demonstrate a basic principle in individual development underlying individual differences: The characteristic of individual development is that it takes place in terms of patterns of operating factors. This is true for the operating factors in subsystems such as the coronary system, the immune system, the brain, and the cognitive system. It is also true for the development of the individual as a whole, where the operating subsystems are organized at the top level in terms of patterns.

This view leads to the conclusion that the main individual differences are to be found in the patterning of operating factors within subsystems, such as those I just described, and in the patterning of subsystems in the totality, for example, in the way the cognitive,

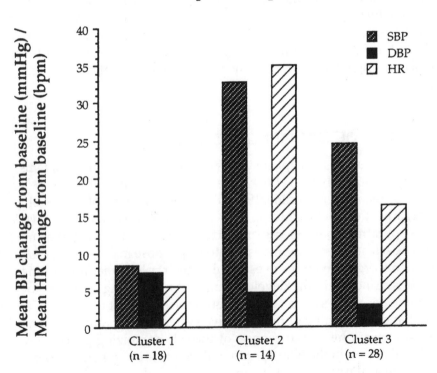

Figure 2

Magnitude of systolic blood pressure (SBP), diastolic blood pressure (DBP), and heart rate (HR) reactivity in cardiovascular response clusters during preparation of a speech (from Graber & Huber, 1994).

the behavioral, and the physiological systems function together in the total functioning of the individual.

The view that development takes place in terms of patterns of operating factors forms the theoretical basis for the application of a person approach in developmental research. The person approach is briefly discussed later.

INDIVIDUAL DIFFERENCES

One of the major goals for scientific work is to arrive at generalizations about the lawfulness of structures and processes in the space of phenomena that are the objects of interest. In psychology, one of the roads to this goal has been the systematic study of individual differences (cf. Cronbach, 1957; Eysenck & Eysenck, 1985).

The Variable Approach

Empirical research on individual differences in the area of developmental psychology has three main characteristics. An understanding of these characteristics is important in order to understand and evaluate the relevance of the results.

The first characteristic is the emphasis on variables in the search for lawfulness of structures and processes in individual functioning and development. The focus of interest is on a single variable or a combination of variables, their interrelations, and their relations to a specific criterion. The problems are formulated in terms of variables, and the results are interpreted in such terms. This is the case in such studies as those on the relationships among variables as a basis for factor analysis, on the stability of single variables across time, on the links between environmental factors and various aspects of individual functioning, and on the developmental background of adult functioning. An example is the research focusing on the relation between various aspects of individual functioning and environmental upbringing conditions, on the one hand, and the development of adult alcohol abuse and criminal behavior, on the other.

The second characteristic is that the lawfulness of structures and processes in individual functioning is studied by the application of various regression models, mainly linear regression models. This approach to the search for lawfulness implies the following interrelated assumptions:

1. Individuals can be compared on a nomothetical, continuous dimension in meaningful ways.
2. Individuals differ only quantitatively, not qualitatively, along the dimension for a certain variable.
3. Relationships among variables and their way of functioning in the totality of an individual is assumed to be the same for all individuals. In a multiple regression equation, each variable has the same weight for all individuals and reflects what is characteristic of the average person.
4. The interrelations among variables studied in nomothetic analyses can be used for inferences about how the variables actually function within individuals.

These assumptions are too seldom made explicit and considered in the interpretation of results from variable-oriented studies. Lewin (1931) discussed the limitations of this approach.

The third characteristic of developmental research is the fact that many, if not most, of the variables studied in empirical analyses are hypothetical variables. A hypothetical variable is an abstraction aimed at delineating a certain aspect of the total functioning of an individual—such as intelligence, aggressiveness, hyperactivity, attachment, shyness—or sometimes of the environment, such as social class or poverty. What is actually assessed as a measure of such an aspect is, of course, defined by the properties of the procedure used for data collection, independent of the wording of the theoretical definition. Hypothetical constructs, in which developmental psychology abounds, run the risk of reification (i.e., to be regarded as tangible and really existing).

One complication of the traditional variable approach, that is, applying regression models for the treatment of data for hypothetical variables in nomothetic analyses, is the existence of collinearity among variables, expressed in sometimes very high correlations among variables (Darlington, 1968). Statistical collinearity is reflected in sometimes very high intercorrelations among operating variables.

One general aim of traditional, variable-oriented studies in developmental research is to estimate the extent to which a specific variable or a set of variables, regarded as independent variables, contribute to the statistical prediction of a specific criterion, regarded and treated as the dependent variable. A study presented by Magnusson, Andersson, and Törestad (1993) was performed to illustrate the problems connected with this approach, in the perspective presented above.

The study was concerned with early person variables as antecedents of adult alcohol problems. On the basis of an analysis of existing literature, seven variables were chosen: aggressiveness, motor restlessness, concentration difficulties, lack of school motivation, disharmony, peer rejection, and school achievement. The data were collected when the boys were 13 years of age. Data for alcohol abuse were obtained from official registers. Both predictor and criteria data were available with insignificant dropout.

In Table 1, the correlation coefficients are presented for the relationship between each of the independent variables and the dependent variable, obtained as point-biserial coefficients. As expected, each of the independent variables had a significant linear relationship with the dependent variable with one exception: peer rejection. Each of the semipartial coefficients presented in the last column reflects the unique relation between the variable under consideration and the criterion when the role of the other independent variables is partialed out. None of them exceeded the level of .10, which means that data for each of the independent variables shared less than 1% with the total variance for registered alcohol abuse at adult age, when the variance common with all of the other variables was removed. Thus, the specific contribution of each single variable per se to the prediction of alcohol problems at adulthood was limited.

As illustrated by the entries in Table 1, the specific role of single hypothetical variables in the developmental process is conspicuously overestimated in studies of single variables in isolation from their context of other, simultaneously operating variables. This

TABLE 1

Point-Biserial Correlations and Semipartial Correlations Between the Independent Variables and the Dependent Variable: Registered Alcohol Abuse Age 18 Through Age 24

Independent variable	Correlation	Semipartial correlation
Aggressiveness	.221	.025
Motor restlessness	.236	.036
Concentration difficulties	.262	.048
Low school motivation	.259	.030
Disharmony	.248	.079
School achievement	−.180	−.018
Peer rejection	.055	−.049

is overlooked too often because, frequently, the roles of only one or a few independent variables are studied at each time. A good prediction is that it would have been possible to publish at least five studies, independent of each other, demonstrating a significant correlation between early individual functioning and adult alcohol problems.

For a statistician, the figures presented in Table 1 are not surprising, considering the intercorrelations among the independent variables. Nor are the results surprising, if they are interpreted in the perspective of a holistic, integrated model for individual development.

The analysis just presented shows the limitations of a simplistic variable approach as a basis for understanding and explaining the functioning and development of the individual. This does not mean that the variable approach can be abandoned in developmental research. It is a useful tool as a first step, in which the goal is to identify possible operating factors in the system that is under consideration as a basis for the application of a person approach.

The Person Approach

As discussed in an earlier section of this chapter, the main characteristics of an individual are in the patterning of structures and functioning of subsystems and cooperating subsystems. A consequence of this view is that the variable approach has to be complemented with a person approach, in which the individual is the basic unit of observation (Bergman, 1988, 1993; Bergman & Magnusson, 1983; Magnusson & Bergman, 1988; Magnusson, Stattin, & Dunér, 1983). In a variable approach, the specific problem under consideration is formulated in person terms and operationalized and studied empirically in terms of patterns of values for variables that are relevant to the problem under consideration. In other scientific disciplines that are concerned with dynamic, complex processes, such as ecology, meteorology, biology, and chemistry, pattern analysis has become an important methodological tool.

The following steps are included in a pattern analysis:

1. Identification of the system to which a pattern analysis is to be applied. This implies specification of the level of analysis, that is, if the interest is in the patterning of variables in a subsystem at a microlevel, such as a subsystem of the brain; in the patterning of variables at a more general level, for example, in the system of manifest behavior; or in the patterning of subsystems forming a system of higher order.

2. Identification of possible operating factors at the specified level of analysis to constitute the pattern to be studied.

3. Application of a statistical method for pattern analysis, for instance, grouping the individuals in categories that are homogeneous with respect to their patterns of values for the variables included in the analysis.

An empirical illustration of a person approach, concerned with the patterning of factors in the cardiovascular system, was presented in Figure 2. Another demonstration, which also offers a comparison with a variable approach, can be obtained from Magnusson and Bergman (1988), who used a person approach to the study of early problem behaviors as precursors of adult adjustment problems, among them, alcohol problems. Thus, the general purpose, the study of early antecedents of adult problems, was the same as that of the study presented by Magnusson, Andersson, and Törestad (1993), referred to above. The result of the pattern analysis is presented in Table 2.

The patterns in Table 2 are based on data for six variables, which cover different aspects of problem behaviors: aggressiveness, motor restlessness, concentration difficulty, low school motivation, underachievement, and peer rejection. Empirical studies indicate that each of them is a possible operating factor in the developmental processes underlying adult maladjustment. Data for each of the variables have been transformed to a scale with values ranging from 0 to 4, reflecting levels of seriousness of problem behaviors for boys at the age of 13. The methodology and results of the pattern analysis were discussed in detail in Magnusson and Bergman (1988). Here, only a few comments, pertinent to the discussion in this chapter, will be made.

Table 2 demonstrates that the boys could be grouped into eight distinctly different groups with reference to their pattern of values for the variables under study. An inspection shows that four out of six problem behaviors did not appear as single problem clusters for the boys at age 13. For example, aggressiveness and motor restlessness, which have been studied extensively in the variable-oriented tradition as separate indicators of maladjustment in both a cross-sectional and in a longitudinal perspective, appear only in combination with other indicators. This result is an illustration of the first basic proposition of a holistic model for individual functioning and individual development: A certain aspect of the total process cannot be finally studied and understood in isolation from its context of other, simultaneously operating factors. A certain factor, say aggressiveness, does not have a significance of its own per se, independent of the context of other factors simultaneously working in the individual. It gets its significance from its context. This became even more apparent in the follow-up study to the age of 24, which was reported by Magnusson and Bergman (1988). The long-term significance of a certain factor was not in the factor itself, it was in the total pattern in which the factor appeared at the individual level. For example, only when in combination with other severe problem behaviors at the age of 13 was aggressiveness a precursor of adult problems.

A number of methods for pattern analysis have been presented and applied: multivariate P-technique factor analysis (Cattell, Cattell, & Rhymer, 1947), Q-sort technique (Asendorpf & van Aken, 1991; Block, 1971), latent profile analysis (LPA; Gibson, 1959; Magnusson, Dunér, & Zetterblom, 1975), configural frequency analysis (CFA; Lienert & zur Oeveste, 1985; von Eye, 1990), and cluster-analytical techniques (Bergman, 1993). Use of higher order contingency-table techniques, for example, log-linear analysis, seems to be one fruitful way for the study of configurations of individuals' values (see, e.g., Bishop,

TABLE 2

Clusters of Boys at Age 13 Based on Data for Overt Adjustment Problems

Cluster no.	Size	Average coefficient[b]	Aggressive-ness	Motor restlessness	Conc. diff.	Low school motivation	Under-achievement	Peer rejection
				Cluster mean[a]				
1	296	.12	—	—	—	—	—	—
2	23	.30	—	—	—	—	—	2.4
3	40	.28	—	—	—	—	−2.6	—
4	61	.39	1.3	1.4	—	—	—	—
5	41	.39	—	1.5	2.3	1.9	—	—
6	12	.56	1.7	1.8	2.3	1.9	2.6	—
7	37	.37	2.3	2.3	1.9	1.3	—	—
8	22	.48	2.2	2.7	2.6	2.4	—	1.9
Residue	8		1.5	1.4	1.3	1.3	1.3	2.3

Note. Conc. diff. = concentration difficulty.
[a]Indicates that the cluster mean of a variable is less than 1 in the 4-point scale coded 0, 1, 2, 3.
[b]Average coefficient means average error sum of squares within the cluster.

Feinberg, & Holland, 1975). The methods that are available are mainly applicable to description of patterns and less appropriate for the study of developmental change in process terms (Magnusson & Törestad, 1993). For further scientific progress, development of methods for empirical study of developmental change in process terms is one of the most urgent tasks.

FINAL COMMENTS

A holistic, integrated model for individual functioning and development does not imply that the whole system of an individual must be studied at the same time. The essential function of the model is that it enables us to formulate problems at different levels of the functioning of the total organism, to implement empirical studies, and to interpret the results in a common, theoretical framework. For a long time, the Newtonian view of the physical world has served this purpose in the natural sciences. The implication of the acceptance of that model of nature has never been that the whole universe should be investigated in one and the same study. But it has enabled researchers concerned with very different levels of the total system, for example, nuclear physicists and astrophysicists, to communicate and understand each other. In the same way, an integrated, holistic model for individual development should make it possible for all those concerned with aspects of individual development, from developmental biologists to psychologists focusing on social development, to plan, implement, and interpret research in the same theoretical framework, thus enabling them to communicate with each other effectively.

The complexity of individual functioning and developmental change has brought some researchers to a pessimistic view about the future of psychology as a science (cf. Cronbach, 1975). However, the litmus test of a scientific discipline cannot be whether its phenomena are complex and hard to analyze. The criterion for a science is the appropriateness of the research strategy and methods that are applied in dealing with relevant questions. Whenever processes display order and regularity on the basis of given structures, it is a scientific challenge to map this lawfulness of order and regularity (cf. Bateson, 1978, in press). To do that successfully in research on individual development, a prerequisite for real scientific progress is that we start in careful analysis of the nature of the phenomena that are the objects of our interest; formulate the issues with reference to the result of such analyses; and plan, implement, and interpret the empirical research with reference to a holistic, integrated model for individual functioning and development (Cairns, 1979b, 1986; Magnusson, 1988, 1992; Magnusson & Cairns, in press).

REFERENCES

Angoff, W. H. (1988). The nature–nurture debate, aptitudes, and group differences. *American Psychologist, 43,* 713–720.

Asendorpf, J. B., & van Aken, M. A. G. (1991). Correlates of the temporal consistency of personality patterns in childhood. *Journal of Personality, 59,* 689–703.

Baldwin, J. M. (1895). *Mental development in the child and the race: Method and Processes.* New York: Macmillan.

Baltes, P. B., Reese, H. W., & Lipsitt, L. P. (1980). Life-span developmental psychology. In M. R. Rosenzweig & L. W. Porter (Eds.), *Annual review of psychology* (Vol. 31, pp. 65–110). Palo Alto, CA: Annual Reviews.

Brandtstädter, J. (1993). Development, aging and control: Empirical and theoretical issues. In D. Magnusson & P. Casaer (Eds.), *Longitudinal research on individual development: Present status and future perspectives* (pp. 194–216). Cambridge, England: Cambridge University Press.

Brentano, F. (1924). *Psychologie vom empirischen Standpunkte. Mit ausführliche Einleitung.* Leipzig: F. Meiner. (Original work published 1874)

Brewin, C. R. (1986). *Cognitive foundations of clinical psychology.* Hillsdale, NJ: Erlbaum.

Bronfenbrenner, U. (1977). Toward an experimental ecology of human development. *American Psychologist, 32,* 513–531.

Bronfenbrenner, U. (1979a). Context of child rearing: Problems and prospects. *American Psychologist, 34,* 834–850.

Bronfenbrenner, U. (1979b). *The ecology of human development: Experiments by nature and design.* Cambridge, MA: Harvard University Press.

Bronfenbrenner, U. (1989). Ecological systems theory. *Annals of Child Development, 6,* 185–246.

Bronfenbrenner, U. (1993). The ecology of cognitive development: Research models and fugitive findings. In R. H. Wozniak & K. Fischer (Eds.), *Development in context: Acting and thinking in specific environments* (pp. 3–44). Hillsdale, NJ: Erlbaum.

Bronfenbrenner, U., & Ceci, S. J. (1994). Nature–nurture reconceptualized in developmental perspective: A bioecological model. *Psychological Review, 101,* 568–586.

Bronfenbrenner, U., & Crouter, A. C. (1983). The evolution of environmental models in developmental research. In P. Mussen (Series Ed.) & W. Kassen (Vol. Ed.), *Handbook of child psychology: Vol. 1. History, theories and methods* (4th ed., pp. 357–414). New York: Wiley.

Cairns, R. B. (1979a). *Social development: The origins and plasticity of interchanges.* San Francisco: W. H. Freeman.

Cairns, R. B. (1979b). Toward guidelines for interactional research. In R. B. Cairns (Ed.), *The analysis of social interactions: Methods, issues, and illustrations.* Hillsdale, NJ: Erlbaum.

Cairns, R. B. (1983). The emergence of developmental psychology. In P. Mussen (Series Ed.) & W. Kassen (Vol. Ed.), *Handbook of child psychology: Vol. 1. History, theories and methods* (4th ed., pp. 41–101). New York: Wiley.

Bandura, A. (1978). The self system in reciprocal determinism. *American Psychologist, 33,* 344–358.

Barker, R. G. (1965). Exploration in ecological psychology. *American Psychologist, 20,* 1–14.

Barton, S. (1994). Chaos, self-organization, and psychology. *American Psychologist, 49,* 5–14.

Basar, E. (Ed.). (1990). *Chaos in brain function.* Berlin: Springer-Verlag.

Bateson, P. P. G. (1978). How does behavior develop? In P. P. G. Bateson & P. H. Klopfer (Eds.), *Perspectives in ethology: Vol. 3. Social behavior.* New York: Plenum.

Bateson, P. (in press). Design for a life. In D. Magnusson (Ed.), *The Life-span development of individuals: Behavioral, neurobiological and psychosocial perspectives.* Cambridge, England: Cambridge University Press.

Bergman, L. R. (1988). Modeling reality. In M. Rutter (Ed.), *Studies of psychosocial risks: The power of longitudinal data* (pp. 354–366). Cambridge, England: Cambridge University Press.

Bergman, L. R. (1993). Some methodological issues in longitudinal research: Looking forward. In D. Magnusson & P. Casaer (Eds.), *Longitudinal research on individual development: Present status and future perspectives* (pp. 217–241). Cambridge, England: Cambridge University Press.

Bergman, L. R., & Magnusson, D. (1983). The development of patterns of maladjustment. In *Report from the project Individual Development and Environment.* Stockholm: Stockholm University.

Bertalanffy, L., von. (1968). *General system theory.* New York: Braziller.

Binet, A. (1909). *Les ideés modernes sur les enfants* [Modern ideas about children]. Paris: Ernest Flammarion.

Bishop, Y. M. M., Feinberg, S. E., & Holland, P. W. (1975). *Discrete multivariate analysis: Theory and practice.* Cambridge, MA: MIT Press.

Block, J. (1971). *Lives through time.* Berkeley, CA: Bancroft Books.

Bolles, R. C. (1972). Reinforcement, expectancy, and learning. *Psychological Review, 79,* 394–409.

Bothe, H. G., Ebeling, W., Kurzhanski, A. B., & Peschel, M. (Eds.). (1987). *Dynamical systems and environmental models*. Berlin: Akademie-Verlag.

Bowers, K. S. (1981). Knowing more than we can say leads to saying more than we can know: On being implicitly informed. In D. Magnusson (Ed.), *Toward a psychology of situations* (pp. 179–194). Hillsdale, NJ: Erlbaum.

Cairns, R. B. (1986). Phenomena lost: Issues in the study of development. In J. Valsiner (Ed.), *The individual subject and scientific psychology* (pp. 79–111). New York: Plenum.

Cairns, R. B. (1991). Multiple metaphors for a singular idea. *Developmental Psychology, 27*, 23–26.

Cairns, R. B. (1994, June). Socialization and sociogenesis. In *The life-span development of individuals: A synthesis of biological and psychosocial perspectives*. Symposium, Stockholm.

Cairns, R. B., & Cairns, B. D. (1985). The developmental-interactional view of social behavior: Four issues of adolescent aggression. In D. Olweus, J. Block, & M. Radke-Yarrow (Eds.), *The development of antisocial and prosocial behavior*. New York: Academic Press.

Cairns, R. B., & Nakelski, J. S. (1971). On fighting in mice: Ontogenetic and experimental determinants. *Journal of Comparative and Physiological Psychology, 71*, 354–364.

Camaioni, L. (1989). The role of social interaction in the transition from communication to language. In A. de Ribaupierre (Ed.), *Transition mechanisms in child development* (pp. 109–125). New York: Cambridge University Press.

Cannon, W. B. (1914). The emergency function of the adrenal medulla in pain and the major emotions. *American Journal of Physiology, 33*, 356–372.

Cattell, R. B., Cattell, A. K. S., & Rhymer, R. M. (1947). P-technique demonstrated in determining psychophysiological source traits in a normal individual. *Psychometrika, 12*, 267–288.

Cronbach, L. J. (1957). The two disciplines of scientific psychology. *American Psychologist, 12*, 671–684.

Cronbach, L. J. (1975). Beyond the two disciplines of scientific psychology. *American Psychologist, 30*, 116–127.

Darlington, R. B. (1968). Multiple regression. *Psychological Bulletin, 69*, 161–182.

de Groot, A. D. (1990). Unifying psychology: A European view. In P. J. D. Drenth, J. A. Sergeant, & R. J. Takens (Eds.), *European perspectives in psychology: Theoretical, psychometrics, personality, developmental, educational, cognitive, gerontological* (Vol. 1, pp. 3–16). New York: Wiley.

Durkheim, E. (1897). *Le suicide: Étude de sociologie* [Suicide: A sociological study]. Paris: Alcan.

Eccles, J., & Robinson, D. N. (1985). *The wonder of being human*. Boston: New Science Library.

Edelman, G. (1987). *Neural Darwinism: The theory of neuronal group selection*. New York: Basic Books.

Eigen, M., & Schuster, P. (1979). *The hyper cycle—A principle of natural self-organization*. Heidelberg, Germany: Springer.

Endler, N. S., & Magnusson, D. (1976). Toward an interactional psychology of personality. *Psychological Bulletin, 83*, 956–979.

Epstein, S., & Erskine, N. (1983). The development of personal theories of reality from an interactional perspective. In D. Magnusson & V. L. Allen (Eds.), *Human development: An interactional perspective* (pp. 133–147). New York: Academic Press.

Eysenck, H. J., & Eysenck, M. W. (1985). *Personality and individual differences: A natural science approach*. London: Plenum.

Farmer, J. D. Kaufmann, A., Packard, N. H., &Perelson, A. S. (1987). Adaptive dynamic networks as models for the immune system and autocatalytic sets. In S. H. Koslow, A. J. Mandell, & M. F. Schlesinger (Eds.), *Annals of the New York Academy of Sciences: Vol. 504. Perspectives in biological dynamics and theoretical medicine* (pp. 118–131). New York: New York Academy of Sciences.

Galton, F. (1869). *Hereditary genius: An inquiry into its laws and consequences*. London: Macmillan.

Gibson, W. A. (1959). Three multivariate models: Factor analysis, latent structure analysis and latent profile analysis. *Psychometrica, 24*, 229–252.

Gleick, J. (1987). *Chaos: Making a new science*. New York: Penguin Books.

Gottlieb, G. (1991). Experiential canalization of behavioral development: Theory. *Developmental Psychology, 27*, 4–13.

Gramer, M., & Huber, H. P. (1994). Individual variability in task-specific cardiovascular patterns during psychological challenge. *German Journal of Psychology, 18*, 1–17.

Greenwald, A. G. (1992). Unconscious cognition reclaimed. *American Psychologist, 47*, 766–779.

Gunnar, M. R. (1986). Human developmental psychoendocrinology: A review of research on neuroendocrine responses to challenge and threat in infancy and childhood. In M. E. Lamb, A. L. Brown, & B. Rogoff (Eds.), *Advances in developmental psychology* (Vol. 4). Hillsdale, NJ: Erlbaum.

Hess, B., & Mikhailov, A. (1994). Self-organization in living cells. *Science, 264*, 223–224.

Hunt, J. McV., (1961). *Intelligence and experience.* New York: Ronald Press.

Kagan, J. (1989). *Unstable ideas: Temperament, cognition, and self.* Cambridge, MA: Harvard University Press.

Kagan, J. (1994). *Galen's prophecy: Temperament in human nature.* New York: Basic Books.

Kaplan, M. L., & Kaplan, N. R. (1991). The self-organization of human psychological functioning. *Behavioral Science, 36*, 161–179.

Kauffman, S. A. (1993). *The origins of order.* New York: Oxford University.

Kohlberg, L. (1969). Stage and sequence: The cognitive–developmental approach to socialization. In D. A. Goolin (Ed.), *Handbook of socialization theory and research.* Chicago: Rand McNally.

Lagerspetz, K. M. J., & Lagerspetz, K. Y. H. (1971). Changes in the aggressiveness of mice resulting from selective breeding, learning and social isolation. *Scandinavian Journal of Psychology, 12*, 241–248.

Lerner, R. M. (1991). Changing organism-context relations as the basis of development: A developmental contextual perspective. *Developmental Psychology, 27*, 27–32.

Lerner, R. M., & Kauffman, M. B. (1985). The concept of development in contextualism. *Developmental Review, 5*, 309–333.

Lewin, K. (1931). Environmental forces in child behavior and development. In C. Murchison (Ed.), *A handbook of child psychology* (pp. 94–127). Worcester, MA: Clark University Press.

Lienert, G. A., & zur Oeveste, H. (1985). CFA as a statistical tool for developmental research. *Educational and Psychological Measurement, 45*, 301–307.

Lindberg, U. (1992). *Livet är en interaktion* [Life is an interaction]. Stockholm: Folkuniversitetet.

Maccoby, E. E., & Jacklin, C. N. (1983). The "person" characteristics of children and the family as environment. In D. Magnusson & V. L. Allen (Eds.), *Human development: An interactional perspective* (pp. 75–91). San Diego, CA: Academic Press.

Magnusson, D. (1981). *Toward a psychology of situations: An interactional perspective.* Hillsdale, NJ: Erlbaum.

Magnusson, D. (1988). *Individual development from an interactional perspective.* Hillsdale, NJ: Erlbaum.

Magnusson, D. (1990). Personality development from an interactional perspective. In L. Pervin (Ed.), *Handbook of personality* (pp. 193–222). New York: Guilford Press.

Magnusson, D. (1992). Back to the phenomena: Theory, methods and statistics in psychological research. *European Journal of Personality, 6*, 1–14.

Magnusson, D. (1993). Human ontogeny: A longitudinal perspective. In D. Magnusson & P. Casaer (Eds.), *Longitudinal research on individual development: Present status and future perspectives* (pp. 1–25). Cambridge, England: Cambridge University Press.

Magnusson, D., af Klinteberg, B., & Stattin, H. (1993). Autonomic activity/reactivity, behavior, and crime in a longitudinal perspective. In J. McCord (Ed.), *Facts, frameworks, and forecasts* (pp. 287–318). New Brunswick, NJ: Transaction.

Magnusson, D., af Klinteberg, B., & Stattin, H. (1994). Juvenile and persistent offenders: Behavioral and physiological characteristics. In R. D. Ketterlinus & M. Lamb (Eds.), *Adolescent problem behaviors.* Hillsdale, NJ: Erlbaum.

Magnusson, D., Anderson, T., & Törestad, B. (1993). Methodological implications of a peephole perspective on personality. In D. C. Funder, R. D. Parke, C. Tomlinson-Keasey, & K. Widaman (Eds.), *Studying lives through time: Personality and development* (pp. 207–220). Washington, DC: American Psychological Association.

Magnusson, D., & Bergman, L. R. (1988). Individual and variable-based approaches to longitudinal research on early risk factors. In M. Rutter (Ed.), *Studies of psychosocial risk: The power of longitudinal data* (pp. 45–61). Cambridge, England: Cambridge University Press.

Magnusson, D., & Cairns, R. B. (in press). Developmental science: Principles and illustrations. In R. B. Cairns, G. H. Elder, Jr., E. J. Costello, & A. McGuire (Eds.), *Developmental science*. Cambridge, England: Cambridge University Press.

Magnusson, D., Dunér, A., & Zetterblom, G. (1975). *Adjustment: A longitudinal study.* Stockholm: Almqvist & Wiksell.

Magnusson, D., Stattin, H., & Dunér, A. (1983). Aggression and criminality in a longitudinal perspective. In K. T. van Dusen & S. A. Mednick (Eds.), *Prospective studies of crime and delinquency* (pp. 273–301). Boston: Kluwer-Nijhoff.

Magnusson, D., & Törestad, B. (1992). The individual as an interactive agent in the environment. In W. B. Walsh, K. Craig, & R. Price (Eds.), *Person–environment psychology: Models and perspectives.* Hillsdale, NJ: Erlbaum.

Magnusson, D., & Törestad, B. (1993). A holistic view of personality: A model revisited. *Annual Review of Psychology, 44,* 427–452.

Meyer-Probst, B., Rössler, H. D., & Teichmann, H. (1983). Biological and psychosocial risk factors and development during childhood. In D. Magnusson & V. L. Allen (Eds.), *Human development: An interactional perspective* (pp. 244–259). San Diego, CA: Academic Press.

Miller, N. E., & Dollard, J. (1941). *Social learning and imitation.* New Haven, CT: Yale University Press.

Nesselroade, J. R., & Ford, D. H. (1987). Methodological considerations in modeling living systems. In M. E. Ford & D. H. Ford (Eds.), *Humans as self-constructing living systems: Putting the framework to work* (pp. 47–79). Hillsdale, NJ: Erlbaum.

Nicolis, G., & Prigogine, I. (1977). *Self-organization in non-equilibrium systems.* New York: Wiley Interscience.

Norman, D. A., & Shallice, T. (1980). *Attention to action: Willed and automatic control of behavior (CHIP Report 99).* San Diego, CA: University of California.

Öhman, A., & Magnusson, D. (1987). An interactional paradigm for research on psychopathology. In D. Magnusson & A. Öhman (Eds.), *Psychopathology: An interactional perspective.* New York: Academic Press.

Pedersen, N. (1989). Some evidence regarding the importance of genes and environments during behavioral development. *ISSBD Newsletter, 15,* 3–4.

Pervin, L. (1968). Performance and satisfaction as a function of individual environment fit. *Psychological Bulletin, 69,* 56–68.

Pervin, L. A. (1983). The stasis and flow of behavior: Toward a theory of goals. In M. M. Page (Ed.), *Personality: Current theory and research* (pp. 1–53). Lincoln: University of Nebraska Press.

Pervin, L. A. (1990). A brief history of modern personality theory. In L. A. Pervin (Ed.), *Handbook of personality: Theory and research* (pp. 3–18). New York: Guilford Press.

Piaget, J. (1948). *The moral judgment of the child.* Glencoe, IL: Free Press.

Pickles, A., & Rutter, M. (1991). Statistical and conceptual models of "turning points" in developmental processes. In D. Magnusson, L. R. Magnusson, L. R. Bergman, G. Rudinger, & B. Törestad (Eds.), *Problems and methods in longitudinal research: Stability and change* (pp. 133–166). Cambridge, England: Cambridge University Press.

Plomin, R., Chipuer, H. M., & Loehlin, J. C. (1990). Behavioral genetics and personality. In L. A. Pervin (Ed.), *Handbook of personality: Theory and research.* New York: Guilford Press.

Pulkkinen, L. (1992). Life-styles in personality development. *European Journal of Personality, 6,* 139–155.

Radke-Yarrow, M. (1991). The individual and the environment in human behavioral development. In P. Bateson (Ed.), *The development and integration of behaviour: Essays in honour of Robert Hinde* (pp. 389–410). Cambridge, England: Cambridge University Press.

Rutter, M., & Casaer, P. (1991). *Biological risk factors for psychosocial disorders.* Cambridge, England: Cambridge University Press.

Sameroff, A. J. (1983). Developmental systems: Contexts and evolution. In P. H. Mussen (Ed.), *Handbook of child psychology* (Vol. 1, pp. 237–294). New York: Wiley.

Schneirla, T. C. (1966). Behavioral development and comparative psychology. *Quarterly Review of Biology, 41,* 283–302.

Skinner, B. F. (1971). *Beyond freedom and dignity.* New York: Knopf.

Sroufe, L. A. (1979). The coherence of individual development: Early care, attachment, and subsequent developmental issues. *American Psychologist, 34,* 834–841.

Stattin, H., & Magnusson, D. (1990). *Paths through life: Vol. 2. Pubertal maturation in female development.* Hillsdale, NJ: Erlbaum.

Stern, W. (1911). *Die differentielle Psychologie in ihren metodischen Grundlagen* [Differential psychology in its methodological basis]. Leipzig, Germany: Verlag von Johann A. Barth.

Strelau, J. (1983). *Temperament-personality-activity.* New York: Academic Press.

Stumpf, C. (1883). *Tonpsychologie* [True psychology] (Vol. 1). Leipzig, Germany: S. Hirzel.

Thomae, H. (1988). *Das Individum und seine Welt: Eine Pers onlichkeitstheorie* [The individual and his world: A theory of personality]. Göttingen, Germany: Hogrefe.

Tolman, E. C. (1951). A psychological model. In T. Parsons & E. A. Shils (Eds.), *Toward a general theory of action* (pp. 279–364). Cambridge, MA: Harvard University Press.

Tomaselli, M. (1992). The social bases of language acquisition. *Social Development, 1,* 67–87.

Toulmin, S. (1981). Toward reintegration: An agenda for psychology's next century. In R. A. Kasschau & Ch. N. Cofer (Eds.), *Psychology's next century: Enduring issues* (pp. 264–286). New York: Praeger.

von Eye, A. (1990). *Introduction to configural frequency analysis: The search for types and antitypes in cross-classifications.* New York: Cambridge University Press.

Waddington, C. (1962). *New patterns in genetics and development.* New York: Columbia.

Wapner, S., & Kaplan, B. (1983). *Toward a holistic developmental psychology.* Hillsdale, NJ: Erlbaum.

Watson, J. B. (1930). *Behaviorism* (2nd ed.). New York: Norton.

Weiner, H. (1989). The dynamics of the organism: Implications of recent biological thought for psychosomatic theory and research. *Psychosomatic Medicine, 51,* 608–635.

Weinert, F. E., & Schneider, W. (1993). Cognitive, social, and emotional development. In D. Magnusson & P. Casaer (Eds.), *Longitudinal research on individual development: Present status and future perspectives* (pp. 75–94). Cambridge, England: Cambridge University Press.

Wills, T. A. (1984). Supportive functions of interpersonal relationships. In S. Cohen & L. Syme (Eds.), *Social support and health* (pp. 61–82). New York: Academic Press.

Wilson, J., Williams, N., & Sugarman, B. (1967). *Introduction to moral education.* Baltimore: Penguin Books.

Wortman, C. B., & Dunkel-Schetter, C. (1987). Conceptual and methodological issues in the study of social support. In A. Baum & J. E. Singer (Eds.), *Handbook of psychology and health* (Vol. 5, pp. 33–67). Hillsdale, NJ: Erlbaum.

Zeeman, E. C. (1976). Catastrophe theory. *Scientific American, 234,* 65–83.

Zohar, D. (1990). *The quantum self: A revolutionary view of human nature and consciousness rooted in the new physics.*

Zuckerman, M. (1980). Sensation seeking and its biological correlates. *Psychological Bulletin, 88,* 187–214.

8

TWO IDEAL PARENTING MODELS: MAKING SENSE OF THEM

Helen M. Gore-Laird, Ph.D., University of Houston

The best way to make children good is to make them happy.

—Oscar Wilde

We live in a diverse world with diverse values. While most of us can recognize the diversity, it is much more difficult to accept and tolerate the diversity. These diverse values lead to a variety of ideas on how to parent our children. Our parenting style is influenced by our values and the many experiences we have in life. In the acknowledgments of George Lakoff's (1996) book, *Moral Politics: What Conservatives Know that Liberals Don't*, he relates a conversation that he had with his good friend, Paul Baum, in which he asked Paul what single question could one ask to distinguish conservative from liberal political attitudes. Paul Baum replied, "If your baby cries at night, do you pick him up?" This same question can be asked of parents to determine their attitudes toward parenting their children. It was on the basis of this question that Lakoff identified metaphors of the ideal family which trace the political beliefs of conservatives and liberals. For the conservatives, political metaphors evolve from a strict-father model of the family; for the liberals, a nurturant-parent model. We will borrow from Lakoff's model to understand differences of opinions in how to parent (discipline) one's children.

The family models developed by Lakoff help us gain an understanding as to how people structure their views on gun control, environmental issues, social programs, taxes, abortion, and other issues. These same structures can illuminate the underlying issues in the parenting styles we choose to use when raising our children. For example, the issue of whether to spank our children for misbehaviors or to use alternative methods of discipline.

Baca Zinn and Eitzen (2002) describe two approaches to understanding the variations in families. They examine the issues in terms of class, gender, and race. These approaches are applied to understanding issues in mate selection, marriage, divorce and parenting. They note that "we typically think of families as biological units based on the timeless functions of love, motherhood, and childbearing (Baca Zinn and Eitzen, 2002, p. 296)." Yet, we know that this is a myth. In order to fully understand the implications that the cultural and structural models have on parenting, Lakoff's work, along with the work of Jane Loevinger and Lawrence Kohlberg, will be utilized to examined these issues.

LAKOFF'S MODELS OF THE IDEAL PARENTS

From listening to people, reading newspapers, and watching television, Lakoff began to notice the family-based values used by liberals and conservatives (Engel, 1996). From these observations he developed the models of family that conservatives and liberals use when discussing political issues. These models of the family, while ideals, form the basis of how we view the functioning and roles of families in our society.

The key feature of the conversative or the strict-father model is that the world is a dangerous place and that life is difficult (Lakoff, 1996). Lakoff (1996) notes the main concern of the strict-father model is that of survival, because one sees evil in the shadows of every thing that happens to us or that we do. Evil is especially present in the human soul. Therefore, the moral strength found in families resides in their ability to do battle with evil. This can be seen as the war between good and evil which is fought with self-discipline and self-reliance.

For those who adhere to the strict-father model, the universe has a natural order. This natural order follows the tenets of Social Darwinism, or the belief that the principle of 'survival of the fittest' applies to human societies (Baca Zinn and Eitzen, 2002). This natural order places God as the ultimate father or authority. The moral authority resides in

CULTURAL LAKOFF'S COMPARISON OF MORAL PRIORITIES

STRICT FATHER FAMILY	NURTURANT PARENT FAMILY
THE STRENGTH GROUP **Moral Strength** (war between good & evil) (self-discipline/self reliance) **Moral Authority** (parental/legitimate) **Moral Order** (the "natural" order) (God/Man/Woman/Child/Nature) (Moral People/Immoral People) (Rich People/Poor People) **Moral Boundaries** (freedom within correct path) **Moral Essence** (good character/rotten character) (always the same) **Moral Wholeness** (unity/uniformity/homogeneity) **Moral Purity** (reinforces "wholeness") **Moral Health** (quarantine evil)	**THE NURTURANCE GROUP** **Moral Nurturance** (helping people in need) (self-nurturance as means to that end) **Moral Empathy** (strong "Golden Rule") (feel YOUR pain) **Nurturance of Social Ties** (maintenance of community) **Moral Self-Development** (cultivate abilities and values that help others) **Moral Happiness** (happy people are more empathetic and able to bring joy to others) **Morality as Fair Distribution** (complex combination of models: depends on particular circumstance)
MORAL SELF-INTEREST success is moral if obtained by self-discipline & self-reliance (well-being through independence)	**MORAL SELF-INTEREST** success is a by-product of caring for others; constrained by nurturant morality (well-being through interdependence)
MORAL NURTURANCE reward for obedience punishment for disobedience	**THE STRENGTH GROUP** **Moral Order** (God/all people)

Prepared by Helen M. Gore-Laird, Ph. D. and Glenn W. Laird
From the book, <u>Moral Politics: What Conservatives Know that Liberals Don't</u> by George Lakoff

the father and this can be the only legimate authority. To be moral requires one to be obedient to the father. This obedience will gain you rewards; however, if you fail to be obedient you will be punished. Being good in this model means that you conform to the rules of the legimate authority, the father. Freedom is given, but only if one is on the correct path. This correct path is determined by the legimate authority. This model of parenting strives for homogeneity. Lakoff (1996) notes that in this model the assumption that is made is that "without the incentive of reward and punishment, self-discipline would disappear, and people would no longer be able to make plans, undertake committments, and carry them out (p. 69)."

In the strict father model, it is assumed that children have to learn self-discipline, self-reliance and respect for authority. The metaphor for this can be taken from the 1950s television show "Father Knows Best." The slogan for the strict-father is "Eighteen and you are out." (Engel, 1996). The other common saying in this model is, "as long as you live under my roof, you will abide by my rules." Parents who operate within this model like to control their children like robots. They want their children to do what they want when they want them to do it. Freedom can only be granted within the bounds of the "correct path." When the child reaches adolescence, the second struggle of independence and autonomy, a struggle for control usually ensues between the adolescent and his or her parents. When working for a large social service agency, I ran a transitional living program for single, homeless mothers. Very often the young mother was homeless because she became pregnant and the parents punished her by "kicking" her out of the house. The view was she broke the rule (do not get pregnant out of wed-lock); therefore, she needed to be punished. The strict father refers to this as "tough love."

The strict father pressures their children to conform by comparing them to others and by using labels or global assessments ("You are a slow reader" or "You are really the brains in the family"). They also use criticism, judgments, and evaluations, reprimands and illogical punishments, thought indoctrination, over-controlling behaviors, and recusing. The strict father also fosters and encourages competition. Competition promotes a meritocracy and it is heirarchical (Lakoff, 1996). These techniques send the message to the child that others need to think for them and that they can not trust their own reasoning process. They learn that unless they act exactly like all the others, they are not OK.

Less we sound very negative about the strict-father model, there are some benefits to be gained by having one operate from the strict-father model in certain circumstances. In times of crisis, such as a natural disaster, when quick, decisive action is necessary for survival, having strong leadership is vital. The strict father model is good for survival in the short-term but not necessarily in the long-term. A perfect example of this can be found in Winston Churchill, the quintesential "strict father." No one could have been better for leading Great Britain during World War II. However, once the crisis was passed, his authoritarian style became utterly ineffective in promoting the kind of cooperation necessary to rebuild the social fabric.

The key feature of the nurturant parent is that of care (Engel, 1996, Lakoff, 1996). Lakoff states that this model may have emerged as a "woman's model." Carol Gilligan (1982) and Nell Noddings (1984) both have explored the issue of care. Nel Noddings, in an effort not to be gender specific, chose to use words like "the cared for" and "the caring one." Carol Gilligan noted that the issue of care resides in relationships or connectedness; whereas, justice lies in our ability to reason logically about issues by being disconnected. The nurturant parent sees self-nurturance as a means to helping other people in need. The goal of the nurturant parent is "for their children to be fulfilled and happy in their lives and to become nurturant themselves (Lakoff, 1996, p. 109). Children raised by this model become self-disciplined and self-reliant through the care given to them by their parents. Piaget (1965) noted that it is the allowing of the child to have autonomy that leads to the practical respect of the law. This according to Piaget, comes through cooperation because this leads to the practice of reciprocity in relations with his peers and others. Thus, the nuturant parent will foster a child's sense of autonomy.

Two-way communication is very important to the nurturant parent. They believe that if they are the authority in their child's life, they have an obligation to communicate to their children the reasons why their decisions are in the best interest of the child. At the same time, they also believe in listening to the ideas and concerns of their children. These ideas and concerns are taken seriously and may be considered in the final decision. The nurturant parent realizes that he or she have the ultimate decision, but wants to make that decision in collaboration with their child.

Discipline under the nurturant parent model uses techniques that promote a child's learning internal controls so that they can control their own behavior. This is the opposite of the strict-father model, in which the child's behavior is controlled externally. The nurturant parent uses methods such as natural consequences, time-out, and logical consequences. Spanking is not a choice of discipline for the nurturant parent. As Murphy (1999) noted

> Most child-development experts agree that spanking is not an effective discipline technique because it teaches kids to behave out of fear rather than as a matter of conscience. Spanking also undermines a child's feelings of safety and self-esteem. Perhaps one six-year old summed up the debate when she said, "Spanking makes grown-ups feel better for a while and makes kids feel worse for a long time." (p. 213)

The nurturant parent believes that authority does not come from domiance but is something that is earned as a consequence of their ability to nurture. As Lakoff stated (Engels, 1996) "the purpose is to make children become nurturers, too. Obedience, for children, comes out of love and respect for parents, not out of fear of punishment. Instead of punishment, you have restituion (p. 3)." Respect is earned through care and love, not demanded.

The nurturant parent model does not serve well in time of crises. It is a time consuming process that takes into account the feelings and concerns of others, including children. However, in the survival of the species, in the long term, it is the most appropriate model because it promotes cooperation and understanding.

Both, the strict father and the nurturant parent models, represent ideals. That is, it is like taking an average of numbers. The number you get may not be in the numbers you used to get the average. There are many variations on these models. As Lakoff (1996) states, "[b]oth provide a wide range of variations—an almost dizzying complexity that if looked at from a distance might just seem like a big soup. But when we look closely, we see a great deal of systematic variations (p. 283)." In other words, amidst the complexity and variations, there is evidence of the two parenting models (for a detailed discussion of these variations, see Lakoff, 1996, Chapter 17).

KOLHBERG AND LOEVINGER MODELS OF MORAL REASONING AND EGO DEVELOPMENT

Both Kolhberg's, moral reasoning, and Loevinger's, ego development, theories provide explanations for how individuals derive meaning from life's experiences and why they develop certain behaviors. Thus, their theories can help us better understand why someone would practice either the strict-father model or the nurturant-parent model. What

TWO THEORIES OF HUMAN DEVELOPMENT

KOHLBERG Moral Reasoning	LOEVINGER Ego Development
PRE-CONVENTIONAL	*PRE-CONFORMIST*
1. Punishment/Obedience 2. Instrumental Hedonism (market exchange; "you scratch my back, I'll scratch your back")	1. Symbiotic/Autistic 2. Impulsive 3. Self-Protective
CONVENTIONAL	*CONFORMIST*
3. Good Girl/Good Boy 4. Law and Order*	4. Conformist 5. Self-Aware*
POST-CONVENTIONAL	*POST-CONFORMIST*
5. Social Contract 6. Universal	6. Conscientious 7. Individualistic 8. Autonomous 9. Integrated

Prepared by: Helen M. Gore-Laird, Ph.D.

*Identified Modal levels of development for American Society

Both Kohlberg's and Loevinger's theories provide theoretical explanations for how individuals derive meaning from life's experiences and why they develop certain behaviors. Thus, their theories can help us better understand why someone would follow the Strict Father Model or the Nurturant Parent Model.

these theories tell us is that a person can change over time and that their parenting style can change. Both models developed by Lakoff can be found at all levels of either moral development or ego development, but the strict-father model would most likely be found in the conventional or comformist levels of the theories.

If we examine the strict-father model of parenting through the lens of Kohlberg's theory, we can understand that the strict-father model wants to care for their child. However, the nature of care has an interpersonal focus that is derived from an impersonal view of duty, responsibility, and obligation (Gore-Laird). This attitude is found most strongly situated in Kohlberg's Law and Order stage. At this stage, adherence to the rules simply because they are the rules is paramount. You can not entertain any exceptions or special circumstances. Every one must be treated the same and failure to follow the rules has consequences. The consequences are decided by moral authority; in the family who parents using the strict-father model, this would be the father. This way of understanding the world is found in Loevinger's Conformist Stage. There is a right way and a wrong way, and it is the same for everyone—no exceptions.

The nurturant parent would most likely be found to operate at Kohlberg's Social Contract stage. At this stage, the individual coordinates personal values with the needs of others. Care is derived from a set of self-established standards and will allow for changes in the standards for utility reasons. For Loevinger (1996), the individual can begin to allow for exceptions when they enter the Self-Aware Stage of development. Here the individual can begin to see alternative possibilities. While this stage is still basically a stage of conformity, it can allow for a variation in the strict-father model. As one enters the Post-Conformist levels of ego development, one can allow for more possibilities and is open to cooperation with others. At this level, one is moving still further from the strict father, and more firmly into the nurturant parent model.

Both the strict-father model and the nurturant parent models demonstrate care for their children. The nature of the care takes different forms. For the strict-father model, to care means to hold one accountable to responsibility, duties, and obligations through heteronomous means. For the nurturant parent model, care comes in the form of cooperation that promotes autonomy of the other. As Noddings (1984) noted, "there is invariably this displacement of interest from my own reality to the reality of the other (p. 14)."

Each model serves a particular niche in parenting. A parent may resort to the strict-father model when their child's life is in danger and quick, decisive action is required. But such action only has short-term results. For long-term results that yield understanding, self-restraint, and self-reliance that comes from within the person, the nurturant parent model will yield the best results.

REFERENCES

Baca Zinn, M. And Eitzen, D. S. (2002). *Diversity in Families*. Boston: Allyn and Bacon.

Engel, Mary (1996). *Does George Lakoff Know Something Conservatives Don't?* Retrieved May 2, 2002 from The Bulletin of the Santa Fe Institute: Summer 1996. *http://www.sanatefe.edu/sfi/publications/Bulletins/bulletin-fall96/lakoff.html*

Gilligan, C. (1982). *In a Different Voice*. Cambridge, MA: Harvard University Press.

Gore-Laird, H. M. Unpublished manuscript.

Lakoff, G. (1996). *Moral Politics: What Conservatives Know that Liberals Don't*. Chicago: University of Chicago Press.

Noddings, N. (1984). *Caring: A Feminine Approach to Ethics and Moral Education*. Berkeley, CA: University of California Press.

Piaget, J. (1965). *The Moral Judgment of the Child*. New York: The Free Press.

9

JOBLESS GHETTOS AND THE SOCIAL OUTCOME OF YOUNGSTERS

William Julius Wilson

It is a special honor to participate in a symposium honoring one of the truly creative social scientists of our time. As a sociologist, I have appreciated Urie Bronfenbrenner's awareness of the importance of social structure and culture in a child's development. I therefore read with some delight the opening paragraphs in the chapter by Steinberg, Darling, and Fletcher (13), which describe Bronfenbrenner's reaction to a paper that failed to address adequately the problem of social context. According to Steinberg et al., Bronfenbrenner explained that it makes "no sense at all to control for ethnicity, social class, or household composition in an attempt to isolate a 'pure' process. No processes occur outside of a context. And if we want to understand context, we need to take it into account, not pretend to control it away" (p. 424).

As Brooks-Gunn correctly pointed out in her chapter (14), the neighborhood context has always been deemed important by developmentalists such as Bronfenbrenner. However, in recent years the rapid increase in concentrated inner-city poverty has resulted in an explosion of research examining neighborhood effects on individuals, families, peer groups, and other social networks. An increasing number of scholars, including child development researchers, recognize that neighborhoods matter, but empirical and theoretical discussions of neighborhood effects remain at a rudimentary level. Empirical measures of neighborhood effects are still underdeveloped, and theoretical issues are far from elaborated. This is especially true of the research that measures the effects of neighborhoods on individual outcomes (Elliott et al., 1994).

In this chapter, I would like to build on some of the theoretical issues I have raised in previous writings concerning the effects of neighborhoods on individual outcomes by integrating arguments that feature the concepts *social organization*, and the *new urban poverty*.

The research for this manuscript was supported by grants from the Ford Foundation, the Rockefeller Foundation, the Carnegie Corporation, the MacArthur Foundation, the Spencer Foundation, the William T, Grant Foundation, the Lloyd A. Fry Foundation, the Woods Charitable Fund, the Department of Health and Human Services. Parts of this chapter are based on a larger study, *Jobless Ghettos: The Disappearance of Work and Its Effect on Urban Life*, to be published by Knopf in 1995.

The Importance of Neighborhood Social Organization

By *social organization*, I mean the extent to which the residents of a neighborhood are able to maintain effective social control and realize their common values. There are two major dimensions of neighborhood social organization: *(a) the prevalence, strength, and interdependence of social networks and (b) the extent of collective supervision that the residents direct and the personal responsibility they assume in addressing neighborhood problems.* Both formal institutions and informal networks reflect social organization (Sampson, 1992). *In other words, neighborhood social organization depends on the extent of local friendship ties, the degree of social cohesion, the level of resident participation in formal and informal voluntary associations, the density and stability of formal organizations, and the nature of informal social controls.* Neighborhoods that integrate the adults by an extensive set of obligations, expectations, and social networks are in a better position to control and supervise the activities and behavior of children and to monitor developments (e.g., the breaking up of congregations of youths on street corners and the supervision of youth leisure time activities; Sampson, 1992).

The connectedness and stability of social networks in such neighborhoods transcend the household because the neighborhood adults have the potential to observe, report on, and discuss the behavior of the children in different circumstances. These networks reinforce the discipline the child receives in the home, because other adults in the neighborhood assume responsibility for the supervision of youth that are not their own (Sampson, 1992).

However, as pointed out by Steinberg et al. (this volume, chapter 13), the norms and supervision imposed on children are most effective when they reflect what Coleman (1990) called "intergenerational closure," that is, the overlapping of youth and adult social networks in the neighborhood. Intergenerational closure is exhibited in those neighborhoods where most parents know not only their children's friends, but the parents of those friends as well.

A recent study by Furstenberg (1993) provides support for these theoretical arguments. On the basis of the field research of five of his research assistants, which included "extended open-ended interviews with parents and their teenage children residing in five distinct inner-city neighborhoods" (Furstenberg, 1993, p. 234), Furstenberg concluded that family management is profoundly influenced by the neighborhoods in which the families live. "Ordinary parents are likely to have more success when they reside in communities where the burden of raising children is seen as a collective responsibility and where strong institutions sustain the efforts of parents" (Furstenberg, 1993, p. 257).

For example, Furstenberg (1993) reported that regardless of the parenting skills of the parents, residents in a poor, unstable, and socially disorganized neighborhood in North Philadelphia tended to isolate themselves and their children from the surrounding community and were not part of neighborhood institutions. They distrusted local schools, regarded local services suspiciously, and tended to use supportive services that were outside the community. Largely disconnected from the community, the parents had to "manage on their own" (Furstenberg, 1993, p. 243). Accordingly, children not only suffered greater risks because of less supervision and monitoring, but they also did not have the positive experiences of being connected to the wider community through school, job, and friendship ties.

This is in sharp contrast to another neighborhood Furstenberg's (1993) research team studied in South Philadelphia. In this neighborhood, which was poor but nonetheless socially cohesive, Furstenberg's researchers found the same range of parenting skills as in the neighborhood in North Philadelphia, but the youths, despite similar levels of poverty and similar family structures, faced quite different structural constraints. This neighborhood featured shared parental responsibility, informal social control of youths in public spaces, and kinship and friendship bonds that connected local institutions with the family. Youths in this neighborhood could not easily escape the scrutiny of neighborhood adults, and the mutual support of other parents in the neighborhood reinforced the activities of parents inside the home. In other words, children in this South Philadelphia neighborhood were socialized not solely by parents, but also by friends, relatives, and neighbors.[1]

The families in South Philadelphia were socially integrated; those in North Philadelphia were not. As pointed out by Steinberg and his colleagues (this volume, chapter 13), as a general rule, adolescents seem to benefit directly from the exchange of resources produced by their parents' social integration. However, social integration may not be beneficial to adolescents who live in unfavorable neighborhoods, for example, neighborhoods characterized by bad parenting. Steinberg et al. state the following:

> Although we tend to think of social integration as a desirable endpoint, its desirability depends on the nature of the people that integration brings one into contact with. There are many communities in contemporary America in which it may be more adaptive for parents to be socially isolated than socially integrated. Indeed, some of Furstenberg's (1990) recent work on family life in the inner city of Philadelphia suggests that social isolation is often deliberately practiced as an adaptive strategy by many parents living in dangerous neighborhoods. (p. 459)

However, in tough inner-city neighborhoods, two kinds of social isolation should be distinguished: (a) families who deliberately isolate themselves from other families and (b) families who lack contact with institutions, families, and individuals in the larger mainstream society, regardless of the level of interaction with neighbors.

Research that we have conducted in Chicago suggests that what many of these tough neighborhoods have in common is a relatively high degree of social integration (isolated from extralocal contacts, inner-city Blacks tend to exhibit higher levels of local neighboring) and a low degree of informal social control. We found a positive relationship between the concentration of disadvantages (poverty, welfare receipt, and joblessness) and the density of local networks and a negative relationship between the concentration of disadvantages and informal social control.[2] To repeat, the structurally disadvantaged inner-city neighborhoods in Chicago feature relatively high levels of local neighboring, but low levels of social control.[3] We need more research on the factors involved in these relationships, but a tentative conclusion would be the following: Not only are children in such neighborhoods adversely affected by the lack of informal social controls, but they are also disadvantaged because the social interaction among neighbors is disproportionately

---

[1] Furstenberg (1993) pointed out that many of our social programs focus solely on improving the material, informational, and psychological resources of parents so that they might manage the task of child rearing. Because the full burden of caretaking is attributed to parents, they receive the full measure of blame when their children do not succeed. However, Furstenberg argued persuasively that if we are committed to strengthening the family, more attention must be given to rebuilding neighborhood centers, recreational services, schools, churches, and other local institutions that support families.

[2] Informal social control was measured by a four-item scale that tapped the respondent's perception of whether neighbors would intervene if they saw children getting in trouble, a fight, a burglary in progress, or a drug sale. The data are from the Chicago Neighborhood Project at the University of Chicago. This project is the part of the Successful Adolescent Research Network of the MacArthur Foundation.

[3] These findings were presented in Sampson (1992).

restricted among those who lack the skills, experiences, and resources conducive to healthy child development. I include among these the lack of steady employment, a problem to which I now turn.

THE NEW URBAN POVERTY

Many inner-city neighborhoods are plagued by the highest levels of joblessness since the Depression. Indeed, there is a new poverty in our nation's metropolises. By the new *urban poverty*, I mean poor segregated neighborhoods in which a substantial majority of individual adults are either unemployed or have dropped out of the labor force. For example, in 1990 only one in three adults (35 %) ages 16 and over in the 12 Chicago community areas with poverty rates that exceeded 40% held a job.[4] Each of these community areas, located on the south and west sides of the city, is overwhelmingly Black. We can add to these 12 high-jobless areas 3 additional predominantly Black community areas, with rates of poverty of 29%, 30%, and 36%, respectively, where only 4 in 10 (42%) adults worked in 1990. Thus, in these 15 Black community areas, representing a total population of 425,125, only 37% of all the adults were gainfully employed in 1990. By contrast, 54% of the adults in the 17 other predominantly Black community areas in Chicago, with a total population of 545,408, worked in 1990. This was close to the citywide figure of 57%. Finally, except for one largely Asian community area with an employment rate of 46% and one largely Latino community area with an employment rate of 49%, a majority of the adults held a job in each of the 45 other community areas of Chicago.[5]

The magnitude of the changes can be seen in the neighborhoods of Douglas, Washington Park, and Grand Boulevard on Chicago's South Side. These three neighborhoods were the focus of the ethnographic research in the Drake and Cayton classic study, *Black Metropolis*, published in 1945. In all three areas, a majority of adults were gainfully employed in 1950, but by 1990, only 4 in 10 in Douglas worked, 1 in 3 in Washington Park, and 1 in 4 in Grand Boulevard.

In previous years, the working poor stood out in inner-city ghetto neighborhoods. Today, the nonworking poor predominate in such neighborhoods. Neighborhoods plagued with high levels of joblessness are more likely to experience problems of social organization. The two go hand in hand. High rates of joblessness trigger other problems in the neighborhood, which adversely affect social organization—ranging from crime, gang

---

[4]The figures on adult employment presented in this paragraph are based on calculations from data provided by the 1990 U.S. Bureau of the Census and the *Local Community Fact Book for Chicago*, 1950. The adult employment rates represent the number of employed individuals (14 and over in 1950 and 16 and over in 1990) among the total number of adults in a given area. Those who are not employed include both the individuals who are members of the labor force but are not working and those who have dropped out or are not part of the labor force. The group who is not in the labor force "consists mainly of students, housewives, retired workers, seasonal workers enumerated in an 'off' season who were not looking for work, inmates of institutions, disabled persons, and persons doing only incidental unpaid family work" (Chicago Fact Book Consortium, 1984, p. xxv).

[5]A *community area* is a statistical unit derived by urban sociologists at the University of Chicago for the 1930 census, to analyze varying conditions within the city of Chicago. These delineations were originally drawn up on the basis of settlement and history of the area, local identification and trade patterns, local institutions, and natural and artificial barriers. Needless to say, there have been major shifts in population and land use since then. But these units remain useful to trace changes over time, and they continue to capture much of the contemporary reality of Chicago neighborhoods.

violence, and drug trafficking to family break-ups and problems in the organization of family life.

Consider, for example, the problems of drug trafficking and violent crime. As many studies have revealed, the decline of legitimate employment opportunities among inner-city residents builds up incentives to sell drugs (Fagan, 1993). The distribution of crack in a neighborhood attracts individuals involved in violence and other crimes. Violent persons in the crack marketplace help shape its social organization and its impact on the neighborhood. Neighborhoods plagued by high levels of joblessness, insufficient economic opportunities, and high residential mobility are unable to control the volatile drug market and the violent crimes related to it (Fagan, 1993; Sampson, 1986). As informal controls weaken in such areas, the social processes that regulate behavior change (Sampson, 1986).

Also, consider the important relationship between joblessness and the organization of family life. Work is not simply a way to make a living and support one's family. It also constitutes the framework for daily behavior and patterns of interaction because of the disciplines and regularities it imposes. Thus, in the absence of regular employment, what is lacking is not only a place in which to work and the receipt of regular income, but also a coherent organization of the present, that is, a system of concrete expectations and goals. Regular employment provides the anchor for the temporal and spatial aspects of daily life. In the absence of regular employment, life, including family life, becomes more incoherent. Persistent unemployment and irregular employment hinder rational planning in daily life, the necessary condition of adaptation to an industrial economy (Bourdieu, 1965). This problem is most severe for jobless families in low-employment neighborhoods. The lack of rational planning among a high number of families without a steady breadwinner in the neighborhood reinforces that condition in any single jobless family.

One way in which joblessness affects the organization of family life is through its effect on the children's future attachment to the labor force. A youngster who grows up in a family with a steady breadwinner and in a neighborhood in which most of the adults are employed will tend to develop some of the disciplined habits associated with stable or steady employment—habits that are reflected in the behavior of his or her parents and of other neighborhood adults. Accordingly, when this youngster enters the labor market, he or she has a distinct advantage over the youngsters who grow up in the typical household in new-urban-poverty neighborhoods—a household without a steady breadwinner and a neighborhood that is not organized around work, in other words, a milieu in which one is more exposed to the less disciplined habits associated with casual or infrequent work both within and outside the family.

The problems of family organization and neighborhood social organization in the new-urban-poverty neighborhoods are mutually reinforcing. The social integration of parents in these neighborhoods may hamper, not promote, healthy child development.

I believe that there is a difference, on the one hand, between a jobless family whose mobility is impeded by the macrostructural constraints in the economy and the larger society, but nonetheless lives in an area with a relatively low rate of joblessness and poverty and, on the other hand, a jobless family that lives in an inner-city ghetto neighborhood that is influenced not only by these same constraints, but also by the behavior of other jobless families in the neighborhood. The latter influence is one of culture—the extent to which individuals follow their inclinations—either through forms of nonverbal action, including engaging in or refraining from certain conduct, or in the verbal expression of opinions or attitudes concerning norms, values, or beliefs—as they have been developed by learning or influence from other members of the community to which they belong or identify. In other words, it is not sufficient to recognize the importance of macrostructural constraints; it is also imperative to see "the merits of a more subtle kind of cultural analysis of life in poverty" (Hannerz, 1969, p. 182).

Let me briefly elaborate on this point with a different example of the kind of cultural analysis I am trying to convey. Joblessness, especially prolonged joblessness, is likely to be associated with or produce feelings of low perceived self-efficacy. In social cognitive theory (Bandura, 1986), *perceived self-efficacy* refers to self-beliefs in one's ability to take the steps or courses of action necessary to achieve the goals required in a given situation. Such beliefs affect the level of challenge that is pursued, the amount of effort expended in a given venture, and the degree of perseverance when confronting difficulties.

As Bandura (1982) put it, "inability to influence events and social conditions that significantly affect one's life can give rise to feelings of futility and despondency as well as to anxiety" (p. 140). Self-efficacy theory identifies two sources of perceived futility. People may seriously doubt that they can do or accomplish what is expected, or they may feel confident of their abilities, but nonetheless, give up trying because they believe that their efforts will ultimately be futile owing to an environment that is unresponsive, discriminatory, or punitive. "The type of outcomes people expect depend largely on their judgments of how well they will be able to perform in given situations" (Bandura, 1982, p. 140).

Weak labor force attachment, I would hypothesize, will tend to lower one's perceived self-efficacy. I would, therefore, expect lower levels of perceived self-efficacy in ghetto neighborhoods—plagued by underemployment, unemployment, and labor force nonparticipation—than in less impoverished neighborhoods. Considering the importance of cultural learning and influence, I would also expect that perceived self-efficacy is higher among those who are weakly attached to the labor force in non-ghetto neighborhoods than among their counterparts in ghetto neighborhoods.

In the more socially isolated ghetto neighborhoods, networks of kin, friends, and associates are likely to include a high proportion of individuals who, because of their experiences with extreme economic marginality, tend to doubt that they can achieve approved societal goals. The self-doubts may exist either because of questions concerning their own capabilities or preparedness or because they perceive severe restrictions imposed by a hostile environment. However, because joblessness afflicts a majority of the adult population in the new-poverty neighborhoods, it is likely that problems of self-efficacy among jobless families in low-joblessness neighborhoods may relate more to feelings of low capability because a majority of families in the neighborhood have jobs whereas they do not. As Urie Bronfenbrenner points out (this volume, chapter 19), proximal processes are moderated by "the nature of the development outcomes under consideration" (p. 621).

The central hypothesis is that an individual's feelings of low self-efficacy grow out of weak labor force attachment, and they are reinforced or strengthened by the feelings and views of others in his or her neighborhood who are similarly situated and have similar self-beliefs (e.g., feelings that severe restrictions imposed by a hostile environment hamper their individual progress). The end result, to use a term from Bandura's (1982) work, is a lower sense of *collective efficacy* in the inner-city ghetto.

To repeat, family social integration in a neighborhood plagued by low levels of perceived self- and collective efficacy is not likely to benefit many aspects of child development. Research on the transmission of such views and feelings would represent a cultural analysis of life in poverty. The psychological self-efficacy theory is used here not in isolation, but in relation to the structural problem of weak labor force attachment and the cultural problem of the transmission of self and collective beliefs in the neighborhood.

The transmission of such beliefs is part of what I have called "concentration effects," that is, the effects of living in a neighborhood that is overwhelmingly impoverished (Wilson, 1987). I argue that these concentration effects, reflected in a range of outcomes from degree of labor force attachment to social dispositions, are created by the constraints and opportunities that the residents of the inner-city neighborhoods face in terms of access to jobs and job networks, involvement in quality schools, availability of marriageable partners, and exposure to conventional role models.

The declining proportion of nonpoor families magnifies the problems of increasing and prolonged joblessness in the new-poverty neighborhoods. Basic neighborhood institutions are more difficult to maintain. Stores, banks, credit institutions, restaurants, and professional services lose regular and potential patrons. Churches experience dwindling numbers of parishioners and shrinking resources; recreational facilities, block clubs, community groups, and other informal organizations also suffer. As these organizations decline, the means of formal and informal social control in the neighborhood become weaker. Levels of crime and street violence increase as a result, leading to further deterioration of the neighborhood.

As the neighborhood disintegrates, those who are able to leave depart in increasing numbers, including many working- and middle-class families. The lower population density creates additional problems. Abandoned buildings increase and provide a haven for crack dens and criminal enterprises that establish footholds in the community. Precipitous declines in density also make it more difficult to sustain or develop a sense of community or for people to experience a feeling of safety in numbers (Jargowsky, 1994).

The neighborhoods with many Black working families stand in sharp contrast to the new-poverty areas. Research that we have conducted on the social organization of Chicago neighborhoods reveals that in addition to much lower levels of perceived unemployment than in the poor neighborhoods, Black working- and middle-class neighborhoods also have much higher levels of perceived social control and cohesion, organizational services, and social support. Unlike in the new-poverty neighborhoods, as revealed in our research in Chicago, in the Black working- and middle-class neighborhoods, adolescents seem to benefit directly from the exchange of resources produced by their parents' social integration.

The rise of new-poverty neighborhoods represents a movement from what the historian Spear (1967) called an *institutional ghetto*—which duplicates the structure and activities of the larger society, as portrayed in Drake and Cayton's (1945) description of Bronzeville—to an unstable ghetto, which lacks the capability to provide basic opportunities, resources, and adequate social controls.

In neighborhoods that suffer from a lack of social organization, that is, neighborhoods with weak social controls and weak social monitoring, peer group cultures play a much greater role in shaping the behavior of adolescents, including behavior detrimental to their health, such as alcohol consumption, drug use, gang involvement, and illicit sexual encounters. This is especially true in the new-poverty neighborhoods. Adolescents in the new-poverty neighborhoods not only are influenced by restricted opportunities in the broader society that confront all disadvantaged families (e.g., limited access to employment), but also are influenced by the behavior of other poor individuals and families who face the same constraints.

In my book *The Truly Disadvantaged* (1987), I pointed out that, in poor neighborhoods in which most of the adults are working, perceptive youngsters are more likely to observe individuals regularly going to and from work, see a clear connection between education and meaningful employment, be aware of the presence of many intact families, notice a significant number of nonwelfare families, and recognize that many individuals in their neighborhoods are not involved in the drug trafficking.

However, in the new-urban-poverty neighborhoods, neighborhoods with a paucity of regularly employed families, the chances of children interacting on a sustained basis with people who are employed or with families that have a steady breadwinner are slim. The net effect is that the youths are more likely to see joblessness as normative and perceive a weak relationship between schooling and postschool employment. This environment is not conducive for development of the cognitive, linguistic, and other educational and job-related skills necessary for the world of work in the mainstream economy.

Some of the residents of poor inner-city neighborhoods clearly see and understand the problem facing their youth. The following are quotations from respondents who were interviewed in the Urban Poverty and Family Life Study that I directed at the University of Chicago. Consider the following comments by a perceptive college student who lives in one of the new-poverty neighborhoods on the West Side of Chicago:

> Well, basically, I feel that if you are raised in a neighborhood and all you see is negative things, then you are going to be negative because you don't see anything positive. . . . Guys and Black males see drug dealers on the corner and they see fancy cars and flashy money and they figure, "Hey, if I get into drugs I can be like him."

He made a similar observation when he was interviewed several weeks later:

> And I think about how, you know, the kids around there, all they see, OK, they see these drug addicts, and then what else do they see? Oh, they see thugs, you know; they see the gangbangers. So, who do they, who do they really look, model themselves after? Who is their role model? They have none but the thugs. So that's what they wind up being, you know. . . . They [the children in the neighborhood] deal with the only male role model that they can find and most of the time that be pimps, dope dealers—so what do they do? They model themselves after them. Not intentionally trying to but if, you know, that's the only male you're around and that's the only one you come in close contact with, you tend to want to be like that person. And that's why you have so many young drug dealers.

A 25-year-old West Side father of two who works two jobs to make ends meet raises a similar point:

> They try to find easier routes, uh, and had been conditioned over a period of time to just be lazy, so to speak. Uh, motivation non-existent, you know, and the society that they're affiliated with really don't advocate hard work and struggle to meet your goals, such as education and stuff like that. And they see what's around 'em and they follow that same pattern, you know. The society says, "Well, you can sell dope. You can do this. You can do that." A lot of 'em even got to the point where they can accept a few years in jail, uh, as a result of what they might do. . . . They don't see nobody getting up early in the morning, going to work or going to school all the time. The guys they—they be with don't do that . . . 'cause that's the crowd that you choose, well, that's been presented to you by your neighborhood.

An unemployed Black male, who lives in an impoverished and high-jobless Black suburban community in the Chicago metropolitan area, described how the children in his neighborhood get into drugs and alcohol:

> They're in an environment where, if you don't get high, you're square. You know what I'm saying? If you don't get high some kind of way or another . . . and then, you know, kids are gonna emulate what they come up under. . . . I've watched a couple of generations—I've been here since '61. I watched kids, I saw their fathers ruined, and I seen 'em grow up and do the very same thing. . . . The children, they

don't have any means of recreation whatsoever out here, other than their back yards, the streets, nothing. . . . The only way it can be intervened if the child has something outside the house to go to, because it is—just go by the environment of the house he's destined to be an alcoholic or a drug addict.

A 40-year-old mother of six, who lives in an extreme-poverty tract on the South Side of Chicago, related the problems of children in her neighborhood to the limited opportunity structure:

> There's less opportunities over here: it's no jobs. The kids aren't in school, you know, they're not getting any education, there's a lot of drugs on the streets. So, you know, wrong environment, bad associations. So you have to be in some kind of environment where the kids are more, you know, ready to go to school to get an education instead of, you know, droppin' out to sell drugs because they see their friends, on the corner, makin' money; they got a pocket fulla money, you know. They got kids walkin' around here that's 10 years old selling drugs.

A 37-year-old unemployed Black male from the South Side described the different situation for males and females:

> Some kids just seem like they don't want to learn, but others, they stick to it. Especially the females, they stick to it. The males either become—they see the street life. They see guys out here making big bucks with fancy cars, jewelry and stuff, and they try to emulate them. That's our problem, you know. The males, they're pretty impressionable. That's why they drop out. . . . They see their peers out here, they didn't go to school, they makin' it. But they making it the wrong way.

Ghetto-specific practices such as overt emphasis on sexuality, idleness, and public drinking are often denounced by those who reside in the socially disorganized inner-city ghettos. However, because such practices occur much more frequently there than in middle-class society, owing in major part to social organizational forces, the transmission of these modes of behavior by precept, as in role modeling, is more easily facilitated.

As Prothrow-Stith (1991) argued, in inner-city ghetto neighborhoods plagued by problems of social disorganization, youngsters are more likely to see violence as a way of life. They are more likely to be taught to be violent by exhortation, witness violent acts, and have role models who do not adequately control their own anger. Accordingly, given the availability of and easy access to firearms, adolescent experiments with macho behavior, especially in peer groups that are not subject to neighborhood social controls, often have deadly consequences.

The problems of family management, neighborhood social organization, unsupervised peer groups, and ghetto-specific cultural practices (problems that are enhanced and ultimately shaped by joblessness and poverty) adversely impact the health, health promotion, and development of children. We are just beginning to understand the mutually reinforcing effects of these problems. What is so encouraging is that there are a growing number of developmental psychologists, influenced by the earlier perspectives of Urie Bronfenbrenner, who are now examining these factors.

REFERENCES

Bandura, A. (1982). Self-efficacy mechanism in human agency. *American Psychologist, 37*, 122–147.

Bandura, A. (1986). *Social foundations of thought and action: A social cognitive theory*. Englewood Cliffs, NJ: Prentice Hall.

Bourdieu, P. (1965). *Travail et travailleurs en Algérie* [Work and workers in Algeria]. Paris: Additions Mouton.

Coleman, J. S. (1990). *Foundations of social theory*. Cambridge, MA: Harvard University Press.

Local community fact book for Chicago, 1950. (1953). Chicago Community Inventory, University of Chicago.

Local community fact book Chicago Metropolitan Area, Based on the 1970 and 1980 Censuses. (1984). The Chicago Fact Book Consortium, The University of Illinois at Chicago.

Drake, S., & Cayton, H. (1945). *Black metropolis: A study of Negro life in a northern city*. New York: Harcourt, Brace.

Elliott, D., Wilson, W. J., Huizinga, D., Sampson, R., Elliott, A., & Rankin, B. (1994). *The effects of neighborhood disadvantages on adolescent development*. Unpublished manuscript, University of Colorado, Boulder, and the University of Chicago.

Fagan, J. (1993). Drug selling and licit income in distressed neighborhoods: The economic lives of street-level drug users and dealers. In G. Peterson & A. Harold Washington (Eds.), *Drugs, crime and social isolation* (pp. 99–146). Washington, DC: Urban Institute Press.

Furstenberg, F., Jr. (1990, August). *How families manage risk and opportunity in dangerous neighborhoods*. Paper presented at the 84th annual meeting of the American Sociological Association, Washington, DC.

Furstenberg, F., Jr. (1993). How families manage risk and opportunity in dangerous neighborhoods. In W. J. Wilson (Ed.), *Sociology and the public agenda* (pp. 231–258). Newbury Park, CA: Sage.

Hannerz, U. (1969). *Soulside: Inquiries into ghetto life and culture*. New York: Columbia University Press.

Jargowsky, P. A. (1994). Ghetto poverty among Blacks in the 1980's. *Journal of Policy Analysis and Management*.

Prothrow-Stith, D. (1991). *Deadly consequences*. New York: Harper & Collins Press.

Sampson, R. J. (1986). Crime in cities: The effects of formal and informal social control. In A. J. Reiss, Jr., & M. Tonry (Eds.), *Communities and crime* (pp. 271–310). Chicago: University of Chicago Press.

Sampson, R. J. (1988). Urban Black violence: The effect of male joblessness and family disruption. *American Journal of Sociology, 93*, 348–382.

Sampson, R. J. (1992, August–September). *Integrating family and community level dimensions of social organization: Delinquency and crime in the inner-city of Chicago*. Paper presented at the International Workshop on Integrating Individual and Ecological Aspects on Crime, Stockholm, Sweden.

Sampson, R. J., & Wilson, W. J. (1993). Toward a theory of race, crime, and urban inequality. In J. Hagan & R. Peterson (Eds.), *Crime and inequality* (pp. 37–54). Palo Alto, CA: Stanford University Press.

Spear, A. (1967). *Black Chicago: The making of a Negro ghetto*. Chicago: University of Chicago Press.

Wilson, W. J. (1987). *The truly disadvantaged: The inner city, the underclass, and public policy*. Chicago: University of Chicago Press.

10

THE BASIC TENETS OF POLYAMORY

Lori M. Selzer, M.Ed.

Theresa is a thirty-five year old female who works as a paralegal in a lawyer's office in the downtown area of a large city. She has worked for the same legal firm for the past ten years. She lives in a suburb of the city that houses middle class families. Families that live in this suburb are mostly nuclear in nature—meaning that these families are composed of a male and a female (a mother and a father) and one or two children. Although there are some families in Theresa's neighborhood that are headed by single parents, these are less common due to the income levels needed to live in the area.

Theresa, though, considers herself to be very fortunate. Her family is very different from many of the families that live around her. Theresa does have two children, Jeremy and Janna, but her family does not fit the typical family prototype for her neighborhood. Theresa and her children live with Jose and Adrian. They all live together, each having equal power, in a family form that is known as a "polyamorous family."

The practice of polyamory, also known informally as "poly", can be defined in many different ways, for it can mean many different things to the many different people that choose to live this type of lifestyle. The above ficticious vignette of Theresa and her family is just a single example of how polyamory can be practiced.

To better understand polyamory and what it really means, we can begin by looking at the history of the word itself. Polyamory can be traced back to the 1980's when the term was coined by Morning Glory Ravenheart (Houston Press, 2000). Further, according to Jennifer Mathieu, in her 2000 *Houston Press* article, "Meet Mr. and Mrs. and Mrs. Jones", many have discovered this lifestyle that was first suggested in "science fiction books by American author Robert Heinlein" (Houston Press, 2000). Heinlein's 1960's novels helped to make others "realize there can be alternatives to a two-person marriage" (Houston Press, 2000).

To ultimately define the word, polyamory, one can turn to its literal translation from its basis in both the Greek and French languages, in which it means "many loves" (*http://www.xeromag.com/fvpoly.html*). Given the direct translation from these two languages, it would seem that the definition is quite straightforward. In all actuality, this is the furthest that it can be from the actual practice.

Polyamory is commonly defined as, "the belief that having open, honest, loving relationships with more than one person at a time is a valid lifestyle choice" (McGarey, 1999, p. 4). While this definition seems simplistic and straightforward, it leaves an individual with the ability to create their own sense of what their "polyness" means to them. Thus, another definition can be offered. According to Dr. Deborah Anapol, the founder of the *Loving More* publication, polyamory can also be defined as "responsible no monogamy (Anapol, 1997, p. 3)." Again, this is a vague definition that offers the ability for polyamorists to determine what this lifestyle practice means to them as individuals. To further the quest for a definition that encompasses the true meaning of polyamory, it can be reported that it is "a non-deceiving non-structurally chauvinistic non-monogamy; acting upon lovingly plurally with openness about other loves to each that one loves, especially in a socially egalitarian context." *(http://www3.primushost.com/~anderson/glossaryrelationshipsM. html)*. It is also noted, "Polyamory is associated with non-sexism and respect for individual autonomy; and this is one of the ways in which it differs from polygamy, which tends to be associated with unequal standing of the sexes." *(http://www3.primushost.com/~anderson/ glossaryrelationshipsM.html)*. To put it in more simplistic terms, even though polyamory is often confused with the term, polygamy, it is very different in the sense that polyamory is based upon a system that does not genderize the sexes.

Overall, after reviewing some of the definitions that are typically linked to polyamory, the term seems to have as many different meanings as the many different people all over the world who choose to be "poly."

It can be determined, as a result of the vagueness of definition, that individuality is important to recognize when approaching polyamory and that "polyamorists believe in freedom of choice" *(http://www.polyamorysociety.org)*. The basic idea seems to lie in that polyamory is an individual choice. Each person who makes this lifestyle choice for themselves must also determine what being "poly" means to them and how they want to practice their understanding. This is supported by Easton and Liszt in their book, *The Ethical Slut*, when they report, "some feel that polyamory includes all forms of relationships other than monogamy, others restrict it to committed love relationships (thereby excluding swinging, casual sexual contact, and other forms of intimacy)" (Easton and Liszt, 1997, p. 41).

Perhaps, though, Mathieu's findings help narrow down a more concrete definition of polyamory when she offers what polyamory "is not". According to Mathieu, "It might be easier to describe polyamory by first describing what its practitioners swear it's not. Polyamorists are not swingers. There is no anonymous sex with multiple partners at low-lit parties where names are unimportant." (Houston Press, 2000). To polyamorists, as reported earlier, disclosure, commitment and truth are important elements of their "polyness".

Mathieu continues to share as she reports, "Polyamorists are not cheaters." (Houston Press, 2000). Discussion and understanding is required between all of the involved parties. With this in mind, a determination of what polyamory actually is can be fostered in the direction of the idea of a person's ability to engage in more than one committed, loving, and long term relationship with all of the involved parties building a sense of understanding and support for each other. Further, "Polyamory is about loving more than one and might or might not involve sex . . ." *(http://www3.primushost.com/~anderson/ glossaryrelationshipsM.html)*.

Taking our understanding of the definition of polyamory into perspective, we can now further our understanding of the practice by distinguishing a boundary between the two basic components of polyamory. The practice involves an understanding that boundaries and rules do exist in order for those involved to have a successful polyamorous relationship. For our purposes, these can be labeled as internal "key" components of the relationships and external "key" components of the relationship—often relabeled as the rules that surround the relationships.

While understanding both the internal and external "key" components to the practice of polyamory is important, it is also important to comprehend that the elements are interdependent to the individual(s) who choose a "poly" lifestyle. In other words, each of the "key" components relies on the other in order for the "poly" relationships to function effectively.

INTERNAL "KEY" COMPONENTS OF POLYAMOROUS RELATIONSHIPS

The internal "key" components of the relationships include the high regard for honesty that must exist between all the parties involved in the relationship, the ability to express oneself, the possession of effective communication skills, and the recognition that jealousy is a human emotion that exists. Without these internal "key" components working together, polyamorous relationships will not survive.

Honesty is a "key" internal element that must be present for polyamory to work as it is designed to do. According to Mathieu, "The highest tenet in polyamory is honesty" (Houston Press, 2000). This idea is further supported by Dr. Deborah Anapol when she reports in her book, *Polyamory: The New Love Without Limits: Secrets of Sustainable Intimate Relationships*, that it is important to "realize the secret to keeping any intimate connection alive is simply to be wholly authentic in every moment and to practice radical honesty." (Anapol, 1997, p. 3). She continues to support her stance by offering, "relationships based on truth, self responsibility, and unconditional love can take many forms, but even small withholds will gradually erode any relationship" (Anapol, 1997, p. 3). For polyamorists, the comments that Anapol offers are even more important due to the multitude and the complexities of the relationships. Without honesty, polyamory can simply not function. It is difficult enough to maintain honesty in a one-on-one relationship, but when you add the complexity of more than one relationship, it becomes even more difficult because all of the relationships must function together. In other words, honesty both depends and relies on the effectiveness of communication skills to make polyamory work.

Communication skills are the second "key" internal component that is essential to the function of polyamory. All of the members involved in a relationship must have a strong ability to communicate and express themselves. Human beings are social animals and they must possess the ability to communicate in order to survive. Given this, while adding the additional component of polyamory, it is even more important for polyamorists to communicate their needs, their desires, and their wants to each other so that their relationships can co-exist and function together. As an example, a "poly" relationship only works if everyone involved is happy and, in order to make this happen, all parties involved have a responsibility to communicate to the others what they need to happen for the relationship(s) to work *(http://xeromag.com/fvpoly.html)*. Without this ability to communicate, it affects all of the other needed interdependent internal components, thus affecting the functioning of a successful "poly" relationship.

The final internal "key" component that affects "poly" relationships is jealousy. Jealousy is an emotion that humans possess, but that does not mean that the emotion cannot be managed. The management of jealousy is no different from managing any other human emotion. For an example, take the emotion of anger. As human beings, we are expected to manage and control our expressions of anger, depending on the situation that we are in. To further explain, an individual will typically manage his or her anger differently in a professional situation than in a situation that is separate from the workplace, such as a situation that involves family. This is evidenced by Erving Goffman's findings that are described by Baca Zinn and Eitzen in their text, *Diversity in Families*. Baca Zinn and Eitzen report that humans live their lives in the context of a "front stage" and a "back stage"

(Baca Zinn and Eitzen, 2001, p. 3). The front stage behaviors are those behaviors that we publicly display, such as within the workplace or at school, and back stage behaviors are those that we keep more private, such as within the family (Baca Zinn and Eitzen, 2001, p. 3). This is the same principle that we can apply to the management of our emotions, whether that emotion is happiness, anger or jealousy. Depending on the situation, the rules are set forth by societal expectations as to what behaviors are deemed appropriate in a certain situation.

Jealousy is a human emotion that can be expressed by appropriate means, just as anger can be. According to Goffman's work, jealousy has a "time and a place" and it can be expressed to the individuals involved in a "back stage" area. In other words, jealousy can be managed when those involved in the polyamorous relationships can investigate these feelings in the privacy of the "family" that they have created through the networking of all of the relationships.

Jealousy is such a powerful emotion because it "brings us face to face with the unpredictable nature of life" *(http://www.lovewithoutlimits.com/nre_for_lmm.html)*. To better understand this, a definition is needed. According to Webster's Dictionary, jealousy is defined as "painful apprehension of rivalship in cases affecting one's happiness" *(http://www.websters.com)*. As a result, jealousy can be classified as an emotion that humans express. It just depends on how and when it is expressed and by the degree to which it is expressed. It is also a human emotion that can be recognized and processed through. It depends on the situation (as evidenced by Goffman's work) and one's ability to recognize the emotion. It also depends on the ability of an individual to manage the magnitude of the emotion and to communicate the feelings that surround it, just as you would with any other human emotion.

Overall, the internal "key" components to a "poly" relationship depend on each other. To put this into perspective and as reported earlier, in order to enjoy the "poly" lifestyle and achieve success with its functioning, the relationships must be based in trust and security *(http://www.xeromag.com/fvpoly.html)*. Additionally, "in a poly relationship, it is vital—perhaps even more vital than in a monogamous relationship—for everyone involved to know and understand the rules of the relationship, and abide by them" *(http://www.xeromag.com/fvpoly.html)*.

EXTERNAL "KEY" COMPONENTS OF POLYAMOROUS RELATIONSHIPS

With previously established internal "key" components, we can move on towards the exploration of the external "key" components of a polyamorous relationship. These include the basic rules for the relationships involved, the recognition of these relationships in society, and the effects on others outside of the "poly" relationship.

The rules for polyamorous relationships are set by the individuals who are involved in the relationships. In some instances, the relationships may be identified as "closed", meaning that those involved in the relationships do not actively seek other members to join them. The relationships are closed off to the potential of adding additional members. This closed polyamorous relationship is also identified as polyfidelity, which is defined as "a committed love relationship consisting of three or more partners on equal footing in which the partners pledge to be sexually exclusive to one another . . ." *(http://www3. primushost.com/~anderson/glossaryrelationshipsM.html)*. An example of this would be a polyfidelitous triad (meaning three individuals). This type of relationship may have three people involved, with one person sexually active with the other two, or even with all three people being sexually active with each other. There is a stipulation to this in that, "nobody in the relationship may take an 'outside' lover, just as neither partner in a monogamous relationship is allowed to have an outside lover." *(www.xeromag.com/ fvpoly.html)*. If the relationship is polyfideitous and a member does make a decision to pursue another relationship, the new relationship could be considered as "cheating" (just the same as in a monogamous relationship) if it is not welcomed by the other members of the triad.

Another possibility is that those members involved may choose to keep the relationships open. This is known as an "open" relationship that allows for the possibility of adding additional members. According to Easton and Liszt (1997), open relationships are "relationships in which sexual and romantic connections are not restricted to the members." It is important to note that those involved in the relationships, while welcoming the addition of new members, may place certain restrictions on the admittance of those new members. For example, the rule may be set forth that a possible outside relationship must be approved by all of the others before the relationship is pursued. It may also be decided by the original members involved in the relationships that there are no rules that apply to the "open" possibility of adding additional lovers. Again, this depends on how each of the members define their "polyness" and the rules guiding their open relationship.

Overall, in terms of the relationship being either "closed" or "open", it must be made clear to all involved what the boundaries of the relationship are. This is achieved by revisiting one of the already identified internal "key" components, communication. Communication is important in this instance because it allows for all to understand that you must have the ability to "negotiate a clear, explicit, and unambiguous set of conditions that guides the manner in which your relationships form, and establishes that framework that helps to make sure that everyone's needs are being met and nobody's feelings are disregarded" *(www.xeromag.com/fvpoly.html)*. In other words, communication serves as the vehicle to establish the rules of the relationships.

Another boundary that must be established, beyond whether the relationships will be open or closed, is whether the polyamorous relationships being established will follow a primary/secondary model, a multiple primary partners model, or a multiple non-primary model.

If a primary/secondary model is to be used, a hierarchy to the relationships is established in which the primary couple is identified as the "more significant" couple whose relationship has priority. This means, "other relationships revolve around this couple (McGarey, 1999, p. 79). This type of polyamorous relationship is, according to McGarey (1999), "the most commonly practiced form of an open relationship and is the most similar to monogamous marriage." Typically, the primary couple is married and resides in the same household. The other relationships that the members of the couple possess take a "back seat" to the primary couple (McGarey, 1999, p. 80). To even further awaken our understanding of the primary/secondary model, it can be understood that the primary couple sets the boundaries of the secondary relationships and that those who are engaged as secondary lovers are able to communicate their wants needs and desires, but they do so with the primary couple ultimately making the decisions and rules for the relationships (McGarey, 1999, p. 80).

Another version, the multiple primary partner model, "includes three or more people in a primary relationship in which all members are equal partners (McGarey, 1999, p. 84). This is the model of polyamory that is offered in the scenario about Theresa, Jose, and Adrian at the beginning of this article. In this relationship, all three of them have an equal amount of authority and power. Each member of this triad has the ability "to negotiate for what they want in the relationship, in terms of time, commitment, living situation, financial arrangements, sex, and other issues" (McGarey, 1999, p. 84).

The final model that we will investigate is the multiple non-primary relationship model. This can be identified as a model that offers polyamorists the ability to "essentially remain single, but participate in more than one relationship" (McGarey, 2001, p.89). Basically, what this offers is the ability of an individual to engage in more than one uncommitted relationship. Those who choose to engage in this type of "poly" relationship usually want to remain free of a commitment to a long term relationship. McGarey (1999) helps to solidify a picture of a person who chooses this type of a relationship when he reports, "People involved in this model usually don't make a lot of rules about their relationships, and retain a very high degree of personal freedom and autonomy" (McGarey, 1999, p. 89).

It can be summarized that, no matter what model of polyamory is chosen, each model allows for the exploration and the tailoring of the practice to the desires of the individual who chooses a polyamorous lifestyle. This also offers the ability for an individual to make decisions about how "open" they want to be in terms of their "poly" lifestyle to those in the community that they live in.

Theresa, Jose and Adrian have made the decision to reveal their lifestyle to those in the neighborhood that they live in. They choose to be open and welcoming to all of the questions, thoughts, and concerns that their neighbors may have about their lifestyle. This is not always true for those who proclaim themselves to be polyamorists. Some feel that if they were to reveal their "true" identity, it may hurt others with whom they associate with, they may be looked down upon by society, or they feel that it might affect them in terms of their job security or status in the community. As a result, some polyamorists choose to keep their identity hidden and they remain "in the closet". For Theresa, Jose and Adrian, they chose to "exit the closet" and allow others who live around them to know who they really are. They feel that by doing this, they can educate others about what it really means to love and care for more than one person at a time. Their thought is that, perhaps, one day, within the United States, we can recognize all different types of diversity and be educated about the different types of families that do exist.

At first, many of the neighbors did not recognize any differences beyond the fact that there were two men and a woman living with two children in the same house. It is understood that, in the United States, we live in a predominately monogamy-centrist environment (Easton and Liszt, 1997, p. 40). According to Easton and Liszt, this means that the prevailing idea in most cultures today is that "monogamy is the only moral and sexual pattern, or the normal or highest form of human relationship" (Easton and Liszt, 1997, p. 40). In fact, the concept of the monogamous relationship is so integrated into society, we tend to have an instinct to question any other form of relationship. This has changed over time, as we have begun to recognize that other forms of family exist beyond the traditional nuclear family that was portrayed by the media so well during the 1950's.

When we, as individuals, are first exposed to a new or different type of relationship, we tend to question its authenticity. We are not sure how to "plug it in" to our already established body of knowledge. As an example, we can look to those who have experienced divorce. According to Baca Zinn and Eitzen (2001), divorce rates have risen dramatically in the United States since 1960 (Baca Zinn and Eitzen, 2001, p. 389). Prior to this date, divorce was rarely talked about or acknowledged. If you were a product of a family that had experienced a divorce, you were regarded as a member of a family that did not hold to the traditions of the "American nuclear family." This essentially meant that your family was viewed as being "less than the standard" that was set by the expectations of American society. This phenomenon was also true for those who became pregnant during their teenage years. Before society recognized the single parent family or a family that was created out of adolescent pregnancy, these types of families were also looked upon as "less than perfect" than the traditional American nuclear family. As time has progressed during the last thirty years, American society has begun to recognize that other family forms do exist. In fact, a strong argument can be made that society has even begun to accept non-nuclear forms of family in a more positive light than it once placed them in.

Referring back to the previous statement about the fact that Theresa, Jose and Adrian have chosen to reveal their "polyness", their goal is to educate others about this type of family so that one day, perhaps, this type of family may be accepted and recognized as well.

This is what is happening to another type of family that is different from the traditional nuclear family. As time has evolved, we can now identify an additional example of a family that is being more recognized by society, a family that is composed of members of the same sex. In other words, gay or lesbian families. While many of the more familiar religions in the United States may not recognize these types of families, an argument can be made that society, on the whole, is beginning to recognize that we are a nation of diverse individuals and that these families do exist.

Taking these different examples into perspective, a case can be built that as the polyamorous lifestyle becomes more visible, it may be better understood and accepted by the predominately monogamous society that we live in here, in the United States. While we now recognize families that are created by non-traditional methods, we must realize the potential for additional forms, beyond the ones that we already give credence to. This takes into account additional diverse forms of family, including polyamory.

REFERENCES

Anapol, D. (1997). *Polyamory: The New Love Without Limits: Secrets of Sustainable IntimateRelationships*. San Rafael, CA: IntiNet Resource Center.

Anapol, D. (1997). Retrieved August 27, 2003, from Loving More Magazine web site: *http://www.lovewithoutlimits.com/nre_for_lmm.html*

Anderson, N. (date unknown). *Glossary of Relationship Terms: Marriage, Love Realtionships, and Polykoity*. Retrieved October 20, 2003, from website: *http://www3.primushost.com/~anderson/glossaryrelationshipsM.html*

Baca Zinn, M. and Eitzen, D. (2001). *Diversity in Families*. Boston, MA: Pearson Education.

Liszt, D. and Liszt, C. (1997). *The Ethical Slut: A Guide to Infinite Sexual Possibilities*. San Francisco, CA: Greenery Press.

Mathieu, J. (2000). *Meet Mr. And Mrs. and Mrs. Jones*. Houston Press. Houston, Texas.

McGarey, R. (1999). *Poly Communication Survival Kit: The Essential Tools for Building and Enhancing Relationships*. Austin, TX: Human Potential Center.

Ve Ard,C. and Veaux, F. (2003). Retrieved August 27, 2003, from Xero Magazine web site: *http://www.xeromag.com/fvpoly.html*

11

GROWING UP WITHOUT "DAD"

JoAnn Hazard, M.Ed.

Statistics show that fatherlessness affects 25 million American children (Smith, 2003), but what does this really mean? Growing up without a father in the home may not necessarily represent an absent father because many fathers play an active role in their children's lives while residing in a different location. There are also fathers who live in the same house with their children, but due to job requirements, depression or illness, they find themselves rarely interacting with their children. This article is intended to discuss many facets of this topic and encourage scholarly debate. The following stories will offer examples as to how complex the issue of fatherlessness is to research. Additionally, it is aimed at drawing universal conclusions.

James has been divorced for five years, but lives within a few miles of his former wife's house. This allows the children to spend about equal time with both parents. James goes to all of his children's school functions, coaches his son's ball team, helps with homework, and financially pays out more than the required child support payments.

Jeff is married and a father of three children. Jeff has a job that requires him to be in another city for most of the week. He usually leaves his home on Sunday evening and returns Thursday night. He is typically busy during the weekend, trying to catch up on household duties. He misses many of his children's activities and has never met any of their teachers. Jeff has always felt child-rearing is the wife's job anyway, and he has not felt the need to leave his good paying job. He enjoys visiting with his children on the weekend, but as they are getting older, they are doing more activities with their friends, which annoys Jeff, and has become a source of tension when he is at home.

Billy is eleven years old and cannot remember much about his father. His parents never married and his father left when he was around four years old. His mother has had several boyfriends, but chose not to marry any of them. Billy does have a photo of his dad, but his mother refuses to discuss anything about his father, except to say he is "no good". His father has called a couple of times, but Billy's mother has not let them talk or plan a time to meet.

Juan and Ann are nine year old twins who live alone with their mother. They have many memories of their father who just recently passed away after a heart attack. Their mother has many pictures around the house of their father and they often reminisce about him.

Monique, who is fourteen, has only met her father a few times. Her mother divorced and remarried before Monique was three. Monique's step father has raised her and she feels that he is her "dad". Her mother has had two more children who have been raised with Monique. While Monique is close to her family, this last year she has become curious about her biological father, and his family, and has asked to meet them. As of now, her biological father has not followed through with this request.

While all these situations depict an "absent" father, they illustrate how complex this issue is to study and how the conclusions of the research are hard to interpret. Questions that arise from these stories include: Does age of the child or gender of the child change the consequences of fatherlessness? Is an absent father physically away all the time or most of time? What is the reason for father absence and does that affect development of the child differently? Is a child of a physically absent father affected the same as a child of an emotionally absent father? How important is financial support and stepfathers to healthy development of a child?

Researchers have been trying to answer these questions and the data has been conflicted in areas, no doubt due to the complexity of family life. This paper will try and explore some of the conclusions drawn from researchers who have studied effects of absent fathers.

To begin, research shows that the reasons for an absent father vary. Approximately 90% are split fairly evenly between divorce and out of wedlock birth, while close to 10% of absent fathers are due to death (Popenoe, 1996). Out of wedlock births have increased recently due to the growing number of single women choosing to raise a child alone, without having any previous relationship with the biological father (Fergus, 2003). Many of these women are choosing to adopt while some are choosing to be impregnated through donated sperm from a sperm bank. Mary Ann Fergus (2003) reports in the Houston Chronicle that in 2001 30% of the 51,000 children who were placed in U.S. homes through public adoption were adopted by single women and 56% of those women were Black. Many of these women are older with established careers and are financially secure (Fergus, 2003).

There are also many reasons cited by divorced fathers on why they do not see their child. Researcher Jonathon Bradshaw (1999) reported in his study that most (53%) fathers who had not seen their child for over a year claimed the child's mother obstructed their contact. Other fathers cited the following reasons: they did not know where the child lived, they did not want to see their child or their child did not want to see them, or a court order prevents them from having contact with their child (Bradshaw et al, 1999).

Researcher David Popenoe (1996) begins with a historical perspective. He states that absent fathers were common during the war years, and he estimates that during any one of the war years 20%-25% of the nations families with children were fatherless (Popenoe,1996). This is similar to the 26.6% of children in 2000 living in homes without a father (Sylvester, 2001). The difference here is that most of the wartime fathers returned home, while today, most men do not return home. Popenoe relates that while wartime fatherlessness was largely involuntary, viewed as a male's service to country, today's fatherlessness is usually a lifestyle choice and about personal freedom. When a soldier went off to war (and even if he died) much of his fatherhood remained behind, sustained by memory, in the lives of his children. The absent fathers today, leave little behind and the children may feel their father left because he wanted to leave. Popenoe claims this leaves a different feeling within the child about his/her perceived worth.

While this may be true in some cases where an absent father leaves and never returns, there are also fathers who are physically separated from their children who retain a close connection to them. There are also other males, such as stepfathers, uncles, and grandfathers who may boost the self esteem of these children by their consistent involvement in the children's lives. Again, the complexity of this situation makes many professionals question such broad claims like those made by Popenoe.

Barbara Defoe Whitehead (1993) brings another perspective to why there may be differences between children losing their father to death compared to children losing their fathers due to divorce or separation. Whitehead states that death is usually untimely and tragic, leading to an outpouring of support from friends, family, and even strangers in the form of both financial and emotional assistance (Whitehead, 1993). Widows with children have access to Survivors Insurance which pays more in benefits than Aid to Families with Dependent Children (Whitehead, 1993). Many widows may also have supplemental insurance policies which pay benefits. After death, the children and the surviving parent grieve together which gives each one daily comfort. After a divorce, the parent and child may not be grieving together which may pull them apart initially. The community may not only be less supportive to this family, but the community may reject this family and "blame" the single parent for a failed marriage. This lack of support, both financial and emotional may contribute to adjustment problems seen with many children.

The American culture has varying opinions on the importance of fathering. There is a continuum where on one end fathers are seen as critical to a child's healthy development, and on the other end parenting roles are seen as interchangeable, with neither mother nor father being unique, and either parent has the potential for nurturing children. These differing viewpoints are worthy of discussion since a study in 1996 revealed 79% of Americans believed the "most significant family or social problem facing America is the physical absence of the father from the home" (Horn, 1997 p. 24). This may relate to researchers predictions that soon 50% of the children in America will grow up without a father at home sometime in their life. (Klinger, 1998). These predictions, however, may be premature. Current census figures in 2000 show the percentage of children living in a home without a father declined slightly from 28.1% in 1996 to 26.6% in 2000 (Sylvester, 2001). Those viewing fathers as playing a critical role in child's well-being cite many advantages to children who are raised with a father. I would add that these are likely to hold true when the father is a healthy, functioning adult and the home environment is free from addiction, violence, and abuse. Those viewing the role of father as not essential to a child's well-being cite that researchers have oversimplified the complex relations between father presence and social problems (Silverstein & Auerbach, 1999).

A FATHER'S INFLUENCE

Modeling is probably the most direct influence a father has on his children. Albert Bandura (Boeree, 1999) states that people acquire cognitive representations of behavior by observing others. For sons, a present father models what it means to be a man in our society. When this role model of a "whole" man is not present, the son may be left to idolize the fantasy figures in the movies, on television and in video games (Wassil-Grimm, 1994). Unfortunately, these are also typically violent figures. Pruett (2000) points out that cultures with the least paternal involvement are also the most violent cultures. Many boys with absent fathers place extra responsibility on themselves to protect their younger siblings and mother, especially in crime ridden neighborhoods. These boys may model the more aggressive behavior from the "fantasy men" as the way to handle problems. In neighborhoods with visible fathers, even the boys without fathers are able to have male role models to watch.

A present father is seen as way to enable the son to separate from his mother and develop his male identity (Gutmann, 1999). Scholars point to the importance of a present father who assists males through pubertal transition where boys migrate away from the mother and go towards the ways of men (Gutmann, 1999). Without a father as a guide, some young males may not separate from their mothers and consequently find it hard later on to have an intimate relationship with another woman. Other young males may force the separation in a more dramatic fashion through abuse of drugs or alcohol or through "tests" of manhood designed by peers (many which are gang related) which can include violence toward others in order to prove courage and strength (Gutmann, 1999). A father's influence as a role model is also shown in the way he relates to his wife. When a father and mother live together, they show their children how males and females interact. For daughters as well as sons, interactions between their parents can show how adults handle conflict, resolve problems, use compromise and work as a team. They can see that frustrations are normal even in a loving relationship. The children learn the values and rewards that come from a committed relationship.

Modeling is also seen in the intergenerational transmission of the fathering role. Furstenberg and Weiss (2000) cited young fathers were less likely to be living with their children if their own fathers had not lived with them throughout childhood. Also, men who did not grow up living with their fathers had a higher rate of becoming a father at a young age, during the teen years and early twenties (Furstenberg & Weiss, 2000).

Research by Blankenhorn (1995) showed that cognitive development is enhanced for boys when the father is in the home. A study done with infants at five and six months old showed that the baby boys living in homes with fathers scored significantly higher on Bayley Scales of Infant Development, as well as showing greater curiosity and interest in new objects. There are other studies which have found verbal ability, problem-solving skills, social skills, and empathy higher in children with involved fathers compared with children without paternal involvement (Brott, 1999; Pruett, 2000).

There are several findings in the literature that describe common characteristics of boys raised with involved fathers compared to boys raised without their father. The list includes that they handle strange situations smoothly, they balk less at being left with a sitter, they are more popular with their peers, more physical in their play, have stronger self-esteem, are less susceptible to peer pressure, show greater skill and confidence, and are more self-reliant (Wassil-Grimm 1994; Klinger,1998; Myers,2000). Wassil-Grimm (1994) reports that studies show the age of the child when the father left was an important factor in boy's adjustment. Generally, male teens had less adjustment problems than boys under five years old which was most likely because their masculine identities had already been formed before their father left (Wassil-Grimm, 1994).

Some studies have shown there are benefits to daughters who have an actively involved father. A father's love and approval can build a daughter's confidence in her own femininity and helps build her self-esteem (Wassil-Grimm, 1994). A daughter is learning how to interact with males by using the father-daughter relationship as a model. Theorists claim that this allows for greater autonomy for daughters in future relationships with males since these women are less likely to seek male approval and affection which is usually expressed through promiscuous behavior (Wassil-Grimm, 1995). Even when studies controlled for income, fatherless girls were at greater risk for early sexual activity, adolescent childbearing, divorce and lack of sexual confidence (Blankenhorn, 1995; Krohn & Bogan, 2001). Rachel Nowak (2003) recently studied 700 girls and reported that "teenage girls raised without fathers are more likely to suffer from depression, drop out of school and have other behavioral problems." Overall, girls who are raised with an attentive father are more ambitious, more successful in school, and more likely to attain careers of their own (Klinger, 1998).

Some researchers feel there are differences in females' behaviors depending on her age when her father left and whether her father's absence was due to death, separation or divorce. (Krohn & Bogan, 2001). These variables are important because the reasons behind the loss of a father and the age of the daughter at this loss can change her perception of males, the outside world and herself (Krohn & Bogan, 2001). Grimm-Wassil (1994) concluded daughters of divorce seek more attention from men and boys their age, are the most critical of their fathers, and have more aggressive behavior toward both male and female peers. In contrast, daughters of widows avoid contact with males, have the most positive concept of their father and feel saddest about his loss.

There can also be a problem with the father-daughter relationship when the father is present. When a father promotes sexual stereotypes and discourages his daughter's intellectual explorations, she may lose confidence in her intellectual ability (Wassil-Grimm, 1994).

For both sexes, research shows that mothers and fathers do approach parenting somewhat differently and these differences may be beneficial to a child's development (Horn, 1997). Fathers play is more rough and tumble, more challenging, and of a more competitive nature than mother's play (Horn, 1997; Klinger, 1998). These studies mainly used two parent families where gender roles may have been common. When a single parent is raising a child, many of these parents avoid adhering to strict gender roles and future research needs to look at how a single parent may interact with their child to see if the child is really missing this type of play.

One of the major advantages to children raised with a father is the added financial support. When a father lives with his children, his income goes into one house, one family. An immediate consequence of fatherlessness is loss of economic resources. After divorce, the household income declines by about 21% per capita for most families (Popenoe, 1995). This will be lower if there are no child support payments and poverty is higher among unmarried mothers than divorced mothers (Myers, 2000). Current figures have 54% of divorced mothers being awarded child custody payment, while only 15% of never married mothers received an award (Myers, 2000). One explanation may be the connection found between the father-child bond and child support payments. Typically, a stronger relationship relates to more payments (Blankenhorn, 1995). While there is agreement financial support is necessary for the well-being of children, Nancy Dowd (2000) has a critical view of society using economic support as the determinant of a "good enough" father. First, she feels the "breadwinner father" suggests a patriarchal power in the family where the male has control over the female through economic decisions. Second, Dowd states the father's involvement needs to go beyond economics to include emotional support and direct, continuing interaction with his child to promote the well-being of this child. Third, the "breadwinner" model discriminates against certain races who have unequal access to well-paying jobs. Specifically, in the African-American community, there is a different fatherhood model that is not connected to marriage relationship but has examples of fathers involved with their children and examples of mentoring in the community, even in the absence of the ability to provide significant economic support. Dowd (2000) feels there is a negative bias toward this new model even when there is a clear father-child relationship just because this model is not the traditional nuclear model.

There is controversy in the research on whether the negative consequences to children with absent fathers is mainly due to economics. Some theorists believe that successful development of children living with their fathers and children with absent fathers become more similar when income differences are balanced (Young, 1994). Another study by Horn (1997) also controlled for income, but found children with absent fathers fared worse in many areas than children growing up with both parents. Other long term studies following children after divorce who did not have extreme financial deprivation showed these children (now in adulthood) were still facing additional psychological burdens beyond the normative tasks of growing up (Whitehead, 1993).

There is also conflicting research regarding adolescents and crime. Friedman (1998) compared 350 African American adolescents and found more illegal offenses in the group from two parent homes compared to the group from single parent home. However, Klinger (1998) found adolescent boys from single parent homes were two to four times more likely to be arrested for juvenile crime, eleven times more likely to get into trouble for violent misbehavior while in school, and Klinger reports that 85% of all youths in prisons grew up in fatherless homes. Myers (2002) states that even after adjusting for income, race, age, population density and city size, juvenile violent crime is higher in neighborhoods with a high proportion of one parent families. Another report by Cabrera and Peters (2000) describe research where race, income, parent's education and urban residence was kept constant, and "boys with nonresident fathers had double the odds of being incarcerated" (Cabrera & Peters: 298). Critics claim that research does not always include other environmental variables such as poverty, peer group or support networks that exert a strong influence on adolescents. In cases where there was a divorce, some scholars feel it is the level of parental conflict prior to divorce, not the absent father variable that affects the child's well-being (Skolnick & Rosencranz, 1994)). Brown (2000) reports that studies confirm "children whose parents were unhappily married demonstrated the lowest psychological well-being when compared to children whose parents experienced either low stress divorces or happily intact marriages" (Brown, p. 225).

Myers (2000) suggests that lack of income is the major component causing negative consequences to children in single parent homes. He also concludes single parent homes may have too little supervision, less parental involvement, and too much residential mobility and these variables also contribute negatively to a child's well-being (Myers, 2000).

Other professionals are aware of the negative statistics, but caution the reader that correlation does not prove causation (Skolnick & Rosencranz, 1994). Skolnick and Rosencranz (1994) claim that much of the social science research is plagued by methodological problems. These researchers would like to see studies using appropriate comparison groups. An example would be to compare divorced families with intact families in which the parents are unhappily married.

Along with the children, mothers also receive benefits when the father is present in the home. Along with the financial support, the father can support the mother's role by sharing the housework and child-rearing duties, which gives the mother a break from her role and more free time. With this support, the mother has less stress which leads to more positive parenting skills such as more patience, flexibility, emotional responsiveness, and being more available to her children (Pruett, 2000).

While many professionals agree that a child's well-being is enhanced with an additional adult in their lives, this adult does not have to be the father or even a male (Silverstein & Auerbach, 1999). Studies have found that the addition of any adult to a single parent home, whether a relative or friend, will offset many negative consequences associated with fatherlessness (Silverstein & Auerbach, 1999). Urie Bronfenbrenner (2000) also points to the value of a "third party", an additional adult in the lives of a single parent, that can offer the mother a break from her role and helps relieve stress from the physical, emotional and psychological overload of sole care-taking duties. While he suggests this third party be of the opposite sex, it is not imperative for the child's overall well-being.

With the information found in research, society is in a position to help fatherless children and single mothers but there is disagreement on the best way to accomplish this goal. In *Diversity In Families*, Baca Zinn and Eitzen (2001) discuss two approaches to helping families; the conservative approach and the progressive approach. The conservative view sees society's problems as a result of the breakdown of the monolithic family. This decline in traditional family values had "led to the moral decay of society's members (Baca Zinn & Eitzen, p. 458). In the conservative perspective, people need to embrace the traditional family form and stop making selfish choices that ignore the children's needs (Baca Zinn & Eitzen, 2001). The Conservatives also feel that governmental policies have supported this decline of society's values.

The Progressive view states that the various family forms are not better or worse than other periods in society, but they are a result of the present social and economic conditions (Baca Zinn & Eitzen, 2001). The Progressives do not want to focus on the past, but instead, attend to the current problems families are experiencing. According to a progressive view, government should be responsible for helping all types of families and promoting diversity while eliminating moral prejudices (Baca Zinn & Eitzen, 2001). These two approaches can help us understand the many debates between political leaders while they try to develop solutions for family concerns. The following proposals include both a conservative and progressive perspective.

A CONSERVATIVE APPROACH

Blankenhorn (1995) represents a more conservative approach with the proposals he made in 1995 which are still being discussed today. Blankenhorn wants to see a change in America's cultural values by creating a marriage culture. He hopes this will recover the fatherhood idea. He stresses reuniting masculinity with fatherhood to change the current image of "being a man" as someone who is tough (even violent if disrespected), owning possessions bought with money, and sexually active with many women who then have his babies with little consequence to him. Blankenhorn would like society believing "being a man" is someone who cherishes his wife and nurtures his children. His proposals begin with an attitude shift starting at the top, meaning the President, Congress, and other lawmakers.

1. Federal money could be put toward a concept called "safe zones". These would be the impoverished neighborhoods in need of help. Safe zones would be civilian led and dedicated to the reduction of violence. Success would depend on local leadership and their creativity to solve problems. Having male schools and male teachers will bring more positive male role models into a boy's life. Money allocated could go toward more YMCAs, Boy's Clubs, and jobs for teens after school.

2. At state levels, laws could be passed to give priority in public housing to married couples. This is a way for married fathers to help transform public housing. Also controversial, is the proposal to prohibit sperm banks and others from selling sperm to unmarried women. This would give legal support to the hope that every child born will have a father.

3. Outside the political arena, communities could create a "Father's Club", aimed at invigorating fatherhood. An interfaith council of religious leaders could speak up and act on behalf of marriage.

4. Using well known athletes in public service announcements stating the value of fatherhood would reach males, but also the children who will be future parents. The other way to reach young people would be to have prominent family scholars write textbooks for students placing a positive light on marriage and family.

5. Around the country, efforts must be made to increase public awareness on the problems facing families without fathers. Blankenhorn describes efforts that have already begun. In Cleveland, Charles Ballard who heads the National Institute of Responsible Fatherhood and Family Development, has started a mentoring program for young, unwed fathers. The program uses a combination of parenting skills, education, and faith to encourage these young fathers to reenter the lives of their children and support the mothers. MAD-DADS claim 60,00 members in 15 states who support active fatherhood which includes outreach programs for mentoring fatherless children (maddadsnational.com). Another larger group is Promise Keepers with over 1.1 million members who are devoted to inspiring men to be faithful husbands and responsible fathers. Marriage Savers is another national organization which is connected to churches. This idea matches couples in the church with strong marriages to younger couples who they will mentor.

Recently, the 2002 budget proposed by President Bush included grants for $60 billion dollars to put towards supporting responsible fatherhood and strengthening marriage (Meckler, 2003).

A PROGRESSIVE APPROACH

Iris Marion Young represents a more progressive view to solving family problems. She has nothing against two parent families, but she worries if government favors these families, other family forms will be unfairly burdened by decreased financial support and increased discrimination. She feels single mothers are the most stigmatized by the "family values" concept where the heterosexual two parent family is the normal and "right" way for a family to be. "The only antidote to this injustice is for public policy to regard single mothers as normal, and give them the social supports they need to overcome disadvantage" (Young, 1997). The following includes some of Young's proposals:

1. Avoid judging a teen age mother's choice to have a baby. Instead, society needs to give teenage girls alternatives to mothering as her only vocational option. Education and employment policies need to take girls and women more seriously, with job training and vocational education starting in the teen years. All schools, colleges, and vocational institutions need to accommodate childbearing and child-rearing into a woman's education and not discriminate certain women because of their age.

2. An increase in state supported childcare so women can get training for better paying jobs. With good job opportunities, women would leave welfare earlier, instead of waiting to be forced off welfare after a certain time limit. Public policy should also acknowledge that taking of care of children at home is work and then support this work with unstigmatized subsidy where necessary to give a child a decent life.

3. Public policy should support all family forms and dispel the assumption that only heterosexual two parent families are normal. The states could assist single parent support systems so these families are not at such a disadvantage. Young points to a European model that provides "mother's houses" where single mothers share child-rearing and cooking, but also have privacy areas.

4. Men need to be accountable. Men who are not poor themselves, need to be forced through paycheck deductions or bank account deductions to pay child support. While this is possible in some situations, other single mothers can

not even find the biological father. This is why Young wants all men to be encouraged to involve themselves in the lives of fatherless children, regardless of whether a child is his biological offspring.

Silverstein and Auerbach (1999) also have recommendations that represent a progressive philosophy. They offer three suggestions for society to encourage father involvement.

1. The father-child bond would be defined by society independent of the mother-child bond. This would allow for a relationship between a father and child to develop and remain whether the father is married to the mother, separated from the mother or divorced from the mother.

2. The workplace norms would accept that men have equal responsibility for child care and therefore men could be free to restructure their commitment to work to allow for more family involvement with no repercussions.

3. There needs to be an overall government policy to aid all families with children that includes economic support during prenatal leave and financed daycare. The government policies are more likely to be achieved if more women are elected and involved in government.

The debate on is still continuing on the best way to help children in fatherless homes. Some feel certain government proposals means more taxation and others feel society is morally obligated to help all citizens in time of need.

SUGGESTIONS FOR SINGLE MOTHERS

To raise healthy children, a single mother needs financial support, but she also needs emotional support that allows her someone to talk to, learn from, and be able to share her feelings. A single mother needs physical support in the form of relief from day to day physical care of the children.

This kind of help relieves stress and helps her maintain energy. However, the sex of the additional adult nor the biological relationship to the child has not emerged as a significant factor in predicting a positive outcome for the child and therefore, the single mother can draw support from any number of friends or family members (Silverstein & Auerbach, 1999).

There are other scholars who disagree and feel there is a need specifically for male role models in a child's life (Popenoe, 1996). The single mother who may want to find male role models might look in the community to services such as Big Brothers or Mad-Dads, as well as their child's scout leader, sports coach, or even a teacher.

The single mother would benefit from services that offer education on the development of children and on the unique problems associated with raising children alone. She can learn ways to take on some traditionally masculine roles, such as rough and tumble play, encouraging exploration, and avoiding over protecting them. Education could also include ways to give her children independence as some children from single parent homes become the co-parent or the mother's way to fill the void in her life. This enmeshment of mother and child blocks the child's healthy movements toward independence (Wassil-Grimm, 1994).

Pollitt (1993) sums up what single mothers really need; "Single mothers need paid parental leave, daycare, flexible schedules, child support, pediatricians with evening hours, schools that recognize that mothers have jobs, and equal pay (Pollitt: 100).

While the burden on the single mother is great, her nurturing and care is the reason so many fatherless children grow into well adjusted adults. Researchers Silverstein and

Auerbach (1999) concluded that a child's well-being was related to having one responsible, care-taking adult who was consistently there for them and with whom they had a positive emotional connection.

FOR MORE DISCUSSION

GRANDPARENTS AS PARENTS

Grandparents are a rising population that is caring for children due to absent parents. While it is reported that nearly 2.5 million grandparents are currently raising more than 4.5 million grandchildren (census, 2000), exact figures are unavailable because many grandparents do not report this "informal" custody arrangement. Reasons vary, but many grandparents hope their children will want to come back and parent again. Some fear losing "elderly" housing , some fear interference by social service agencies that may take the children away, and some do not want to go to court and declare their child an unfit parent (Dourette-Dudman, 1996). However, without legal guardianship or custody, grandparents cannot access services for children such as enrollment in school and obtaining health insurance (Welch, 2003).

Debra Douchette-Dudman (1996) has interviewed many grandparents raising grandchildren and reported on the many struggles facing this population. The grandparents who gain temporary custody receive much less government money than foster care parents. (Dourette-Dudman, 1996). Many tell stories of discrimination from social service agencies where workers are hostile and even encourage the grandparent to give the children up to foster care. (Dourette-Dudman, 1996). They also relate that some social workers make a judgment that the entire family is dysfunctional because of the behavior of one of its members. Liz Welch (2003), however, finds that social service agencies want to place the children with grandparents because "the grandparent who takes a child in has a deeper emotional commitment to the child than a stranger would"(Welch, 2003:5).

There are other strains placed on the grandparents, with a major strain concerning decisions about their own child, the biological parent. These biological parents typically have serious problems which led to the grandparents raising the children. The grandparents must decide about visitations and worry about the parent wanting the children back before they are ready. Grandparents often express grief at losing their traditional role and losing their expected retirement time (Welch, 2003). The extra large generation gap can cause conflicts with their grandchildren when the grandparent does not understand the "new" way of life in American society compared to when they were young, (Dourette-Dudman, 1996).

CHILDREN RAISED WITH ABSENT MOTHERS

A growing number of fathers are raising their children alone. In 1996, custodial fathers comprised 16% or 1.9 million of the 11.8 million custodial parents in the United States (Hameer & Marchioro, 2002). Some reasons for this growing trend include children removed from the mother due to neglect or abuse, a mother's lack of interest in parenting, and children who actively want to live with their fathers (Hameer & Marchioro, 2002). While the growth in White custodial fathers is an outcome of divorce, the growth of African American custodial fathers has increased because never married single fathers are gaining custody of their children (Hameer and Marchioro, 2002). These two groups do have similar concerns about raising their children alone, but due to African-American males' higher unemployment, more financial difficulties and more health problems, these fathers struggle more than their White counterparts (Hameer and Marchioro, 2000). One problem single fathers face, regardless of race, is lack of formal child support payments from the biological mother (Hameer and Marchioro, 2000). Some fathers apply for public aid, but many fathers tell of the difficulties working with social services. In a study with African American single fathers, Hameer and Marchioro (2000) report these fathers experienced questions from suspicious workers asking about possible inappropriate touching of their daughters. The workers at social service agencies also encouraged fathers to allow the grandmother to take care of the children insinuating living with a single father might be harmful.

Downey and Ainsworth-Darnell (1998) compared children raised in single mother homes with children raised in single father homes to see if the children develop particular characteristics due to the sex of the custodial parent. The researchers admit there are studies supporting the idea that fathers interact differently than mothers with their children, but they claim "there are few important differences that we could detect between children living with a single mother and children living with a single father" (Downey and Ainsworth-Darnell, 1998:11.). However, single fathers do have some advantages over single mothers. On average, single fathers have higher occupational prestige, greater family income, and more years of education (Downey & Ainsworth-Darnell, 1998).

Single fathers need physical and emotional support just as single mothers do and, according to the 2000 Census, single fathers are receiving more live-in support than single mothers. The 2000 Census reports that three out of ten single fathers raising their children had an unmarried partner, compared to one out of ten single mothers who lived with an unmarried partner.

With children being raised in a broad range of family structures, professionals are continually trying to find answers to which structure is best for children. William Smith (2003) cites studies that show "children need at least one, preferably two, responsible adult caretakers, but the caretaker's sex nor their biological relationship to the child was as significant as the stability of the emotional connection and the predictability of the care-taking relationship" (Smith 2003:2).

In conclusion, Downey and Ainswoth-Darnell (1998) state that the sex of the custodial parent does not seem to matter in regard to the children's well being, but family stressors, processes within the family, and available (or lack of) familiar resources are the variables that contribute to differences in children's development and well-being.

REFERENCES

Baca Zinn, M. and Eitzen, D. (2001). *Diversity in Families*. Boston: Pearson Education.

Blankenhorn, David (1995). *Fatherless America: Confronting Our Most Urgent Social Problem*. New York: Harper Collins.

Boeree, C. George, (1998) Personality Theories. electronic e-textbook. Shippensburg University.

Bradshaw, Jonathon; Stimson, Carol; Skinner, Christine; and Williams, Julie (1999). *Absent Fathers*. New York: Routledge Press.

Brott, Armin (1999). "Not Just Another Pair of Hands" in *The Fatherhood Movement*. Edited by Wade F. Horn, David Blankenhorn, Mitchell B. Pearlstein. New York: Lexington Books

Cabrera, Natasha, Peters, Elizabeth H. (2000) "Public Policies and Father Involvement" in *Fatherhood: Research, Interventions and Policies*. Edited by Elizabeth H. Peters, Gary W. Peterson, Suzanne K. Steinmetz, Randall D. Day. New York: The Haworth Press, Inc.

Doucette-Dudman, D. (1996) *Raising Our Children's Children.* Minneapolis: Fairview Press.

Dowd, Nancy E. (2000). *Redefining Fatherhood.* New York: New York University Press.

Downey, Douglas, B., Ainsworth-Darnell, James, W. (1998) "Sex of Parent and Children's Well-being in Single Parent Households". *Journal of Marriage and Family.* V. 60 I. 4

Fergus, Mary Ann (2003). "Adopting Parenthood, Alone". *Houston Chronicle* 8(3) pp. 1E, 3–4E

Friedman, A., Ali, A., McMurphy, S. (1998) "Father Absence as a Risk Factor for Substance Use and Illegal Behavior by the Adolescent Sons". *Journal of Child and Adolescent Substance Abuse.* 8(2), 79–95

Gutmann, David L. (1999). "The Species Narrative" in *The Fatherhood Movement.* Edited by

Hameer Jennifer, and Marchioro, Kathleen. (2002) "Becoming Custodial Dads: Exploring Parenting Among Low-income and Working Class African American Fathers". *Journal of Marriage and Family.* V. 64, I.1

Horn, Wade (1997) "You've Come a Long Way, Daddy". *Policy Review* 7 (8), 24–30.

Horn, Wade, Blankenhorn, David, Pearlstein, Mitchell, B. (Eds) (1999): *The Fatherhood Movement.* New York: Lexington Books

Klinger, Ron (1998). "What Can Be Done About Absentee Fathers?". *USA Today Magazine.* 7(1).

Krohn, Franklin, Bogan, Zoe (2001). "The Effects Absent Fathers Have on Female Development and College Attendance". *College Student Journal.* V. 35 I. 4, 598.

Myers, David (2000). *The American Paradox: Spiritual Hunger in an Age of Plenty.* New Haven: Yale University Press

Nowak, Rachel (2003). "Absent Fathers Linked to Teen-age Pregnancies". *New Scientist,* 5(17) V. 178 I 2395, 13.

Pollitt, Katha (1993). "Single Motherhood is a Legitimate Choice" in *Single Parent Families.* Edited by Karin L. Swisher. San Diego: Greenhaven Press, Inc.

Popenoe, D. (1996). *Life Without Father.* New York: Pressler Press.

Pruett, Kyle (2000). *Fatherneed.* New York: The Free Press.

Silverstein, Louise B., Auerbach, Carl, F. (1999) "Deconstructing the Essential Father". *American Psychologist.* V.54 (6) 397–407.

Skolnick, Arlene, Roosencrantz, Stacey (1994). "The Harmful Effects of Single Parent Families are Exaggerated" in *Single Parent Families* edited by Karin L. Swisher, San Diego: Greenhaven Press, Inc.

Smith, William, C. (2003) "Dad's Want Their Day". *American Bar Association Journal.* V. 89, I 2

Wassil-Grimm, Claudette (1994). *Where's Daddy?* Woodstock: Overlook Press.

Welch, Liz (2003). "Grandparents to the Rescue". *Parade Magazine* 7(20), 4–5.

Whitehead, Barbara Defoe (1993) "Single Parents are Harmful" in *Single Parent Families.* Edited by Karin L. Swisher, San Diego: Greenhaven Press, Inc.

Young, Iris Marion (1994) "Single Parent Families Have Been Unfairly Stigmatized" in *Single Parent Families.* Edited by Karin L. Swisher, San Diego: Greenhaven Press, Inc.

12

PARENTING IN DIVERSE CULTURES

Tommy J. Hamner

The term *culture* refers to the sum total of the attainments and learned behavior patterns of a specific people, regarded as expressing a traditional way of life. The behavioral patterns of a given culture are believed to be transmitted from one generation to the next, subject to gradual and continuous modification. In the United States, many diverse groups exist that manifest distinct behavioral patterns and can be clearly designated as subcultures. These include racial/ethnic groups, religious groups, socioeconomic classes, and geographic populations. In most subcultures certain aspects of the lifestyle deviate to some extent from that of the dominant culture. However, it is important to note that subcultures within the United States are probably similar in more ways than they are different. Socioeconomic differences are included in the following discussion of cultural diversity because poor families may display cultural behavior patterns that are different from expectations implicit in the larger middle-class culture. Class differences exist in all racial minority groups and are believed to be a more fundamental barrier than race or ethnicity to structural integration into American society.

SOCIOECONOMIC DIFFERENCES IN PARENTING

A serious contemporary concern is the growing number of children in the United States, especially younger ones, who live in poverty. The proportion of children living in poverty has increased steadily since 1975 and only recently has begun to level off. In 1997, 19 percent of all dependent children (under age 18) and 22 percent of children under the age of 6 lived in families below the poverty line, a rate almost twice as high as that in most other industrialized nations. Of all children under 18 in 1997, approximately 37 percent of African American, 36 percent of Hispanic, and 11 percent of White children were poor. Figures were not provided for Native American children, but based on older data, the figure probably is close to 40 percent. Ten percent of all children in married-couple families are poor, whereas 49 percent in female-headed households are poor. A staggering 63 percent of Hispanic and 55 percent of African American children living in female-headed households are poor. Eleven percent of the nation's families live below the poverty line, and an additional 15 percent live at 125 percent of the poverty level (Forum on Child & Family Statistics, 1999; U.S. Bureau of the Census, 1998).

The three groups of families significantly represented in the poverty population are single-mother families, minority-group families, and families with preschool children. Other factors related to family poverty are young parents, low level of educational attainment, and unemployed status.

The largest percentage of poor families are single-parent families. Single parents have a 40 percent poverty rate, but the low number of poor single-parent men masks the high rate for single-parent mothers. Families headed by single-parent females are three times more likely to be in poverty than those headed by single-parent men. The majority of poor single mothers live independently with their children rather than cohabiting or living with relatives or friends, and at least 25 percent of those who have children under the age of 6 are not receiving any kind of government benefits. For those who are, benefits account for less than 7 percent of their aggregate income (U.S. General Accounting Office, 1992).

Three reasons have been given for the increase in child poverty rates: Economic changes have eliminated many blue-collar jobs that pay well; the percentage of children living in single-mother families has increased; and government benefits have steadily declined. Poverty is a conglomerate of conditions and events that amount to a pervasive stressor, often including exposure to poor health conditions, inadequate housing and homelessness, environmental toxins, and violent or unsupportive neighborhoods. The impact of poverty, however, can vary with race, gender, and ethnicity. The employment of one, or even two workers, is not necessarily sufficient to bring family income above the poverty line because the minimum wage is too low (Garrett, Ng'andu, & Ferron, 1994; Huston, McLoyd, & Coll, 1994).

For several decades researchers have been investigating differences in parenting practices among lower, middle, and upper socioeconomic classes. Particularly in the 1960s, in conjunction with the federal government's War on Poverty, there was a multitude of research on children from low-socioeconomic-status families and how best to help them. One of the difficulties of these studies was that socioeconomic status often was confounded with race or minority-group membership. Nevertheless, the picture that emerged, and subsequently the services that were provided, assumed a generalized image of poor families and poor children. Specifically, the emphasis was on the detrimental effects of early experiences of "deprived" children. The terms *progressive retardation* and *cumulative cultural deficit* were commonly used to describe what would ultimately happen to poor children in an academic setting if intervention did not occur. Programs were designed to assist poor children in "catching up" so that they could match middle-class standards. Little attention was given to the strengths of poor families, and indeed poor children were assumed to be lacking in cognitive and affective strengths altogether.

Much of the research in the 1960s has been criticized for its biases, assumptions, and faulty methodology. The current perception is that social-class groups are not homogeneous and that social-class levels differ from one section of the United States to another. Some researchers contend that there is as much variation in child-rearing patterns within a given social class as there is between social classes. It has been concluded that assertions on the effects of social class on child development represent probabilities, not inevitabilities. More recent research has introduced statistical sampling controls for socioeconomic status when assessing the effects of race or ethnicity in an attempt to untangle the two variables, and little research has focused on differences within ethnic groups. However, evidence for variability within a given social class or a given ethnic or racial group is beginning to emerge.

Quality of the Home Environment

Research in the 1960s and 1970s focused on the differences in mother-child interaction between low- and middle- to upper-income families, especially in the areas of language patterns and discipline techniques. Fairly consistent differences emerged. Lower-class mothers were found to be less instructive and more imperative than middle-class mothers in their control systems with children, more critical, more restrictive, and less sensitive to their children's needs. Middle-class mothers were found to be less intrusive and to give more reinforcement to their children's behavior and responses, and these behaviors were reflected in their language patterns and those of their children. The most consistent differences were found in the degree and quality of verbal interaction (Bee, Van Egeren, Streissguth, Nyman, & Leckie, 1969; Clarke-Stewart, 1977; Hess & Shipman, 1965).

Several more-recent researchers have focused on differences in the quality of the home environments of low-income and middle- and upper-income children because this variable has been consistently related to school success. It has been asserted that the more time children live in families with incomes below the poverty line, the lower the quality of the home environments, and improvements in income have the strongest effects on the home environments of chronically poor children (Huston et al., 1994). McLeod and Shanahan (1993) found that the length of time spent in poverty was an important predictor of children's health even after current poverty status was taken into account. Stress was a function of the duration of poverty, and harsh discipline, including paternal abuse, was more prevalent in persistently poor families, accounting for children's mental-health problems. Persistent poverty significantly predicted children's internalizing symptoms above and beyond the effect of current poverty, but only current poverty predicted externalizing symptoms. These researchers concluded that poor children appeared to experience the same parenting disadvantages regardless of race.

The availability of stimulating toys and books, and encouragement and support for intellectual accomplishments, factors known to contribute to a child's language development and later school performance, have been reported to occur less often in the homes of families living in poverty. Low-income parents are also reported to play fewer language games that are conducive to early language learning and to press their children for language less often. To further exacerbate the problem, teachers in some schools with large numbers of low-income children devote less daily time to instruction in basic academic skills, such as reading. Variations in exposure to language in the home and academic instruction in the school as influenced by socioeconomic status over time are predictors of subsequent child language, IQ, and achievement (Walker, Greenwood, Hart, & Carta, 1994).

Results of a study that was a 5-year extension of a 10-year longitudinal study showed that cumulative language spoken in the home was a key predictor of later school outcome. Children reared in lower socioeconomic environments had fewer early language experiences associated with later optimal language outcomes. The constraints placed on their language development in the context of early parenting may have compromised their growth in both early language and intelligence, as well as later success in reading and spelling achievement, in particular. The elementary school results showed that the earlier differences were predictive 7 years beyond the initial measures. Children from low-income families continued to demonstrate lower performance on language and reading-related achievement across grades in the elementary school, suggesting that initial differences were further maintained in the context of schooling. The authors pointed out that the differences found in this study were attributable to socioeconomic status factors and not specifically to their minority or cultural background (Walker et al., 1994).

Kaiser and Delaney (1996) confirmed that impoverished children exhibit poorer language development and facility and poorer cognitive functioning—which translates into lower academic achievement, more mental and physical health problems, and poorer social adjustment. Bolger, Patterson, Thompson, and Kupersmidt (1995) studied outcomes associated with persistent economic hardship among a group of children over a 4-year period. Children who experienced persistent family economic hardship started out behind other children on every measure of school-based competence and generally stayed behind throughout the study. Overall, the greatest difficulties in adjustment were shown by children whose families experienced intermittent economic hardship; the fewest difficulties were shown by those families who did not experience economic hardship. Children who experienced persistent economic hardship had difficulties in peer relations, showed conduct problems at school, and reported low self-esteem. Both White and African American boys were more affected than were girls by family economic hardship, at least in externalizing behavior problems. However, to some extent parental characteristics mediated the effects. For example, maternal involvement was predicted by mothers' own levels of educational attainment, which in turn predicted children's intelligence scores.

Miller and Davis (1997) examined the relationship among depth or timing of poverty, mother's marital history, and quality of the home environment for children 6 to 9 years of age. They found that the quality of the home environment was substantially lower for poor children than for children who were not poor and that the quality of the home environment increases with increasing income up to approximately three times the poverty level, even when other sociodemographic attributes are taken into account. Low educational level of the mothers in this study was significantly and negatively associated with the quality of the home environment, even when poverty history was controlled, although the estimated effects of maternal education were notably smaller than the poverty effects. The number of children in the household and minority identification also were negatively associated with home-environment quality. Results suggested that poverty has a more important effect on the provision of material and other learning resources than on the quality of the parents' interactions with the child. Further, children who had experienced marital disruption had markedly lower home-environment quality, especially on emotional support, and children of never-married mothers fared less well than children of married mothers.

Neighborhood quality, as well as family income, appears to affect cognitive development and IQ. Klebanov, Brooks-Gunn, McCarton, and McCormick (1998) found that as early as age 1, the accumulation of family risks was associated with lower infant-development test scores. By age 3, neighborhood income entered as the third strongest environmental influence on test scores, just after family poverty.

Another study found that neighborhood income level was found to influence IQ by age 5. Living in more affluent neighborhoods raised IQ 1.6 points for each 10 percent increase in the proportion of affluent neighbors. Conversely, living in a poor neighborhood did not negatively affect age-5 IQ. These authors noted that the effects of persistent poverty on children are 60–80 percent greater than the effects of transient poverty, and the apparent effects of female headship of families on child cognition are due mostly to the lower incomes of female-headed families rather than to family structure (Duncan, Brooks-Gunn, & Klebanov, 1994).

These and other studies emphasize the importance of a home environment for young children that is stimulating, both in materials (toys and books) and in interactions with adults that are rich in language experiences. The pattern, first noted in the 1960s, of lower academic achievement and early school failure that is disproportionately experienced by children of poor families was confirmed by research in the 1990s. And it appears that many children are at risk for progressive and cumulative poor performance in elementary school as a result of early home environments that fail to stimulate language and cognitive development, and the risk is compounded when children grow up in poor-quality neighborhoods.

Parenting Behaviors

The impact of poverty on children is mediated by the behavior of adults—how they react to inadequate financial resources structures the consequences of poverty for children. The same level of income or material comfort may be perceived quite differently, depending on whether parents communicate worries about economic insecurity or whether children often are denied objects and experiences because the family lacks money (Garrett et al., 1994; Huston et al., 1994). Nevertheless, a large body of data indicates that poverty has profound effects on parenting, largely because of high levels of stress.

There has been little emphasis in the literature on the parenting behaviors of low-income fathers, but it has been suggested that loss of income for fathers may result in their becoming punitive and unnurturing, which results in children developing socioemotional problems, somatic symptoms, and reduced aspirations and expectations. Parents may react to financial stress by overemphasizing obedience, withholding affection, relying on corporal punishment as a means of control, and failing to be responsive to the socioemotional needs of children (Garrett et al., 1994). Using a national sample, Hashima and Amato (1994) found that the likelihood of punitive parental behavior decreased as household income increased. Parents at low-income levels were especially likely to report behaving in a punitive and unsupportive fashion toward their children.

Conger, Ge, Elder, Lorenz, and Simons (1994) found that aversive behavior toward children is a spillover effect of marital conflict. Earlier research had suggested that economic stress may increase conflict and irritability in family interactions. The study by Conger and his associates found that economic pressure is associated directly with parent-adolescent financial conflicts as well as indirectly through parent depressed mood and hostile interactions in the marriage. Both marital conflict and financial conflict were found to be significantly related to parent hostility toward the child.

There is far more emphasis in the literature on the parenting behaviors of low-income mothers and how they affect children. Many studies of diverse samples report that mothers experiencing high emotional stress exhibit diminished nurturance and sensitivity toward their children and, in disciplinary encounters, rely less on reasoning and loss of privileges and more on aversive, coercive techniques. Economic loss has adverse, indirect effects on children's behavior and socioemotional functioning through increasing negative parenting behaviors, which is consistent with the evidence that children of parents who use harsh, punitive, and inconsistent discipline are prone to a number of behavioral and psychological problems (Kalil & Eccles, 1998; McLoyd, Jayaratne, Ceballo, & Borquez, 1994).

Epidemiological researchers have found consistent relationships between low socioeconomic status and early-onset behavior problems in childhood. It has been speculated that low-income mothers employ harsh disciplinary practices at a high rate because of urgent needs to try to prevent their children from becoming involved in antisocial activity, either as victims or as perpetrators. Stress induced by economic disadvantage may lead to increased coercive exchanges between parent and child. Many researchers have found that harsh and punitive parenting is associated with child aggressive behavior, and this relationship holds in diverse cultural groups and with children in five different countries. The stresses of socioeconomic disadvantage may cause a parent to be less attentive to the child's needs and thus less warm toward the child. Some studies have found maternal warmth to be negatively correlated with low-socioeconomic status, which is associated with child aggressiveness. Children also may learn aggression from models; violence often is readily observed in low-socioeconomic marital dyads and neighborhoods, and observation of adult conflict is associated with both immediate and long-term adverse effects on children (Dodge, Pettit, & Bates, 1994).

Researchers have found that children in the lowest socioeconomic class received teacher-rated externalizing problem scores significantly above the national mean; more than 60 percent of the low-status children received a score in the clinical risk range at some time during elementary school. In fact, the lower the socioeconomic status, the greater the behavior problems. Low-status children were more likely than their more advantaged peers to receive harsh discipline from their parents, to observe violence in their extended families and neighborhoods, and to have unstable peer groups and friendships. They received less cognitive stimulation in their home environments; mothers were less warm and experienced more life stressors, perceived less social support and greater isolation, and were more likely to believe that aggression is an appropriate and effective way to solve problems. These findings held even when the effects of single parenthood were controlled statistically, revealing their direct relationship to economic disadvantage. Harsh discipline was the strongest predictor of behavior problems (Dodge et al., 1994).

Felner, Brand, DuBois, Adan, Mulhall, and Evans (1995) found that young adolescents from families characterized by lower levels of occupational status reported greater maternal rejection, less sense of belonging at school, and greater exposure to major stressful events than their more advantaged peers. Parental education had a different and more pervasive pattern of association with risk experiences. Specifically, adolescents from homes in which neither parent had graduated from high school reported more developmentally negative experiences, including higher levels of rejection from both parents, less social support and emphasis on intellectual-cultural issues in their families, more negative feelings about school, and heightened levels of exposure to both major and relatively minor stressors. These findings suggested that household occupational status and parental educational attainment each had unique influences on children's academic performance and achievement. Further, parental education also associated significantly with several other indices of socioemotional functioning where household occupational status did not.

Because it appears to inhibit the capacity of families with adolescents to achieve informal social control, poverty increases the likelihood of delinquency. Strong family social controls may serve as an important buffer against structural disadvantage in the larger community. The fundamental causes of delinquency are consistent across time and rooted not in race but in generic family processes—such as supervision, attachment, and discipline—that are systematically influenced by family poverty and structural disadvantage (Sampson & Laub, 1994).

When economic hardship is accompanied by social isolation, parents are more likely to become neglectful of and abusive toward their children. The reported incidence of maltreatment is disproportionately large among families living in poverty, and socially isolated families have higher rates of child abuse than other families do (Hashima & Amato, 1994). Several studies have pointed out the buffering effects of social support on the negative parental behaviors associated with the stresses of economic deprivation. Social support appears to have a positive effect on parenting behavior by making mothers feel less isolated and overwhelmed by their parenting situation, more gratified with the maternal role, and more satisfied with their children (McLoyd et al., 1994).

The preceding evidence suggests rather strongly that there are documented differences between the home environments and the parenting behaviors experienced by poor children and their more economically advantaged peers. This contemporary research has used statistical controls that help to untangle the variables of income/socioeconomic status and race/ethnicity. The results, therefore, point more clearly to differences in income as the major factor influencing these differences. Lack of financial resources causes increased stress, leading to negative parenting behaviors, which result in adverse outcomes for children.

However, parenting behavior may be related to other factors, such as education, health status, and biological differences. We conclude that consistent differences have been observed among different social-class levels but that many other factors influence children's behaviors and abilities. Further, conditions associated with poverty, such as slum neighborhoods, inferior employment, poor health, unstable marriages, and high birthrates, serve to devastate the child's well-being as much as specific parenting behaviors.

Finally, there appear to be "within-class" differences that might be as significant as "between-class" differences. Clearly, lower-class parents lack resources in parenting equal to those of middle- and upper-class parents—financial, educational, psychological, and medical resources. And this lack of resources surely has some impact on the way in which they interact with their children.

PARENTING IN AFRICAN AMERICAN FAMILIES

In 1997 there were approximately 8.5 million African American families and more than 34 million African Americans in the United States. Most reside in the inner-city sections of the largest cities (U.S. Bureau of the Census, 1998). According to many researchers, African Americans constitute a distinctive culture that represents an interaction between strong African cultural derivatives and the influence of American cultural imperatives (Greene, 1995). The tendency to have dual or even several social systems or structural arrangements for access to, and receiving, resources and for enforcing laws has reinforced the

HIGHLIGHTS

Positive Home and Parental Characteristics

QUALITY OF HOME ENVIRONMENT
Provision of stimulating toys and books
Encouragement and support for intellectual accomplishments
Early language stimulation
Living in an affluent neighborhood
Low level of financial stress

PARENTING BEHAVIORS
High levels of nurturance and maternal warmth
Low likelihood of punitive behavior toward children
Reliance on reasoning and loss of privilege as discipline techniques
Absence of violence in home and neighborhood
Social control, e.g., supervision, guidance, attachment
Economic security

development and continuance of a distinct African American culture. However, as a group, African Americans are geographically and socioeconomically diverse, but they share cultural origins and negative racial barriers in a variety of ways (Greene, 1995).

Demographics

There have been enormous changes among African Americans over the past two decades: a rise of their underclass, a rise of their middle class (more than one-third of African Americans are classified as middle-class), and the demise of their stable blue-collar working class. Social scientists have emphasized the underclass, manifested by increased unemployment, poverty, and female-headed families. African American poverty was dramatically reduced between 1959 and 1979 by the combination of an expanding economy, greater educational opportunity, more government programs for the poor, and the enforcement of civil rights and affirmative action. Since 1979, however, these trends have been reversed, and by 1985 poverty among African Americans had reached unprecedented levels. More than half of all African American households earned less than $25,000 in 1996. Twenty-eight percent of all African Americans now live below the poverty line. The situation is worse for children. Thirty-seven percent of African American children in all family types live in poverty, and more than half who live in mother-only families live below the poverty line. The younger the child, the more likely she is to be impoverished (U.S. Bureau of the Census, 1998).

The exceptionally high rate of unemployment for African Americans and their relatively low level of education account for the fact that their median household income is approximately 59 percent of Whites'. African American males have almost three times the rate of unemployment that Whites males do. At the present time the median family income in constant dollars for African Americans is only $2,000 per year more than it was in 1970. Although African American women make a much greater contribution to the economic standing of their families than White women do, even when both groups are married to working husbands, African American women earn less than White men and women and African men (U.S. Bureau of the Census, 1998). Even when African Americans complete 4 years of college, their incomes do not equal those of some other racial groups with comparable education.

Traditionally, African Americans have begun their childbearing much earlier than other racial groups; they continue their childbearing longer and have a higher average number of children ever born than Whites or Hispanics do. Further, African American females are more likely to be never-married mothers and to divorce if they do marry than Whites or Hispanics and are less likely to remarry than Whites. Separation and divorce occur at younger ages for African Americans than for other groups, and the period of separation before divorce is longer. Even so, African American families are represented by great diversity in lifestyle. In their struggle for equality and justice, African Americans have survived by living in a variety of family forms—two-parent households, common-law marriages, extended families, male-headed families, and female-headed families.

Since the 1970s, however, there has been a dramatic increase in both teenage pregnancies and out-of-wedlock births among African Americans of all social classes. Seventy percent of all African American babies are born out of wedlock; nearly one-fourth are born to teenagers, and most of those teens are unmarried. Births to single African American women are two and one-half times higher than to single White women even though these rates in the White population have risen drastically in the past 6 years (U.S. Bureau of the Census, 1998). Research has pointed out, however, that "multiple mothering" is commonplace in African American families. That is, aunts, cousins, close friends, and fictive kin provide mothers with a range of modeling and tangible support, so that these families may be unlike the typical White model of a single parent (Greene, 1995).

Diverse Viewpoints of the African American Family

African American families have immense differentiation in cultural values and regional differences. Several viewpoints of the African American family have been held by social scientists and have influenced research, policy, and programs. Until 1965–1970 the major image of these families, particularly of poor African American families, was one of pathology and deviance. Most of these ideas developed because researchers failed to distinguish between factors of culture and class in family lifestyles. For many years it was believed that family structure determined social achievement.

Amuzie Chimezie (cited in Hale-Benson, 1986) believes that theorists of African American culture are divided broadly into two categories—negative and affirmative. Negative theorists deny the existence of an African American culture and attribute differences to class position; degree of poverty; and attendant social pathologies, that is, the *cultural deviant* approach.

In 1965 Daniel Patrick Moynihan published a report, *The Negro Family: The Case for National Action*. Moynihan's position was that slavery had destroyed African cultures and family patterns. The efforts of African American males to protect and support their families were so undermined that the men were not authority figures in their families; therefore, a matriarchal family emerged. The bond between the mother and the child became the most durable and meaningful feature of African American family life. The African American male did not have an opportunity to become acculturated to the dominant nuclear family form. The huge migration of African Americans to northern cities before World War I and later to inner-city sections of large cities in the United States only created more difficulties as African American men were thrown into highly competitive and racially discriminating situations. The family structure was further weakened, and desertion and divorce, sexual promiscuity, illegitimacy, crime, delinquency, and welfare dependency were thought to be characteristic of African American families.

Other writers, such as Frazier (1939) and Rainwater (1966), also contributed to the unfortunate idea that African American families were unstable, structurally weak, socially disorganized, and handicapped in performing essential family functions. In addition, African American families were said to be seriously deficient in necessary resources and competencies. It was felt that the extremely persistent negative conditions in which these families lived caused them to resort to adaptive strategies that produced expressive and violent behavior within the family as well as tendencies toward depression and a sense of fatalism. These attitudes were perpetuated from one generation to another. The idea of a cycle of poverty was a prevalent one in the 1960s. Those individuals who still hold to the viewpoint that African American families in general are deviant and pathological feel that the situation is growing steadily worse, because the number of African American divorces, out-of-wedlock births, and unemployed are increasing (Frazier, 1939; Moynihan, 1965; Rainwater, 1966; Staples & Mirandé, 1980).

On the other hand, the affirmative theorists subscribe to at least four different viewpoints. The first is the African Heritage theory, which is based on the assumption that certain African traits have been retained by African Americans and are evidenced in kinship patterns, marriage, sexuality, child rearing, and so forth (Hale-Benson, 1986). This viewpoint is sometimes referred to as the *cultural variant* approach and views African American families as culturally unique units.

The affirmative New World Experience theory attributes distinctiveness to the experiences of blacks in America rather than to African traditions. The Biculturation theory views African American culture as composed of African American and Euro-American elements in that African American children are socialized in both African American and Euro-American culture. However, there is lack of consensus about the importance of each culture to them.

The Eclectic theory recognizes a distinctive African American culture and attempts to identify the salient factors that are theoretically responsible for its cultural elements. These theorists believe that certain aspects of African American culture are African retentions and others arise from American experience. They emphasize that many factors influence and affect Black ways of life (Hale-Benson, 1986). Finally, some subscribe to the *cultural equivalent* approach, in which African American families are seen as culturally equivalent if they adhere to the White, middle-class lifestyle.

If one subscribes to the African Heritage theory, then one would contend that the development and behavioral styles of African American children differ as a result of growing up in a distinct culture. Hale-Benson (1986), an African Heritage theorist, pointed out a number of characteristics unique to African American culture that have roots in West Africa, which have resulted in the emergence of a distinct language system and particular behavioral characteristics. Apparently the aspects of African culture that have survived and been transmitted have occurred without conscious effort and so subtly that they are not thought of as Africanisms but may influence the manner in which African American children are parented (see Highlights).

Functions of African American Families

African American families are varied and complex. Depending partly on socioeconomic status, some families are adaptable and stable and are effective socializers of their children; others are marginal, operating close to their limits. The families who live in poverty have few resources and may demonstrate some of the negative characteristics that have been attributed to them. On the other hand, many families are resilient and resourceful, even in the absence of adequate financial resources (Greene, 1995).

Many people believe that the major function of African American parents is to transmit the cultural heritage of Africa and African America to their children, often in the form of accounts of the struggles, achievements, and defeats of African American heroes. Bicultural socialization often occurs, whereby both the aspects of African heritage and the realities of America are integral aspects. When rearing children, African American parents may have to resolve basic conflicts between European and African views, often being forced to ignore White child-rearing norms that are irrelevant to the existing situation of their children. Clearly, ethnic image is critical to promoting self-image (Greene, 1995; Hale, 1991; Julian, McHenry, & McKelvey, 1994).

Most African Americans have a large network of relatives and fictive kin (Padgett, 1997). Upward mobility does not seem to erase the sense of reciprocal obligation to kin, which suggests that the extended family is a cultural rather than an economic phenomenon. One study, controlling for income, found extended living arrangements twice as common among African American as among White households (cited in Taylor, Chatters, Tucker, & Lewis, 1991).

African Americans are more likely to socialize children without strict differences determined by the gender of the child and to share in child care and in decision making about

HIGHLIGHTS

Unique Traits of African American Families

Funerals	Motor habits—walking, speaking, dancing, burden carrying, and so on
Magical practices	
Folklore	Hairdressing—wrapping, braiding, cornrowing
Dance	Respect for elderly
Song	
Wearing of kerchiefs, scarves	

Source: Hale-Benson, J. (1986). *Black children: Their roots, culture, and learning styles* (Rev. ed.). Provo, UT: Brigham Young University Press.

child rearing (Allen & Majidi-Ahi, 1989). A study of rural two-parent African American families showed that fathers often are involved in child rearing, and men and women are beginning to share household tasks, even though the women still assume a greater share of the responsibility. However, a 1997 study by Padgett found that African American married women do two-thirds of the housework as compared to their husbands' one-third, and the division of labor was not affected by children's involvement in household work. Nevertheless, research has emphasized the gender-role flexibility of African American families as an important adaptive strategy that derives from valuing interdependence among group members (Greene, 1995).

Finally, African American families historically have valued education, hard work, achievement, and social mobility, though the gap is widening between those who are able to take advantage of educational opportunities and those who are not even aware of them.

Characteristics of African American Culture That Affect Parenting

Because of the emphasis on affective, interpersonal relations and the emotional, people-oriented characteristics of African American people, children are likely to grow up to be feeling-and people-oriented and more proficient in nonverbal communication skills than White children are. White children are more likely to be object-oriented, since they have had numerous opportunities to manipulate objects and to discover their properties and relationships. African American babies experience considerable human interaction with people of all ages. Babies often are encouraged to feel or to rub the holder's face, and a game of "rubbing each other's face" ensues. Infants and young children often sleep with their parents. There is a rhythm of sleeping and eating, with each activity being of short duration and the pattern repeated frequently.

Many African American parents expect early assumption of the child's responsibility for his bodily functions and personal feelings (Julian et al., 1994). Therefore, toilet learning is normally begun early and is stringent. This pattern is in startling contrast to that experienced by White infants whereby, after many months of paying no attention to wet and soiled diapers, the mother suddenly interferes and begins the toilet-learning process.

Verbal communication during infancy may be less important than other types of communication, such as looking deeply into the child's eyes and caressing the baby. Looking into the eyes is used by the mother to impress a point on the child. When African American school children refuse to look at their teachers, they may be trying to sever an intense level of communication that is typically shared among their people. Or, the child may feel that it is disrespectful to an authority figure to look him or her in the eye.

Cultural-specific values of African American families have been found in such areas as discipline, expectations regarding age- and sex-appropriate responsibilities, kin net-

HIGHLIGHTS

Characteristics of African American Culture That Affect Child Rearing

Feeling orientation	High degree of human interaction
People orientation	Biculturation
Proficiency in nonverbal communication skills	Multiple environmental stimuli

work, and awareness of racism. There is special emphasis in child rearing on respect for authority figures; strict discipline; a high value on a variety of responses, abilities, and talents; open receptivity to multiple environmental stimuli; and expression of emotions by both males and females. Many writers have emphasized that African American families use corporal punishment more than White families. However, many of these studies generalized the child-rearing behaviors of low-income African American mothers to all African American mothers, suggesting that African American families were a monolithic group (Bradley, 1998). Further, historically, models of child rearing developed with respect to the ethnic majority have been used as standards in comparing or evaluating minority parenting practices. Only recently have studies begun to focus on within-group differences. Blue-stone and Tamis-LeMonda (1999) found that substantive variation existed among African American parents in disciplinary strategies. The most common disciplinary strategies used with working- and middle-class African American mothers was reasoning—a characteristic of authoritative parenting. Physical punishment was reported relatively infrequently. Maternal depression and negative child-rearing histories were negatively associated with child-centered parenting styles, and higher levels of maternal education were positively associated with child-centered parenting.

Bradley (1998) also found that the middle-income African American parents (mothers and fathers) in her sample preferred to use nonphysical forms of discipline. However, parents did use an "order child not to" disciplinary technique that seems more associated with an authoritarian style. Several scholars have suggested that demanding obedience from African American children in some cases is imperative, given the life circumstances imposed on African American youth in a discriminatory society. Parents in this study used as disciplinary techniques only the belt and spanking with an open hand in severe contextual situations. In fact, physical punishment was used only when a child directly challenged the authority of the parent. This finding is consistent with the African American value of respecting elders and authority figures. Another study examined the parenting practices of low-income, White urban mothers with children 3 to 6 years old. The results indicated that all these mothers could not be characterized as "parent-centered" as opposed to "child-centered," a distinction often made between African American and White mothers. Some did use authoritarian control practices and demonstrated attitudes emphasizing obedience, but the correlations between these two characteristics were not significant—that is, they existed independently. Mothers who took the child's perspective in disciplinary encounters were as likely to use power assertion as those who were parent-centered, but mothers varied widely in their attitudes toward physical punishment. In this study, religious mothers were more likely to be child-oriented. Younger, less educated mothers who were raising their children alone and were less involved in religion placed more emphasis on respect for obedience and were more likely to use a parent-oriented approach, whereas older, more educated married mothers appeared to emphasize more autonomous behavior and use a more child-oriented democratic approach (Kelly, Power, & Wimbush, 1992).

Therefore, it appears that the most significant factors in differentiating parenting styles of African American parents are socioeconomic status, level of education, their own parenting histories, and presence or absence of depression.

African American Mothers

A strong bond seems to exist between African American mothers and their children. African American heritage emphasizes that children represent the continuity of life, and the mother role is highly valued. Whereas some researchers have described the African American family structure as matriarchal, with a domineering, pathological female as head, others have described the African American mother as strong, particularly in the sense that she has been able to maintain the dual role of wage earner and manager of a household. Contrary to the dominant cultural norm of women remaining at home to raise children, African American women have always worked outside the home (Greene, 1995).

The increasing out-of-wedlock birthrate may suggest that more young African American women desire to achieve the status of parenthood without becoming involved in the marital role. Even though most African Americans do not view childbearing outside of marriage as socially desirable, long-term shame and stigma are uncommon. In addition, African American females have a more restricted field of marriage eligibles and often marry less-educated men (Littlejohn-Blake & Darling, 1993). The accessibility and assistance of the kin network is particularly important to African American single mothers, especially if they are young and/or poor.

However, a recent study concerning African American mothers and grandmothers found surprising results that are in marked contrast to results of studies a decade ago (Chase-Lansdale, Brooks-Gunn, & Zamsky, 1994). The study included African American multi-generational families living below the poverty line. Contrary to expectations, the researchers found that grandmothers' parenting was not superior to that of the mothers, despite their age and experience. For mothers and grandmothers that co-resided, the correlations between mothering and grandmothering behaviors involved only the negative dimensions of parenting, especially for the younger childbearers and grandmothers. Harsh parenting showed continuity across generations, suggesting that negative ways of treating children are readily learned and modeled. However, mothers and grandmothers who lived apart were somewhat more likely to be similar in the positive dimensions of parenting. Co-residence seemed to have negative consequences on the quality of both mothers' and especially grandmothers' parenting for the sample as a whole. However, the age of the mother at first birth was a factor: When the mother was very young, co-residing grandmothers offered higher-quality parenting than non-co-residers—for example, positive emotional expression, more expert teaching skills, greater involvement and support, and warmth combined with appropriate discipline. But when mothers were older at first birth, the grandmothers' parenting quality was higher when their daughters lived independently with their children. It appears, then, that co-residence of mothers and grandmothers does not always have positive results.

Despite the large percentage of African American single-mother families, there has been considerable misinformation about the causes and consequences of this family type and a tendency to focus on their problems, ignoring the diversity that exists among African American families and their resilient, adaptive characteristics. Sudarkasa (1993) pointed out the importance of understanding the earlier African extended families out of which contemporary family structures evolved. Households headed by single parents, mostly women, were embraced as well as households headed by couples. The notion that female-headed households are the major cause of the deplorable conditions of poverty, crime, and hopelessness found among African Americans in many inner cities must be refuted. African American female-headed households have always had bases of support in other households and received critical support from brothers, sons, and uncles.

The frequent African American practice of informally "adopting" children not biologically related probably stems from the days of slavery when children often were separated from their parents without regard for family ties. These extended networks of kinship between biological and unrelated family members still exist today and carry with them networks of obligation and support (Greene, 1995).

Even though much has been written about the matriarchal theme in African American families and its consequences, in reality the egalitarian family pattern is common in intact families. Although it is not clear how prevalent the egalitarian pattern is, it does appear to be the norm for middle-class African American families.

African American Fathers

African American fathers have been neglected in the research on African American families, probably because they have not been as accessible as White fathers and have been perceived as being less significant persons to their families. Historically, African American fathers have been depicted as peripheral to family and as performing poorly in the family role of spouse and father. However, some investigators have found that the role of economic provider was a frequently cited role among both middle-income and blue-collar African American men. For middle-income fathers, central to their self-perceptions of being better providers for their families is the goal of exceeding the socioeconomic status of their own fathers. Personal income and age have been found to be associated with the likelihood that African American men will perceive themselves as good providers for their families. Having a higher personal income is associated with being married among African American men and satisfaction with family life among African American husbands (Taylor et al., 1991).

McAdoo (1991) has noted that when African Americans marry, they are expected to work cooperatively for the good of the marital unit; the family's survival depends on spousal cooperation. His research has found that couples share equally in decision making, demonstrating the same kind of decision-making pattern as other groups. Other research has shown that both fathers and mothers are involved in the racial socialization of their children (cited in Taylor et al., 1991).

Fathers' involvement in the basic caregiving of their preschool children in intact middle- to lower-income African American families was examined by Ahmeduzzaman and Roopnarine (1992). Their data revealed that fathers spent about one-third as much time as their wives in primary caregiving, and father's educational level, family income, communication, extrafamilial support, and length of time married were the chief variables associated with different dimensions of men's involvement with children. Men with higher incomes and better education and who had been married for longer periods of time were more likely to be involved with their preschoolers than those who had lower incomes and less education and who had been married for shorter periods of time. Men's ability to communicate in productive ways within the family was positively linked to their involvement with children. The stronger the commitment to the family, the more likely fathers were to rate their overall involvement and participation in child care as being greater. The more support fathers received from extrafamilial members, the more invested they were in the socialization and care of their children.

African American adolescent fathers are a diverse group in terms of age, timing of fatherhood in relation to work and education, number of children, length of fatherhood experience, relationship with the child's mother, and marital experience. One study found that young African American men were more likely than Hispanics or Whites to have had a nonmarital first birth and were least likely to live with that child. However, in comparison with other adolescent fathers, African Americans were more likely to complete high school. Another researcher suggested that the father's absence from the home of the mother and child does not necessarily reflect noninvolvement with parenting; minority fathers were more likely to be involved than were White fathers (cited in Taylor et al., 1991).

The recent research on African American fathers, though limited, does not support the stereotypical view that they are invisible and uninvolved with their children. In fact, African American married men are more likely to share housework and child care than White men are; there is more egalitarianism in household tasks between couples when the wife's employment status, earning power, and sex-role attitudes are controlled for. The greater the economic security of the family, the more active the father becomes in child rearing (Ahmeduzzaman & Roopnarine, 1992).

Rearing African American Children

African American children today are more likely than ever before to be born into devastating conditions of poverty and to be born to a mother who is not married and who lacked adequate prenatal care. These children are twice as likely as White children to die in the first year of their lives and three times as likely to be misplaced in classes for educable mentally retarded. They are twice as likely as White children to have a parent who is unemployed and to live in a substandard housing. African American teenagers are more likely today than 10 years ago to drop out of high school and to be unemployed. They are four times as likely as White teens to be incarcerated (Goduka, 1990).

These risks to the healthy development of children, especially those in inner cities, seem overwhelming. Yet, despite the odds, many African American children grow up to be well adjusted. The literature and the media do not emphasize the diversity of African American youth as individuals who come from different families, neighborhoods, communities, and socioeconomic backgrounds, but instead have focused on the problems identified earlier. As a result, little is really known about various aspects of the development and socialization of African American children (Taylor et al., 1991).

African American parents, like all other parents, play a crucial role in helping their children learn to participate successfully in society. As in other cultures, male and female African American children are reared differently. By the age of 3, most of them are no longer treated as babies. Early independence is valued, and many children assume responsibility for the care of younger siblings. For males the peer group is more important in the socialization process than for females. Male children are socialized into the peer group earlier and more completely than are females.

An important rite of passage into manhood by African American males is that of "playing the dozens," a verbal duel in which two males make derogatory comments about each other's family. Onlooking peers urge each on. The skills of each player are appreciated and judged by the peer group. To master this game, the boy must control his emotions so that he can think quickly and counter with an even more clever remark about a family member of his opponent. Learning to control one's emotions is an important aspect of socialization of the African American male (Hale-Benson, 1986). Urban youth have developed other ritualized games, such as "ribbin," "jivin," and "shuckin," possibly to cope with the stresses and strains of their environment.

In traditional families African American girls usually are given responsibility for the care of younger siblings and the household at an early age. Daughters are expected to be independent and capable of shouldering family responsibilities very early. African American mothers advocate acceleration of development. This emphasis helps to develop a strong motherhood orientation. Girls are not expected to have jobs outside the home until adolescence. The most frequent jobs for younger African American girls are baby-sitting and other domestic duties. In many families there is a strong emphasis on personal uniqueness. Girls are taught to develop their own style, sexuality, and personal distinctiveness. What one does and how it is done are both viewed as important. Personal attributes are considered more important than status or office.

Stevens (1997) noted that the socialization experiences of African American families are anchored in an African American cultural idiom. The girls in her study were observed employing ritual insult games, mostly verbal, to organize the context of their social environments. Most of these games centered on boys and were a means of exercising some control over their environments. The girls' assertive behavior was an emotive stylistic expression that is cultural, and they saw "arguing" as a demonstration of self-assertiveness and a sense of power. Self-esteem concerns were salient in the management of sexuality and gender development. Girls saw themselves competing with one another for a boy's attention or interest, and as a result, they engaged in physical fights and verbal insult games with their female peers. Stevens concluded that many African American females, at the onset of adolescence, experience a normative crisis of connection/disconnection with parents and their fictive kinship group as they try to negotiate relationships within the dominant culture for cultural/bicultural competence.

The peer group exerts a strong influence on both African American boys and African American girls. The peer group is critical for the continuation of the socialization process begun by the parents. It is a much more significant influence in families in which the father is absent or unemployed. African American fathers have been found to have somewhat distinct influences on the development of their sons and daughters. Father involvement is relevant for helping sons to avoid problem behaviors, whereas for daughters involvement helps to prevent psychological distress (Salem, Zimmerman, & Notaro, 1998). Identification with the peer group is achieved earlier and more completely for boys than for girls. For both sexes it is a significant influence during the teen years. Boys, particularly, affiliate with informal gangs and are likely to be dependent on and influenced by them greatly. Concepts of womanhood and manhood are learned from the peer group. Friends are viewed as the source of rewards, both material and nonmaterial. In many families, dating has begun by age 12, as well as a heavy commitment to a peer group of the same sex. By adolescence an intensely sexual, frequently exploitative, web of informal social relations may have developed between the sexes.

In summary, African American parents instill in their children respect for authority figures, a strong work ethic, emphasis on achievement, a sense of duty and obligation to kin, a strong religious orientation, self-esteem and pride in their cultural heritage, and the importance of coping skills and resiliency (Julian et al., 1994; Kane, 1998).

Resources for African American Families

A number of researchers have pointed out that one of the strengths of African American families is the extensive support system provided by a network of relatives, friends, and neighbors. This system provides emotional support and economic supplements, better enabling the family to handle adverse external forces. Since the majority of both African

American men and African American women work, this support system is even more important. The kin network has been vitally important as a coping strategy for large numbers of these families. The extended network is a more salient structure for African American than for White families. African Americans see more of their kin other than their parents than do White families. More Whites have living parents than African Americans do. Aunts frequently become mother substitutes in African American families (McAdoo, 1993).

Even though many African Americans are reared in nuclear families, a large number still receive instrumental or task-oriented help from a significant adult other than the parents. The unmarried, divorced, or widowed are most often integrated immediately into the extended-kin network. Some of the services provided by this expanded network system include assistance with finances; help in making important decisions; assistance in planning and carrying out special occasions; and providing clothing, food, furniture, and transportation to various places. Usually help is extended in the areas of greatest need. Among poor African Americans, the extended family assists in the socialization of children (McAdoo, 1993).

Kinship networks may be declining. The size of African American families is decreasing. Young women giving birth out of wedlock are more likely now to move into their own households than to stay with their families. In addition, greater numbers of divorced or widowed men and women who can support themselves are living by themselves.

Some African American researchers have noted that the extended family also can be a liability for the African American family. In some instances it may deter upward mobility. Once a family has achieved a higher status, the family may be expected to provide help for other extended-family members. Thus, professional and social upward mobility may be limited to some extent because of the necessity of providing physical and financial resources to members of the larger family. The dilemma of upward mobility versus meeting the everyday needs of extended-family members is a very real one.

It is felt by some experts that if the welfare of African American children in this country is to be significantly enhanced, a national commitment will have to be made to full employment, a guaranteed minimum income, a comprehensive program of child development and child care, meaningful education, decent housing, a restructuring of the health-care system, and reconsideration of foster-child placements. Further, this commitment will have to be translated into public policies and comprehensive programs at the national level. Most of these ideas were debated in the 1990s, but little progress has been made.

In sum, varying viewpoints of African American families in the United States are represented by the cultural deviant, cultural equivalent, and cultural variant approaches. Despite the lack of agreement among these approaches, it seems clear that the families are characterized by a number of behavior patterns and traditions that are significantly related to child-rearing practices.

There is considerable evidence to refute the persistent image of the African American family as being matriarchal. Egalitarianism in family roles seems to be more common than once believed, especially among the middle class. Nevertheless, African American mothers seem to be especially close to their children, and the differences in child-rearing patterns for male and female children seem to be especially visible. The network of relatives, friends, and neighbors who provide a support system for the families is seen as being a particular strength, but some believe that it has been a factor in limiting upward mobility.

Clearly it can be concluded that many African American families have been the victims of racism, poverty, and limited education, which accounts for many of the stereotypes that have held sway, and both future research and new programs are needed to completely replace these attitudes.

Future Research Needs

Over the last two decades a more balanced depiction of African American family life has emerged, with growing appreciation of the diversity of these families in both status and form. The tendency to compare African American families with the White middle-class family norm is just beginning to be replaced by research that examines differences within African American families. Research must consider the impact and interrelationships among factors that operate at varying levels and potentially manifest themselves through diverse behaviors and phenomena—for example, linkages between changes in family structure and alterations in family relationships and functioning. Research must occur within expanded disciplinary frameworks to avoid viewing African American family phenomena in isolation and separate from other perspectives. The tendency to view African American families as a collection of the problems and challenges they face has diverted attention from important and basic issues of family functions, structure, and relationships and has largely restricted the research focus to that of "problem Black families." Critics of African American family research have noted that simply making racial comparisons in which White behaviors are designated as the standard of baseline research invariably indicates the presence of deficiencies in African Americans. Future research must avoid this temptation (Taylor et al., 1991).

PARENTING IN MEXICAN AMERICAN FAMILIES

The principal origins of Hispanic people in the United States are Mexico, Puerto Rico, and Cuba, and the descendant population of all three groups is scattered widely. High immigration rates and birthrates have increased considerably the nation's Hispanic population in the last two decades. In 1996 Hispanics in the United States totaled more than 27 million, almost doubling since the 1980 census. Hispanics are concentrated in nine states, led by California and Texas (U.S. Bureau of the Census, 1997). Census data have often failed to distinguish the three Hispanic populations from one another by identifying a Hispanic as one with a Spanish origin, one with a Spanish surname, and/or one who uses the Spanish language. However, it has been pointed out that Hispanics of Mexican descent are considerably different on a number of characteristics from non-Mexican Hispanics.

In 1995 there were almost 18 million Mexican Americans, representing by far the largest Hispanic subgroup in this country. Ninety percent of Mexican Americans live in the West and the South. Though recent data suggest that Hispanics, especially those between the ages of 25 and 34, are getting much closer to non-Hispanics in completing high school and college, data reported in 1996 indicated that Mexican Americans (both males and females) complete fewer years of formal education and are less likely to graduate from high school than other Hispanics. Fifty-three percent of Mexican Americans have less than a high school education. Further, they are considerably lower on the occupational scale than other Hispanics, with Mexican Americans having higher percentages of manual laborers and farmers. Median incomes of Mexican American women are lower than those of all other, non-Mexican Hispanic women, and Mexican American men earn less than Cubano men (U.S. Bureau of the Census, 1997). It has been said, however, that Mexican Americans represent the nation's second largest and most rapidly growing ethnic group. Because of the differences among Mexican Americans and other Hispanics and because of the large number of Mexican Americans in this country, we have chosen to limit our discussion to parenting in Mexican American families.

Demographics

There are a number of demographic characteristics that differentiate the Mexican American family from the dominant White family in the United States. The first is its high fertility rate. Mexican Americans have the highest fertility rate of any major ethnic and racial group in the United States (U.S. Bureau of the Census, 1998). Attitudes and normative beliefs (what others think one should do) of significant others, combined with motivation to comply with those reference groups, have a relationship to whether Mexican American women will or will not have more children. Those with lower incomes, less education, lower parity, and of the Catholic faith are more influenced in fertility by their normative beliefs. Further, evidence suggests that the church's influence on the fertility of Mexican American women is considerably less than might be expected.

In 1996, 72 percent of Mexican American children under 18 lived with both parents in intact families, a figure higher than the population in general, but down from 81 percent in 1980. In 1996, 21 percent of Mexican American families with children under 18 were headed by females and 7% were headed by males. Recent data have challenged the long-held notion that Hispanic families have lower rates of marital disruption than others. Though the actual divorce rates for Mexican Americans are lower than for non-Hispanic Whites, when separations are included, the differences disappear. Marital stability is inversely related to level of education among Mexican Americans (U.S. Bureau of the Census, 1998).

In 1996, 76 percent of Mexican American males earned less than $25,000 per year, and the majority of females earned less than $20,000 per year. Thirty-one percent of all Mexican Americans and 34 percent of all Mexican American children live below the poverty line (U.S. Bureau of the Census, 1997).

Family Roles and Relationships

Many descriptions of Mexican American family life have presented negative, stereotypical views, with little optimism for the ultimate fate of Mexican American children. That image persisted for some time, but beginning in the late 1970s, a number of researchers began to challenge it. First, earlier researchers may have been guilty of using the dominant family structure as a yardstick by which to measure "deviant" family patterns in minority groups, failing to be sensitive to other cultural or ethnic systems. Second, many recent researchers have contended that earlier research was based on persistent traditional stereotypes rather than on convincing empirical evidence. Even when differences from the traditional images were found, they were attributed to the Mexican American family's acculturation or modernization, as if an acculturated family was somehow "more correct." Or data that did not fit the picture were ignored, discarded, or considered irrelevant (Mirandé, 1997; Zinn, 1979). In fact, one writer concluded that the works he reviewed on Mexican American culture and family life constituted an exercise in social science fiction and presented a distorted view of Mexican Americans as passive, masochistic vegetables controlled by traditional culture (Romano, 1973).

A very different image of Mexican American family life has emerged. Mexican American writers argue that *la familia* is a warm and nurturing institution rather than an unstable, pathological one. The traditional concept of *machismo* has been redefined in terms of family pride, respect, and honor rather than in terms of male dominance. In fact, this view asserts that the family is the most important unit in life and individuals are likely to put the needs of the family above their own. The family, then, is depicted as a stable structure in which one's place is firmly established and cooperation among family members is emphasized. An important part of the concept of machismo is seen as the father's using his authority within the family in a fair and just manner. If he misuses his authority, he risks losing respect within the family and the community (Staples & Mirandé, 1980).

The family orientation of Mexican Americans has been a consistent theme in the literature for decades and has led to the traditional extended-family stereotype. In attempting to clarify many of the assumptions and interpretations that have produced pejorative images of these families, recent researchers have maintained that despite the adaptive requirements of acculturation and urbanization, Mexican Americans still enjoy large extended-family networks. It has been found that they participate in relatively large kin networks and engage in high rates of visiting and exchange. They are more willing than some other ethnic groups to agree that the family should be the resource for dealing with problems. Because of geographic closeness, kin are available and are used for meeting instrumental and affective needs. Whereas non-Hispanics have a tendency to migrate away from kin networks, Mexican Americans have a tendency to migrate toward them. Kinship ties seem to be an enjoyable and expected set of practices and attitudes (Vega, 1991).

Education and income have been reported to be the best predictors of more available support and more contact with network members. Historically, a case has been made for kinship networks as exchange systems for people who are economically marginal, but researchers have noted emotional support as the main outcome of familism (the tendency to favor interaction and social support over other alternatives). Several researchers have reconfirmed the familistic orientation of Mexican Americans by noting that the family is the major source of advice and help across generations, but the acculturation process has created distinctive intergenerational expectations (Vega, 1991).

There is both evidence for continuity in traditional cultural gender expectations and evidence of more egalitarian relationships. In fact, studies have found a range of gender roles, from a patriarchal, role-segregated structure to an egalitarian, joint-role structure, with many combinations of these two polar opposites evident (Vega, 1991). It has been found that the availability of employment is the most important determinant of whether Mexican American women work. Chilman (1993) noted that a woman's power in relationships within and outside the family tends to increase when she is employed outside the home and has acquired a high level of education and independent income. When these roles shift, there may be considerable stress involved. Many investigators emphasize, however, that Mexican American families, like other Hispanic families, are adaptive, and gender-role expectations change as social conditions require.

Some scholars have described Mexican American family systems as extended, enmeshed, dense, and self-reliant (Vega, Kolody, & Valle, 1986). Recent studies have indicated that familism, and hence the availability of social support, increases with each generation living in this country. These findings contradict earlier views that the highest degrees of familism correlate with "Mexicanness" and Mexican birth and would become weaker in subsequent generations (Vega et al., 1986). Nevertheless, the consequential role of familism among Mexican Americans, especially with regard to expressive support, cannot be overemphasized. Mexican American families have been described as "closed systems," with intense, multiplex relationships and with members who underutilize mental-health services. Perhaps this is due to the stress-buffering qualities of an endogenous support system. Familism is a basic source of emotional support for children. "Family" includes not only parents but also aunts and uncles, grandparents, cousins, and even friends. In fact, there is little distinction made between relatives and friends—often they are one and the same. The custom of compadres that dates to the colonial times remains intact in many families, with Mexican American adults reporting at least one, two, or three such relationships. Often these friends serve as godparents to the children. This kinship web imposes the obligation of mutual aid, respect, and affection (Ramirez, 1989).

Few important differences have been found between non-Hispanic Whites and Mexican Americans on marital satisfaction, wife labor-force participation, role expectation, family dynamics, or conjugal power (Vega et al., 1986). Further, few major differences have been found between Whites and Mexican Americans on dimensions of family functioning, such as cohesion and adaptability. Mexican American families are well functioning and resilient. Cohesion has been found to be highest at the early stages of the family life cycle, to decrease as children reach adolescence and thereafter, but to rise again as children leave home. Adaptability also decreases as families move through the child-rearing years and increases again when children leave home (Vega et al., 1986).

It is important to emphasize that there is no one typical Mexican American family, just as there is no one typical White family. Obviously such factors as education, income, age, geographic location, and time of migration to the United States contribute to a diversity of family types. In fact, time of immigration seems to have a fairly significant impact on the socialization of children (Buriel, 1993).

Rearing Mexican American Children

Only a few studies have been conducted on the child-rearing attitudes and practices of Mexican American parents, and those that exist fail to provide consistent conclusions. Some researchers have concluded that Mexican American parents are primarily permissive, whereas others have suggested that traditional values and authoritarian practices are more prevalent. Still others describe Mexican American families as nurturing and affectionate within a patriarchal, authoritarian family structure, with unusual respect for males and the elderly (Martinez, 1988).

One writer (Ramirez, 1989) noted that *el amor de madre* (motherly love) is a greater force in Mexican American families than wifely love; that is, the parent-child relationship is more important than the spousal relationship. Most homes are child-centered when children are young. Though there is an emphasis on good behavior, much nurturance and protection are provided to young children. There is a basic acceptance of the child's individuality and a relaxed attitude toward achievement of developmental milestones. As children approach the latency period and later (age 5 or so until puberty), parents begin to expect more responsible behavior from children; they are assigned tasks or responsibilities in accordance with their age and ability.

A recent observational study of predominantly lower-class mothers and their young children found few permissive Mexican American mothers, and authoritative and authoritarian mothers were about equal in number. Authoritative parents use rational, issue-oriented discipline techniques and set firm limits within a loving context. This style of child rearing is characteristic of White middle-class mothers but is thought to be inconsistent with the communal values of Mexican Americans. Although these results suggest that at least some Mexican American mothers resemble White mothers in their child-rearing patterns, others clearly do not (Martinez, 1993).

HIGHLIGHTS

Characteristics of Mexican American Families

Strong family ties
Migration toward kin networks
Emotional support
Two-parent participation in child rearing
Range of gender roles
Mutual aid, respect, affection

Authoritative, authoritarian, and permissive
  child-rearing styles
Differences in child rearing according to gender
  of child
Deference and respect accorded to fathers

Dumka, Roosa, and Jackson (1997) examined mothers' parenting and children's adjustment in low-income Mexican immigrant and Mexican American families. Mothers' supportive parenting was found to partially mediate the effects of family conflict on children's depression. High levels of supportive parenting were linked to low levels of children's depression and low levels of child conduct disorders, whereas high levels of inconsistent parenting were related to higher levels of children's depression and conduct disorder. Further, higher maternal acculturation was related to greater consistency in discipline, which then led to reduced depression in children.

The home environment of Mexican American children may vary according to their generation status. Shared cultural variables, particularly Spanish-language background and achievement aspirations, vary as a function of generational status. Surprisingly, first- and second-generation children often perform better in school than their third-generation counterparts, suggesting that immigrant parents, particularly mothers, may pass on high aspirations to their children (Buriel, 1993). Further, there is substantial variation in the degree of Spanish retention in each generation. One study found that personal aspirations were by far the most potent predictors of first, second, and third generations of Mexican American students, and that socioeconomic status was unrelated to most measures. These results seem to suggest that the strength of the relationship of socioeconomic status to achievement may be greater for White students than for Mexican American students (Buriel & Cardoza, 1988).

However, Buriel (1993) later found that child-rearing orientations of Mexican Americans differed with parents' education and income, but significantly with whether children were first-, second-, or third-generation immigrants. On average, years of schooling and family incomes are highest in the third generation. Further, changes in language usage may correlate with changes in child-rearing styles. Buriel found that mothers born in Mexico (where children were first- and second-generation immigrants) stressed early autonomy, productive use of time, strictness, and permissiveness more than mothers of third-generation children. Fathers of first- and second-generation children are similar to their spouses in areas of autonomy, strictness, and support. By contrast, fathers of third-generation children expect early autonomy of daughters only and less strictness of sons. Further, foreign-born parents score high on valuing responsibility, whereas U.S.-born parents score high on concern. Emphasis on a concern style reflects a shift toward the child-rearing norms of mainstream Euro-American society, arising from acculturation. However, the author concluded that a child-rearing style resembling responsibility may be crucial in fostering healthy social and academic development in Mexican American adolescents because delinquency and school achievement seem to be two serious problems among Mexican American adolescents who are third-generation immigrants.

As with other ethnic minority groups, there appear to be gender differences in the rearing of Mexican American children that become especially prominent at adolescence. Mothers seem to be particularly close to their daughters, and this closeness extends into and beyond puberty. The mother-son relationship is close but not as strong as that of mother and daughter. Fathers appear warm and affectionate when children are young and are playful companions. Some evidence suggests, however, that fathers become more aloof as children approach puberty, assuming the role of primary disciplinarian. Sons often are pampered and indulged more than daughters during childhood, and at adolescence they have far more freedom than girls do. Males often are encouraged to gain worldly knowledge outside the home, whereas females are likely to remain close to home and be protected and guarded in their contacts outside the family to preserve femininity and innocence (Ramirez, 1989).

One study suggested that Mexican American adolescents undergo the identity process somewhat differently from the way White adolescents do. Specifically, Mexican Americans have been found to be more "foreclosed" than Whites are on ideological identity, even when socioeconomic status is held constant; that is, they tend to adopt wholesale the commitments of others, usually their parents, without first testing the fit for themselves. Males are inclined to be more foreclosed and less "identity achieved" than females. This phenomenon may be due to the fact that minority status exposes Mexican Americans to a narrower range of available occupational and ideological roles and commitments than Whites, or there may be actual cultural differences in ways the two groups develop identity because of parental socialization techniques. The differences between the two groups in resolving difficulties such as sex roles, dating, friendship, and recreational preferences were less than differences related to issues of political and religious ideology, philosophical lifestyle, and occupation. Foreclosure is associated with warmth and support, but also a highly controlling parental style is optimal for effectively guiding youth into preconceived roles (Abraham, 1986).

Peers contribute significantly to the socialization of adolescent males, whereas adolescent females are more confined to the home and rely more heavily on mothers and sisters. The value of premarital chastity for females still exists, but its enforcement is more difficult than in the past. Even though strong role differentiation for males and females has persisted, there is evidence that many young Mexican Americans are challenging their traditional roles, thereby establishing more equality customs, governance, language, income, and religion. Therefore, there are no absolute universal cultural norms for Indians (Dykeman & Nelson, 1995; Pipes et al., 1993).

Demographics

Contrary to popular belief, Native Americans are not a dying breed. At the present time, they number 22.3 million and are expected to reach 4.6 million by the year 2050. Between the 1980 and 1990 census, there was an increase of 38 percent in the Native American population. Approximately 35 percent of American Indians live on reservations or other tribally controlled land (U.S. Bureau of the Census, 1997), and an additional 13 percent live near or adjacent to Indian reservations (Pipes et al., 1993). The Bureau of Indian Affairs (BIA) has noted that more Indians have recently been returning to the reservations and that fewer are leaving. This phenomenon—combined with fewer infant deaths, better health services, and high fertility rates—accounts for part of the increase in population. Though American Indians can be found throughout the United States, five states contain the majority of Native Americans residing on reservations: Arizona, New Mexico, South Dakota, Montana, and Washington. American Indians have the longest tenure in this country of all racial minorities.

In 1996, 66 percent of family households were married couples, 26 percent were headed by single males. In 1990 the average family size was 3.6, with household size varying on the reservations from 3.5 (Blackfeet) to 4.6 (Zuni). Rural Indian families are larger than urban ones, sometimes having five or more children, and Indian families as a group have more children under the age of 18 than does the general U.S. population. About half of Indian households include other relatives, and about one-fourth include individuals unrelated to the family (U.S. Bureau of the Census, 1993, 1997).

American Indians are among the most impoverished groups in the United States. Median income varies across tribes, ranging from just over $13,000 (Navajo) to just under $25,000 (Cherokee), with an average median income being $21,619. Thirty-one percent of Native American individuals and 27 percent of families are below the poverty line (U.S. Bureau of the Census, 1997). The 1990 census reported that more than half of American Indians living on reservations were below the poverty line, but there are vast differences among the reservations. For example, 49 percent on the Hopi reservation were poor as compared with 67 percent on the Pine Ridge reservation. In 1990 the per capita income for Native Americans living on reservations was $4,478, ranging from a low of $3,113 to a high of $4,718. It is estimated that 50 percent of families maintained by females are below the poverty line (U.S. Bureau of the Census, 1993).

In 1990, 69 percent of all American Indian males older than 16 were employed, but the figure fell to 62 percent on the reservations, again with considerable variation among the reservations. The proportion of females in the labor force increased from 48 percent in 1980 to 55 percent in 1990. Educational attainment has increased; in 1980, 56 percent of the population had graduated from high school, and in 1990, 67 percent had diplomas. On the 10 largest reservations, the figure for high school graduates drops to 54 percent, with a high of 66 percent (Blackfeet) and a low of 37 percent (Gila River) (U.S. Bureau of the Census, 1993).

Native Americans have an alcoholism rate 3.8 times that of the other ethnic groups; cirrhosis of the liver is 4.5 times higher. The homicide rate is 2.8 times higher than in other groups, and the suicide rate is 2.3 times higher. The mortality rate from motor vehicle accidents is 5.5 times higher, and the infant mortality rate is twice the national average. One-third of Native Americans are classified as illiterate (LaFromboise & Low, 1989). Native Americans have the highest birthrate in the United States and the highest mortality rate. In 1990 only 8 percent of the American Indian population was 60 years or older, which is about half the proportion for the total U.S. population.

Housing, sanitation, and health characteristics are significantly inferior for many Native Americans, especially those that live on the reservations. Some dwellings lack water and electricity, and at least one-fifth of reservations lack complete plumbing. On the Navajo and Hopi reservations, respectively, 49 percent and 47 percent of the homes still lack complete plumbing (U.S. Bureau of the Census, 1993). Marginal incomes, substandard housing, poor transportation, and inadequate nutrition make American Indians more vulnerable to a variety of health problems. In 1955 the Indian Health Service assumed responsibility for Indian health care. Although death rates due to health problems are considerably higher than for the U.S. population as a whole, there has been a marked decrease since 1955. It can be concluded that even though conditions are improving for American Indians, as a group they are the most in need of services of all groups in this country.

Family Structure

Native American families are extremely diverse. Family structure, values, and roles and relationships differ from tribe to tribe. Actually, little is known about Native American families, and the knowledge is fragmented, anecdotal, descriptive, and often overpowered by poor understanding of tribal cultures. However, there is little disagreement among researchers that the family remains the basic unit of Native American society and community. Extended-family ties are very strong (Dykeman & Nelson, 1995). Native American families represent a combination of traditional beliefs, languages, and practices. They are characterized by a unique history and lifestyle and are supported by the strengths of their individual and tribal identity.

The traditional Native American family system is vastly different from other extended-family units in this country. These networks are structurally open, assume a village-type characteristic, and are usually composed of clans, which include several household of relatives. "Family" is defined by some tribes in terms of household composition, the extended family through second cousins, and clan membership (Carson, Dail, Greeley, & Kenote, 1990). The roles of family members and the structure of the extended family vary across tribes. Traditionally, they live in relational networks that serve to support and nurture strong bonds of mutual assistance and affection. Many engage in the traditional system of collective interdependence, with family members responsible not only to one another but also to the clan and the tribe (La Fromboise & Low, 1989).

Relationships between family members and the community can be complex. The degree of social and governing control exhibited by women or men depends on the tribe. Some tribes are more matriarchal, and others, patriarchal (LaFromboise & Low, 1989). Although the extended-family network is rapidly changing on many reservations, it is still a major factor contributing to family strengths. Guidance and wisdom received from elders facilitate family cohesion and resiliency, and the personal support from extended-family members and the community, especially during times of crisis, contributes immensely to family strengths (Carson et al., 1990).

Some Native American family systems can cover a broad geographic region and in fact represent an interstate family structure, with several households in each of several states. Still other family structures represent a small community in an urban area; for example, several households of the same family may be in close proximity to one another within an urban community. Finally, family households may be spread among several communities or cities of a metropolitan area. All these types of family structure represent lateral extension. Nevertheless, the family remains a repository of values and guides behavior through all stages of the life cycle (London & Devore, 1988).

Native Americans view their extended family as a source of strength and perennial support, offering multiple opportunities for the effective socialization of children, but some feel that the extended-family system is greatly misunderstood by human-service professionals. There have been numerous attempts to impose the traditional Western model of the nuclear monogamous family or Native Americans, but they have struggled continuously to maintain their tribal identities and at the same time their special relationships with the federal government. Generally, Native Americans have not wanted or acquiesced to acculturation and assimilation into mainstream society. Instead of being viewed as a culturally variant but well-functioning society, they have largely received societal ridicule for their resistance to the norms and models of middle-class American society.

Value Orientation

The value systems of Native Americans as a group have consistent themes, with tribal-specific expectations. Common among all tribal groups are tribal loyalty, respect for elders, reticence, humility, avoidance of personal glory and gain, giving and sharing with as many as three generations of relatives, precedence of group goals over individual goals, rich oral traditions, group cohesion and consensus, and an abiding love for their land (Dykeman & Nelson, 1995; London & Devore, 1988; Pipes et al., 1993).

Other values include responsibility, courage, patience, optimism, and contentment that is derived from a cosmic identity, a spiritual orientation to life, and traditional religious practices. Living in harmony with all of nature, including human beings, is paramount, and the world of nature often is used as a tool for learning both within and beyond the family (Carson et al., 1990). Native Americans may feel indifferent toward acquiring material goods. Traditionally, the acquiring of "things" for the sake of ownership or status is not as important as being a good person (Little Soldier, 1992).

Many Native Americans tend to view time as flowing and relative—things are done as the need arises rather than by the clock or according to some future-oriented master plan. Time is perceived as flexible and geared to the activity at hand. There is a tendency to live in the present and seek immediate gratification (Little Soldier, 1992).

Most Native Americans value noninterference. Any kind of intervention (for example, by social workers) is contrary to Indians' strict adherence to the principle of self-determination. The less assimilated and acculturated the individual, the more important this principle is to him or her. Further, the majority culture norm of quick self-disclosure in therapeutic intervention does not extend to American Indians (Dykeman & Nelson, 1995). These phenomena characterize Navajos; the tribes of the northern and southern plains; and to some extent, other tribes and the Pueblo Indians. It is not clear from the literature how much can be generalized based on these values (Strauss, 1986).

Parent-Child Interactions

Perhaps because of the diverse nature of American Indians, there is little systematic knowledge about parenting styles and how they vary from tribe to tribe. Further, because few widely used developmental tests have been standardized for American Indian populations, we have little insight into the development of American Indian children. However, child-rearing practices are shaped largely by Indian worldviews, which regard children as beloved gifts. Native Americans are described as having a "beautiful blindness" toward children with disabilities (Pipes et al., 1993). Time spent caring for, playing with, and

HIGHLIGHTS

Characteristics of Native American Families

High poverty rates
Diverse values, roles, and relationships across tribes
Family is the basic unit of society and community
"Family" includes household residents, extended family, and clan members
Relational networks support and nurture strong bonds of mutual assistance and affection
Elders provide guidance and wisdom
Many individuals participate in child rearing
Living in harmony with nature is valued
Participation in tribal ceremonies and rites of passage
Group-oriented philosophy

admiring children is cherished. Native Americans celebrate milestones in early childhood, such as the first steps, first smile, first word, and so forth, but no pressure is felt over the timing of these events (LaFromboise & Low, 1989).

The most striking difference in child rearing and socialization is the exposure of children to a wide array of persons to whom they can become attached—parents, siblings, aunts, uncles, cousins, and grandparents—thus protecting children and providing them with the assurance of love (Dykeman & Nelson, 1995). Grandmothers and aunts, and in some tribes men, share in child care. The extended family plays as much a role in child rearing, supervision of children, and the transgenerational transmission of teachings and customs as do parents. Grandparents perpetuate the oral tradition—they are safekeepers of tribal stories. They engage in purposeful activities with grandchildren that are geared toward passing on cultural values and beliefs and educating children about the physical, social, and spiritual world. There also are indirect lines of communication about children's behavior—for example, from the mother to the aunt or uncle—that serve to protect the bonds between parents and youth (Carson et al., 1990; LaFromboise & Low, 1989).

Children are regarded as important to the family and are accorded as much respect as adults—adults rarely hit children. In fact, physical punishment usually is not condoned. Parents more often use facial expressions and other body language to indicate disapproval, or they use social shame (embarrassment). Shouting when correcting a child is disapproved of. Autonomy is highly valued, and children are expected to make their own decisions and to operate semi-independently at an early age. Parents give children choices and allow them to experience the natural consequences of them. The impact of the child's behavior on others is emphasized. Children are not socialized to expect praise for that which is already required of them; parents reserve praise for special accomplishments. It is these characteristics of parenting that sometimes are perceived as overly permissive or negligent by nontribal social workers.

Families encourage children and youth to participate in tribal ceremonies, and parents devote considerable time and effort to making items for children to wear or to use in ceremonies. Traditional rites of passage that are symbolic of entrance into adulthood are common, and these practices are an integral part of the maintenance of individual, family, and tribal identity (Carson et al., 1990).

Native American children demonstrate lower school achievement than most other groups, and they have the highest dropout rate. These problems are due to a number of factors, including health and family problems, geographic distances from schools, absenteeism (sometimes because of tribal ceremonies), and lack of culturally relevant instructional materials and approaches to learning. White teachers who are unfamiliar with tribal cultures frequently interpret language and cultural differences as deviant. For example, most White teachers focus on verbal instruction, whereas most Indian children learn better through visual means. Lack of eye contact is the most notable difference frequently cited between White and Native American children. Some tribes consider it rude and disrespectful to make direct eye contact with authority figures. A bowed head is a sign of respect (Pipes et al., 1993).

As Indian children enter school, they often feel stranded between two cultures. Many speak a first language other than English, practice an entirely different religion, and hold different cultural values, yet they are expected to perform successfully according to conventional White criteria. Native American children in the upper elementary grades often are perceived as uncommunicative, but silence is comfortable in traditional Native American culture. Further, when there is pressure for a right answer, Native American children would rather remain silent than risk being called upon and being embarrassed and ridiculed. Since these children have grown up with a group-oriented philosophy, striving for individual achievement is foreign to their world outside of school. They prefer anonymity, harmony, and cooperative rather than competitive learning. Because children are likely to feel marginal in both cultures, biculturalism must become an educational priority (Little Soldier, 1992). During the past two decades, Indian education has come under increasing tribal control, and there is more emphasis on tribal history, Indian languages, and increased self-esteem.

The Indian Child Welfare Act

The Indian Child Welfare Act (ICWA) became law in 1978, after 4 years of congressional lobbying. The intent of Congress was to increase the probability that tribal children would grow up in tribal environments. Research had indicated a high correlation between children's removal from tribal cultural settings and subsequent problems with parenting, alcoholism, and suicide (Blanchard & Barsh, 1980). However, passage of the act has caused concern, controversy, and misunderstanding among social workers, particularly between Indians and non-Indians. They cannot agree on how much American Indian children and families benefit by provisions of the act.

American Indians themselves have been gravely concerned about the barriers that have existed to the reunification of American Indian families after separation of a staggering percentage of children from their families. Placing children in non-Indian homes, not allowing parents to visit their children while the children are in substitute care, placing children at great distances from their homes, a series of foster-care placements over a short time, and the disruptive responses of children following visits by their parents have all been viewed as obstacles to family reunification. Thus, the ICWA was initiated. The law returns to tribes the responsibility for and jurisdiction over American Indian children.

According to Goodluck (1989), the enactment of the ICWA brought about the following improvements: an increase in tribal family and children's programs, an increase in tribal service delivery systems on the reservation for abused and neglected children, and an increase in ICWA training and leadership opportunities for direct staff and administrators. In addition, significant case law has been developed that confirms the original act's goals and objectives, specifically to promote the security and well-being of children within the tribal context and to prevent the unnecessary breakup of extended families. The findings of three national centers that have researched and surveyed the impact of the act indicate that it has made a difference, but many problems continue. Their findings show that Native American children are still being placed at a higher rate, but the placements are at the direction of the tribal systems, under the supervision of tribal workers, and within Native American homes, which encourage tribal value systems.

In sum, it is difficult to make generalizations about parenting in American Indian families. Because of their diversity, family lifestyles cannot be studied easily; and because of Native Americans' resistance to being studied by non-Indian researchers who are critical and biased, even less data are available. To be sure, there are strengths in traditional Native American values and practices that have not been emphasized in the literature by those with little understanding of this minority culture. And further, the status of Native American families is in a state of transition. Nevertheless, it seems imperative that educators, social workers, psychologists, and health personnel make an effort to understand and appreciate the heritage of Native American families so that those children can experience a sense of competence and self-satisfaction in on- or off-reservation situations.

Further Research Needs

There is no doubt that adaptive behavior must be understood within a sociocultural environment. Future research must test treatments that are adaptable to both tribal and non-tribal environments. Researchers require deeper insight into the Native American heritage of values and family structure and the role of culture in the child's overall development. Assistance programs must provide support to Native American families in the form of child care, counseling, homemaker services, alcohol- and drug-abuse programs, respite care, foster-care and adoption subsidies, legal counseling, and protective services programs for children. And, finally, Native Americans themselves must be given greater opportunity to prepare for careers as psychologists, health personnel, social workers, and anthropologists so that the body of really insightful data can be enlarged.

PARENTING IN ASIAN AMERICAN FAMILIES

The literature on Asian American families is scant in comparison with the research on other cultural groups, especially African American and Mexican American families. Asian Americans have been described as the "model minority." In fact, they represent a diverse, heterogeneous population, including Japanese Americans, Chinese Americans, Filipino Americans, Korean Americans, Vietnamese Americans, and other Southeast Asian refugees. Therefore, there is considerable variation among these groups in demographic characteristics, values, family traditions, and parent-child interactions. Further, the time of immigration to the United States seems to affect the degree of acculturation and assimilation into mainstream American culture, with third- and fourth-generation Asian Americans demonstrating more similarity to the majority culture than first- and second-generation immigrants. This section will focus primarily on Japanese Americans and Chinese Americans and Chinese Americans, the two groups for whom the most data exist.

Historical Perspectives

Chinese immigrants came to the United States in two streams of different character: The first began in the 1820s when impoverished rural Chinese came to work on the railroads and in the mines; the second began in 1847 and consisted of middle- and upper-class Chinese who came to seek higher education or to join relatives who had professional degrees (Young-Shi & McAdoo, 1993). Another influx of Chinese immigrants into the United States began to occur in the 1960s.

Early Japanese immigration to California was similar to that of the Chinese. Large-scale emigration of Japanese people to America began in the late 1880s. After the passage of the Chinese Exclusion Act in 1882, Japanese laborers were brought in to replace the departing Chinese laborers.

The Chinese system of patrilineal descent divided household property and land equally among adult sons, usually upon the marriage of the youngest son. Responsibility for the support of aging parents was shared by all the sons. Conversely, daughters married out of the village, did not inherit property, and were not responsible for the support of elderly parents. For those fortunate enough, ownership of property and land provided a strong tie to the Chinese village of emigration. Therefore, to ensure a continuing bond to family and village, emigrating Chinese men were expected to leave their wives and children behind. "Without the establishment of families in America, there was little incentive for early Chinese immigrants to invest in acquiring the cultural and social skills necessary to get on in Anglo society" (Nee & Wong, 1985, p. 289).

Like the Chinese, early Japanese immigrants came to America as temporary residents, to earn the higher wages available here and to return to Japan upon completion of their work contracts. However, differences in Japanese and Chinese rural social structure resulted in a weaker tie to family and village for Japanese immigrants. The Japanese inheritance system was one in which one son, usually the oldest, inherited the property and land and was responsible for the care of aging parents. Younger sons could pursue their fortunes elsewhere; therefore, the extended-kinship system in Japanese villages was much weaker than in Chinese villages. By the second decade of sustained Japanese immigration, the formation of families became important. The weaker tie to family and village in Japan permitted the early formation of Japanese family life in America, and by 1920, there was a sizable second generation of Japanese Americans in this country.

These differences had implications for the well-being of the two groups in America. As long as the Chinese viewed their American experience as temporary, failing to establish families and produce a large second generation, they retained the characteristics of low educational attainment and high illiteracy. To make matters worse, a strong anti-Chinese movement emerged, characterized by ethnic antagonism and violence, culminating in the passage of the Chinese Exclusion Act in the early 1880s. Thus, it was more than 80 years after the beginning of large-scale immigration of Chinese and the formation of immigrant families in America before significant socioeconomic gains occurred (Nee & Wong, 1985).

On the other hand, by 1920 the sizable second generation of Japanese American children began to enter American public schools and to achieve the high educational goals that still characterize this population. The transition from Japanese sojourner to settler was much more rapid, then, than that for Chinese immigrants. Nevertheless, both groups experienced considerable discrimination and hostility. Since World War II, all Asian Americans have made significant socioeconomic gains. However, the large influx of Chinese immigrants in the 1960s has had the effect of lowering the overall socioeconomic profile of Chinese Americans, compared with that of Japanese Americans (Nee & Wong, 1985).

Demographics

Chinese Americans—the largest Asian American population, numbering approximately 2.3 million—are an extremely heterogeneous group socially, politically, and culturally. They emigrated from a number of provinces in China and countries in Asia and thus speak a variety of dialects. The majority of the population now resides along the East and West coasts and around metropolitan areas. Chinese Americans have among the highest incomes of many ethnic minorities, with the median family income being approximately $38,000 in 1990 (U.S. Bureau of the Census, 1993). However, many are unemployed or underemployed, receiving lower wages than their peers for comparable work, especially recent immigrants. Therefore, they span the range of socioeconomic status. Even though education is highly valued, there is still a high percentage of Chinese American illiterates (Huang & Ying, 1989). Seventy-four percent of Chinese Americans 25 years and older have finished high school, and 41 percent have bachelor's degrees or higher (Lee, 1998).

Japanese Americans are the third largest Asian American population—numbering approximately 925,000, behind Chinese Americans and Filipino Americans—and are concentrated in the West and in Hawaii. However, the Japanese American population has been declining—from 21 percent of all Asian Americans in 1980 to 10 percent in 2000. The outmarriage rate of Japanese Americans (rate of marriages to persons outside their population) is greater than 60 percent. With the declining population and the increasing outmarriage rate, many worry that the Japanese American culture and values will disappear altogether. Hawaiian Japanese Americans live in an environment with many Asian Americans and tend to preserve their Japanese culture to a greater degree than their mainland counterparts. Differences also exist between those in Los Angeles, where there is a concentrated population, and those in Chicago, where they are widely dispersed (Lee, 1998).

Educationally, Japanese Americans are above the national average, with almost all of the population finishing high school. Not surprisingly, they have one of the highest incomes of all groups (median family income was nearly $52,000 in 1990) and one of the lowest poverty rates (7 percent in 1990). In fact, it has been reported that Japanese American households have the second highest income in the country, second to Jews, presumably because of outstanding achievement in educational attainment. Another factor contributing to their economic status is low rates of separation and divorce, resulting in 85 percent of children under 18 living with two parents. Still, some Japanese Americans are underemployed, making less than their non-Asian peers. Japanese Americans have low rates of delinquency, and they are underrepresented in child-abuse statistics (Lee, 1998; Nagata, 1989).

Chinese American Families

Family Characteristics. The historical and cultural antecedents of Chinese family characteristics derive from Confucian traditions, passed from one generation to the next, which still impose an Eastern philosophy on Chinese American families. Confucian philosophy dictated a sense of order and prescribed role relationships in Chinese society. Guidelines were provided for specific family relationships and patterns of communication. Negotiations with the outside world were delineated, with the goal of harmonious existence in society.

There was strong emphasis in traditional Chinese society on specific family roles and the proper behavior associated with each. The role structure was vertical and hierarchal, with the father as the undisputed head of the family. The obligations, responsibilities, and privileges of each role were clearly delineated. The father's authority was unchallenged, and he received total respect and loyalty from all family members. In return, he assumed maximum responsibility for the family's social status and economic well-being. The mother was responsible for emotional nurturance of family members and for their psychological well-being, her primary role being to serve her husband and rear the children. Though she was less removed and distant than the father, she was accorded respect by the children. She was discouraged from working outside the home. In traditional Chinese families, there also were gender and birth privileges, with sons more highly valued than daughters. Lineage was passed through the male, whereas females were absorbed into the families of their husbands. The role of female was less rewarding because females did not gain status and respect until they became mothers-in-law (Huang & Ying, 1989; Yau & Smetana, 1996).

As China has modernized, these roles have changed radically, and only derivatives of them may be found in Chinese American culture. For example, contemporary fathers may be figurative heads of families, with the mother as the driving force and the decision maker behind the scenes. Male/female role distinctions are far less glaring. Many Chinese Americans have attempted to reconstruct the kin network, with the extended family as the primary unit, but these relationships often have become disrupted. Some still see the extended family as an important source of social and sometimes financial support, but others see it as a burden and a restriction of autonomy.

In traditional Chinese families, gender and age governed the degree of open expression allowed, as well as the structure of the language used and the topics discussed. Even now, expression of emotion generally is frowned upon and suppression of undesirable thoughts or emotions is highly valued, views that are in stark contrast to the American value of speaking one's mind. Reciprocity in interaction that is obligatory and unspoken is still of paramount importance. Behavior is often dictated by a sense of obligation or, conversely, to avoid being in a situation of obligation. Shame and loss of face are guiding principles of behavior and powerful motivating forces for conforming to family and societal expectations. Even honesty and truthfulness are secondary to saving face for self and for others. Interdependence is the foundation of Chinese culture, with group values being more highly valued than individual desires (Huang & Ying, 1989; Miller, Wiley, Fung, & Hui Lang, 1997; Yau & Smetana, 1996).

Parent-Child Interactions. Individuals in Chinese society are believed to have the potential from within to achieve fulfillment and happiness. A sincere effort to conduct oneself morally and to develop one's potential brings personal satisfaction. *Filial piety* is a central Confucian concept and has governed intergenerational Chinese families for centuries. It is a complex system that involves a series of obligations of child to parent—most centrally to provide aid to, comfort to, affection to, and contact with the parent and to bring glory to the parent by doing well in educational and occupational areas, that is, achieving success in the outside world. It means that children are expected to satisfy their parents, to respect and to show reverence for elders in all situations (Kelley & Tseng, 1992; Lin & Liu, 1993). The concept of filial piety, or *hsiao*, is deeply ingrained in Chinese culture and has served as the moral foundation of interpersonal relationships in China for centuries: "To encourage the hsiao of a son to his parents is also to encourage the loyalty of the people to the ruler" (Lin & Liu, 1993, p. 272).

Miller et al. (1997) described how storytelling functions as a means of socialization, but in different ways, for Chinese and American parents of 2-year-olds. Chinese parents were much more likely than American parents to tell stories about their children's transgressions, apparently viewing the child's transgressions as a way of teaching young children the appropriate rules of conduct. American parents were more likely to use the child's past experiences in stories for entertainment and affirmation. Other research has noted the subtle nature of Chinese American mothers' interactions with their children.

Chinese parents are very concerned about the education of their children and want them to do well academically. Traditional parents frequently insist that children learn a Chinese language. The parents' attitudes toward their heritage in a dominant society have always been considered to play a significant role in the children's cognitive development and mental health. Young-Shi and McAdoo (1993) found that parents' attitudes toward Chinese culture and language usage with children were significantly correlated with boys' self-concept.

According to Kelley and Tseng (1992), Chinese parents tend to be warm, affectionate, and lenient toward infants and young children, but once they reach the "age of understanding," discipline becomes much more strict. Children are taught mutual dependence, group identification, self-discipline, and good manners, as well as the importance of education. Departure from parental goals is seen as a reflection on the parents; therefore, parents take complete responsibility for the development of their children and are very involved in child rearing. They view the parenting role mainly as one of teacher.

Gorman (1998) noted that even though Chinese parenting historically has been seen as more authoritarian than mainstream American parenting, some research suggests that authoritarian parenting may be a Western concept that does not accurately depict Chinese socialization. Gorman found little rule setting for adolescents among the Chinese mothers in the study, suggesting that these mothers did not characterize their roles as including domination and control. Rather, these mothers perceived that they were training their children, giving them guidance, and helping them to make good decisions; that is, they provided pertinent information and arguments but left the final decision in their children's hands. This approach is consistent with the Chinese cultural value of individual responsibility. Expectations for their children were based on mothers' deep desires for children's successful adjustment rather than on a need to dominate their children. Mothers were concerned about making sure their children became productive members of society and were not negatively influenced by their peers. Lack of concern over their children's academics was striking. Few mothers reported problems with their children's academic behavior, suggesting that influences on academics may be more indirect and subtle than traditionally identified means of involvement and influence. Mothers preferred the indirect approach to dealing with differences of opinion, rather than badgering, arguing with, or coercing their children. This style of interaction appears to reflect the cultural value of self-sufficiency and the importance of reaching the "age of understanding."

The author concluded that Chinese parenting is characterized by an interaction of expectations and filial obligation rather than parental control and child submission. Though the expectations were communicated in subtle ways, they appeared to be understood clearly by the children. This balance between subtle expression of parental expectations and compliance stemming from a deep sense of filial obligation appears to be at the root of many of these mothers' interactions with their adolescents.

Yau and Smetana (1996) examined adolescent-parent conflict in lower-class Chinese early, mid-, and late adolescents. They noted that adolescent-parent conflict reflects the development of autonomy during adolescence in both Chinese and American cultures. Conflicts over everyday issues of family life occurred frequently and were of moderate intensity. Conflicts emerged primarily over issues of exercising or maintaining personal jurisdiction. In this study, conflicts over homework and academic achievement and over teen behaviors (smoking, leisure activities, relations between parents and themselves) were reported more frequently by Chinese than American adolescents. Further, Chinese teenagers were more subtle and indirect in expressing disagreements with parents than American adolescents. Girls reported more conflicts than boys, and conflicts were primarily with mothers rather than fathers. Chinese adolescents reported their parents as warm but controlling, and mothers were warmer than fathers.

The father-son dyad is prominent in Chinese society, and parents often have a strong voice in the son's selection of a spouse. Even into adulthood, Chinese children remain emotionally and often financially attached to their parents. It is common for the adult child to move into an occupational position provided by family contacts. Whereas cooperation and obedience are highly valued, independence training is not. There is frequent giving and receiving of help between the generations—an indication of family solidarity. The Chinese maintain their self-esteem by having someone to depend on. The Chinese elderly are highly influential and highly valued; their experience is the major source of knowledge to children, and they are seen as a link to the gods (Lin & Liu, 1993).

Kelley and Tseng (1992) compared the child-rearing practices of immigrant Chinese and White mothers. The results suggested that the two groups had similar child-rearing goals, but immigrant Chinese mothers relied on traditional Chinese methods of socialization to achieve those goals. These mothers were maintaining strong bonds to Chinese culture, as evidenced by their participation in a church where Chinese was spoken and their children's attendance at a Chinese-language program. Chinese mothers reported a higher degree of physical control over their children, including the use of harsh scolding. However, both groups of mothers reported reliance on rule setting, with White mothers relying more heavily on this approach. Chinese mothers also reported less nurturance, responsiveness, and consistency and were more restrictive with their children than White mothers.

The use of reasoning was reported by both groups. The authors believe this approach to be uncommon in traditional Chinese families and suggest that this finding represents a shift in younger-generation Chinese away from traditional child-rearing patterns. Again, contrary to historical perceptions, no differences were observed in the degree to which mothers emphasized obedience. Also contrary to the results of previous research, abrupt changes in Chinese parenting behavior did not occur when the child entered primary school.

The subjects in the Kelly and Tseng study were first-generation Chinese Americans. Even so, some departure from traditional parenting practices was found. A complete understanding of parent-child relationships in these families will not be possible without continued research that includes second-, third-, and even fourth-generation Chinese American families from a range of socioeconomic levels.

Japanese American Families

Family Characteristics. Japanese American adults typically have been perceived to be successful, well acculturated, and mentally healthy, and their children often are seen as being obedient and educationally successful. Though these families have tended to remain intact, generational changes and outmarriage rates have affected the nature of family characteristics. Families vary enormously in the extent to which they have maintained the characteristics of the traditional family, which are as follows: emphasis on the household as the most important entity for early socialization and upbringing; emphasis on the group rather than the individual; loyalty; importance of rank and status; emphasis on ascribed and contractual obligations; vertical relationships (meaning that relationships are clearly defined to those above or below one's social status); conformity to societal norms; and social control based on shame and guilt. Authority of the traditional family is vested in the father and older male children (Nagata, 1989).

It has been said that Japanese American values, skills, attitudes, and behavior do not differ markedly from those of the average American. A possible explanation is that as white-collar and professional jobs opened to Japanese Americans in post-World War II, they moved into White residential suburbs and assimilated into American society. Their dispersed pattern reduced visibility as a racial minority and promoted higher outmarriage rates. Further, the concentration of family-run small businesses provides the economic basis for stable family life and resources to support high educational attainment. The combination of values compatibility, high educational attainment, and family stability account for the socioeconomic parity that Japanese Americans have achieved with middle- and upper-class Americans, despite a history of discrimination, and that is quite unlike the status of other minorities (Lee, 1998; Nee & Wong, 1985). Each successive generation of Japanese Americans is more acculturated than the last, and today's Japanese Americans probably are more influenced by American society than by their parents and grandparents (Nagata, 1989).

Parent-Child Interactions. Both middle-class White mothers and Japanese American mothers are child-centered; however, they tend to perceive and treat very young children in fundamentally different ways. The Japanese mother is likely to organize her interactions with her infant so as to consolidate and strengthen a mutual dependence between herself and her infant, and her goal is a passive, accommodative, placid baby. Some researchers maintain that in traditional Japanese families, training in behavioral deportment begins in infancy. Cross-cultural researchers have concluded that because of different patterns of interaction with their mothers in the United States and Japan, infants have learned how to behave in different and culturally appropriate ways by 3 to 4 months of age (Bornstein, 1989).

Japanese American mothers expect early mastery of emotional maturity, self-control, and social courtesy in their preschoolers. Culturally specific goals that Japanese American parents have for their school-age children include patience, persistence, and accommodation. There is an emphasis on prolonged dependency, obedience and conformity, and indirect, nonconfrontational techniques of parenting that rely on nonverbal communication. There is a reluctance to praise achievements and a hesitancy to speak out or to ask questions. Emotions tend to be repressed or internalized rather than expressed (Nagata, 1989).

A pervasive Japanese cultural value is to know one's role, accept one's place in society, and work hard to perform faithfully one's assigned task. Okagaki and Sternberg (1993) noted that both Japanese and White middle-class mothers value independence in children. For White mothers, the independence takes the form of assertiveness; for Japanese mothers, independence means that the child is able to enter into relationships of mutual sympathy, trust, and consideration—consistent with the central values of interdependence, cooperation, and collaboration. In their recent study, these researchers found that both White and Japanese American mothers gave higher importance ratings to the goals on teaching first and second graders socially conforming behaviors (e.g., following directions and obeying school rules) than to teaching socially autonomous behaviors (e.g., how to make friends and how to make decisions). However, unlike White parents, the Japanese American parents saw noncognitive attributes (such as motivation, social skills, and working hard) as important as or more so than cognitive skills.

One can conclude that middle-class White parents and traditional Japanese parents share many of the same goals for their children, notably educational achievement and economic security, but differ dramatically in the ways in which they reach those goals.

HIGHLIGHTS

Characteristics of Asian American Families

CHINESE AMERICANS	JAPANESE AMERICANS
Father is undisputed head of family	Authority vested in father and older male children
"Saving face" an important guiding principle	Emphasis on group as opposed to individual
Role differentiation	Loyalty
Gender and birth privileges	Child-centeredness
Obligatory reciprocity in interactions	Emphasis on prolonged dependency, obedience,
Interdependence/group values	conformity, and nonconfrontational parenting
Filial piety (*hsiao*)	techniques
High achievement expectations	High educational and achievement expectations
Value on cooperation and obedience	High family stability
Elders are highly valued	High level of parental education and income

However, generational status and acculturation level apparently influence the degree to which contemporary Japanese Americans maintain traditional child-rearing philosophies.

Summary

The Asian American population in the United States, which represents about 4 percent of the total population, consists of Chinese Americans, Filipino Americans, Japanese Americans, Korean Americans, Vietnamese Americans, and other Southeast Asian refugees. They are, then, a diverse and heterogeneous population, speaking many different languages and dialects. This section has focused on Chinese Americans and Japanese Americans, whose emigration patterns were very different, which accounts for some of the differences between the two groups today.

Emphasis on education and achievement in both groups has resulted in a high standard of living, at least for Japanese Americans. Families tend to remain small (1.1 to 1.4 children per family) and intact, and great emphasis is placed upon interdependence in family relationships, creating prescribed obligations of children to their parents. Fathers and sons (especially eldest sons) are the authority figures, and the social structure is vertical.

Although the child-rearing values between Asian American parents and middle-class American parents are similar in some ways, the particular child-rearing patterns used between the groups appear to differ. However, the longer Asian American families have resided in the United States, the more likely they are to be influenced by American behaviors. It is important, however, to emphasize that in some families, there is uncertainty about identification with the old and new cultures, and role relationships may become confused. Identifying differences in values and social norms among cultural groups and explicitly acknowledging the difficulties of simultaneously living in two social worlds may help children to succeed in creating a way of life that reflects the traditions, values, and languages of both cultures (Okagaki & Sternberg, 1993).

SIMILARITIES AND DIFFERENCES AMONG CULTURES

Because there are many subcultures in the United States, we do not have a single identifiable pattern of parent-child interactions or child-rearing techniques. Because we are a democratic society that values freedom of religion, freedom of speech, freedom of the press, and freedom of unique family values, cultural differences in parent-child interactions are evident. Each subculture has unique language patterns, each has traditional rituals, and each has its own perceptions of family structure, roles, and functioning.

In many ways the similarities among cultures are striking. Children are valued and respected, but the outward manifestations may be quite different. White cultures seem to value individualism over familism, whereas African Americans, Mexican Americans, Native Americans, and Asian Americans demonstrate strong relational bonds with family members. The traditional stereotype of African American families as matriarchal and of Mexican American families and Asian American families as patriarchal has been replaced by a more contemporary attitude of egalitarianism. Many members of African American, Mexican American, Native American, and Asian American cultures have become acculturated to the degree that they resemble the majority culture more than they do their own minority culture.

Most differences in parenting style are related less to ethnic background than to geographic location, level of education, and income. Recently there has been an attempt to preserve much of the cultural heritage of these minority groups. Surely one's cultural heritage affects one's life in many ways, regardless of the effort to become "assimilated" or "acculturated" into mainstream society. Even greater emphasis may need to be put on the preservation of language, values, rituals, and ethnic traditions in our pluralistic society. At the least, greater effort should be made to understand, appreciate, and cultivate the unique characteristics of our minority populations.

SUMMARY

Variations in parenting attitudes and styles are evident among the diverse cultural groups in the United States. This chapter has addressed the characteristics of and similarities and differences among four such groups—African Americans, Mexican Americans, Native Americans, and Asian Americans. Many other cultures exist in this country; unfortunately, space prohibits the discussion of additional groups.

A key variable relating to parenting practices in any ethnic or cultural group is the socioeconomic status of the families constituting that group. The literature of the 1960s and the early 1970s identified significant differences among lower- and middle-class parents in several areas. Contemporary research has found that the quality of the environment in low-income families is generally lower than for middle- and upper-class families. Fairly consistent differences in parental behavior also have been found. Many observers have emphasized that within-class differences may be as great as between-class differences.

The four ethnic groups discussed in this chapter clearly have distinctive characteristics; some derive from the cultural heritage of the group itself, and some are more related to the minority status the group has experienced for an extended period of time. However, those families that have been assimilated into the majority culture and have achieved middle-class status tend to use parenting practices that are similar to those of White middle-class society.

More objective research and support are needed to emphasize the strengths of culturally diverse groups and to determine how best to preserve these strengths through healthy parent-child relationships. Only then will damaging stereotypes be eliminated.

REFERENCES

Abraham, K. (1986). Ego-identity differences among Anglo-American and Mexican-American adolescents. *Journal of Adolescence*, 2, 151–166.

Ahmeduzzaman, M., & Roopnarine, J. (1992). Socio-demographic factors, functioning style, social support, and fathers' involvement with preschoolers in African-American families. *Journal of Marriage and the Family*, 54(3), 699–707.

Allen, L., & Majidi-Ahi, S. (1989). Black American children. In J. Gibbs et al. (Eds.), *Children of color* (pp. 148–178). San Francisco: Jossey-Bass.

Bee, H., Van Egeren, L., Streissguth, A., Nyman, B., & Leckie, M. (1969). Social class differences in maternal strategies and speech patterns. *Developmental Psychology*, 1, 726–734.

Blanchard, E., & Barsh, R. (1980). What is best for tribal children? A response to Fischler. *Social Work*, 25, 350–357.

Bluestone, C., & Tamis-LeMonda, C. (1999). Correlates of parenting styles in predominantly working- and middle-class African American mothers. *Journal of Marriage and the Family*, 61(4), 881–894.

Bolger, K., Patterson, C., Thompson, W., & Kupersmidt, J. (1995). Psychosocial adjustment among children experiencing persistent and intermittent family economic hardship. *Child Development*, 66, 1107–1129.

Bornstein, M. (1989). Cross-cultural comparisons: The case of Japanese-American infant and mother activities and interactions. What we know, what we need to know, and why we need to know it. *Developmental Review, 9,* 171–204.

Bradley, C. (1998). Child rearing in African American families: A study of the disciplinary practices of African American parents. *Journal of Multicultural Counseling and Development, 26*(4), 273–282.

Buriel, R. (1993). Childrearing orientations in Mexican American families: The influence of generation and sociocultural factors. *Journal of Marriage and the Family, 55*(4), 987–1001.

Buriel, R., & Cardoza, D. (1988). Sociocultural correlates of achievement among three generations of Mexican-American high school seniors. *American Education Research Journal, 25*(2), 177–192.

Carson, D., Dail, P., Greeley, S., & Kenote, T. (1990). Stresses and strengths of Native American reservation families in poverty. *Family Perspective, 24*(4), 383–400.

Chase-Lansdale, P., Brooks-Gunn, J., & Zamsky, (1994). Young African-American multigeneration families in poverty: Quality of mothering and grandmothering. *Child Development, 65*(2), 373–393.

Chilman, C. (1993). Hispanic families in the United States. In H. McAdoo (Ed.), *Family ethnic Strength in diversity* (pp. 141–163). Newbury Park, CA: Sage.

Clarke-Stewart, A. (1977). *Child care in the family review of research and some propositions for policy.* New York: Academic.

Conger, R., Ge, X., Elder, G., Lorenz, F., & Simons (1994). Economic stress, coercive family process and developmental problems of adolescents. *Child Development, 65*(2), 541–561.

Dodge, K., Pettit, G., & Bates, J. (1994). Socialization mediators of the relation between socioeconomic status and child conduct problems. *Child Development, 65*(2), 649–665.

Dumka, L., Roosa, M., & Jackson, K. (1997). Risk conflict, mothers' parenting, and children's adjustment in low-income, Mexican immigrant, and Mexican-American families. *Journal of Marriage and the Family, 59,* 309–323.

Duncan, G., Brooks-Gunn, J., & Klebanov, P. (1998 Economic deprivation and early childhood development. *Child Development, 65*(2), 296–318.

Dykeman, C., & Nelson, J. (1995). Building strong working alliances with American Indian families. *Social Work in Education, 17*(3), 148–159.

Felner, R., Brand, S., DuBois, D., Adan, A., Mulhall P., & Evans E. (1995). Socioeconomic disadvantage, proximal environmental experiences, and socioemotional and academic adjustment in early adolescence: Investigation of a mediated effects model. *Child Development, 66,* 774–792.

Forum on Child & Family Statistics. (1999). *American children: Key national indicators of well-being, 1999* [On-line]. Available: *http://www.childstats.gov/.*

Frazier, E. (1939). *The Negro family in the United States.* Chicago: University of Chicago Press.

Garrett, P., Ng' Andu, N., & Ferron, J. (1994). Poverty experiences of young children and the quality of their home environment. *Child Development, 65 (2)* 331–345.

Goduka, I. (1990). Racialization of poverty—American apartheid: Where does it leave the black child? *Family Perspective, 24*(4), 373–382.

Goodluck, C. (1989). Social services with Native Americans: Current status of the Indian Child Welfare Act. In J. Gibbs et al. (Eds.), *Children of Color* (pp. 217–226). San Francisco: Jossey-Bass.

Gorman, J. (1998). Parenting attitudes and practices of immigrant Chinese mothers of adolescents. *Family Relations, 47,* 73–80.

Greene, B. (1995). African American Families. *National Forum, 75*(3), 29–33.

Hale, J. (1991). The transmission of cultural values to young African American children. *Young Children, 46(6),* 7–15.

Hale-Benson, J. (1986), *Black children: Their roots, culture, and learning styles* (Rev. ed.). Baltimore: Johns Hopkins University Press.

Hashima, P., & Amato, P. (1994). Poverty, social support, and parental behavior. *Child Development, 65*(2), 394–403.

Hess, R., & Shipman, V. (1965). Early experience and the socialization of cognitive modes in young children. *Child Development, 36*, 869–886.

Huang, L., & Ying, Y. (1989). Chinese American children and adolescents. In J. Gibbs et al. (Eds.), *Children of color* (pp. 30–66). San Francisco: Jossey-Bass.

Huston, A., McLoyd, V., & Coll, C. (1994). Children and poverty: Issues in contemporary research. *Child Development, 65*(2), 275–282.

Julian, T., McKenry, P., & McKelvey, M. (1994). Perceptions of Caucasian, African-American, Hispanic, and Asian-American parents. *Family Relations, 43*, 30–37.

Kaiser, A., & Delaney, E. (1996). The effects of poverty on parenting young children. *Peabody Journal of Education, 71*(4), 66–85.

Kalil, A., & Eccles, J. (1998). Does welfare affect family processes and adolescent adjustment? *Child Development, 69*(6), 1597–1613.

Kane, C. (1998). Differences in family of origin perceptions among African American, Asian American, and Hispanic American college students. *Journal of Black Studies, 29*(2), 93–106.

Kelley, M., Power, T., & Wimbush, D. (1992). Determinants of disciplinary practices in low-income black mothers. *Child Development, 63*(3), 573–582.

Kelley, M., & Tseng, H. (1992). Cultural differences in child rearing. *Journal of Cross Cultural Psychology; 23*(4), 444–455.

Klebanov, P., Brooks-Gunn, J., McCarton, C., & McCormick, M. (1998). The contribution of neighborhood and family income to developmental test scores over the first three years of life. *Child Development, 69*(5), 1420–1436.

LaFromboise, T., & Low, K. (1989). American Indian children and adolescents. In J. Gibbs et al. (Eds.), *Children of color* (pp. 114–147). San Francisco: Jossey-Bass.

Lee, S. (1998). Asian Americans: Diverse and growing. *Population Bulletin, 55*(2), Washington DC: Population Reference Bureau.

Lin, C., & Liu, W. (1993). Intergenerational relationships among Chinese immigrant families from Taiwan. In H. McAdoo (Ed.), *Family ethnicity: Strength in diversity* (pp. 271–286). Newbury Park, CA: Sage.

Littlejohn-Blake, S., & Darling, C. (1993). Understanding the strengths of African American families. *Journal of Black Studies, 23*(4), 460–472.

Little Soldier, L. (1992). Working with Native American children. *Young Children, 47*(6), 15–21.

London, H., & Devore, W. (1988). Layers of understanding: Counseling ethnic minority families. *Family Relations, 37*(30), 310–314.

Martinez, E. (1988). Child behavior in Mexican American/Chicano families: Maternal teaching and childrearing practices. *Family Relations, 37*(3), 275–280.

Martinez, E. (1993). Parenting young children in Mexican-American/Chicano families. In H. McAdoo (Ed.), *Family ethnicity: Strength in diversity* (pp. 184–192). Newbury Park, CA: Sage.

McAdoo, J. (1993). Decision making and marital satisfaction in African American families. In H. McAdoo (Ed.), *Family ethnicity: Strength in diversity* (pp. 109–119). Newbury Park, CA: Sage.

McLeod, J., & Shanahan, M. (1993). Poverty, parenting, and children's mental health. *American Sociological Review, 58*, 351–366.

McLoyd, V., Jayaratne, T., Ceballo, R., & Borquez, J. (1994). Unemployment and work interruption among African American single mothers: Effects on parenting and adolescent socioemotional functioning. *Child Development, 65*(2), 562–589.

Miller, J., & Davis, D. (1997). Poverty history, marital history, and quality of children's home environments. *Journal of Marriage and the Family, 59*, 996–1007.

Miller, P., Wiley, A., Fung, H., & Hui Liang. (1997). Personal storytelling as a medium of socialization in Chinese and American families. *Child Development, 68*(3), 557–568.

Mirandé. A. (1977). The Chicano family: A reanalysis of conflicting views. *Journal of Marriage and the Family, 39*(4), 747–756.

Moynihan, D. (1965). *The Negro family: The case for national action*. Washington DC: U.S. Government Printing Office.

Nagata, D. (1989). Japanese American children and adolescents. In J. Gibbs et al. (Eds.), *Children of color* (pp. 67–113). San Francisco: Jossey-Bass.

Nee. V., & Wong. H. (1985). Asian American socioeconomic achievement: The strength of the family bond. *Sociological Perspectives, 28*(3), 281–306.

Okagaki, L., & Sternberg, R. (1993). Parental beliefs and children's school performance. *Child Development, 64*(1), 36–56.

Padgett, D. (1997). The contribution of support networks to household labor in African American families. *Journal of Family Issues, 18*(3), 227–250.

Pipes, M., Westby, C., & Inglebret, E. (1993). Profile of Native American students. In L. Clark (Ed.), *Faculty and student challenges in facing cultural-linguistic diversity*. Springfield, IL: Thomas.

Rainwater, L. (1966). The crucible of identity: The lower class Negro family. *Daedalus*, 95, 258–264.

Ramirez, O. (1989). Mexican American children and adolescents. In J. Gibbs et al. (Eds.). *Children of color* (pp. 224–250). San Francisco: Jossey-Bass.

Romano, O. (1973). The anthropology and sociology of Mexican-Americans: The distortion of Mexican-American history. In O. Romano (Ed.), *Voices: Readings from El Grito, a journal of contemporary Mexican-American thought* (pp. 43–56). Berkeley, CA: Qunto Sal.

Salem, D., Zimmerman, M., & Notaro, P. (1998). Effects of family structure, family process, and father involvement on psychosocial outcomes among African American adolescents. *Family Relations, 47*, 331–341.

Sampson, R., & Laub, J. (1994). Urban poverty and the family context of delinquency: A new look at structure and process in a classic study. *Child Development, 65*(2), 523–540.

Staples, R., & Mirandé, A. (1980). Racial and cultural variations among American families: A decennial review of the literature on minority families. *Journal of Marriage and the Family, 42*(4), 887–903.

Stevens, J. (1997). African American female adolescent identity development: A three-dimensional perspective. *Child Welfare, LXXVI*(1), 145–172.

Strauss, J. (1986). The study of American Indian families: Implications for applied research. *Family Perspectives, 20*(4), 337–350.

Sudarkasa, N. (1993). Female-headed African American households. In H. McAdoo (Ed.), *Family ethnicity: Strength in diversity* (pp. 81–89). Newbury Park, CA: Sage.

Taylor, R., Chatters, L., Tucker, M., & Lewis, E. (1991). Developments in research on black families: A decade review. In A. Booth (Ed.), *Contemporary families: Looking forward, looking back* (pp. 275–296). Minneapolis: National Council on Family Relations.

U.S. Bureau of the Census. (1993). *Statistical abstract of the United States: 1993* (113th ed.). Washington, DC: U.S. Department of Commerce.

U.S. Bureau of the Census. (1997). *Statistical abstract of the United States: 1997* (117th ed.). Washington, DC: U.S. Department of Commerce.

U.S. Bureau of the Census. (1998). *Statistical abstract of the United States: 1998* (118th ed.). Washington, DC: U.S. Department of Commerce.

U.S. General Accounting Office. (1992). *Poverty trends. 1980–88: Changes in family composition and income sources among the poor*. Washington, DC: Author.

Vega, W. (1991). Hispanic families in the 1980s: A decade of research. In A. Booth (Ed.). *Contemporary families: Looking forward, looking back* (pp. 297–306). Minneapolis: National Council on Family Relations.

Vega, W., Kolody, B., & Valle, R. (1986). The relationship of marital status, confident support, and depression among Mexican immigrant women. *Journal of Marriage and the Family, 48*(3), 597–605.

Walker, D., Greenwood, C., Hart, B., & Carta, J. (1994). Prediction of school outcomes based on early language production and socioeconomic factors. *Child Development, 65*(2), 606–621.

Yau, J., & Smetana, J. (1996). Adolescent-parent conflict among Chinese adolescents in Hong Kong. *Child Development, 67*, 1262–1275.

Young-Shi, O., & McAdoo, H. (1993). Socialization of Chinese American children. In H. McAdoo (Ed.), *Family ethnicity: Strength in diversity* (pp. 245–270). Newbury Park, CA: Sage.

Zinn, M. (1979). Chicano family research: Conceptual distortions and alternative directions. *Journal of Ethnic Studies, 7*(3), 59–71.

13

VIETNAMESE AMERICAN FAMILIES

Nazli Kibria

With the settlement of about 0.5 million refugees from 1975 to 1985, Vietnamese Americans became one of the largest Asian-origin populations in the United States. In 1990, they were estimated to be the sixth largest Asian American group, numbering 593,423. In the decades to come, Vietnamese Americans are expected to be a significant presence, particularly in California and Texas.[1] This chapter provides a descriptive overview of the family life of Vietnamese immigrants in the United States, paying particular attention to the effects of the migration process on Vietnamese American family patterns. Data from historical and demographic studies of Vietnamese refugee families are supplemented with materials from an ethnographic study, based on in-depth interviews and participant observation of Vietnamese refugees in Philadelphia during the mid-1980s (Kibria 1993).

The chapter begins with a brief description of the historical context of Vietnamese settlement in the United States. This is followed by a discussion of the key demographic characteristics of the Vietnamese American population, such as its age and gender composition and rates of marriage, divorce, and childbearing. The next sections of the chapter deal with family and household structures and the dynamics of family roles and authority.

THE VIETNAMESE EXODUS

The exodus of refugees out of Vietnam, which began in 1975 and continued through the 1990s, is a process that has deep and complex roots in the contemporary history of Vietnam, including the military, political, and economic involvement of the United States with South Vietnam. Vietnam was colonized by France in 1883. The French presence in Vietnam continued until 1954, when the country was partitioned across the middle into the "North" and the "South." South Vietnam became closely allied with the West, particularly with the United States, which was interested in supporting the South Vietnamese government's efforts to defeat the Communist regime that had been established in the North. The U.S. military, political, and economic involvement in South Vietnam escalated during the 1960s as the conflict between the two Vietnamese regimes grew in scope. The long war ended in 1975, soon after the military withdrawal of the United States from Vietnam, when Northern forces gained control of the South and the country was reunited under Communist rule. Shortly before the fall of Saigon to Communist rule, about 130,000 Vietnamese were flown into the United States as part of an evacuation effort designed to aid South Vietnamese employees and associates of the U.S. government. Often referred to as the "first-wave" refugees, the 1975 arrivals tended to be from the elite strata of South Vietnamese society, with high levels of education and occupational attainment (Baker and North 1984).[2]

Largely unanticipated by the U.S. government was the continuing flow of refugees out of Vietnam after the 1975 evacuation. These later waves of Vietnamese refugees were driven to leave the homeland by the political and economic policies of the Communist government. Many of these refugees had been persecuted by the new government because of association with the former South Vietnamese government. For example, some were sent to the "reeducation camps" set up by the new government to indoctrinate and punish those associated with the former regime. Those South Vietnamese who had drawn on the urban business and service sectors for their livelihood were also affected by the new government's economic policies, particularly the efforts to nationalize businesses. These policies particularly impacted the Chinese minority in Vietnam, a group that had been prominent in commerce and trading activities. In the late 1970s, the Chinese were also subject to discriminatory policies such as reduced food rations and the forced closure of Chinese-language newspapers and schools. As a result, during the 1978 to 1979 period, the Chinese Vietnamese accounted for about 70 percent of the "boat people" leaving Vietnam (Wain 1981). Another factor that spurred the outflow of people from Vietnam was the compulsory military draft imposed by the Vietnamese government in the late 1970s in order to cope with ongoing military conflicts in the region. Motivated by a desire to escape compulsory military service, young men constituted a large portion of Vietnamese arrivals to the United States during the 1980s.

As a group, post-1975 Vietnamese refugees differ from the 1975 evacuees in a number of ways. Unlike the 1975 evacuees, these later arrivals (often referred to as "boat people") have left Vietnam via covert boat journeys, taking them to nearby asylum countries such as Thailand, Malaysia, and Hong Kong. In the refugee camps that had been set up by those countries, they have waited for resettlement decisions, for periods of time ranging from six months to more than two years. The major countries of Vietnamese resettlement have included Australia, Canada, China, and the United States. In order to cope with the growing number of refugees from Vietnam (as well as Cambodia and Laos), in 1980 the U.S. government instituted the Refugee Act, which specified a set of formal guidelines for the entry, resettlement, and assistance of refugees.

This brief discussion of the history of Vietnamese migration to the United States provides some background for understanding the characteristics of Vietnamese family life in the United States. As suggested by the discussion, Vietnamese refugees are a diverse group. There are, for example, significant differences in the socioeconomic background of the 1975 wave and the later arrivals. Whereas many of the first-wave Vietnamese had held white-collar or high-level military jobs in Vietnam, a large proportion of those who have arrived since 1977 had occupied blue-collar or sales/service positions. Levels of educational attainment and English language proficiency have also been lower for the later arrivals (Rumbaut 1989; Strand and Jones 1985). Furthermore, the Vietnamese refugees include the Chinese Vietnamese, a group that has in many ways a cultural identity and experience distinct from those of the ethnic Vietnamese. In Vietnam, many Chinese had maintained a distinct identity from Vietnamese by living in enclaves and maintaining their own schools and newspapers. We can expect these differences in social class and ethnic background to enter into the family patterns of Vietnamese Americans in important ways.

Besides the diversity of the Vietnamese American population, what is also relevant to understanding the group's family patterns is the fact that migration from Vietnam has, in the recent past, been a selective process. The costly, secretive, and hazardous nature of the boat journeys out of Vietnam has meant that it has not usually been possible for entire family units to migrate. The process of resettlement from refugee camps has also contributed to family disruption, given the greater favor with which resettlement officials have viewed smaller family units (Haines 1988). Since the 1990s, there have been important political changes in Vietnam, easing the ability of Vietnamese nationals to apply through regular immigration channels to come to the United States, often to join family members already present here. However, the migration-related disruptions of family structure just described remain an important part of the Vietnamese American family experience.

DEMOGRAPHIC TRENDS

Age and Gender Composition

Both the age and the gender compositions of the Vietnamese American population have some unusual qualities. The Vietnamese American population has been young, reflecting both the greater proclivity of young persons to undertake the difficult journey out of Vietnam and the high rates of fertility among the group. In 1984, the Office of Refugee Resettlement (1985: 10) reported that the median age of all Vietnamese arrivals was 20 years. Data from a longitudinal study of Southeast Asian refugees in San Diego County show that for the 93 Vietnamese households surveyed in 1983, children under 18 years of age comprised 44 percent of the total household members. In 1984, for the same group of households, the percentage of children (42.4 percent) had changed little (Rumbaut 1989). The 1990 census reports a median age of 25.6 years for Vietnamese Americans.

During the 1970s and 1980s, a predominance in the number of men over women was another important characteristic of the Vietnamese American population. In 1975, males composed 49 percent of the general U.S. population. In comparison, 55 percent of the first-wave Vietnamese settlers to the United States were men. The proportion of Vietnamese men to women climbed to 58.4 percent among 1982 arrivals, reflecting in part increasing efforts of young Vietnamese men to escape the compulsory military draft (Baker and North 1984: 25). From the study in San Diego, Rumbaut (1989) reported a gender ratio of 120 males to 100 females for the Vietnamese. Evidence also showed the gender ratio to be particularly skewed for Vietnamese Americans aged 12 to 24 years. For example, the Office of Refugee Resettlement (1985) reported that among the Vietnamese who entered the United States in 1984, men outnumbered women by more than two to one in the 12 to 24 year age group.

The 1990 census shows 53 percent (311,858) of the Vietnamese American population to be male, thus indicating a gradual shift away from the sharply male-dominated gender ratio of the 1980s. However, most observers would agree that the "skewed" gender ratio has shaped family life for many Vietnamese Americans. Besides affecting the ability of men in certain age groups to find Vietnamese American marriage partners, the male-dominated gender ratio may also be part of the organization and ideology of gender roles and relations in the group (for a discussion of the effects of gender ratios on gender relations, see Guttentag and Secord 1983). An ethnographic study of Vietnamese refugees, conducted in the 1980s, showed that although married Vietnamese refugee women did not derive benefit from the high gender ratio, young unmarried women did experience greater power in their sexual relationships with men owing to the "shortage" of women in the group (Kibria 1993).

Marriage, Divorce, and Childbearing

Because the marriage and divorce patterns of Vietnamese Americans have not been widely explored, information on this topic is preliminary in nature. There may be some special problems in gathering accurate information on marital dissolution because of the stigma attached to divorce in Vietnamese culture, particularly for women.

In an analysis of data on the 1975 Vietnamese arrivals, Baker and North (1984) report 49 percent of those 15 years or older to be married at the time of arrival. A small number of the group, all women, indicated that they were divorced (0.3 percent) or widowed (0.1 percent). From his survey study in San Diego, Rumbaut (1988) reported the average of age of marriage for Vietnamese Americans as 21.4 years for women and 25.8 years for men. The study also shows extremely low rates of marital dissolution through either death or separation/divorce. For example, of the 157 Vietnamese adults who were surveyed in 1983, none were divorced or separated, and less than one percent indicated that they were widowed. The same respondents were questioned about what their marital status had been in 1975. Sixty-four percent indicated that they were married in 1975, compared with 87.3 percent in 1983. There was little difference in the proportion of widowed and divorced persons in 1975 and 1983. A Bureau of Social Science Research study (Dunning and Greenbaum 1982; Dunning 1986) of 555 Vietnamese refugees (including Chinese Vietnamese) in the New Orleans, Houston, and Los Angeles areas also reveals fairly low rates of marital dissolution. The study found that of those who had ever been married, 83 percent were with their initial spouse at the time of the study. The 1990 census showed about 40 percent of the eligible Vietnamese American population to be married, and 1.1 percent divorced or widowed.

Far more information is needed to clarify the marriage and divorce rates of Vietnamese Americans and the variations of these patterns within the group due to differences of social class and ethnicity. Contrary to the picture of stability and continuity suggested by the preceding information, a number of qualitative, in-depth studies suggest that there has been a rise in separation and divorce due to the strains on marriages generated by settlement in the United States (Gold 1989; Kibria 1993; Kinzie 1981; Masuda and others 1980).

Fertility rates in Vietnam are significantly higher than in the United States (Rumbaut and Weeks 1986). For Vietnamese Americans, rates of childbearing continue to be high, owing to both the large proportion of persons of childbearing age and traditional values concerning fertility. The 1980 census shows the number of children ever born per 1,000 Vietnamese American women (aged 15 to 44) as 1,785. This figure is close to that recorded for Hispanic (1,817) and African American women (1,806) and higher than that of the general U.S. population (1,429) or that of other Asian American groups (Gardner and others 1985: 17). Rumbaut and Weeks (1986) suggest that the 1980 census figures (which provide information mainly on the 1975 arrivals) may underestimate the current fertility rates of the Vietnamese because of the higher socioeconomic background of the 1975 arrivals, a condition that tends to depress rates of childbearing. Using data from a study in San Diego, they report a child-to-woman ratio[3] of 574 children (aged 0 to 4) per 1,000 Vietnamese American women of childbearing age. This figure is somewhat higher than that found for the Chinese Vietnamese (511) and substantially higher than that of the general U.S. population (309). They found the subgroup of 1975 arrivals within their sample of Vietnamese respondents to have lower fertility rates than later arrivals. The authors also found that increased length of residence as well as a higher level of economic and cultural adaptation to the United States significantly lowered childbearing rates. On the basis of these findings, they predict a decline in childbearing over time for Vietnamese Americans. However, given current rates of childbearing, we can expect a large proportion of children and young persons to be an important characteristic of the Vietnamese American population in the near future.

HOUSEHOLDS AND EXTENDED FAMILY

In traditional Vietnamese culture, the family was seen as an extended structure, a group that stretched beyond immediate or nuclear family ties to include a wide range of kin (Haines 1984; Luong 1984; Whitmore 1984). Households, which could include nuclear or extended family members, were enmeshed in a large and an active web of kinship relations in the neighborhood and general vicinity. These relations with kin often functioned as important sources of economic and social support (Hickey 1964).

A number of studies have emphasized the continued significance of extended family ties for Vietnamese in the United States. Data on the size and composition of Vietnamese American households provide some evidence for this idea. The 1980 census reports an average household size of 4.4 for Vietnamese American. Other relatives beyond the householder's immediate family (that is, households, spouse, children) were found to account for 55 percent of total household members. Seven percent of those living in the household were found to be unrelated to the head of household. In comparison, among whites, the immediate family accounted for 94 percent of total household members (Gardner and other 1985:23). A Bureau of Social Science Research study (Dunning and Greenbaum 1982) reports an average household size of 4.5 for Vietnamese refugees. For purposes of comparison, respondents were also asked about the size and composition of their households in Vietnam. Average household size in Vietnam was larger (6 persons), and there were also a greater number of three-generational households in Vietnam than in the United States.

From his study in San Diego, Rumbaut (1988; 1989) reports a mean household size of 5.5 for the Vietnamese American sample in 1983. Nuclear family member accounted for about four, and extended family members for one, of all household members. Unrelated persons composed a relatively small proportion (0.43) of total household members. There was little change in these figures in 1984, when the same respondents were questioned again (Rumbaut 1988). Data from the study also show few differences in household size and composition between the first "wave" and later arrivals. However, the average household size of the Chinese Vietnamese sample was somewhat larger than that of the Vietnamese. Further investigation is needed into both the diversity and the processes of change that are most likely occurring in the composition of Vietnamese American households.

The resurfacing of extended family household structures in the United States is in some ways unexpected, given the considerable disruptions to family relations that have been part of the migration process for the group. Studies suggest that the presence of extended family ties in the United States has been made possible by the vigorous efforts of Vietnamese Americans to rebuild their families in the face of the disruption to family ties caused by the migration process (Gold 1989; Kibria 1993). One expression of this family reconstruction process is the heavy secondary migration of Vietnamese Americans within the United States to areas of the country where kin and friends reside. Crucial to this process of reuniting and rebuilding has been the popular Vietnamese conception of family as a large and an inclusive circle of significant kin. In effect, this fluid and inclusive conception has allowed for the incorporation of people into the extended kin network who would perhaps not have been part of it in the past. More specifically, Kibria's (1993) study show three means by which family networks are reconstructed. First, relationships with distant kin are elevated in importance. In other words, relatives who were previously marginal members of the family circle in Vietnam are incorporated into the network of active kin relations. Second, compared with the past, distinctions based on paternal versus maternal descent or the ties of blood versus marriage were considered less important in determining the closeness of family ties. Third, close friends were incorporated into the family circle and treated as kin members.

The efforts to reconstruct kin networks clearly reflect the cultural importance placed on familial relations by Vietnamese Americans. But in addition, studies have suggested that extended family ties have material significance for Vietnamese Americans, in that they play an important part in the processes by which the group copes with the economic conditions and institutions of U.S. society. Kin are often involved in relations of mutual aid with each other, exchanging goods, services (for example, child care, cooking), and information on how to deal with such U.S. institutions as hospitals and welfare agencies. Family members are often a source of job referrals as well as investment capital for opening small business or purchasing homes (Finnan and Cooperstein 1983; Gold 1989; Haines and others 1981; Kibria 1993).

FAMILY ROLES AND AUTHORITY

The rebuilding of kinship ties highlights the continuities of Vietnamese American family life and the ways in which families may be a source of support in the process of adaptation to U.S. society. At the same time, many aspects of the traditional Vietnamese family, particularly patterns of family roles and authority, are being challenged by the conditions of life in the United States. The following sections explore the effects of migration to the United States on intergenerational and gender relations in the family.

Intergenerational Relations

The traditional Vietnamese ideal of the family, derived from Confucian principles, was of a hierarchical entity in which the young were subordinate to the old, as were women to men. For the young, ideal behavior entailed obedience to the elderly and the submission of individual needs and desires to those of the family collective. These principles were given meaning and legitimacy through the practice of ancestor worship, in which rites were performed to remember and honor the spirits of ancestors. For Vietnamese, the practice of ancestor worship helped to socialize children into ideal family values through its symbolic expression of the unified, sacred, and hierarchical quality of the kin group. Slote (1972) further suggests that traditional modes of child-rearing in Vietnamese families helped to generate qualities of dependence rather than independence in children, thus supporting the prescribed behaviors of obedience and submission to the family collective.

In the United States, these core traditional familial values—the authority of the old over the young and the primacy of the family collective over the individual—continue to be emphasized by the older Vietnamese immigrant generation in their interactions with the young. However, a number of conditions have eroded the ability of parents and other family elders to influence the younger generation. First, there is the youthful age structure of the Vietnamese American population and the small number of Vietnamese elderly in the United States (Eckles and others 1982). And particularly in recent years, many Vietnamese youth have arrived in the United States without older family members. Migration to the United States has thus often created situations in which the elderly are simply not present to enforce their authority over the Vietnamese American young. The growth of Vietnamese American youth gangs is at least partly a reflection of the significant number of young Vietnamese refugees who are in the United States without their parents or other family guardians (Vigil and Yun 1990).

Besides an absence of guardianship, settlement in the United States has also enhanced the economic and social resources of the young compared with those of the old. In a number of Vietnamese American families observed (Kibria 1993), the better language skills, opportunities for education and job training, and familiarity with U.S. cultural norms have placed children in a position of greater advantage than that of their parents in dealing with the institutions of U.S. society, a condition that has eroded parental authority. Along with their diminished power and authority over the young, Vietnamese American parents and other family elders also complain about the cultural assimilation of the young, fostered by such powerful cultural agents as U.S. television, popular music, and schools. Of particular concern to the Vietnamese immigrant generation is the growing individualism of the young. Studies document intergenerational clashes within Vietnamese American families, involving attempts by parents or older guardians to ensure that the young behave in ways that meet traditional Vietnamese cultural expectations (Indochina Refugee Action Center 1980; Kibria 1993; Pennsylvania Department of Public Welfare 1979).

However, to suggest that the intergenerational relations of Vietnamese Americans are characterized solely or even primarily by change and conflict would be misleading. A study by Simon (1983) pointed to the considerable consensus of values and expectations between Vietnamese American parents and their adolescent children. Kibria's study (1993) found considerable attachment among younger Vietnamese Americans to traditional Vietnamese family values, including the collectivist and hierarchical qualities of traditional Vietnamese family life.

Gender Relations

The ideal traditional Vietnamese family, modeled on Confucian principles, was one in which women were subordinate to men in all phases and aspects of their lives. The realities of traditional Vietnamese family life of course deviated from this normative model in many ways. For example, older women often exercised considerable power in their household. As part of their domestic caretaking role, women often controlled the family budget and exerted influence over the family economy. And although men controlled key economic institutions, Vietnamese women did have access to economic resources through their extensive involvement in small business and trading. Even though such activities may have enhanced the resources and power of women in the family, there is little evidence that they weakened fundamental subordination and dependence of women on men (Kibria 1990).

Scholars have observed that migration to the United States has challenged traditional Vietnamese bases of male authority and thus generated a rise in conflicts between men and women. They note how there has been a reversal of traditional male/female roles, a situation that has given rise to conflict. More specifically, Vietnamese American women often assume the "breadwinner" role because service sector jobs are more easily available than the kinds of unskilled blue-collar or professional jobs that men seek. In some cases, the woman economically supports the family while the man undergoes educational or technical training for a skilled job (Gold 1989; Kinzie 1981; Masuda and others 1980).

Although the employment rates of Vietnamese women in the United States are relatively high (see Haines 1986), it is not clear that the economic activities of women have taken on primary significance compared with those of men. The unemployment rate of

Vietnamese American women is higher than that of the group (Dunning and Greenbaum 1982; Haines 1987). Perhaps the crucial difference in Vietnamese refugee men's and women's employment is revealed in a comparison of their wages and income. For example, the Bureau of Social Science Research study (Dunning and Greenbaum 1982) showed the wages and income of women to be far less than those of men. Whereas, on average, the income of women constituted 36 percent of total household income, the comparable figure for men was 64 percent. Kibria's (1989) study also showed Vietnamese refugee women to be working in unstable, low-paying jobs, often in the underground or informal economy. In short, the evidence suggests that the elevation of Vietnamese American women's economic activities to primary significance compared with men's activities may be a reality for only a small number of families.

Although migration may not have generated a sharp reversal in the economic roles of Vietnamese refugee men and women, it has certainly resulted in a decline in men's ability to obtain jobs that ensure a middle-class standard of living for their families. By the mid-1980s, those Vietnamese immigrants who had arrived as part of the 1975 evacuation had achieved parity in their household income levels with the general U.S. population (Office of Refugee Resettlement 1988:147). The later cohorts of Vietnamese refugees, however, have had less economic success (Haines 1987). The 1990 census reports 23.8% of Vietnamese American families to be below the poverty level. A 1984 survey of Vietnamese refugees in San Diego found 22.4 percent of respondents to be unemployed and 61.3 percent to have incomes below the poverty level. Of those who were employed, 29.2 percent indicated that they received no fringe benefits at work, and 48.7 percent said that there was no possibility for promotion at their jobs (Rumbaut 1989). Caplan and others (1985) note that although the economic self-sufficiency of Vietnamese American families tends to rise over time, this condition is usually achieved not through a rise in individual wages but through the use of multiple wage-earner household strategies. Tensions concerning traditional conceptions of male authority may become apparent when men who were the sole or primary family breadwinners in Vietnam find themselves dependent on the income of other wage-earners in the household. More generally, we can expect the conditions of economic scarcity and insecurity faced by many Vietnamese American families to be a source of strain on marriages and other family relationships.

Besides economic conditions, other factors have affected gender relations in Vietnamese American families. Kibria's (1993) study shows how the cultural and legal conceptions of male authority that are prevalent in the majority U.S. society may work to challenge and shift Vietnamese American normative attitudes regarding men's and women's behavior. Also important was the expansion of Vietnamese refugee women's homemaking activities beyond such traditional work as child care and housework to include negotiation with social institutions located outside the household, such as schools, hospitals, and welfare agencies. The expanded "intermediary" role played by women is a potentially important source of power for women in their relations with men.

CONCLUSIONS

This chapter provides overview of research on Vietnamese families in the United States. Many studies of Vietnamese American family life have focused on patterns of continuity as evidenced, for example, by the presence of extended family household structures. In these studies, the continued significance of the traditional values and organization of Vietnamese family life in the U.S. context is emphasized. In contrast, other studies have stressed the theme of conflict, or the clashes between traditional expectations of family life and the conditions and orientations of U.S. society. Incorporation of these two themes into a unified perspective may provide a better understanding of ongoing processes of change or the ways in which Vietnamese American families are being shaped and constructed by both the past and the present.

Future research on Vietnamese American families must take into account some distinctive aspects of the Vietnamese experience prior to arrival in the United States. This observation includes not only the group's complex cultural and historical heritage but also the somewhat unusual conditions that have surrounded the migration from Vietnam. For example, the predominance in number of young persons and of men will most likely have important effects on Vietnamese American family life for some time into the future. Also relevant is the considerable disruption of family ties experienced by most Vietnamese refugees. Because of the difficulties of leaving Vietnam, chain migration processes or the gradual migration of entire family units has been less prevalent among the Vietnamese than among many other immigrant groups.

Finally, the diversity of the Vietnamese American population is another important key to understanding the group's family life. As has been discussed, there are significant differences of social class among Vietnamese Americans in terms of both past and current socioeconomic status. Differences between the Chinese Vietnamese and ethnic Vietnamese are also important to consider. In short, rather than viewing Vietnamese Americans as a monolithic population, future research must take into account the differences in social class and ethnic background within the group and the ways in which those differences are affecting family experiences.

NOTES

1. The 1990 census showed California to be home to 45.6 percent of the Vietnamese population in the United States, with Texas following at 11.3 percent.

2. Baker and North (1984) present information on the socioeconomic background of the 1975 arrivals. They found that 19 percent of the adults had had postsecondary (13 to 16 years) education, whereas 51 percent had received secondary (12 years) level education. Twenty-five percent had held professional jobs in Vietnam. Others had held mainly clerical and service sector jobs.

3. Child-to-woman ratio = (Total number of children aged 0–4) / women of childbearing age $\times$ 100.

REFERENCES

Bach, Robert L. 1984. "Labor Force Participation, Household Composition and Sponsorship among Southeast Asian Refugees." *International Migration Review* 20:381–404.

Baker, Reginald P., and Davis S. North. 1984. *The 1975 Refugees: Their First Five Years in America*. Washington, DC: New Transcentury Press.

Caplan, Nathan, John K. Whitmore, and Quang L. Bui. 1985. *Southeast Asian Refugee Self-Sufficiency Study: Final Report*. Ann Arbor, MI: The Institute for Social Research.

Donoghue, John D. 1962. *Cam An: A Fishing Village in Central Vietnam*. Saigon, Vietnam: Michigan State University Vietnam Advisory Group.

Dunning, Bruce B. 1986. "Vietnamese in America: Domain and Scope of Adjustment among 1975–79 Arrivals." Paper presented at the Annual Meeting of the American Association for the Advancement of Science. Philadelphia, Pennsylvania.

Dunning, Bruce B., and J. Greenbaum. 1982. *A Systematic Survey of the Social, Psychological and Economic Adaptation of Vietnamese Refugees Representing Five Entry Cohorts, 1975–1979*. Washington, DC: Bureau of Social Science Research.

Eckles, Timothy J., L. S. Lewin, D. S. North, and D. J. Spakevicius. 1982. *Portrait in Diversity: Voluntary Agencies and the ORR Matching Grant Program*. Lewin and Associates: Office of Refugee Resettlement Report.

Finnan, Christine R., and Rhonda Cooperstein. 1983. *Southeast Asian Refugee Resettlement at the Local Level*. Office of Refugee Resettlement Report.

Gardner, Robert W., Bryant Robey, and Peter C. Smith. 1985. "Asian Americans: Growth, Change and Diversity." *Population Bulletin* 40.

Gold, Steven J. 1989. "Differential Adjustment among New Immigrant Family Members." *Journal of Contemporary Ethnography* 17: 408–434.

Grant, Bruce. 1979. *The Boat People*. New York: Penguin Books.

Guttentag, Marcia, and Paul F. Secord. 1983. *Too Many Women? The Sex Ratio Question*. Beverly Hills, CA: Sage.

Haines, David. 1984. "Reflections of Kinship and Society under Vietnam's Le Dynasty." *Journal of Southeast Asian Studies* 15:307–314.

———. 1986. "Vietnamese Women in the Labor Force: Continuity or Change?" In *International Migration: The Female Experience*, edited by R. J. Simon and C. B. Brettell. Totowa, NJ: Rowman & Allenheld.

———. 1987. "Patterns in Southeast Asian Refugee Employment: A Reappraisal of the Existing Research." *Ethnic Groups* 7:39–63.

———. 1988. "Kinship in Vietnamese Refugee Resettlement: A Review of the U.S. Experience." *Journal of Comparative Family Studies* 19:1–16.

Haines, David, Dorothy Rutherford, and Patrick Thomas. 1981. "Family and Community among Vietnamese Refugees." *International Migration Review* 15:310–319.

Hendry, James B. 1954. *The Small World of Khanh Hau*. Chicago: Aldine Publishing Co.

Hickey, Gerald C. 1964. *Village in Vietnam*. New Haven, CT: Yale University Press.

Indochina Refugee Action Center. 1980. *An Assessment of the Needs of Indochinese Youth*. Washington, DC: IRAC.

14

AIN'T MISBEHAVIN':
DISCIPLINE AND PARENTING

Annie C. Beal

Linda Villarosa

Alison Abner

Stern, strict discipline has long been an accepted way of parenting in our community. This legacy stems from the past, when an undisciplined child could—literally—lose his or her life. Emmett Till's lynching in 1955 for allegedly talking "fresh" to a white girl sent shock waves through black America, confirming everyone's worst fears about the price of falling out of line. Life-threatening incidents such as this and countless others since slavery forced black parents to be exceptionally strict and even harsh with their children, demanding that they obey rules for their own protection.

Because even seemingly small incidents could mean the difference between life and death, African-American parents didn't have the luxury of explaining the whats and whys of their rules. Children who didn't obey were usually physically punished, no questions asked.

Times have changed, but has our parenting style? By and large, our children don't face the same kinds of risks our parents and grandparents did, so does strict, harsh discipline still make sense? Are parents who attempt to reason with their children, and who spend time explaining why certain behavior is unacceptable instead of administering a good, old-fashioned "whipping," adopting "white" parenting styles and spoiling their children?

This chapter will explore some of our attitudes about parenting and discipline and demonstrate through studies and advice from experts ways that you can discipline your child to get the behavior you want. Keep in mind that there is no magic method and that all parenting takes patience. Our goal is to give you choices so you can choose the styles that work best for you as you move toward your ultimate goal: to raise a safe, happy, respectful, emotionally healthy child.

OUR JOB AS PARENTS

Parenting, as you've probably already figured out, is a full-time job—whether or not you have full-time hours to devote to it. Not only are we required to meet every physical need of our children when they're babies, but as they mature, they require a tremendous amount of emotional care, guidance, and affection. "Children are a part of us," explains Morgan State University psychology professor Henrietta Hestick, Ph.D. "We are a large tree, and our young children are our branches and get all their sustenance from us." According to Hestick, our primary function is to provide nurturing, love, protection, guidance, understanding, and flexibility in order to raise healthy, productive adults who can make positive contributions to society. No wonder we're tired!

As black parents our role is more complex. "Black parents have to raise their children with an understanding of how society really is," says Bryan Nichols, Ph.D., clinical psychologist and instructor in the Effective Black Parenting Program at the Center for Improvement of Child Caring in California. "While there are no great differences between black and white children's behavior, there are much greater consequences for more minor infractions if a black child doesn't adhere to society's standards." That leaves black parents to face a strange juggling act: Though we disagree with society's double standards, we must still find ways to help our children succeed within these limitations—and eventually work to change those standards.

THE FOUR WALLS PARENTING QUAD

Parenting is the structure by which we raise our children and it is made up of four walls: discipline, limit-setting, consistency, and love. When balanced and used together, they help us develop our children's behavior, self-control, and ability to make good decisions. Here's a brief description of each wall and how it benefits our kids:

Discipline. In the minds of many—and many of us—discipline is synonymous with rigidity, toughness, punishment, and anger. (The image that comes to mind is Louis Gossett, Jr., as the never-smiling, unbending drill sergeant barking orders in the movie *An Officer and a Gentleman*!) In reality, discipline actually means to teach and as parents, we definitely should think of it that way. With small children, our role is to show them how to respond in different situations, to guide them toward the right choices and help them learn to think for themselves.

Limit-setting. This means laying down the ground rules and establishing consequences for your child's conduct. Setting these boundaries helps your child learn concepts like "right and wrong" and that other people have feelings. Children may test and protest limits many times before they actually learn to live within them. This is completely normal and repetition is part of how children learn. It is also how they gain a sense of security, because they know that when they can't exercise self-control, you'll be there to help them.

Consistency. This is the broken-record concept. You will find yourself repeating phrases your mother said to you, like "I'm not going to tell you again," when in fact you will probably have to remind your child many more times not to touch that plant, or to hold your hand while outside. Being consistent also provides your child with a sense of comfort, as youngsters thrive on knowing what comes next, and will often test you just to make sure you react the same every time.

Love. This is the most important of all four components in parenting, because more than any other, your child needs to feel a special bond with you. As the foundation for healthy parenting, love will help you to act in your child's best interests (despite her protests), and help her to understand that you are close by to support and comfort her.

UNDERSTANDING DISCIPLINE

With discipline, your main goal should be teaching, not punishing. While we each have our own rules and beliefs, basically, there are four identified parenting styles:

Authoritarian. This style of parenting is based on many rules with few explanations and no challenge to the authority of the parents. Parents who favor this style also don't use a lot of praise when the child behaves well because she's "supposed to do it anyway." This style tends to create children and adults with a strong sense of order but who struggle to think for themselves and to express their emotions.

Lax. The lax parent usually demands little to nothing from her child. There are few clear limits set and children often receive praise and rewards when they may not be warranted. These children often go on to lead chaotic lives; they also lack direction and are generally insecure.

Abusive/Neglectful. This is really a nonparenting style, in which the parent doesn't assume proper responsibility for the child. The child is left to fend for himself before he has the judgment and maturity to make decisions. These children are considered abused and, unless helped, often lack the social skills needed to succeed.

Authoritative. This term was coined by University of Berkeley researcher Diana Baumrind, as she tried to describe the parenting style that worked best with subjects of her studies. Authoritative parents demand responsible behavior from their children by setting high yet reasonable standards according to their children's personality and development. These parents set firm rules but were open to their children's opinions about the rules. Family values and morals are discussed as the basis for the family rules (except in obvious cases in which safety is an issue), and children are expected to behave responsibly (for instance, cleaning up after play, pitching in on family chores). At the crux of this style are parental love, support, and commitment. Research shows that children raised with this style tend to be creative, competent, and experimental as well as responsible.

As a whole, black parents tend toward the authoritarian style of parenting, but many parents are integrating positive discipline techniques into their parenting styles. "Black parents are accused of causing everything that's wrong in society," says Nichols. "I like to remind parents that they are already doing a lot of things right, but just need to add things." Like Nichols, Hestick sees ways that African-American parents can improve on their disciplining techniques with the addition of "new tools." "Children these days are exposed to so much," explains Hestick. "Given that, parents need to communicate with their kids in a much more sophisticated manner than their parents did." Both suggest that we move more toward the authoritative model of parenting.

DON'T SHAKE

You should never, ever shake your baby. Shaken baby syndrome describes the injuries that result when an infant is shaken vigorously, usually when the baby won't stop crying. Since infants have weak neck muscles and relatively large heads, shaking an infant causes the brain to "rattle" within the skull. This causes brain injuries that can result in serious consequences, including death.

Our babies are programmed to cry to have their needs met. And that sound is programmed to get on our nerves so that we'll meet those needs. Unfortunately, some people are less tolerant of hearing a baby's cry, and some babies have temperaments that make them cry a lot. If you feel your self getting frustrated with your child, put him down and walk away. No baby ever cried himself to death, but some have been shaken to death.

Shaken baby syndrome does not happen when you bounce your baby in your lap, during a rough car ride, or by falling while learning to walk. So you shouldn't be afraid to touch and play with your baby. Another important fact to note: Studies show that father and/or boyfriends are twice as likely to cause shaken baby syndrome, followed by female babysitters, and then mothers. Also, baby boys are twice as likely to be victims than are baby girls.

To prevent shaken baby syndrome:

- Make sure your baby's caretakers don't have quick tempers and are patient.

- Try to have more than one adult around your infant. People are less likely to become violent while another adult is watching. The other adult can also provide some relief to the caretaker.

- Recognize when you are angry or frustrated and find someone else to help you. Or put your baby in a safe place such as his crib and walk away.

- If you feel like you're going to lose it, count to ten and take deep breaths.

- Let your baby cry, but check on him every few minutes to make sure he is OK.

HOW TO DISCIPLINE

As you move toward the authoritative model, you will need to find new ways to discipline your child. In the Effective Black Parenting Program, Nichols teaches parents seven-step strategies for praising and reprimanding their child. Mirror images, Nichols's strategies are simple and effective ways to guide children toward the behavior you want.

When **praising** your child:

1. *Look at her*. Eye contact lets your child know you're sincere and that you are giving her your full attention.
2. *Get close*. Bring yourself down to her eye level, if possible, but at least get close enough to touch.
3. *Show physical affection*. A kiss, a rub on the back or head, or a hug accompanying praising words make a loving impression on a child.
4. *Smile*. This is one of the most powerful nonverbal ways of showing your approval.
5. *Use positive words*. Your words greatly impact how a child feels about herself. Use pleasant phrases, such as "Wow, what a great drawing" and "I'm so proud of you," while avoiding critical comments, like "Finally you did what I asked"

or "You're smarter than I thought." Be upbeat and excited about your child's accomplishment, and this will add to his feelings of pride.

6. *Praise behavior, not your child.* This means don't tell your daughter she's "a good girl" for brushing her teeth. This will lead her to believe she's only good when she's doing what you want, and "bad" when she's misbehaving. Your child should feel she's always good, whether she's misbehaving or not. Instead, tell her that what she's just done, hung up her coat or used the potty, is wonderful.

7. *Do it within five seconds.* Immediacy is crucial. The sooner you praise your child after she has completed the act, the better. Because children have very little sense of time, it's important to get to them immediately so they will remember what they did and be more likely to repeat the same behavior next time.

When reprimanding your child:

1. *Look at him.* As with praise, looking at your child, rather than yelling from across the room, lets him know you're serious and you're paying attention.

2. *Get close.* This helps assure that he has heard and understood you.

3. *Show facial disapproval.* Young children learn about anger, disappointment, and other emotions by associating them with our facial expressions. Frowning or having a stern look will bring your point home.

4. *Use a disapproving gesture.* Point, put your hands on your hips, hold up your hand, or do whatever comes naturally to show that you don't like the behavior without hurting your child.

5. *Make a brief statement about the behavior.* Nothing will lose your child's attention faster than a lecture. By using short statements—not questions like "Didn't I just tell you not to do that?" or "What did I just say?"—you will be most effective. Try "Stop that or I'll have to take it away" or "No hitting."

6. *Remain calm and serious.* Without being either too extreme (yelling) or too polite (pleading), convey your disapproval and what you want to happen. Use what Nichols calls the Clint Eastwood style: firm, not loud, and very direct.

7. *Do it within five seconds.* Immediate action is more likely to get results. If too much time passes, a child may forget what he did and not understand why he's being chastised.

THE WELL-BEHAVED CHILD: FIFTEEN WAYS TO GET RESULTS

The following section covers what we consider to be the most effective ways to apply some of the information mentioned above to everyday situations. With time and repetition (a component of consistency), your child will incorporate these methods into his own behavior and you will have less correcting to do. Remember, however, that above and beyond these suggestions, your own behavior—how you treat others, how much you value yourself, and what you actually *do*—is the best way to model the behavior you want.

1. *Baby-proof the house.* This is critical during the first three years of your child's life. Young children don't understand the meaning of danger or the value of precious objects. At the same time, they are innately curious and exploratory, and when they are young, their main way of gathering information is through taste, touch, and sight. When your son grabs your priceless vase from atop a

Appropriate Discipline for Your Child's Age

The following are some guidelines to help you understand what your child understands in the way of discipline. Keep in mind that understanding rules, knowing right from wrong, and being honest are developed after many years of consistent parenting and don't actually begin to take shape until after age three or four.

0–Age 1: While you will no doubt run into situations that call for setting limits and rules, babies don't understand the concept of rules and consequences yet. Don't use punishment; instead use words in the positive, which give direction and clear explanation. Babies aren't able to be intentionally mean, hurtful, or "naughty," but their natural curiosity and impulses can take over. They need your judgment and guidance to steer them away from harm and into an interesting activity. You will find yourself repeating rules many times until you see even small progress. Be patient.

Age 1–3: Children this age are delighted to know that their actions can produce reactions, although they don't yet understand that biting and hitting aren't ways to greet others. Tone of voice and clear words help children this age learn what is appropriate behavior. Consequences, such as removing children from a situation, can also help them learn what will happen if they continue unwanted behavior. Some children begin to display aggressive behavior at this age in the form of tantrums or losing control (see p. 116 for more on tantrums). This is a natural part of development and is more an expression of inner tension than outward anger. This is the age at which clear and consistent limits are crucial to avoid conflicts and power struggles, because children test over and over to be sure what the rules and consequences are. You will continue to repeat rules many times before they are followed. Praise positive behavior as a way to encourage what you want.

Age 3–5: Children this age are more able to express their feelings, reason, and understand explanations for rules. When a child misbehaves, using time-outs or revoking privileges of certain toys can be very effective. Explain what you expect from your child ("I expect you to keep your food in your bowl, not throw it.") and then describe the consequences if it occurs ("If you throw food, you'll have to clean it up and have a time out.") Children are much more likely to follow rules more carefully at this stage (or try to sneak if you're not around), but you will still have to repeat your expectations and rules often. If you can, find out why your child is misbehaving, because often she has a perfectly good reason (in her own mind) that might not occur to you.

table and watches it crash, he has no sense of the danger he faces or how much the vase means to you. His mind is processing the sound the vase makes when it hits the floor, all the shiny pieces that have just appeared, and that objects fall when they aren't attached or resting. And this information is extremely valuable when it's learned in a safe environment; babies use it to expand their knowledge of the world. Limiting your child's world by expecting him to learn what's off limits and continually punishing him—either by spankings, "no's," or constant admonishment—will squash his natural curiosity and his motivation to learn or try new things. This, in turn, will limit his desire and ability to accomplish new goals.

The best way to keep children safe while teaching them about danger is to protect them and their surroundings. Eventually your child will learn what's OK and not OK to touch, but until he's old enough to really understand, why not put your valuables out of reach and create a safe environment where he can explore? You'll feel better too.

2. *Find distractions.* This is one of the best ways to avoid an escalating power struggle. A typical scenario goes like this: Your toddler takes something she's not supposed to have out of your purse, like lipstick. You tell her to give it

Testing the Temperament

No two children (or people for that matter) are exactly alike, and parents who have more than one child understand this completely. One of the many ways children differ from one another is that each has a different temperament. Established in infancy, temperament consists of three major areas: energy level, adaptability, and frustration tolerance. Minor areas of temperament are sensitivity, regularity (such as with sleeping and eating schedules), and distractibility.

Knowing where your child fits in each of these categories (and where you fit) can improve your relationship with your child because you can adjust your parenting style and expectations accordingly. While there are no good or bad temperament traits, some may be considered problematic until both you and your child learn how to deal with them positively.

An article in *Parenting* on-line magazine, by Ginny Graves, outlined the five basic temperament categories that begin to emerge around six months but become fully recognizable after the first year, with tips for parents:

- *The yo-yo* is generally active and hard to settle down (especially when learning new skills), has a hard time with even small changes unless she's in control, and has irregular schedules (with eating and sleeping, for example).
  Your best bet: Let her burn off energy, help her find ways to calm herself (she may need some hugs from you), and stick with a routine. Don't force her to eat when she's not hungry, and try not to confine her to a high chair for very long. Give her plenty of space and time to learn skills her way.

- *The whirlwind* is like a cyclone of emotion, with very high highs and low lows. He wants to be in control and finds it difficult to move on to the next activity.
  Your best bet: Allow your child to express himself strongly and try not to overreact. Help him find ways to calm down (maybe a favorite blanket or stuffed toy), establish a routine he can count on, and give transition warnings to prepare him for what's coming next.

- *The tiptoer* doesn't like to jump into anything without completely checking it out. She may say "no" to any situation that's new until she gets used to it, in large part because she's incredibly sensitive—to fabrics, foods, and too many people.
  Your best bet: Don't force her to do anything uncomfortable and respect her sensitivities. She's not just making them up. Help her by giving her plenty of space and time to get used to people, allow her to make decisions in her own time, and buy her food and clothing that she can tolerate.

- *The footdragger* tends to be quiet and deliberate, taking his time with tasks. He has a hard time with change and a low frustration level.
  Your best bet: Encourage him to use his quiet time constructively (buy books, puzzles, art supplies), set a routine, and give warnings about changes or transitions. Give him space to learn skills on his own time without pressure.

- *The trooper* is generally easygoing and calm and can handle spontaneous changes.
  Your best bet: Don't overlook her needs just because she doesn't require a lot of attention, and teach her how to express her wants when others assume she's "fine."

If you'd like more information about your child's temperament, Preventive Ounce, a research group in Oakland, provides free on-line assessments. You can get a free evaluation of your child's temperament on-line at *http://www.preventiveoz.org*

back, but she refuses and is intent on taking the cap off and putting the lipstick on like Mommy does. If you snatch it from her, she's sure to cry. If you demand it back from her, she'll probably ignore you and continue to prove to you she's independent enough to do it anyway. But if you find something appropriate to trade with her, like a favorite toy, or pick her up and play pat-a-cake while quietly taking the lipstick away, she's less likely to protest. You will have accomplished your goal and avoided a tantrum or hurt and angry feelings. Other distraction tactics:

- Sing a song.
- Remove her from the trouble spot by saying, "Hey, I know something fun we could do."
- Use a stuffed toy to play a game.

3. *Fight the bad with the good.* Be sure to put the focus on what your child is doing right instead of what he is doing wrong. This is a very effective way to give your child positive reinforcement while boosting his self-esteem. For instance, if your child is pulling your hair for fun, get him to stop by telling him it hurts and showing him a more gentle way to touch. Every time you see him use that gentle touch, tell him how good it feels and how proud you are that he's learning so well. If you ask him to help you pick up his toys and he does, praise him for being a good listener. Small children thrive on their own accomplishments, so if you go out of your way to praise rather than criticize, you'll help him feel good about himself and encourage him to do more for your praise.

   As you praise your child, choose your words carefully. Here are some brief guidelines:

   - *Remember: There are no good or bad girls or boys.* Praise the "good" deed, and correct the "bad" one.

   - *Try not to overdo it.* Every action a child makes doesn't call for a cheerleader. Pick effective times to use praise or else the praise becomes meaningless. Your child will look for praise when he doesn't deserve it or will only be motivated by other people's wishes.

   - *Avoid using praise as a bribe.* If you get locked into a battle and promise a gold star or special sticker if your child takes a bath, you're sending the wrong message. Praise is meant to help children feel good when they do something for the right reasons (such as picking up their toys so nobody gets hurt), not just to get gifts or prizes.

4. *Let children work out their differences themselves.* How many times have you watched two small children engage in a nonviolent argument, over a toy for instance, and resolve it without anyone stepping in? Probably not very often because parents generally don't give kids a chance to work things out by themselves. But recent studies show that when a child takes a toy from another child, the owner of the toy almost always gets it back without too much aggression, if parents don't interfere. This hands-off approach, of course, only applies when there is no danger of either child getting hurt; if an argument turns into a hitting or biting brawl, both children need separation and a break.

5. *Explain what feelings mean.* Discussing and exploring emotions is key to raising a healthy, well-behaved child. From the early months, babies learn about different emotions from their parents' facial expressions, exaggerated smiles and frowns that mirror their babies' moods. As children get older, they learn

to attach words to their feelings. But they don't really begin to grasp the difference between happy, sad, and mad until they are old enough to speak. It's important to help your children recognize their feelings early on so they won't be overwhelmed, frightened, or frustrated by them, and so you can avoid clashes. Here are a few great ways to help children understand their emotions:

- *Name feelings as they come up.* If you see your daughter bouncing on her tiptoes and singing, you can say, "You look really happy right now." Likewise, if she's angry about not getting her way, you can acknowledge her feelings by saying, "I know you're really frustrated/angry/mad that you can't have that right now."
- *Look at picture books.* Show her pictures of characters expressing their emotions and ask her to help you identify how the characters feel. Then explain each emotion by noting tears, smiles, frowns, etc.
- *Play the happy, sad, mad game.* By using your own facial expressions you can help her figure out what you're feeling. Then let her pick the feelings and show you.

6. *Teach your child to problem-solve.* As your child gets older, try giving her tools to help her think for herself. Myrna Shure, Ph.D., author of *Raising a Thinking Child* (Pocket Books, 1994) and *Raising a Thinking Child Workbook,* has developed a method called ICSP ("I Can Solve a Problem") to teach children as young as four years old how to solve problems for themselves by getting them to come up with solutions on their own. Problem-solving cuts down on frustration levels and gives your child a sense of independence, which is usually what's at stake when she challenges you. Here are the steps:

- There's a problem, for example, Aisha took a toy from Michael. Michael runs and tells Mommy.
- Mom presents Aisha with the problem by saying, "Michael tells me you took his toy. What happened?"
- Mom listens to Aisha's explanation and asks more questions, such as "Why did you take the toy from Michael while he was playing with it?"
- This gives Mom new information, such as that Aisha was playing with it first when Michael snatched it, or they had agreed to share but Michael took too long with the toy.
- Mom helps Aisha understand how she made Michael feel by saying, "How do you think Michael feels when you take his toys like that?"
- After hearing Aisha's answer, Mom helps her understand the consequences of her actions by asking, "What happened when you took his toy?"
- Aisha may say he cried and told. Mom then helps Aisha understand her own feelings by asking, "And how did that make you feel?"
- When Aisha answers, Mom asks her to think of a different way to get Michael to give her the toy.
- With each answer, Mom asks Aisha, "And what do you think might happen then?" If it's a positive solution, Aisha will problem solve to get the results she wants without negative consequences for anybody.
- Mom praises Aisha for coming up with such good ideas.

Tempering Tantrums

Imagine if you had all the feelings you do now, but no words to explain them. This is how young children feel before they are able to speak well. Throughout the day, these feelings build and are released in spurts we know as tantrums. And your child is more likely to have one if he's sleepy, hungry, off-schedule, sick, or made to sit still.

Although tantrums are a normal part of early childhood (they begin between one and three years old and end at about age four), many parents react to them with anger or worry. Many African-American parents think tantrums are a challenge to their parental authority. But for the sake of our children's healthy development, we need to let our children "get it all out" at a young age when we can still help them identify what they're feeling. Otherwise, they will learn to keep their emotions bottled up—only to be released in more dangerous ways. Once children learn to speak and identify their feelings, their tantrums decrease. In the meantime, remember that tantrums are never easy to deal with. But as the parent, you must keep your cool.

Try applying these suggestions the next time your child explodes, but know that there will be times when none of these methods works:

- *Stay calm.* Your child is out of control and though it may be hard to believe, she's looking to you for help. The calmer you are, the sooner the tantrum will subside. But if you get angry and yell, she'll do the same.

- *Try distractions.* Immediately try to get him interested in something else, like a toy or song, before the tantrum gets full blown.

- *Ignore it.* As long as her outburst doesn't put her in danger of hurting herself or someone else, try to ignore the behavior until she's calmed down.

- *If you can't ignore it, be understanding.* Put yourself in his shoes by remembering times in your life when you've gotten very, very frustrated. Think about what you wanted most: to vent your feelings with someone who would be sympathetic and caring. You can even say to your child, "I understand you're angry because I wouldn't buy you that toy." That helps him identify what he's feeling and lets him know you understand him. If you can, calm him by picking him up and giving him a warm hug. After a tantrum, children crave reassurance.

- *Don't give in.* If your child isn't too hysterical, try asking why she's upset. If it's because she wanted candy and you don't allow it, for instance, don't give in just to stop the tantrum, even if you're in public. Tell her you understand her feelings but stay firm. If she has a tantrum in a public place, pick her up and get her out of there as soon as you can.

After reading about ICSP above, you may be thinking "oh come on," but think again. Although her method may make you feel like "Dr. Freud," Dr. Shure has twenty years of experience with ICPS, and she insists that it's more effective and its benefits last longer than those of spanking or yelling.

7. *Do something zany.* Sometimes you just can't get your child to pay attention or cooperate no matter how much you ask. Before you get too annoyed and stressed and the two of you start to tangle, try taking a sharp left turn and do something off the wall. In other words, take "distraction" to a new level. For example, if your baby's fussing at the diaper-changing table, put a sock on your hand and make a puppet. (Or put it on your head!) Or if your preschooler is pouting about not getting another bowl of ice cream, pick him up and start

dancing. Not only will you be able to maintain control over the situation, you'll both have a lot more fun.

8. *Don't take your child's behavior personally*. Much of parenting requires self-control and patience and the ability to take your child's behavior in stride. For black parents this can be tough, considering the challenges we face outside the home that we are forced to dismiss. By the time we get home, many of us take *every-thing* personally! Although there is no easy answer to dealing with aggressive or negative behavior (except to address it firmly according to your household rules), understand that it's a normal part of childhood, and that your child isn't trying to hurt you.

9. *Provide choices, unless there aren't any*. As parents, we become so used to making decisions for our children we sometimes forget that they have their own preferences. Letting your child decide—within limits—which shirt to wear, which juice to drink, or which book to read helps him feel he has some control over his world. A child who feels like he has a partnership with you is less likely to throw a tantrum. For example, many children fight about getting dressed. If you ask your child which pair of pants he wants to wear and hold out two for him to choose from, he's more likely to cooperate, because he's part of the decision-making process.

   When it comes to more critical situations, such as whether or not to take medicine, there is no choice. But you can still give him the option of using water or juice to wash it down. Other times, when there are no options, you can explain why there isn't a choice—"no playing with knives, because they'll cut you"—and be prepared for some disappointment.

10. *Give a countdown for transitions*. Transitions between activities often provoke tantrums and because small children love routines and consistency, it's important to give them time to prepare for change. Countdowns and good-byes work amazingly well in helping young children move from one activity to the next. Depending on your child's temperament, you may have to use this technique for both large and small events.

    Here are some suggestions for easing transitions:

    * *Give your child a two-minute warning before changing locations or activities.* You can either set a timer or look at a clock, but try to stick as close to your time limit as possible so that your child will come to know how long two or five minutes is.

    * *Say good-bye.* Once the time limit is up, you can tell your child to say good-bye to her toys, friends, the park, or whatever she was doing and think of a way to help her look forward to the next event. Saying goodnight to family, dolls, and toys can help your child let go of the day and go to bed more easily. If your child has picked up a toy in the store and is having a hard time putting it back, let her examine it for a minute and then tell her it's time to say bye-bye to the toy. You'll be surprised how many times this works.

11. *Don't let "no" make you crazy*. Many African-American parents feel that when their children tell them "no" they aren't showing proper respect. "Don't tell me no when I tell you to do something" is a phrase many of us heard growing up, and we knew our parents meant it. But toddlers don't understand the concepts of defiance and "talking back" the same way older kids and teenagers do. When she says "no" she means "I don't want to" or "Do I have to?" Rather than punishing her or engaging in a power struggle, take a deep breath, ignore

the "no's" and guide her toward the action or behavior you want her to take. And do yourself another favor: Teach her the word "yes."

12. *Ignore unwanted behavior that isn't dangerous.* Much of the time children will do whatever it takes—good or bad—to get your attention. And any parent who has ever been stressed or busy knows how small children can pick the worst times to act out. One way to deal effectively with some of these small problems is to do your best to ignore the behavior as it's happening. Here's how:

   - *Identify the behavior you want changed and when it happens.* Does she always whine for candy in the supermarket? Or scream until you get off the phone? Either avoid those situations or talk to her before they happen and tell her how you expect her to behave.

   - *Be conscious of your previous response and try a new one.* You may have tried to placate your whiner to get her to stop, or chastised your screamer, or just given her a stern look. These are all reactions that your child picks up on, and she will repeat her behavior in order to get your attention. Instead, try to resist the urge to say or do anything, no matter how loud she becomes, and no matter how many people are around.

   - *Act as if it isn't happening.* At first this may aggravate her even more, but if you continue to ignore the behavior each time it occurs, she'll eventually see it's not going to get your attention.

   - *Praise her for correct behavior.* When she asks you, without whining, if she can have a candy bar, praise her for being a big girl while reminding her of the "no candy" rule. Or tell her how proud you are of her for playing quietly until you got off the phone. She may fall into old habits again, but use this method and it should help her behavior the next time around.

13. *Try not to set too many rules.* Even if you decide upon a strict parenting style, be aware that the rules you set should be appropriate for your child's age. Babies and very young children don't understand rules and need to be guided away from harm toward safety. Children don't even begin to understand the meaning of rules until around age two or three, and, even then, their impulses are so great they can't always be expected to follow them. In general the rule about rules is that the more you have, the more opportunities there will be for your child to break them. This doesn't mean you shouldn't set any rules or limits, it just means that you should limit rules to the most important ones until your child is old enough to understand them.

14. *Use time-outs effectively.* Time-outs aren't just for white families; they can be an effective way to calm your child when she gets out of control. While some parents use time-outs as punishment, it's best to use them as a way to help your child shift gears from unpleasant behavior into a more quiet state. Children, especially preschoolers, need help bringing themselves down before they get overly excited. When you see your child spinning out of control, try these tips:

   - *Stay cool.* This is the key to getting your child under control and behaving the way you want. Yelling will only make it worse.

   - *Take your child away from the activity.* You could take him to another part of the room or into his bedroom. Anywhere works as long as it allows him enough quiet to take a break.

"Have time-outs worked every time? No. Have I been frustrated? Yes." —Anne's Story

As a pediatrician, I have always counseled parents to use "time-outs" to discipline children and steered them away from hitting or spanking. However, when my daughters were born, I learned that in the real world, using time-outs rather than hitting requires a great deal of time and energy from a parent. It's harder than I thought.

First, I found that my children didn't begin to understand the concept until they reached age two. Trying to got them to sit down and take some time to calm themselves didn't really work before then. What *did* work was holding them when they were crying and upset and telling them to take a deep breath to calm themselves. When things got out of hand and they had tantrums or were really testing their limits, I put them in their playpen and told them they had to stay there until they had calmed themselves. "You're getting a time-out!" I would say.

My oldest child quickly learned that if she wanted to get out of "jail," she had to calm herself and listen to her mother. But my youngest would cry and holler and carry on, taking forever to get herself together.

What I liked about using the playpen was that I knew they were safe and I could leave the room— to give myself a time-out. However, it became a problem when they were big enough to climb out, or when I needed to discipline them outside our home. By the time they were two, they had learned how to calm themselves and better understood the time-out concept. This is when time-outs began to work and make sense.

The conventional wisdom says that the length of the time-out depends on the age of the child: two years = two minutes, three years = three minutes, and so on, but I gave them as much time as they needed to get themselves together, and it was different for each child. Now that they are four and five, I use time-outs not only as a way to calm them, but also to give them time to think about why they are being punished.

Have time-outs worked every time? No. Have I been frustrated? Yes. Have there been times when I slipped up and popped them on the butt? Yes. But now that they're older, I can really see they know how to control themselves and understand how to behave in a way that is considerate and respectful of others. I like to think that all the talking and reasoning is bearing fruit as my daughters grow older and become thoughtful young girls.

- *Let him go once he's calm.* A time-out can be as short as thirty seconds.

- *Try not to use time-outs as punishments.* They are really meant as chill time, not as a temporary prison sentence.

- *Tell him what a good job he's done when he's behaving well.* Once he's calm, give him a hug and kiss and let him go back to what he was doing before he started misbehaving.

Of course, there are times when you're the one who needs a time-out, when all you want to do is scream or lash out. Before you lose it, it's usually best to separate. Place your child somewhere safe, a crib or playpen, and then go into another room where you can take a few deep breaths and let your blood pressure return to normal. This will protect both of you from doing something you'll regret. Call a friend, take a quick shower, or lie down and meditate until you feel you are able to return to your child and calmly handle the situation. If you're having a particularly difficult day, let your child know

Are the Twos Really So Terrible?

Think back to when you were a teenager. If you were like most, you probably had power struggles with your parents, wanted to do things your own way, and began making your own decisions about your likes and dislikes—however much they clashed with those of your family. Now think about any two-year-old child. The similarities are striking enough that many experts call the twos the first adolescence. But are the twos really so bad?

According to Dr. Jay Belsky, Distinguished Professor of Human Development at Pennsylvania State University, who conducted research with sixty-nine families and their two-year-old boys, "A few bad apples have given every other two-year-old a bad reputation." His studies revealed that most parents don't have problems with their children's behavior at this stage, which is marked by children "stepping out of infancy to assert themselves, take control over their bodies, and decide what they want." Using his favorite word, "no," is a short and effective tool for him to achieve this new independence.

Belsky's study showed that only 20 percent of parents had a difficult time with their two-year-olds, and these families tended to have high levels of stress anyway, and therefore lacked the emotional resources to effectively discipline their children. Additionally, parents with very strict or authoritarian styles tended to have problems at this stage as well.

Rather than struggling over authority with a two-year-old, Belsky suggests you acknowledge her wishes. "What most kids want when they say 'no' is for you to hear them, not necessarily go along with them." Just saying "I understand you don't want to do this" and then giving a short explanation as to why and what you are going to do can cut down on the number of battles. "Saying you understand how your child feels isn't the same as giving in to his desires," says Belsky.

Two is also the age when children begin to bit, hit, throw things, and basically act out their aggressive impulses, actions that are understandably troubling to many parents. But this behavior is normal, too, and a part of human development. Parents need to understand that although your child can sometimes act out of anger, he still can't grasp that he's hurting you or even stop his own Impulses. Here are some ways to help your two-year-old's aggressive urges:

- *Be patient and firm.*
- *Talk to him.* Explain which behavior you find unacceptable (like hitting), why (because it hurts), what you'd like him to do instead (touch gently, or punch a pillow if he's angry), and that if he continues he'll have to be removed from the situation. You'll need to repeat this process many times until your child really gets the concept of hurting someone else, and understands that your rules apply to many different circumstances.

- *Praise him when he shows the correct behavior.*

Power struggles and constant "no's" aren't always fun to deal with, but this behavior will pass quickly. In the meantime, support your child's assertiveness while channeling it in a positive direction, appreciate his struggle for independence, and keep a sense of humor.

and explain what you would like to happen. If you still find you can't cope, call a friend or relative to come and relieve you for a while. Or call the National Family Violence Helpline at (800) 222-2000.

15. *Give lots of hugs, kisses, and reassurance.* Like most African-American parents, you work, so most of your free time is spent cooking, cleaning, going to the doctor, shopping, paying bills—the list seems endless. The amount of time and energy it takes to run a home and raise a family can be so overwhelming that it's easy to forget how important it is to take time with your child. Those

Don't Spank!

According to a 1994 Gallup poll, only 68 percent of parents approve of spanking, compared with a 1964 survey in which 94 percent approved. And recent studies show that as a child grows older and continues to be spanked, the greater the chance that spanking will escalate into greater violence because the child will hit back. Despite these facts, black parents—women especially—are more likely to spank children compared with our white counterparts. Regardless, we're taking a hard line, and one that many folks won't agree with: Don't ever spank your child. Here are all the reasons we believe you shouldn't spank your child:

- *Spanking teaches children to use violence to solve their problems.* Parents often spank when they are frustrated or irritated and trying to get a child to do something they want. And since we teach through our actions, this sends a message that when you're angry, frustrated, or bigger than someone is, physical pain is the way to get what you want. If parents who spank were to iron out their problems with other adults in the same manner, they would be breaking the law. So why should it be OK to do the same to a small person—not to mention your own child?

- *Spanking really doesn't work.* Several studies reveal that spanking is less effective in helping teach proper behavior to children than discipline without spanking. The results point out that parents who started spanking their children before age one spanked their four-year-old children just as often as parents who began spanking later. In other words, children who get spanked aren't learning the proper behavior or parents would have to spank them less for the same problem. And in a 1995 study funded by the National Institute of Child Health and Human Development, parents who used physical punishment had children who were more unruly than those who didn't hit.

- *Love and affection are more effective than pain and fear.* Children who are spanked generally feel angry, resentful, humiliated, fearful, and helpless. These feelings don't foster healthy self-esteem, nor do they help your child learn respectful behavior.

- *Spanking is dangerous.* For babies, it can lead to shaken baby syndrome, a deadly problem that can cause brain damage or death. If you are very angry and out of control, you can injure or—at very worst—kill your baby. It's better to not get in the hitting habit at all.

- *Other methods of discipline work better.* Spanking may have immediate results, but it doesn't help your child learn to think. If you have tried all the methods mentioned earlier in this chapter and still feel the urge to hit, try clapping your hands together, or hitting your knee or a table. The loud sound alone may startle your child and you will have avoided hurting her.

- *Spanking will negatively affect your child later in life.* The Family Research Laboratory at the University of New Hampshire has found that the amount of physical punishment people receive as children directly affects their level of income. This means the more a person was physically punished as a child, the less he earns as an adult. What's more, children who are spanked often are at risk for using violence with their siblings, their spouses, and with someone outside the family when they get older. These children are also more likely to face depression, criminal behavior, and impaired learning compared to those who aren't spanked.

times when your child seems clingy, overly frustrated, is acting out or feeling anxious, he's probably in need of reassurance. It's surprising how something so small as a hug or a kiss can produce great results. It lets your child know you haven't forgotten about him, that despite your harried pace you love him, and that he's not the reason for your stress. Hugging also helps you, because it forces you to slow down, calm down, and connect with your child.

Taking the Trauma Out of "Good-Bye" (and "Hello")

Separation is one of the biggest challenges for both children and parents. Working mothers are especially vulnerable to feeling guilty for "abandoning" their teary-eyed children. But working or not, all of us must experience the pain of separation from our children whether we leave them with a sitter or simply say goodnight. Separation anxiety is a natural stage of a child's emotional development.

Newborns have very little concept of where they end and you begin, and therefore don't understand the idea of separation until about six months. At the same time, six-month-old babies are just beginning to grasp the idea that when you two separate you don't just disappear, but are actually somewhere else. When babies fully understand this concept, called "object permanence," they will reach for a ball you have shown them hidden behind your back. A baby who now knows that you are somewhere else will miss you and want you with him. And since your baby has no real understanding of time, he will wonder when you will return. All of these developmental factors come together at around nine months when your baby will begin to show signs of separation anxiety, marked by excessive crying, clinging, and acting out just before and after you leave.

Toddlers, whose hallmark of development is independence and exploration, also experience a fear of separation. They are beginning to understand how vast (and sometimes scary) the world is. While they need to satisfy their curiosity, they also need the security of your presence. In this "rubberband method" of exploring, children will go away to investigate and return after a couple of minutes to check in, sit on your lap, or get a hug, all of which gives them the courage to continue their discovery.

Fortunately, as children mature they also learn through experience that you will return. Time, or at least the sequence of predictable events, becomes a clear marker for when you will come back. Both of these new developments generally mean that separation is easier, though not always painless, especially in the case of family transitions. (See Chapter 12.)

If your child hasn't shown any real difficulty with transitions, you may be one of the lucky ones—at least for now. Some children who have gotten through infancy without much anxiety still may experience separation anxiety later. Often children who are highly sensitive to their surroundings or have difficulty with transitions in general may be more likely to have separation anxiety. Although separation may never be fun, there are ways to make parting less sorrowful:

- *Face your own separation anxieties.* Children are masters at sensing our discomfort, even when we think we're masking it. Think first of what your own feelings of separation are (such as guilt about working, guilt about enjoying time alone, fear of abandoning your child, fear of "damaging" your child). If there are reasonable explanations for your decisions or ways to resolve your feelings, your sense of security will be more clearly communicated to your child. And remember that many of these issues will need to be revisited throughout parenthood.

- *All separations are hard for small children at first.* Have faith that the most difficult period is brief, and that after time your child will grow accustomed to the routine, and even rely on it.

- *Stick to a routine.* This is the key to easing your child's fears. When she knows what to expect—that you will return after her nap and snack at day care, for instance—she is less likely to be fearful when you drop her off. Likewise, have a set routine for drop-offs and pick-ups. A ritual of a familiar phrase ("I love you" or "Daddy will be thinking of you all day"), song, or activity before you leave can help your child settle into her new environment or say good-bye when it's time for her to go.

- *Respect your child's feelings.* Your child's response to separation can cause frustration. Resist any urge to reprimand your child. It will only make her more fearful and upset. Reassurance is the only way to ease your child's fears, so be patient and loving. Enlist the support of your child's caregiver in helping you comfort your child. She can distract your child, or involve her in a special activity.

- *Make coming home less stressful.* Reuniting at the end of the day is especially hard for parents, who feel pressured to both decompress from the end of the day and reconnect with their children. Take a few moments to focus on yourself and bring your day to an end. Then you can focus on your child.

- *Share your day.* Encourage your child to share the day's events by talking about your own highlights of the day. Ask lots of questions about her friends, teachers, and activities and listen carefully.

- *Have lots of cuddle time.* Having your child sit on your lap or hugging and kissing can reassure your child and help you both relax. Giving your child emotional and physical attention is a vital part of gaining your child's cooperation and helping your child to feel content enough to play alone while you attend to other family matters.

- *Keep it simple.* Don't overload yourself with too many chores when you get home. Get your child to pitch in with the few chores you do have, such as cooking dinner or picking up, as a way to spend time together. After completing the essentials, take a break until after you put your child to bed.

RESOURCES

Recommended Reading for Parents

Becoming the Parent You Want to Be: A Sourcebook of Strategies for the First Five Years, Laura Davis and Janis Keyser (Broadway Books, 1997). Cheerful, culturally inclusive, and often funny, this sourcebook includes a section called "The Problem with Spanking."

Good Behavior Made Easy: 1,200 Solutions to Your Child's Problems from Birth to Twelve Years Old, Stephen W. Garber, Ph.D., Marianne Daniels Garber, and Robyn Freedman Spizman, Ph.D. (Great Pond Publishing, 1992). This book includes problem/solutions sheets, readiness tests, and motivational charts. It's easy to use with lots of ideas for how to work with your child in a positive way.

The Moral Intelligence of Children: How to Raise a Moral Child, Robert Coles, Ph.D. Random House, 1997). The book's premise is that the most important skill a child must learn is to be a kind person. The author is the Pulitzer Prize-winning author of *The Spiritual Life of Children.*

Parenting the Strong-Willed Child: A Self-Guided Program for Children Who Are Often Disruptive, Rex Forehand and Nicholas Long, Ph.D. (Contemporary Books, 1996). This program helps improve a child's behavior while encouraging a better family relationship.

Raising Black Children, James P. Comer, M.D. and Alvin F. Poussaint, M.D. (Plume, 1992). As the cover says, "Two leading psychiatrists confront the educational, social, and emotional problems facing Black children today." This is one of the few books that confronts racism in America as a major obstacle to the health and safety of black children. These two authors are respected experts who answer many of the most common questions asked by black parents.

Raising Your Spirited Child, Mary Sheedy Kurcinka (HarperPerennial, 1991). This book looks at how parents can evaluate and live with a child who is "more intense, sensitive, perceptive, persistent, or energetic" than the average child.

Ready, Set, Cooperate, Marlene Barron (John Wiley & Sons, 1996). The author is the head of the West Side Montessori School in New York City. The book provides instructions for sixty playful activities that encourage your child to get along with others.

Smart Parenting, Peter Favoro, M.D. (Contemporary Books, 1995). This book gives stories of real-life problems and shows how they were resolved. Favoro coaches caregivers on how to help children "survive and thrive in a difficult and demanding world." He includes sections on building confidence, self-esteem, a sense of responsibility, and social skills.

Teaching Your Child the Language of Social Success, Marshall P. Duke, Ph.D., Stephen Nowicki, Jr., Ph.D., and Elisabeth A. Martin, M.Ed. (Peachtree Publishers, Ltd., 1996). This book helps caregivers recognize and understand their children's nonverbal language. It explains how children can be encouraged to use their nonverbal language in ways that will become the basis for having satisfying relationships and social success throughout their lives.

Touchpoints, T. Berry Brazelton, M.D. (Addison-Wesley Publishing, 1992). Starting with pregnancy and continuing through childhood, this book lays out issues and questions concerning all stages of chidrearing. It also shows ways that aggressive children can learn to control their own behavior and shows parents how to "reorganize" when they make mistakes.

Twenty Teachable Virtues, Barbara C. Unell and Jerry L. Wyckoff, Ph.D. (Berkley Publishing Group, 1995). Some of the virtues this book focuses on are empathy, fairness, humor, respect, patience, honesty, resourcefulness, self-discipline, responsibility, self-motivation, peacemaking, cooperation, and loyalty. The authors believe it's important to start teaching these virtues as early as possible.

Why Children Misbehave and What to Do About It, Christine Adams, Ph.D., and Ernest Fruge, Ph.D. (New Harbinger Publications, Inc., 1996). The authors teach parenting methods that send messages of love and respect for oneself and others. Children learn how to "do the right thing." The book includes lots of photographs of children in various situations, attitudes, and moods that you will recognize.

ORGANIZATIONS

Center for Anti-Corporal Punishment, (215) 579-4865. This is an organization that promotes the concept that it is never OK to hit a child.

Center for Improvement of Childcaring, 11331 Ventura Blvd., Suite 103, Studio City, CA 91604-3147, (818) 980-0903. This organization has the "Effective Black Parenting Program" for instructors who help teach parenting skills to African-American parents.

Family Communications, Inc., 4802 5th Ave., Pittsburgh, PA 15213, (412) 587-2990. Family Communications, Inc., produces materials to facilitate communication between parents and children. Its booklet series topics include moving, going to school, discipline, separation, divorce, and death. For one free booklet, indicate your choice of subject matter and send a self-addressed, stamped, business-size envelope.

Family Resources Warm Line, (800) 641-4546. This hotline provides answers to nonmedical, nonlegal childrearing questions and concerns about children from birth to twelve years old. They have a counselor on hand to give advice from 9 A.M. to 9 P.M. weekdays and from 1 P.M. to 5 P.M. on Saturdays and Sundays. They also give referrals for emergencies.

Fatherhood Project (FP), Families and Work Institute, 330 7th Ave., 14th floor, New York, NY 10001, (212) 268-4846.

> Website: *www.fatherhood project.org*
>
> The Fatherhood Project encourages the participation of males in childrearing by operating a national clearinghouse on fatherhood. It includes information about programs and resources in areas of employment, law, education, health, adolescent fathers, and social services. Referrals to programs that deal with the father's role in parenting are available upon request.

National Committee to Prevent Child Abuse, 332 S. Michigan Ave., Suite 1600, Chicago, IL 60604, (800) CHILDREN, (800) 55-NCPCA, or (312) 663-3520.

> Website: *www.childabuse.org*
>
> This organization runs a program called "Healthy Families America" for new parents which focuses on parenting skills, child development, child health, and other aspects of family functioning. They also publish material on parenting and child abuse prevention.

Parent Training and Children's Social Skills Program, UCLA Neuropsychiatric Institute, 300 UCLA Medical Plaza, Los Angeles, CA, 90024, (310) 825-0142. This is a program run out of UCLA offering individual counseling and parenting classes for parents of children ages two through twelve.

Parents Anonymous (PA), 520 Lafayette Park Pl., Suite 316, Los Angeles, CA, 90045. PA is a self-help program for parents under stress and for abused children. There are no fees, and no one is required to reveal his or her name. Group members support and encourage one another in searching out positive alternatives to the abusive behavior in their lives. To locate a PA group in your area, call toll-free outside California (800) 421-0353.

Parents United/Daughters and Sons United, 232 E. Gish Rd., 1st floor, San Jose, CA 95112, (408) 280-5055. Parents United is a national self-help organization with many local groups throughout the United States. It provides assistance to families dealing with child sexual abuse and also sponsors self-help groups for adults who were sexually abused as children.

Parents Without Partners, Inc. (PWP), 8807 Colesville Rd., Silver Spring, MD, 20910, (800) 637-7974, (301) 588-9354.

> Website: *www.parentswithoutpartners.org*
>
> PWP has activities and mutual help groups for single parents and their children in all fifty states, Canada, and overseas. Bibliographies, resource lists, and information about a PWP group in your area are available.

15

THE TWO SEXES AND
THEIR SOCIAL SYSTEMS

Eleanor E. Maccoby

In the mid-1950s, when Ted Newcomb and I set about organizing the third edition of the *Readings in Social Psychology* (Maccoby, Newcomb, & Hartley, 1958), we invited Urie Bronfenbrenner to do a chapter on socialization, asking him to put the issues in a larger context than the usual intrafamilial one. That chapter was in some ways a starting point for the themes that Urie presented in his influential book on the *Ecology of Human Development* (1979). I have had many spirited conversations with Urie, as well as exchanges of letters, before and after that book was published, and I can say with some confidence that the ecology book, even though it occupies a central place in Urie's theorizing, represents only one segment of his larger intellectual agenda. In that book, he placed individual behavior and family functioning in a nested set of sociocultural contexts, something that much needed to be done. But he strives to understand organism—environment interaction in a more comprehensive sense: to understand how an ecological point of view can be integrated with the driving forces of individual growth and development. Effective contexts change with development, not only because individuals at different stages take different things from the same environment, but because they create and select different social networks by which they are then affected. When we consider social environments, we know that individuals are subject to the demands and constraints of significant other persons at every point in the life cycle, but also that individuals exercise their own influence on those who are making these demands and setting these constraints. In other words, the bidirectional perspective is especially important for thinking about social ecology.

What I want to discuss relates to Urie's more comprehensive agenda. I want to consider the social environments that are constructed by, and constructed for, children of the two sexes and, in turn, the way these distinctive social environments shape the interpersonal relationships of male and female persons as they progress through several stages of the life cycle.

Sex, of course, is both a biological and social characteristic. Although hermaphrodites exist, biological sex is almost completely binary; so is *social sex*—that is, the gender label that is given by others to an individual child. In the vast majority of cases, biological and

---

Parts of the empirical groundwork for this chapter were presented in two previous papers (Maccoby, 1990; Maccoby & Jacklin, 1987); additional documentation will be included in forthcoming work.

social sex coincide. I suspect it is the very fact that sex is binary that helps to make it so powerful as an organizing dimension for social identity and social interactions. However, the relevance of an individual's sex to that individual's social networks is not a constant through the life course. The relevance of an individual's gender waxes and wanes at different points in development (see also Cairns & Kroll, 1994). And, although we do not have good research evidence on the continuity of sex typing from one period of development to another, I will take it as a given that there is continuity in this sense: The experiences that an individual has as a member of a gender-differentiated social network at one period will have an impact on the way that individual functions within the social networks that are formed at subsequent periods of time.

INFANCY AND TODDLERHOOD

I want to focus now on the succession of social networks within which individuals of the two sexes live their lives as they progress from infancy to mature adulthood. In the first 2 or 3 years of life, the social system of greatest importance to the child is the nuclear family. For many children, it is the only social system within which the child's daily life is enacted at this early time. True, the parents are usually part of several more extensive social systems, but from the standpoint of the child, it is the network of relationships between the child and the parents and siblings that constitute the child's social world. For the majority of children, the network includes both a mother and a father; for a minority, only one parent.

We are accustomed to thinking that the social networks of boys and girls take on a different quality even from the first few months of life. The developmental literature is replete with claims of differential treatment of male and female infants by their parents, or differential responses by children of the two sexes to their parents' socialization efforts. I want to claim that, on the contrary, the social relationships experienced by male and female children within the nuclear family during the first 2 years of life are remarkably similar. Of course, the nuclear family is seldom a gender-neutral structure, if one considers the different roles of the two parents. But from the standpoint of the children, the roles of young boys and girls in the family structure appear to be much the same. We know that boys and girls develop the same kinds of attachments to their parents in early childhood and that their attachments serve the same functions. The child's sex may seem important to the parents, and they may have different expectations regarding the future of a male or female child. But when it comes to day-to-day interactions, they treat children of the two sexes very much alike. The only well-documented differences are that boys are handled somewhat more roughly, and girls are talked to about emotions—their own and others'—more frequently. But parental responsiveness, total amount of interaction with a child, the standards set for the child's behavior, the restrictions and controls imposed, and the modes of discipline—all these aspects of socialization vary considerably from one family to another, but are essentially unrelated to whether a parent is dealing with a young son or daughter. Of course, it is possible that young boys and girls react differentially to the same parental input. But the evidence to date does not reveal any strong or consistent Sex X Environment interactions of this kind. During infancy and toddlerhood, then, male and female children can be seen as functionally equivalent members of the nuclear family, and we see only pale foreshadowings of the differentiation that will take place in the ensuing years.

CHILDHOOD

Whether the nuclear family continues to be a structure that is gender neutral (from the standpoint of the child's position in it) depends, I think, on how early children are inducted into sex-differentiated work and patterns of deference (Edwards & Whiting, 1988). Whenever young boys are taken by their father to join men in herding large animals, for example, the boys begin to become part of a male social structure; whenever young girls are recruited by their mother into female domestic work or agricultural field work not assigned to boys or whenever girls are taught to defer to and wait on their father and brothers and other older males, the nuclear family becomes a different social structure for male and female children. In modern Western societies, however, this kind of differentiation of boys' and girls' roles within the family is rare. The social positions of boys and girls in the nuclear family are probably somewhat more differentiated than they were in the first 2 years of life, but still are primarily similar.

It is when children become part of the new social structures created by peers that the social experiences of the two sexes truly diverge. The years from age 3 to about age 12 are a crucial, highly active time from the standpoint of gender differentiation. Let me now set out the major themes that seem to me to emerge from the vast literature on boys and girls in this age period:

1. In some cultures, children have many opportunities to spend unstructured time with age-mates; in others, they have very few. The relative influence of peers probably depends on how much unstructured time children spend with their age-mates.

2. When with peers in situations not structured by adults, children tend to segregate themselves by sex, selecting same-sex playmates. In the early preschool years, there is a considerable amount of play in mixed-sex groups, but by age 5 or 6, gender segregation is strongly in place (Maccoby & Jacklin, 1987).

3. The social structures that emerge in male and female peer groups are different. Male groups tend to be larger and more hierarchical. The modes of interaction occurring in boys' and girls' same-sex groups become progressively differentiated, and the different styles appear to reflect different agendas (see Maccoby, 1990, for summary). Boys are more concerned with competition and dominance, with establishing and protecting turf, and with proving their toughness, and to these ends they are more given to confronting other boys directly, taking risks, issuing or accepting dares, making ego displays, and concealing weakness. Among boys, there is a certain amount of covert sexy (and sexist) talk, as well as the elaboration of homophobic themes (Thorne & Luria, 1986). Girls, though of course concerned with achieving their own individual objectives, are more concerned than boys with maintaining group cohesion and cooperative, mutually supportive relationships. Their friendships are more intimate than those of boys.

4. Boys are more oriented toward their same-sex peers than are girls. In saying this, I do not mean to imply that girls' peer relations are in any sense less important to them than are boys' peer relations to them. I mean rather to imply two things: Boys' groups are more gender differentiating than those of girls, and boys distance themselves more from adults—not only from their nuclear families, but also from teachers and other adults. Boys strongly reject girls and girlish activities and become relatively unresponsive to influence attempts from girls (at least, if other boys are watching). Girls are more gender neutral

in their activities and interests, and there is some evidence that they are equally responsive to influence attempts from male and female peers. Boys' stronger peer orientation appears to involve a certain indifference to and distancing from adults (particularly female adults), whereas girls remain oriented toward both adults and female peers. For example, Grant (1985), while observing 6 first-grade classrooms, reported the number of teacher contacts and peer contacts for each child. In each class, the boys had more contacts with peers than teachers, whereas the pattern for girls was usually the reverse. Thus, the agendas of male peer groups are more incompatible with maintaining a simultaneous orientation to adults than are those of girls.

The age period of 3 to about 12 is unique in many ways. There is no other time of life when gender segregation is so extreme, and the social structures of the two sexes so different, as in middle childhood. Sroufe and colleagues (Sroufe, Bennett, Englund, Urban, & Shulman, 1993) listed the rules that children appear to maintain concerning which kinds of cross-sex contacts are allowable and which are not. For example, contact is acceptable if it is clearly accidental, if a child is acting under instructions from adults, or if a child has recruited a same-sex partner to go along when speaking to a child of the other sex. These rules, which children monitor rigorously among themselves, are not what children observe in their home or among adults in other settings. Children have their own culture. It would seem obvious that the social behavior of male and female children of this age cannot be regarded as merely derivative reflections of the gender arrangements of adult society.

From where then do these distinctive behavior patterns come? It is not possible to present and discuss here the several relevant theories and evidence. My own conclusion is that although we do not understand the etiology very well, what we do know points to a complex causal nexus—including some biological predispositions that differ by sex and have a specifiable time course, some differential social pressures applied by adults to children of the two sexes, and a large component of self-socialization on the basis of gender cognitions, that is, on clusters of attitudes, knowledge, and expectations that make up a gendered self system that has a developmental trajectory. For our present purposes, the main point is that the social structures of middle childhood provide the foundation for those that develop at subsequent points in the life cycle.

So far, I have depicted the nuclear family—and adults more broadly—as playing a rather minor role in the gender differentiation of childhood and have argued that same-sex peer groups are much more powerful. This has not always been so. In many patriarchal societies, men manage and control the life of boys in their groups (witness boys' boarding schools or segregated male living quarters in some preliterate societies). In socialist societies, peer groups may be co-opted by adults to become avenues for socializing children into the communal values of the adult culture (witness Bronfenbrenner's, 1970, report on Russian youth groups in *Two Worlds of Childhood*, and the functioning of the Little Red Soldiers in China). In these two settings, youth groups were usually composed of both boys and girls. In other settings, adult-managed youth groups are gender segregated. But we in modern Western societies have cut youthful peer groups free from adult involvement and influence to an extraordinary degree. The gender differentiation I described above is what happens under conditions of minimal adult involvement, in the context of a larger society with a rapidly changing pattern of sex-role differentiation.

ADOLESCENCE

In adolescence and young adulthood, there is progressive disengagement from the nuclear family and progressive movement toward involvement with opposite-sex peers. In many settings, early cross-sex contexts occur in the context of mixed-sex groups of young people who have not yet explicitly paired off. The rate at which pairing off occurs for youth of the two sexes, of course, depends greatly on the social organization of the society of which the young person is a member. Also, the fact that girls reach sexual maturity at an earlier age than boys is relevant, but more relevant in some societies than in others. In traditional societies, girls were married soon after they reached puberty, often to men considerably older than themselves—men who commanded resources permitting them to support a family. In societies in which marriage was delayed beyond the girl's puberty, various social customs and arrangements were in place to keep the sexes apart; girls were sequestered and chaperoned, and in many parts of the world, fathers and brothers had the responsibility of protecting the girl's virginity until her marriage. Thus, a girl was kept closer to her nuclear family than were boys and young men.

In the modern world, there are progressively fewer restrictions on the social activities of adolescents. What then is happening to the nature of the social networks of which they are a part? In terms of the adolescent's position in the nuclear family, Youniss and Smollar (1985) and Steinberg, Darling, and Fletcher (this volume, chapter 13) have noted that *disengagement* is probably not the right word to use. Rather, what happens is a shift from hierarchical parent—child relationships to more egalitarian ones. Young people continue to live at home even after they have been "emancipated" from parental control to a considerable extent and, in many cases, after they have become sexually active.

The relationships of adolescents with their parents continue to be quite similar for youth of the two sexes, with certain modifications. Youniss and Smollar (1985) noted one respect in which the social relationships are not the same for the two sexes: Fathers seem to distance themselves somewhat from daughters who have reached sexual maturity, whereas this does not happen with sons. In view of the fact that girls, but not boys, are at risk for pregnancy, one might expect that girls would be more closely monitored than boys. The evidence that this is so is, so far, surprisingly weak and contradictory. I am prepared to believe that, in modern Western societies, girls are probably still monitored somewhat more closely than their male counterparts. On the whole, however, it would appear that, in modern Western societies, the nuclear family continues to be a social structure that functions in largely the same way for male and female adolescents.

From about age 12 till the time they leave home, adolescents spend progressively less time in joint activities with their parents and more with their peers. In adolescence, young people continue to congregate largely with same-sex peers and only gradually build up relationships with the opposite sex (Larson & Richards, 1991). Interaction with same-sex peers shows considerable continuity with the styles developed in middle childhood: Interactions among males in their peer groups and between pairs of male friends continue to be qualitatively different from those among adolescent girls, and one sees considerable continuity with the patterns that were apparent in middle childhood. What changes is that there is progressively greater variation among the peer groups of a given sex. Young people find and congregate with others with similar interests and goals. Individuals become known as members of distinctive groups or cliques, the "jocks," the "brains," and the "nerds" (Brown, 1990; Steinberg et al this volume, chapter 13). There are youth subcultures in which boys loathe respect among their peers if they show softness or romantic interest toward girls; instead, they gain points through sexual exploits that do not involve intimacy. (See Anderson's, 1991, book, *Streetwise*, and recent relations concerning the Spur Posse in the White, middle-class community of Lakewood, CA; "Where 'Boys Will Be Boys,' " 1993.) In other youth subcultures, a young man's special relationship with his girlfriend is understood and respected, even though in other respects the male group may endorse exploitative attitudes toward women. In other words, membership in certain male subcultures is incompatible with forming an intimate reciprocal, egalitarian relationship with a girl, but this is by no means true for all (probably not for most) male peer groups. Membership in a female subculture is almost always compatible with the formation of an intimate relationship with a male.

When youths of the two sexes encounter each other in adolescence and begin the exploration toward romantic bonds, we can see the process as the formation of a new kind of social structure. Many young people are understandably wary at first, and not altogether comfortable with the other sex. But as members of male-female pairs continue to spend time together their relationships become progressively more intimate, and I believe that the majority of boys establish relationships with their female partner that are much more intimate and reciprocal—less guarded—than those they have had with male friends. For girls, cross-sex relationships can all achieve deep intimacy, but for both sexes, the intimacy is of a qualitative different kind than they have known before. Of course, the sexual element in cross-sex relationships is of enormous importance, but the requirement of forming a smooth cross-sex relationship go much beyond negotiation of sexuality.

What is also necessary is to find a way to integrate the two different interaction styles that the new partners have brought with them from the childhood history of interaction with same-sex partners. Girls' reciprocal socially supportive style may put them at something of a disadvantage in dealing with boys' more direct, confrontational style, but couples vary greatly with respect to who is dominant in the relationship. Students of family relationships have found it very difficult to identify which member of a couple has more power. The relationship that any individual couple will construct, of course, depends on a myriad of factors: the temperament and physical attractiveness of each person; each person's history of earlier failed or rewarding cross-sex relationships; and the images, scripts, and messages each person has absorbed from television and other culturally available sources.

In addition to these factors, I think that there are two kinds of interpersonal experiences at earlier points in the life cycle that have an impact. Children construct internal representations of their parents' relationship, and even though these representations probably have little relevance to the same-sex interactions of middle childhood, they no doubt do come into play as couples construct their new cross-sex relationships. I suggest that the nature of cross-sex relationships will be strongly affected by the models presented in the nuclear family of each member of the youthful pair, concerning how adult male and female partners can and do relate to one another. Up until now, I have been arguing that because children of the two sexes are exposed to pretty much the same models of family interaction in childhood, they ought not to be affected differentially by the environment provided in the nuclear family environment. And to some extent, I think that even with respect to relationships with the other gender, the nuclear family continues to be a fairly gender-neutral source of influence. That is, experiencing in childhood a model of harmonious interparental relationships can foster the potential of both young men and women to construct similar relationships with their own romantic partners. In addition, however, there is the question, do young men and women adopt primarily the stance of their same-sex parent? The implication would be that the son of an abusive father will become abusive toward his wife or girlfriend or that the young woman who has watched her mother submit to a dominant husband will be disposed to do the same. It is an easy and common assumption that these continuities prevail, but I think we have not considered sufficiently the possible influence of the cross-sex parent. Both boys and girls can learn nurturance and intimacy from observing whichever parent most displays these qualities and nagging or abusiveness from either parent. I think we should question the assumption that boys and girls identify mainly with the same-sex parent with respect to these matters.

More gender differentiating, I believe, are each person's experiences within the same-sex peer groups of childhood. Peer group experience is probably more uniform within sexes, and more different between sexes, than is nuclear family history. Not only is it true that certain interpersonal styles developed and consolidated within segregated peer groups carry over into cross-sex adult relationships but probably also that some of the attitudes and beliefs concerning the other sex that pervade childhood peer groups are carried over as well. In any case, there is enough variation in both nuclear family experience and peer group experience to produce an almost infinite variety in the nature of the interpersonal solutions that are arrived at by different couples.

CHILDLESS YOUNG ADULTHOOD

The social structure formed by a young, adult, heterosexual couple who live together and do not yet have children can be an extraordinarily powerful one. In Western middle-class societies, such couples spend almost all of their nonworking time together, either at home or in the company of other couples. Although they retain connections with their two sets of parents—perhaps somewhat closer connections with the woman's parents—these connections with the earlier generation fade into the background and have little impact on daily life.

The same-sex social groupings that prevailed before the couple came together become relatively weak. In other words of the old song, "wedding bells break up old gangs," and the bachelor party the night before the wedding is meant to symbolize the end of the carefree days of male companionship and the beginning of a new spousal way of life. In the modern world, both men and women, of course, spend a great deal of time at work outside of the home during the childless young adult period. Working relationships sometimes develop into friendships and become a work-related social network that offers social support to its members. These networks are largely same-sex groupings, either because the workplace itself is gender segregated or because men and women who work together usually maintain a somewhat guarded stance toward one another if they do not want their work relationship to develop overtones of sexual attraction.

Whether or not childless young adults are part of a same-sex work group, the pair bond is their primary social structure in modern societies. The roles of the two persons within this structure need not be greatly differentiated, although many couples do adopt a gender-related division of labor within the household. But joint activities, interests, and goals are the predominant mode of this period. Within this framework of relative undifferentiation, however, there do persist differences in interactive style, which carry forward the distinctions seen in childhood and adolescence.

PARENTHOOD

Some couples feel that the birth of a child brings them closer together: They now have a new joint agenda, a new major enterprise that calls for new kinds of cooperation.

However, the usual experience is that even for couples who attempt to maintain equal roles and responsibilities, the birth of a child seems to force a greater division of labor—a greater differentiation of the roles of the two adults—than had been the case before child-bearing began. This pull toward differentiation seems to be based on at least four major forces:

1. *The biology of reproduction.* Probably the primary biological distinction between the sexes in mammalian species is that females gestate fetuses and give birth to infants whereas males do not. There has been considerable debate concerning whether this basic biological fact implies any sort of difference between mothers and fathers in terms of the power of parental instincts or the readiness to bond with infants and respond sensitively to them. Lactation adds a further biological element: When mothers breast-feed, it provides a unique form of interaction with infants that no doubt contributes to the intimacy of the mother-infant bond. Work with nonhuman primates certainly points to a biological element in the more nurturant behavior of females toward the young, but it also indicates that males have a potential for competent nurturance of the young, which can be called into play under exceptional circumstances.

2. *Human culture and social expectations.* Every known society assigns more child-rearing responsibility to women than to men, and girls everywhere grow up with the expectation that they will carry this responsibility if they have children. If we look at the parental roles of the two sexes cross-culturally, we see that there is a great deal more variation among men than among women in terms of their involvement with infants: Women are primary caregivers for infants and young children in every known society. Modern experience shows us that men can become equally competent, committed caregivers for infants and toddlers, but in most societies they seldom do so. It is as though cultures respond to the universal biological role of women in childbearing and lactation by setting up universal cultural arrangements that place women and children together, not only during infancy, but beyond. Thus, societies reinforce women's primary role in childbirth and early nurturance with a network of cultural expectations and demands. Societies have usually assigned different kinds of parenting responsibilities to fathers and to mothers, but expectations for paternal behavior have been changing radically over the past two centuries in the modern industrialized world (see Griswold's 1993 book: *Fatherhood in America*). Paternal roles are cross-culturally highly variable and currently very much in flux.

3. *The economics of family support.* The practicalities of earning a living create pressures for differentiation of maternal and paternal roles. Even for couples in which both have been working full-time, the men usually earn more than the women, often considerably more. When children are born, it usually becomes necessary for one parent to cut back on work time to care for young children (unless, of course, the family can afford a full-time nanny). It makes economic sense that it be the lesser earner who stops working or goes to part-time work. Also, complications of pregnancy sometimes dictate that a mother cut back on work hours before a child is born, and time is needed to recover from childbirth. All these factors imply that childbearing will take a greater toll on a woman's out-of-home work life than a man's.

4. *Male and female interaction styles.* A fourth element contributes to a differentiation of parenting functions: the interaction styles that males and females developed at earlier points in their developmental history. As we all know,

mothers usually become the managers in the family, setting up time schedules for children's baths and sleep and for meals, household chores, recreation, and out-of-home child care. When both parents are home, fathers often play with the children, but they usually leave to the mothers the job of directing the child through the routines of the day. This would suggest that mothers are, on average, more directive than fathers, and from one standpoint this is true. Certainly the old "instrumental—expressive" distinction with which Parsons (1955) sought to characterize paternal and maternal roles does not come close to fitting the realities of family life. Fathers are at least as warm and affectionate with their children as mothers are (Collins & Russell, 1991). Yet observations of mothers and fathers in family situations show that fathers use more imperatives when dealing with the children, whereas mothers use more suggestions and inductions. Interchanges between mothers and children are more reciprocal and less hierarchical.

Youniss and Smollar (1985), in their study of several large samples of adolescents, give a clear description of the way mothers and fathers relate to their adolescents, noting how different these relationships are:

> The modal relation with fathers appears to be an extension of the structure of unilateral constraint that was in place at the end of childhood. . . . Fathers seem to have a narrow view toward their sons and daughters, thinking of them as potential adults and caring most about their progress toward productive adulthood. As a result, fathers share only a small part of adolescents' here and now interests. . . . Mothers, no less than fathers, hold adolescents to performance standards that refer ultimately to impending adulthood. . . . But this aspect of the relationship is only one aspect of its full character and it is communicated in a different style than is common in the paternal relationship. . . . Mothers maintain regular contact with their sons and daughters. . . . Mothers engage themselves in adolescents' interests, whatever they might be. Mothers closely monitor their sons and daughters. . . . Mothers do not solely take the role as authorities, but serve as confidantes who share experiences—with the end result being empathy. Mutuality enters the relationship. . . . The mark of the mother-adolescent relationship is conversation for its own sake—the kind of conversation in which ideas and feelings are exchanged, not instructional episodes that are designed to influence or persuade. (pp. 89–91)

To my mind, the parallels between the way parents behave with their children and the way they behaved in their peer groups when they were children are unmistakable. At each of these life stages, it is the females who seem to work from a dual agenda: to maintain a norm of reciprocity and positive affect while at the same time working to achieve the instrumental objectives of the moment. For males, the instrumental objectives is foremost, and the authority aspect of the parental role is a natural extension of the male-male confrontational, didactic interaction style. Mothers are more likely to listen to a child's point of view, and children, for their part, seem to feel more free to negotiate with their mother. It is not surprising, then, that Youniss and Smollar have found that, by the time children become adolescents, they feel closer to their mother and feel that their mother knows them better, even though they love and respect their two parents equally. In keeping with this literature, we (Buchanan, Maccoby, & Dornbusch, 1992), too, in our studies of divorcing families, have found that adolescents report feeling closer to custodial mothers than to custodial fathers.

It is not my intention to suggest that one of these parental styles is better for children than the other. My intuition is that children of both sexes benefit from being exposed to both styles. But true to the Bronfenbrenner tradition, what I am trying to do is to focus our attention on a neglected aspect of the social ecology of childhood. I think that, in trying to understand adult sex roles and adult gender differentiation, we have relied too heavily on an individual–differences perspective, thinking about gender as an aspect of the individual personality rooted in individuals' interactive histories within their nuclear families. We need to expand our horizons by giving greater attention to categorical membership, with its roots in both the gender-segregated peer groups of childhood and the categorical perceptions and conceptions that govern so much of our thought and behavior.

No doubt, many of you will already have identified a weakness in the argument of this chapter to date. It is too static. Elder (this volume, chapter 4) has alerted us to the importance of historical time: Large societal events and climates have an impact on the way social contexts such as families and peer groups affect children's development. Furthermore, biological time matters, too: Societal events have a different impact depending on the age of a child at the time they occur. My guess is that the forces of segregation in childhood are so powerful that they are not likely to be cancelled out by large societal events, though they may be modified. (A question: What is the gender composition of the street gangs of homeless children in Brazil? Do the pressures of hunger and homelessness take precedence and make gender irrelevant to social relationships in such groups?) Considering adolescents, it must surely be the case that the widespread availability of contraceptives and the revolution in sexual mores that has taken place in the last several decades in Western societies have profoundly changed the processes of mate selection and cross-sex relationships in young adulthood. We do not know what implications this has for any continuities growing out of the events of the middle-childhood period. It is to be hoped that the next phases of gender research will give us some answers.

Much of what I have said about the sequence of gendered social systems may seem obvious—that is, may be part of the growing consensus among developmental scientists. However, I hope I may have issued at least a few invitations to controversy. If I have, this too would be in the Bronfenbrenner tradition.

REFERENCES

Anderson, E. (1991). *Streetwise*. Chicago: University of Chicago Press.

Bronfenbrenner, U. (1958). Socialization and social class through time and space. In E. E. Maccoby, T. M. Newcomb, & E. L. Hartley (Eds.), *Readings in social psychology* (3rd ed., pp. 400–424). New York: Holt.

Bronfenbrenner, U. (1970). *Two worlds of childhood: U.S. and U.S.S.R.* New York: Russell Sage Foundation.

Bronfenbrenner, U. (1979). *The ecology of human development*. Cambridge, MA: Harvard University Press.

Brown, B. B. (1990). Peer groups and peer cultures. In S. S. Feldman & G. R. Elliott (Eds.), *At the threshold: The developing adolescent* (pp. 171–196). Cambridge, MA: Harvard University Press.

Buchanan, C. M., Maccoby, E. E., & Dornbusch, S. M. (1992). Adolescents and their families after divorce: Three residential arrangements compared. *Journal of Research on Adolescence, 2,* 261–291.

Cairns, R. B., & Kroll, A. B. (1994). A developmental perspective on gender differences and similarities. In M. Rutter & D. Hay (Eds.), *Development through life: A handbook for clinicians*. Boston: Blackwell Scientific Publications.

Collins, W. A., & Russell, G. (1991). Mother-child and father-child relationships in middle childhood and adolescence: A developmental analysis. *Developmental Review, 11,* 99–136.

Edwards, C. P., & Whiting, B. B. (1988). *Children of different worlds*. Cambridge, MA: Harvard University Press.

Grant, L. (1985). Gender, status, classroom interaction and children's socialization in elementary school. In Wilkinson & Marrett (Eds.), *Gender influences in classroom interaction*. New York: Academic Press.

Griswold, R. L. (1993). *Fatherhood in America*. New York: Basic Books.

Larson, R., & Richards, M. H. (1991). Daily companionship in late childhood and early adolescence: Changing developmental contexts. *Child Development, 62,* 284–300.

Maccoby, E. E. (1990). Gender and relationships: A developmental account. *American Psychologist, 45,* 513–520.

Maccoby, E. E., & Jacklin, C. N. (1987). Gender segregation in childhood. In H. Reese (Ed.), *Advances in child behavior and development* (Vol. 20, pp. 239–287). New York: Academic Press.

Maccoby, E. E., Newcomb, T. M., & Hartley, E. L. (Eds.).(1958). *Readings in social psychology* (3rd ed.). New York: Holt.

Parsons, T. (1955). Family structure and the socialization of the child. In T. Parsons & R. F. Bales (Eds.), *Family socialization and interaction process* (pp. 35–131). Glencoe, IL: Free Press.

Sroufe, L. A., Bennett, C., Englund, M., Urban, J., & Shulman, S. (1993). The significance of gender boundaries in preadolescence: Contemporary correlates and antecedents of boundary violation and maintenance. *Child Development, 64,* 455–466.

Thorne, B., & Luria, Z. (1986). Sexuality and gender in children's daily worlds. *Social Problems, 33,* 176–190.

Where "Boys Will Be Boys" and Adults Are Bewildered. (1993, March 29). *The New York Times.*

Youniss, J., & Smollar, J. (1985). *Adolescent relations with others, fathers, and friends.* Chicago: University of Chicago Press.

16

FAMILY TIME, FAMILY VALUES

Mark Mellman

Edward Lazarus

Allan Rivlin

In 1989 the Massachusetts Mutual Life Insurance Company commissioned from our firm, Mellman & Lazarus, Inc., a comprehensive investigation of family and family values in America. We sought answers to a number of questions. What do people mean when they talk about family? What are "family values" today and how important are they? What are the threats to the American family? What can be done to strengthen family values in America?

In both focus-group discussions and in a major national survey, we found general agreement with the view, put forward by countless politicians in recent elections, that declining family values are at the heart of our nation's major problems. When asked, "Which of the following do you think best explains the incidence of crime and other social problems in the United States today?" the top two answers were "parents failing to discipline their children" (20%) and "declining family values" (17%). Thus, approximately 37% of respondents located the causes of social problems in the family. The next largest number of respondents (13%) cited "poverty," followed by "the influence of TV and movies" (12%) (see Table 1).

Other major findings included the following:

- Family is the central element in the lives of most Americans.

- There is a high degree of consensus on those values that can properly be called family values: love and emotional support, respect for others, and taking responsibility for actions.

- Opposition to abortion and support for prayer in schools do not rank among the top family values.

- The values Americans call "family values" are the most important values to most Americans.

Mark Mellman, Edward Lazarus, and Allan Rivlin are with Mellman and Lazarus, Inc., a Washington, D.C.-based consulting firm whose clients include corporations, public interest organizations, and political candidates. The authors are grateful to Katherine B. Rohrbach and Leonard H. Ellis, Vice Presidents at Fleishman Hillard of New York City, for their contributions to this essay.

TABLE 1: CAUSES OF SOCIAL ILLS

Which of the following do you think best explains the incidence of crime and other social problems in the United States today?

Parents failing to discipline their children	20%
Declining family values	17
Poverty	13
The influence of TV and movies	12
Judges who are too soft or lenient	10
Increased greed and materialism	9
Problems with our educational system	6
Too many government social programs	4

Survey respondents picked lack of family discipline and declining family values as the principal causes of crime and other social problems.

- Americans see a dramatic decline in others' families but do not report a decline in their own family. In other words, when it comes to families, Americans are saying, "I'm O.K., but you're not."

- Lack of time together is recognized as the greatest threat to the American family.

- Americans say they need help from outside institutions to cope with stresses on the family.

- Americans have little faith that government and other institutions, as they exist today, can help them.

These findings are based on a series of four focus-group discussions in Baltimore, Maryland, and Denver, Colorado, and on a survey of 1,200 respondents.[1] The focus groups were used to explore attitudes toward family values without interviewer preconceptions. The range of opinions expressed in the focus groups were then presented to the survey respondents as options in many of the questions.

THE CENTRALITY OF THE FAMILY

Family is central in the lives of most Americans; it is both the source of our greatest joy and the cause of our greatest worries. When asked what gives them the greatest pleasure, 64% of our sample said family. Another 17% identified family as the second greatest joy. Friends were the next most frequently mentioned. However, only 7% said friends were their greatest source of pleasure; another 23% said friends were their second greatest source of happiness. Furthermore, more than three-quarters (77%) of parents said that their children were "the main satisfaction in my life."

More than half (51%) said providing financial security for themselves and their families was one of two things they worried about most. Another 17% cited declining family values as a major concern. Thus, the worries of approximately two of every three Americans revolve around family.

This family-centered perspective permeates every segment of the American public. Although older people are less concerned about financial security for their families than are younger people, their families' financial security is still the single most important concern among older people. Moreover, family was by far their greatest joy. Almost all married people (90%) find their greatest joy in family, but so do 56% of single Americans and 74% of those who are currently divorced.

Comments of Some Focus-Group Participants

"When I think of family, I like to think of things like support and love and guidance."

"One thing about my family and my family's values is that my parents love me no matter what."

"[I think of] an ideal family as being one in which there's love, mutual respect, and communication. I don't care if there's one parent, two parents, etc. If those things are there, that's an ideal family. On the other hand, where the children don't feel love and they don't communicate with each other, that's not a very ideal situation. I think you need to define it in those contexts, not just the physical structure of who and where."

"I have the best memories of my childhood. When I was younger, every night my mom would come in after I was put to bed and she'd kiss me good night and she'd sit there for a couple of minutes and we'd talk a little bit and she would leave. Then my dad would come in and kiss me and we'd talk a little bit and he'd leave. And I used to look forward to their coming into my room for those few minutes. I remember that like it was yesterday. I know my parents love me. I know that. They've said it. And I feel comfortable telling them that, and I think they feel comfortable telling me."

"Self-confidence comes from emotional support, because if you've got someone who's always putting you down, you're going to have this much [very little] self-confidence and you're not going to be worth anything to anybody, but if you get support from the family, that helps."

WHAT DO FAMILIES DO?

In the eyes of our respondents, the family performs two principal functions. First, the family is the base for caring and nurturing. Second, the family is the place where values are taught and learned.

When we asked respondents to tell us how well various words and phrases describe their families, some common denominators quickly emerged. Table 2 displays the average score for a range of phrases and terms. A score of four means that the phrase describes the respondent's family "very well," whereas a score of one means "not at all well." Thus, a score of three suggests that the average response was "pretty well."

People see words like "caring" and "loving" as being most descriptive of their families. Interestingly, respondents are less inclined to believe that their families provide emotional support, are close, or communicate well. Although one might think that these latter items are prerequisites for being caring and loving, the public does not seem to see it that way. It seems that in many families members have the positive feelings but lack the skills to express these feelings to one another. They feel love and concern but do not communicate it well or report actions that are associated with these emotions.

The other primary function of family is teaching family values. More than nine of ten (95%) agree with the proposition that "family is the place where most basic values are instilled" (61% agree strongly). This sense of family is also reflected in respondents' descriptions of their own families. Items such as "provided me with good ethical values" and "taught me responsibility," "respect for authority," and "discipline" tend to be at the top of the chart. Indeed, families seem to be as much about teaching as they are about support and closeness.

Many analysts have focused on the family as a haven from the outside world. Although the public does focus on the emotional bonds that tie families together, they do not see their families as being a refuge from "the pressures of the outside world" in any substantial way.

TABLE 2

How well does each describe your family? (Rank ordered by mean)

Positive Attributes

Caring	3.73
Loving	3.72
Honest	3.63
Provided me with good ethical values	3.57
Can always be counted on to help when needed	3.57
Taught me responsibility	3.56
Taught me respect for authority	3.55
Fun to be with	3.55
Respectful of each other	3.53
Taught me discipline	3.52
Provides emotional support	3.51
Close	3.50
Understanding	3.47
In touch with each other	3.44
Lets me be myself	3.36
Helps me financially when necessary	3.33
Spends time together	3.30
Tolerant	3.26
Doing things together	3.26
Communicates well	3.25
Is a place to get away from the pressures of the outside world	3.22
Has traditions	3.17
Makes decisions democratically	3.14
Religious	2.95
Financially secure	2.93
Financially well-off	2.74

Negative Attributes

Argumentative	2.35
A source of frustration	2.18
A source of guilt	1.80
Meddles too much in my life	1.71

Respondents' biggest complaint was that their families are "argumentative." But none of the negatively loaded terms were seen as more descriptive of respondents' families than even the least descriptive positive term; that is, people tend to see their families in a positive light.

WHAT ARE FAMILY VALUES?

The term *family values* is often used but rarely explicated. Politicians and pundits of various stripes have attempted to co-opt the term in pursuit of their own agendas. To date, no one has asked the American public what "family values" mean to them. We presented respondents with 28 value statements and asked how well the term "family value" described each one. The value statements were based on responses of the focus group participants. The value items represent a sampling of the things people told us are important personal values to them.

Table 3 displays the average score for various terms. A score of 4 means that "family values" describes this term "very well," whereas a score of 1 means "not at all well." A score of 3 would indicate that the average response was "pretty well." The higher the score, the more that particular value is thought of as a family value.

TABLE 3

How well does the term "family value" describe each particular value? (Rank ordered by mean)

Being able to provide emotional support to your family	3.67
Respecting one's parents	3.66
Respecting other people for who they are	3.65
Being responsible for your actions	3.64
Being able to communicate your feelings to your family	3.61
Having a happy marriage	3.59
Respecting one's children	3.59
Respecting authority	3.52
Living up to my full potential	3.46
Having faith in God	3.45
Leaving the world to the next generation in better shape than we found it	3.40
Being married to the same person for life	3.39
Following a strict moral code	3.37
Having good relationships with your extended family, including aunts, uncles, and cousins	3.31
Being physically fit	3.30
Being married	3.28
Having a rewarding job	3.28
Having children	3.28
Being well educated and cultured	3.27
Being independent	3.25
Earning a good living	3.23
Being financially secure	3.19
Having leisure time for recreational activities	3.14
Helping your community or neighborhood	3.14
Being in favor of prayer in school	2.92
Having nice things	2.75
Opposing abortion	2.72
Being free of obligations so I can do whatever I want to do	2.33

We found significant agreement among respondents on the values that can be properly called "family values." When Americans talk about family values, they tend to think in terms of the nature and quality of relations with others. Providing emotional support, offering respect—for parents, others, children, and authority—and being responsible for one's actions top the list of family values. Self-oriented values—being free of obligations, being well-educated and cultured, having a rewarding job—and material values are much less likely to be thought of as family values.

Religion falls toward the middle of the list. The items "having faith in God" and "following a strict moral code" received a comparable score to "being married to the same person for life" and "leaving the world to the next generation in better shape than we found it." The number of respondents who felt that these traits defined family values "pretty well" was about equal to those who picked "very well."

Some in the political community have tried to define family values in terms of opposition to abortion and support for school prayer. The public does not accept this construction. These items rank near the bottom of this list.

It is important to note that family values are not just about "family," as narrowly or legalistically defined. "Respecting other people for who they are" is as much a family value as is "respecting one's parents." Similarly, "being responsible for your actions" is more of a family value than is "having good relationships with your extended family."

To push deeper and understand what people have in mind when they respond to these value items, we return to the focus groups for a richer explanation of the values Americans call family values.

Comments of Some Focus-Group Participants

"You were taught at home when you were spoken to, you did it. You knew it wasn't asked a second time. And you knew to say "yes sir" and "no sir" or "yes ma'am" and "no ma'am" to your elders. You better not step out of line. It taught us respect. It didn't kill us. In fact, it taught us respect. It taught us that you don't do that next time."

"Many children today are not brought up with respect. Parents used to say, 'This is the way it is and that's the way it's going to be.' Well, I kind of raised my kids that way, and all three of them turned out to be an asset to the community. No dope. They don't even smoke cigarettes. They're great. Just drive into a parking lot today. Watch your car. As soon as somebody pulls in next to you, the door opens and crash. That all goes to respect."

"I think the children should have respect for each other; so often you'll find conflicts between each other, where there should be some way to instill respect for their siblings."

"I think you have to respect your children's opinions sometimes, and not always be right, but you got to give them their chance. Sometimes they're right. Sometimes they're wrong. Just because you're older, don't make you right. People are not listening to their children."

"You respect your children, you want your children to respect you. They have to feel they're someone without having a convertible. That has to be reinforced in the family."

"How you manage your money and how you treat other people, and that sort of thing. You don't walk in others' flowers. You don't hurt their dog. You be nice to each other. Respect is part of a real family."

"We are uniquely individual human beings and because you think certain things are right, doesn't mean that everybody is the same way. I think we have to respect individual differences."

Love, Caring, Nurturing, and Emotional Support

In the focus groups, a great deal of discussion revolved around the emotions that exist within a family. Love was given primary importance as the key element in a healthy family. Many of the comments about love and support took the form of fond reminiscences about past family rituals. The view of the focus groups seemed to be that when children grow up in a family in which little love is expressed, they will carry feelings of self-doubt rather than self-worth into adult life.

Respect for Others

The issue of respect was raised continuously throughout the focus groups. Three broad themes emerged. The first is respect for authority. In this view, young people learn to avoid punishment by showing the proper respect for parents, teachers, their elders, and others with the authority to command respect. In the view of some of the older participants, there is far less of this type of respect today than there was in the past.

The second view is mutual respect, which takes the form of parents respecting their children as much as they expect respect from their children.

The third view is a generalized respect for all other people. In this view, all people are due the sort of respect described in the Golden Rule: "Do unto others as you would have them do unto you." Many focus-group participants seemed to believe the second and third views of respect are connected. Teaching either one is the same as teaching both.

Comments of Some Focus-Group Participants

"Responsibility in a family means you have to think about somebody besides yourself. You've got people waiting for you. You've got people to make money to pay the bills for. Those are family responsibilities that you have."

"I'm the one who's working, and if I don't work, and just take off work with no pay—I've got responsibility both financially and to be there to help her with the kids. My wife and I are equal, but it's on me to make sure I bring home the paycheck."

"Responsibility to me would be a person who has a child, they have to be responsible to bringing that child up. A responsible person is—when you do something, you have to stick to what you're going to do. You make a decision that you're going to try to make it the best way you can."

"I think before, your responsibility was to the family, now it's making the money to pay for everything. They're pushing it more toward money to pay for the house. They worry about the house payments before they worry about the kids."

"It goes both ways too. It's not just parent-child, it's every member of the family. As a part of a family, you've got a responsibility and obligation to each member of that family. My sister and I grew up and we couldn't stand each other. We still can't in a lot of ways. But I know that if my sister ever had a problem, [snap] I would be there like that. If she asked, I'd be there like that."

"Responsibility really has an impact on everybody. Everybody's responsibility has an impact on somebody else. If I don't get up and go to work tomorrow, I know some guy in my squad can't get off because I didn't feel like going to work. It affects everybody."

Living up to Responsibilities

For many, living up to responsibilities means going to work each day to earn money to support a family. Others cited the responsibility of family members to be there when needed to provide emotional support.

In many ways the discussions of responsibilities mirrored those concerning respect in that several common subthemes emerged: traditional responsibility that flows from authority, mutual responsibility among family members, and generalized responsibility to co-workers and society at large.

An interesting generational difference became clear in Americans' views of respect and responsibility. For older participants, one is exchanged for the other: parents are responsible for providing for their children. In return, their children respect them. Younger participants see more mutuality in both areas; for example, parents give respect to children in order to receive it back from them. Similarly, younger participants spoke of the responsibilities that all family members have toward one another.

FAMILY VALUES ARE AMERICANS' MOST IMPORTANT PERSONAL VALUES

Believing that a particular value is a family value is not the same as considering that value to be personally important. In practice, though, we see a strong correlation. A comparison of Table 3 with Table 4 shows that items defined as family values also tend to be the most important values in people's personal lives.

For this question, a five-point scale was used, in which "one of the most important values" is awarded 5 points, "very important" 4 points, "somewhat important" 3, "not too

TABLE 4

How important is each of the following values to you? (Rank ordered by mean)

Being responsible for your actions	4.35
Being able to provide emotional support to your family	4.32
Respecting one's parents	4.32
Respecting other people for who they are	4.30
Having a happy marriage	4.30
Respecting one's children	4.27
Being able to communicate your feelings to your family	4.23
Having faith in God	4.15
Respecting authority	4.13
Leaving the world to the next generation in better shape than we found it	4.12
Living up to my full potential	4.11
Being physically fit	4.02
Being married to the same person for life	4.00
Following a strict moral code	3.99
Being independent	3.97
Having a rewarding job	3.95
Being well educated and cultured	3.94
Earning a good living	3.92
Having good relationships with your extended family, including aunts, uncles, and cousins	3.84
Being financially secure	3.83
Having children	3.81
Helping your community or neighborhood	3.75
Having time for leisure activities	3.73
Being married	3.60
Being in favor of prayer in school	3.39
Having nice things	3.21
Opposing abortion	3.11
Being free of obligations so I can do whatever I want to	2.67

important" 2, and "not at all important" gets 1 point. Thus a mean score of 4 indicates that, on average, respondents found it to be "very important." The higher the score the more important the value.

People's highest values are family values. From top to bottom, the two lists are quite similar. We see responsibility, respect, and the ability to provide emotional support and communicate emotions within the family at the top of both lists. These are Americans' highest values, and they are the values that Americans tell us they regard as family values. Figure 1 illustrates this point dramatically. Here, values that are thought to be family values are toward the right-hand side. (Values that are not seen to be family values are toward the left.) Values that are the most important are found at the top of the chart. The fact that the points fall close to a line sloping up indicates that the more a value is thought to be a family value, the greater its importance to most Americans.

Another interesting finding emerges from Figure 1. The emotional quality of family relationships is felt to be more important than the formal status of those relationships. Psychological criteria, in short, outweigh formal criteria. Having a happy marriage is more highly valued than is being married. Respecting one's children ranks higher than does having children. The inner qualities of relationships are valued more than is the simple existence of the relationships.

This emphasis on psychological gratification as a central—perhaps the central—rationale for the family should be recognized, in historical terms, as a relatively new direction for our culture. Moreover, this trend contains profound and multiple consequences for the family as a social institution. People increasingly believe, to take just one example, that divorce is a better solution for an unhappy marriage than is staying together for the sake of children. On the other hand, it may be true that today's marriages that do not end in divorce are in fact happier than were marriages in earlier eras.

THE POLITICS OF FAMILY VALUES

Ever since the emergence of the conservative "pro-family" movement in the late 1970s, as epitomized by the Moral Majority, the Eagle Forum, and other religious and grass-roots organizations, the debate over family values has been divisive and often confusing. Many people feel that they are being asked to choose between two polarized sets of values, neither of which they fully endorse.

The Moral Majority criticized self-centered values, condemning the materialism, sexual freedom, and drug use that they see harming American society and that are featured in television, magazines, and movies. The alternative they proposed emphasizes strong faith in God, opposition to abortion, and support for prayer in the public schools.

Many people are uncomfortable with these choices. Though they reject drug use and other self-centered excesses and feel a strong commitment to their family and often to religious institutions, they are not interested in what was the Moral Majority political agenda. In our poll, the majority believe in family values without accepting the prescriptions of many of today's most outspoken moralists. To understand American family values in the 1990s, therefore, we must leave behind the old polarizations and political symbols of the 1970s and 1980s. We need, in short, a better framework for understanding the choices people make and the issues about which they are concerned.

Toward this end, we sought to elicit people's attitudes toward various values by applying multivariate statistical procedures to the data from the survey. This exercise resulted

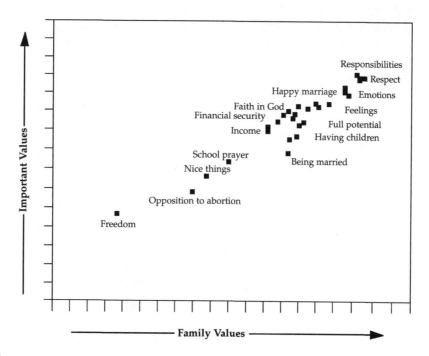

Figure 1
American's Most Important Values Are Family Values
A scatterplot of value items shows that the more an item is judged to be a "family value," the more it is viewed as important. Note: to avoid congestion, not all points are labeled.

in a new values "map"—one that we believe to be far richer than the traditional dichotomies of left versus right, conservative versus liberal.

A VALUES MAP

The map, displayed in Figure 2, was made with a standard multidimensional scaling routine[2] in two dimensions. All of the results are based on responses to the question: "How important are each of the following?"

The map was constructed by a computer program that looks for patterns in the importance different people place on each of the value items. Distances on the map between any two items represent the level of similarity of the items in the minds of the respondents. If two items are close together on the map, like "being married" and "having children," then we know that people who placed a high value on "being married" also placed a high value on "having children." In addition, we know that people who placed a low value on "being married" also placed a low value on "having children."

For two items that are far apart in the map, such as "being married" and "independence," we know that responses to the items tended to go in the opposite direction. If someone said that "independence" was "one of the most important" values to them, they were not likely to place a high value on "being married." Similarly, from the distance in the map we know that people who placed a high value on "being married" probably placed a low value on their "independence."

We added lines that group several of the items together. These groupings are based on a separate statistical routine that clusters items that engendered similar responses.[3] The two procedures use different statistical methods to achieve similar, though not identical, results. Two items that are close in the map may not be in the same cluster. Some rather strange shapes had to be drawn to twist around some items and their labels. (The shape of the clusters has no significance.) The simple explanation for this is that several clusters may occupy the same region of the map. If we were to expand the model to three dimensions instead of two, the model could allow more room for some of the overlapping clusters.

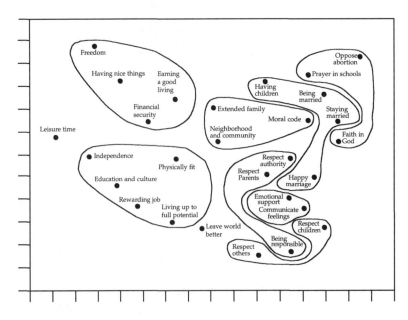

Figure 2
Values Map

How do we interpret the map? First, we must label the axes (see Figure 3). To the left, or west, we find a series of items that address personal self-interest: "leisure time," "freedom," "independence," "having nice things," "a rewarding job," and "living up to my full potential." On the right, or east, we find other-oriented concerns: "opposing abortion," "staying married," "having faith in God," "respecting one's children," and "being able to communicate feelings within the family." Accordingly, we label the east-west axis "self" and "others."

As described above, many of today's moralists claim the entire east side of the map as their territory and condemn those who find the other values important. However, this is not the whole story.

The significance of the north—south axis becomes clear when we consider some pairs of items. For example, in the north we find "having children"; in the south, "respecting one's children." In the north we see "being married"; in the south, "having a happy marriage." On the "self-oriented" side, in the north we find "earning a good living"; in the south, "having a rewarding job." In all these cases, the northern item describes objective status: one is either married or not, has children or does not. Perhaps to a lesser degree, we can say that the level of one's salary is far more objective than is the level of one's job satisfaction.

By contrast, the items in the south—"a rewarding job," "a happy marriage," and "respecting one's children"—are subjective or psychological goals. The values in the southern part of the map address the quality of life and include words that are more statements of feelings than statements of fact.

Several conclusions emerge from careful study of this map. First, the family cannot be found on the western side of the map. Respondents are clearly indicating that there is a trade-off between personal freedom and family commitments. Those whose primary values are career, leisure time, and material well-being are fundamentally different from those whose primary values are faith in God and emotional closeness in family and children.

But on the east side of the map, we find the family in both the north and south quadrants. In the northeast quadrant, flanked by "a strict moral code," "faith in God," and "prayer in schools," we find "having children," "being married," and "being married to

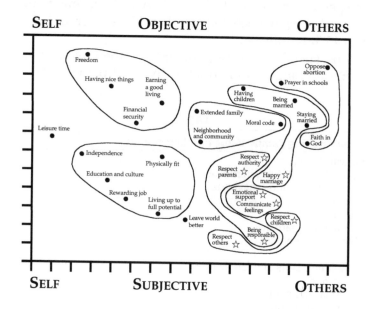

Figure 3

the same person for life" (shortened to "staying married"). Again these are the more objective, descriptive aspects of family. These aspects of family—children and marriage for life—are most closely associated with morality and religion.

In the southeast region of the map we find those who value the family but not the Moral Majority's political positions. Here, the view of family involves mutual respect, emotional sharing, and the quality of family life. These are the items that respondents describe as "family values."

Nationally, the eight items that top the list of values that people call "family values" are all located here in the southeast corner. These are also the values that are most important personally to respondents. At the center we find "being able to provide emotional support to your family," "being able to communicate your feelings to your family," and "having a happy marriage." Arrayed around this emotional center, we find respect and responsibilities, the key concepts that were thought to be most important by the focus-group respondents. Here, we find "respect for others," "respect for one's parents," "respect for one's children," "respect for authority," and "living up to one's responsibilities." This constellation of eight stars represents the ideal family—the norms of family life—for which the majority of Americans are searching.

IMPROVING FAMILY LIFE: TIME IS THE KEY

Americans do perceive threats to the family. The most important threat is lack of time. In particular, American families suffer from a lack of time together as a family. In the focus-group research, we heard a consistent story. In recent years, the number of single-parent families and two-career families has increased dramatically. These changes mean that people, especially parents, have less time for family. The survey results support this assertion.

The deeply felt need for more family time is clearly evident in Table 5, in which most respondents favor "spending more time with family" as the most effective way to strengthen family values. Eighty-six percent agree with the view that "families seem to spend less time together than they did 30 years ago"; 52% agree strongly.

Respondents indicated that during a normal week they spend an average of 47% of their waking time with their families. Not surprisingly, there are important demographic differences. Men spend an average of 41% of their waking time with family compared with 53% for women. Among women younger than 45, the average is 55%, whereas among men younger than 45, it is only 38%.

Married persons spend an average of 53% of their waking hours with family compared with 35% for singles and 36% for divorced persons. The time pressure on

TABLE 5

Effectiveness in Strengthening Family Values (% Extremely)	
Spending more time with family	54%
Providing better role models on TV and in movies	32%
Teaching family values in church and synagogue	30%
Full-time parent raising kids	28%
Teaching family values in school	23%
Improving financial situation of families	21%
Allowing more flexible work schedules	18%
Providing day care	8%
Teaching kids about their ancestors and family tree	18%
Full-time relative raising kids	15%
Living closer to other family members	13%
Allowing workers to do more at home	10%

single-parent families is particularly evident from the fact that married couples with children spend an average of 52% of their time with family compared with 41% for single parents. That difference is exaggerated further when one recognizes that with two-parent families, the percentage represents 52% of two individuals' time compared with 41% of a single parent's time.

Americans clearly feel this time pressure. Forty-six percent of our respondents state they do not spend enough time with their families. Forty-seven percent believe they spend the right amount of time with family, and 5% say they spend too much time with their families.

The amount of time one spends with the family is related to personal satisfaction with family. Those who are satisfied with their family life spend an average of 50% of their waking time with family. Those who are dissatisfied spend only 39% of their time with family. More to the point, 32% of those who say they spend the right amount of time with family are "extremely" satisfied with their family lives compared with only 18% of those who feel they spend too little time with family. Americans see the need for more family time not only within their own families, but also in families generally. When asked to identify the most important reason for the decline in family values, the largest number (35%) selected "parents having less time to spend with their families." (The reason selected next most frequently was lack of discipline, at 22%.)

The reported family-time shortage is related, people believe, to economics. Nearly eight in ten believe that "it is getting to be impossible to support a family on just one income." More than half (52%) agree strongly with this statement.

Today, the average working wife contributes 28% of her family's income. Wives who work full time fill 40% of the family purse. The median income for families with married partners and a working wife is 50% higher than that for families with married partners in which the wife does not work.

Approximately half (46%) of respondents say that employed married mothers are working "because their families need the money to afford basic necessities." Another third (36%) say married women with children work "to enable their families to afford some of the nicer things in life." Approximately 15% take the view that these women work "because they find it personally satisfying."

In sum, a majority of Americans believe that economic pressures cause more family members to work harder. This pressure has taken time away from the family, which in turn has caused a decline in the quality of family life, a weakening of family values, and a diminution of satisfaction with one's own family.

On the other hand, few of our respondents indicated that they would refuse a job that offered more money and/or more prestige but entailed less time with the family. All of our respondents were asked to imagine that they were 38 years old and had just been

A man in Denver expressed a common theme of all four groups:

"I think the thing that affects family values, currently, is the fact that there are no more full-time parents any more. The economy is forcing more two-income families, there is a lot more single parents, a 50% divorce rate. You're going to have a lot of kids that aren't getting any parental guidance. They're getting all their guidance from a video game or TV."

Like many others, a man in the Baltimore group believes there has been a change in values:

"I think before, your responsibility was to the family, now it's making the money to pay for everything. [People] worry about the house payments before they worry about the kids."

offered a new job in a field they enjoyed. The downside is that "the new job would require you to work more hours and therefore keep you away from your family more often." Three different "upside" scenarios were given, each one to a random third of our total sample. One group was told simply that the new job was "more prestigious than the one you hold now." Another third of the sample were told the job was more prestigious and would result in a 15% raise. The last group was told that the job was more prestigious and carried a 35% salary increase. All respondents were then asked whether they would take the new job.

Among all three groups, nearly two-thirds said they would be at least somewhat likely to take the new job. Overall, 63% said they would be likely to take the job. Only about a third said they would be unlikely to take it. Even among those who would get no raise, approximately 65% said they would be likely to take the job, whereas approximately 35% said they would be unlikely to take it. Thirty-eight percent said they would be very likely to take the new job, but not one person reported she or he would be very unlikely to accept it. Respondents with high incomes were a bit more likely to take the job. These results suggest an apparent conflict between stated values and actual behavior—between generalized ideals and real-life decisions—and illustrate the financial pressure that seems to play such an important role in contemporary American families.

OTHER WAYS TO IMPROVE FAMILY VALUES

Although a majority of Americans do not place primary blame for family problems on the media, the data point to an undercurrent of dissatisfaction with the images presented in the movies and on television. When asked to cite the major causes of crime and other social problems, a small but significant minority (12%) chose "the influence of television and movies." This was the fourth most popular response to the question presented. These data are presented in Table 1. Nearly a third believed that "providing better role models on television and in the movies" would be an "extremely effective way to strengthen family values." Women seem more convinced than men of the value of better role models, with 39% of women as opposed to 26% of men choosing "extremely effective." Similarly, blacks seem particularly conscious of the importance of role models, with 46% of this group choosing "extremely effective."

Educating people about family values, particularly through religious institutions, is also seen as valuable. Those who are most satisfied with their own family lives are particular partisans of this approach.

When asked to identify the major reason for the weakening of family values, the second highest number (22%) said, "parents are not disciplining their children enough." (The most frequent response was not enough time with families.) Moreover, an overwhelming 84% agreed that "parents today are too lenient and permissive with their children." Nearly half (47%) agreed strongly, whereas only 13% expressed any level of disagreement.

CONCLUSIONS

We live in a family-centered society. At a personal level, family is the source of Americans' greatest joys and most significant worries. At a societal level, Americans locate the root causes of our most pressing social problems in the family. The family is the base for caring and nuturing. It is also the place where values are taught and learned. Disrupting either of these functions can produce individuals and societies with serious pathologies.

There is a high degree of consensus as to which values can properly be called "family values." These center on love and emotional support, respect for others, and taking responsibility for one's actions. The same values that Americans call "family values" are also the values that the public holds most dear.

An analysis of Americans' underlying value preferences reveals two central fault lines. The first is self versus others; the second is objective status versus psychological feelings. Most Americans profess values that are other-oriented and concerned with subjective feelings.

To perform family functions, families must have time together. A lack of time is seen as the core threat to American families. Finding ways for families to spend more time together is a central challenge to preserving the family and strengthening family values in our society.

NOTES

1. Interviews were conducted between June 20 and 27, 1989. Respondents were chosen by means of random-digit dialing techniques, such that each telephone household in the nation had an equal probability of being called. The margin of error for the sample as a whole is less than plus or minus 3.5%; however, the margin of error for subgroups is larger.

2. The scaling routine was Kruskal's stress formula 1 in two dimensions, on a Pearson correlation matrix.

3. The clustering procedure was hierarchical clustering of stimuli, based on a matrix of Pearson correlations, with "centroid" linkage.